Inside Book Publishing

How do publishers work and make money? Why do they exist?

This expanded and thoroughly revised fourth edition of *Inside Book Publishing* is designed for students of publishing, authors needing to find out publishing secrets, and those wanting to get in or get on in the industry. It addresses the big issues – the globalization of publishing, the impact of the internet – and explains publishing from the author contract to the bookshop shelf.

It covers:

- how the present industry has evolved,
- publishing functions – editorial, design and production, marketing, sales and distribution, and rights,
- the role of the author,
- copyright and contracts,
- the sales channels for books in the UK, from the high street to ebooks, and
- getting a job in publishing.

It features:

- topic boxes written by expert contributors,
- a glossary of publishing terms,
- suggestions for further reading,
- a directory of publishing organizations, and
- a companion website – www.insidebookpublishing.com.

The book is an essential tool for anyone embarking on a career in publishing, and a useful handbook for those who are in the industry and for authors.

Giles Clark is the Copublishing Adviser, Learning and Teaching Solutions, at The Open University.

Angus Phillips is Director of the Oxford International Centre for Publishing Studies, Oxford Brookes University.

Inside Book Publishing

Giles Clark and Angus Phillips

Fourth edition

LONDON AND NEW YORK

First published 1988 by Blueprint

Second edition published 1994
Reprinted 1995, 1996, 1998

Third edition published 2001
Reprinted 2002, 2004, 2005

This edition published 2008
by Routledge
2 Park Square, Milton Park, Abingdon, Oxon OX14 4RN

Simultaneously published in the USA and Canada
by Routledge
270 Madison Ave, New York, NY 10016

Routledge is an imprint of the Taylor & Francis Group, an informa business

© 1988, 1994, 2001 Giles Clark
© 2008 Giles Clark & Angus Phillips

The right of Giles Clark and Angus Phillips to be identified as the Authors of this Work has
been asserted by them in accordance with the Copyright, Designs and Patents Act 1988.

Copy-edited, designed, typeset in Scala and Scala Sans, proofread and project-managed by
The Running Head Limited, Cambridge, www.therunninghead.com
Printed and bound in Great Britain by
Cpod, Trowbridge, Wiltshire

British Library Cataloguing in Publication Data
A catalogue record for this book is available from the British Library

Library of Congress Cataloging in Publication Data
Clark, Giles N. (Giles Noel)
    Inside book publishing / by Giles Clark and Angus Phillips.
    p.   cm.
    Includes bibliographical references and index.
Publishers and publishing. 2. Publishers and publishing—Vocational guidance.
3. Publishers and publishing—Great Britain. I. Phillips, Angus II. Title.
Z278.C557 2008
070.5—dc22

                                                                            2007048604

ISBN10: 0–415–44156–0 (hbk)
ISBN10: 0–415–44157–9 (pbk)
ISBN10: 0–203–34154–6 (ebk)

ISBN13: 978–0–415–44156–8 (hbk)
ISBN13: 978–0–415–44157–5 (pbk)
ISBN13: 978–0–203–34154–4 (ebk)

Contents

Expert, focus and skills boxes

Tables

Illustration credits

The publisher would like to thank the following companies and individuals for permission to reproduce the following illustrations:

page 23, Random House Group; page 28 (left and right), Random House Group; page 32 and throughout, the open book and laptop computer 'icons' are wood engravings by Andy English (www.andyenglish.com); page 35, Pearson Education; page 43, Palgrave Macmillan; page 50, Bloomsbury Publishing, Jason Cockcroft © Bloomsbury 2007; page 55, A & C Black; page 83, The Friday Project; page 90, John Taylor; page 98, Random House Group; page 103, John Taylor; page 120, Routledge; page 136, The Running Head; page 138, The Publishing Training Centre; page 141 (left), page 71 from *Oxford English Mini Dictionary* (2007), by permission of Oxford University Press, © Oxford University Press; page 141 (right), page 131 from *Paperback Oxford Large Print Dictionary* (2007), by permission of Oxford University Press, © Oxford University Press; page 143, Pearson Education; page 144, The Running Head; page 160, Heidelberg UK; page 162, A & C Black; page 165, Hobbs the Printers; page 166, Lightning Source; page 170, John Taylor; page 171, National Literacy Trust; page 175, Profile Books; page 176, Lonely Planet; page 182 (top), Kate Wheeler; page 182 (bottom) Finn Beales; page 220, Sue Pandit; page 224, Angus Phillips; page 227, Mladinska Knjiga, Ljubljana; page 233, John Taylor; page 239, Jaffé and Neale bookshop; page 241, Waterstone's; page 242, John Taylor; page 257, John Taylor; page 269, John Taylor; page 272, John Taylor.

Preface to the fourth edition

When *Inside Book Publishing* was first published in 1988 it was not conceived as a textbook; but its annual sales pattern came to show the characteristics of a textbook with orders peaking before the start of the teaching year in the autumn. The expansion of respected publishing courses, the adoption of the book by lecturers and its purchase by students have kept it growing. This fourth edition responds to the main student market and the needs of teachers. The publisher Routledge has increased the size of the book to a larger format and redesigned the typography to give it a textbook feel.

Textbook publishing is long term. Publishers need to issue new editions of successful books to keep them current, to fend off competition and to overcome the attrition in sales from the used book market. They also face the possibility that the original author may not have the time to undertake yet another new edition alone, or more problematically, be able to consider their work afresh. Katrina Chandler, the development editor at Routledge, found for Giles Clark a new co-author, Angus Phillips, who has brought significant new ideas for additional content, structural reorganization, publishing knowledge, and teaching and illustrative approaches. Her successor, Aileen Storry, saw the book through from the contract with the authors to publication. The redesign of the book to match market needs and the finding of a new co-author of complementary strengths to work alongside the original author in a highly productive way, are good examples of a publisher adding value, a theme which runs throughout this book.

This fully updated and bigger edition breaks the subject matter into twice the number of chapters (each of which is shorter than in the previous edition), and it includes additional chapters and special features. Although this book is stocked in some campus bookstores and a few main bookshops, it is a specialist book which lends itself to internet selling, not just by Amazon but also by the specialist sites advising authors about publication, a market interest taken account of here. Amongst the many new features, 25 industry experts have been commissioned to contribute their views and knowledge on particular topics. These pieces are framed in boxes. The larger margins provide space for sidebars, and a glossary has been added. Greater use is made of tables, illustrations and commissioned cartoons to enliven the subject. The associated website (www.insidebookpublishing.com) has been redesigned for the new edition.

For this new edition, the book is now supported by a certificated course from The Publishing Training Centre. Called *Train for Book Publishing*, the course is largely completed online. It summarizes key learning points from the book and reinforces the learning through a series of self-test exercises, before requiring delegates to submit an essay or project on a book-related topic for final assessment and grading. For further information please visit the website: www. train4publishing.co.uk or call the Publishing Training Centre on 020 8874 2718.

ACKNOWLEDGEMENTS

We are indebted to cartoonist John Taylor for his wit; to Carole Drummond and David Williams at The Running Head for their editorial and design expertise; and to Aileen Storry, Susan Dixon, Sarah Hartley, Christoph Chesher and other colleagues at Routledge for producing, marketing and selling this book.

A number of friends and colleagues have given their help with the new edition of *Inside Book Publishing*. The following read chapters in draft and offered many useful comments on the text: David Attwooll, Adrian Bullock, Clare Fletcher, Mario Fortini, Sally Hughes, Sheila Lambie, Peter Mothersole, Lynette Owen and Beverley Tarquini. The illustrations are credited separately but in all cases there was a cheerful and prompt response to the authors' requests. A variety of people helped the search, including Clare Christian, Kath Donovan, David Fickling, Camilla Garton, Jonathan Glasspool, Ruth Killick, Sheila Lambie, Richard Ogle, Sue Pandit, Richard Samson and Beverley Tarquini.

All the contributors of the boxed panels deserve our gratitude for their readiness to have their arms twisted to write for the book.

Angus would like to thank Ann, Matthew, Charlotte and Jamie for their patience and support during the writing of the book.

Preface to the first, second and third editions

In the 1980s, the Society of Young Publishers (SYP) asked Giles Clark to write a book for the benefit of its members, to give an overview of publishing and the careers available. His employer, The Open University, supporting the project, gave him special leave to undertake the primary research: over 150 publishing managers were interviewed.

The publishing history of this book is indicative of the dramatic and sometimes fraught changes that have occurred in the industry since the 1980s. The first contract was with Allen & Unwin, a long-established, family-owned publisher of medium size and diversity most noted for its general list, including the classic works by J. R. R. Tolkien – *The Lord of the Rings* and associated titles. This publisher also had a respected school textbook list, and higher education and professional titles in the earth sciences and the social sciences. By the time Giles had pulled together his research, Allen & Unwin had been taken over by another privately owned company and became Unwin Hyman. The first editor Adam Sisman left the restructured company (later going on to write a well-received biography of A. J. P. Taylor), and the new editor cancelled the contract and paid compensation. Unwin Hyman was then bought by HarperCollins, the international book publishing imprint of Rupert Murdoch's News Corporation. The Tolkien classics joined the ranks of other famous dead and living authors of HarperCollins and were to become in the next century reissued bestsellers tied in to the international film series, but at the time of purchase the staff were surplus as were the more specialist titles. A few of the Unwin Hyman managers formed University College London Press, which was later acquired by Taylor & Francis, and the social science titles were acquired from HarperCollins by Routledge, the respected academic imprint of the International Thomson Organization.

Giles was thankfully saved from the wilderness of being unpublished by Gordon Graham, then President of The Publishers Association and Chief Executive of Butterworths (legal and technical publishers) and subsequently the founder of the renowned publishing journal *Logos*, who introduced him to Dag Smith of the Book House Training Centre (renamed the Publishing Training Centre), who in turn contacted Blueprint Publishing – a new small publisher spearheaded and owned by Charlotte Berrill. She successfully focused on books on publishing and printing. Giles' work was adapted to the brief they drew up. The first edition of *Inside Book Publishing* (1988) was energetically published and sold by Blueprint.

Blueprint Publishing was later acquired by Chapman & Hall, the scientific and professional book imprint of Thomson. In 1993, Vivien James (the publisher in charge of the Blueprint list) needed a thoroughly revised second edition, which duly appeared in the autumn of 1994. German translation rights were sold to Hardt Wörner, which published their edition in 1996. During the summer of 1995, International Thomson conducted a reorganization which included combining the business and management lists of Routledge and Chapman & Hall into a new company, the International Thomson Business Press, and the transference of Blueprint to the media studies list of Routledge under the editorship of Rebecca Barden. By the autumn of 1995 the first printing of the second edition of *Inside Book Publishing* had fortuitously sold out, enabling the reprint to appear under the Routledge imprint. A management buy-out of Routledge occurred in 1996, supported by the venture capitalist Cinven. In 1998, the UK journal and book publisher, Taylor & Francis bought Routledge. The third edition appeared in 2001 and reprinted three times. In May 2004, Taylor & Francis and Informa merged under the public listing of Informa to provide specialist information to the global academic and scientific, professional and commercial communities via publishing, events and performance improvement.

Thus since conception, the copyright of *Inside Book Publishing* has passed through six changes of outright publishing ownership, has appeared under five publishing imprints and been worked on by six editors. This story is not unique in publishing today.

Special thanks are therefore due on the first edition to all Giles' friends in the SYP, to The Open University, Gordon Graham, Dag Smith and Charlotte Berrill; on the second edition to Vivien James; on the third edition to Rebecca Barden; and to Iain Brown for establishing the website www.insidebookpublishing.com. Furthermore he is indebted to the many dozens of people who have helped him with *Inside Book Publishing* over the years, and now supremely to co-author Angus Phillips who has made this much enhanced fourth edition possible, opening a new phase in the book's development.

THE AUTHORS

Giles Clark, with a family background in publishing, works at The Open University, Milton Keynes, where he is the Copublishing Adviser, Learning and Teaching Solutions. He organizes copublication arrangements between the University and a wide range of publishers from small to large, across most academic disciplines. The partnerships forged with commercial publishers extend the university's readership internationally, reduce its costs and give it entrepreneurial income. In a private capacity, he chairs the Graham Greene Birthplace Trust in Berkhamsted and serves on other grant-aiding charities.

Angus Phillips is Director of the Oxford International Centre for Publishing Studies and Head of the Publishing Department at Oxford Brookes University. He has degrees from Oxford and Warwick Universities, and many years' experience in the publishing industry including running a trade and reference list at Oxford University Press. He has acted as consultant to a variety of publishing companies, and trained publishing professionals from the UK and overseas in editorial, marketing and management. Angus is the editor, with Bill Cope, of *The Future of the Book in the Digital Age* (2006) and *The Future of the Academic Journal* (forthcoming).

CHAPTER 1

Introduction

This book addresses the needs of four audiences:

- *students* on publishing courses at undergraduate and graduate level,
- *graduates* seeking a career in book publishing,
- *newcomers to the industry* and those wanting to broaden their professional knowledge, and
- *authors* who would like a better understanding of how the industry works.

The subject matter of this book relates to the highly competitive business of developing and marketing books for profit, in the UK and for export, and this includes the university presses operating along similar lines. UK publishers sold 855 m books in 2007 (both at home and export) with a value of £2.995 bn; the value of the home market, at end-purchaser prices, was £3.5 bn. The number of titles published in 2006 was 115,522. In 2004 the book publishing industry employed around 35,000 people.

Commercial publishing is not a slow-paced genteel hobby to nurture literature or poetry without reference to the market, or a continuance of academic study, or a vehicle to express and propagate one's own particular views. Risk taking is inherent in the business: while prepared for failures, a publisher, as an eternal optimist with a short memory, forever searches for and expects success – sure in the belief that future rewards will more than exceed past losses – the last mistake seemingly the worst.

'To publish' is commonly defined as 'to make public'. Most publishers operate successful and profitable businesses. Their *primary* business model is based overwhelmingly on the copy sale – or 'transaction sale' – of books: complete packages of information. The business model of learned journal publishing is based on selling subscriptions to academic libraries. The *secondary* business model is licensing various rights in authors' works to others. These business models are relatively stable and recession resistant in comparison to that of the newspaper and magazine publishers, dependent on fluctuating advertising revenues. However, the advent of digital publishing poses both threats and opportunities to such conventional business models. In 2007 the president of the American publisher John Wiley said they had tried more business models over the last 10 years than in their previous 200 years of publishing.

The book publishers that prosper in good times and bad are those which have developed and maintained a core group of long-lasting titles – their *backlist* – delivering handsome margins. However, they are not overdependent on such past successes and also focus on producing new, high-quality books – their *frontlist*. Many of the most interesting and successful books are those that are exceptional, not a slavish imitation of other books. Book publishing is a complex interplay of the creative and economic. The book is an enduring medium through which ideas and knowledge are communicated, and a society's culture portrayed; and as such it is a primary resource for the student, the general reader and sometimes for the media. The diversity of books and publishers is vitally important to a democracy.

At the time of writing there is much speculation about the arrival of the ebook and the potential of an iPod type device that will transform the industry. Other industries such as music and photography have been fundamentally altered by digital developments. Paradoxically, in the case of the book, internet bookselling and digital printing have so far helped the sale and survival of minority interest titles in print form. The printed book scores over other communications media by its permanence, portability, robustness, browsability, accessibility, overall general convenience, physical attractiveness, status in society and relative cheapness. It has no need for a power source, an after-sales service or maintenance and, unlike electronic media, it transcends ever-changing and dating technologies. And as Stephen Fry says, 'people can be dippy about all things digital and still read books'. Book publishing, as a long-established industry, has a worldwide distribution system through which its output can be traded profitably in a continuing and largely regulated and controlled way. But publishers have to compete vigorously against other forms of entertainment, learning processes and information sources.

> Stephen Fry says: 'people can be dippy about all things digital and still read books'

Book publication continues to attract authors who want to communicate their ideas, thereby gaining recognition. Book publishing serves the million-copy fiction writer and the specialist author with sales of under 500 copies. Books can be published profitably for tiny markets which though limited in scale are limitless in number.

Elements underpinning UK book publishing are copyright protection; a plethora of talented living (and dead) authors; the freedom to publish; the English language, shared by much of the world; and a multiplicity of varied micro-markets, as opposed to a few mass markets, that arise and change rapidly and give opportunities for a wide range of publishers.

Publishers are not mere 'middle men' interjecting themselves between authors and readers while creaming off the profits. They add value to authors' works. Publishers commission authors (often before manuscripts are written), confer the authority of their brand on authors' works, finance the production and marketing, and sell the works wherever possible. The publisher, aiming to make a profit for the owners/shareholders and to carry on publishing:

- researches the markets in which it specializes and builds contacts,
- seeks authors (in competition with other publishers) and is sought by them,
- matches marketable ideas to saleable authors,
- assesses the quality of the author's work (sometimes externally refereed), costs of production and sales prospects,

- decides whether to risk its investment funds in projects to appear under its brand,
- edits and designs books to meet market needs,
- specifies, buys and oversees the work of print suppliers (in the UK or abroad) which manufacture the books,
- exploits new technology to reduce costs and stock levels, develop new products, and expand its sales and marketing techniques,
- builds a worldwide sales network,
- promotes and publicizes books to their intended users, the media, and to the intermediaries (retailers, wholesalers, and overseas firms) – the channels through which the books are mainly sold,
- sells the books face-to-face to intermediaries,
- holds bulk stock of titles, where necessary, to satisfy demand, and
- fulfils orders, distributes the books and collects the money, paying royalties to authors on sales made.

Additional income benefiting the publisher and author may be made from various licensing arrangements which enable other organizations at home and abroad to exploit the author's work in different ways, media and languages.

Although the specialist staff of large publishers carry out all the above activities, some work (such as the detailed editing of books) is often contracted out to freelancers or possibly to other firms. Smaller publishers may not have the resources to employ their own sales representatives or to distribute the books themselves so they may use larger publishers, or specialist firms. Apart from the decision to publish a book and raising the finance, all the other work could conceivably be outsourced, under the publisher's direction, to freelancers or separate firms. Publishers of all sizes have increasingly outsourced work in order to reduce their staff overhead costs, a process that began in the editorial departments. But there are potential drawbacks: the publisher may have less control over the way the books are produced; lose the marketing emphasis projected by its own employees committed solely to its books; run the risk of outsourcing core competences; and contribute to the profit margins of sub-contractors.

Publishers come in all shapes and sizes; but in order to give a comprehensive review this book concentrates on commercial publishing in medium and large firms with their specialist departments. Such firms account for most of the industry's sales. Small publishers are generally started up by people with particular expertise: the information contained here, covering the way in which larger firms with more resources tackle other areas, could still be invaluable to them.

If you catch the bug, publishing is fun and exciting. It involves working with (but not universally for) congenial people and provides opportunity for individuality, creativity, and considerable responsibility for the young. The workforce is fluid, there are many possibilities for changing jobs early on, scope to go freelance, and for some high-fliers, the building of empires. Even quite junior jobs call for the management of people, products and money. Such skills combined with ideas, effective communication and organization are marketable.

Starting salaries are low, staff work hard and long hours, formal career structures are uncertain, middle-ranking salaries are usually modest, and there is little job security in some firms. Yet there is intense competition to secure junior jobs, and many people are hooked for much of their working life – though rarely in the same firm. The appeal and fulfilment lie in serving people's entertainment, educational and informational needs, and sometimes in influencing the future course of events, in discovering and moulding new writing talent, and creating new markets. Publishers are continually dealing with many new products, each of which presents its own challenge in the way it can be produced and marketed for a particular audience. All jobs include routine and boring work. It is the infinite variety that fascinates. Every book presents its own issues to be solved at both the macro and micro levels. Success depends on personal contacts with authors, illustrators, printers, customers and colleagues – networking is a vital publishing skill.

The publishing industry has successfully undergone many changes. But the pace of change affecting the publishers' businesses and the professional lives of their staff is quickening at an unprecedented rate. The application of new technologies to the production of books, to their marketing and selling in various print and digital formats – and the pervasiveness of the internet – are impacting on every aspect of the business. Will the digital revolution be a seismic shift for the industry on a par with earlier pivotal moments? These include the introduction by Caxton of the printing press into England in 1476, the development of the English novel in the eighteenth century, and the first Penguin paperbacks, the brainchild of Allen Lane, published in 1935. At present no one can predict the effects, for example, of the digital retailers and technology companies – Amazon, Google and Microsoft – offering readers the ability to buy segments of books online.

The industry was traditionally broadly based with many medium-sized firms, but by the mid-1980s and after a spate of mergers and acquisitions, ownership became far more concentrated. A small handful of very large international publishing groups now control well over half the home market and the market for English language books throughout the world. The breadth of choice of companies for both authors and employees is narrowing.

Chapters 2 and 3 provide a background to the development of the publishing business from the latter half of the twentieth century to the present day. Chapter 2, 'A short history of modern trade publishing', reveals the forces that have shaped the publishers of general books for the consumer. Chapter 3, 'The consolidation of non-consumer publishing', describes the business drivers affecting the educational, academic, scientific, technical and medical (STM), and professional publishing sectors. In these areas, publishers are moving beyond the publishing of content to the provision of services.

The globalization of publishing and the consolidation of publishers to create ever larger enterprises is a continuing trend. As publishers used to compete with each other across Bedford Square in London, now they compete across the world. A striking feature is the rise of the European-owned publishers – the British, Dutch, French and German – that have bought American publishers and others elsewhere to create world-class market-leading companies. Large publisher size gives economies of scale in production, marketing, sales and distribution. Size provides the resources to finance and market the major books which dominate the sales charts; the ability to source and sell products internationally; and of growing significance, to make large investments in the digital delivery of large amounts of content and in the support of related services.

Negative impacts of the takeovers of small and medium publishers include the cancellation of authors' contracts, staff redundancies and in some cases the virtual or actual demise of once respected imprints. On the other hand, some bought firms survive relatively intact, are rejuvenated, and take full advantage of being part of a larger enterprise. Some authors, too, benefit from increased sales and higher royalties on sales made by the constituent firms of an international group.

While the trend is towards larger publishers, there will always be room for innovative, imaginative and entrepreneurial small publishers which, with lower overheads, are more agile than some large ones that can be overburdened with bureaucracy, slow to respond to fast-changing markets and fearful of innovation and technological development. The larger the giant publishers become, the more niches they leave open for smaller publishers to exploit. Small publishers, with less resources and small margins of error, tend to be more specific in the books they publish. They must work hard at choosing and marketing their titles carefully, and at developing authors and books which endure on the backlist. They can offer a more personal service to authors, who can receive less special attention from the larger publishers. All publishers give most attention to their important frontlist titles, especially in respect of marketing and sales effort. An author, or book, ranked lowly on a large publisher's list may be given greater prominence on a smaller publisher's. Small publishers may, however, ultimately lose their successful authors to larger publishers.

A sign of a vigorous industry is the frequent start-up of new firms – compared with many industries, publishing needs only a little equipment and a relatively small amount of investment capital. Some new firms arise from management buy-outs of lists or imprints surplus to a large firm; others are newly created from their former employees. No professional qualifications are needed to be a publisher – entry is unrestricted.

Publishing is intimately interwoven with society, touches on every aspect of knowledge, often reaches a worldwide market and produces books for tiny tots through to high-powered lawyers. But publishers specialize in producing products for particular markets, the dynamics of which differ. The key characteristics of the main publishing sectors are described in Chapter 4.

Some commentators state that it is now so easy for authors to self-publish there is no need for publishers. They say that publishers increasingly look like dinosaurs in the age of the internet. Much 'good enough' content is already available online for free. Poetry has escaped into the wild on the internet from which their creators receive no income. It will be the end of media businesses, such as publishers, which derive their earnings and profitability from paid-for content. Do such views have credence or are they based on simplistic ignorance? In Chapter 5, 'Creating and protecting value', we start with the publishing value chain and highlight the main ways publishers add value to authors' works, and go on to discuss the impact of the internet, risk and the financial performance and valuation of publishing companies. We then examine the topic of intellectual property, and the copyright regime which provides the legal framework underpinning the earnings of authors and publishers, and the ways in which it is practised and challenged by technological and social change.

Fundamentally publishing rests on the creativity and knowledge of authors. However, authors may feel that they are outsiders and kept in the dark by their

The novel *Shadowmancer* (2002) by G. P. Taylor was originally self-published before being taken on by Faber publishers. We hope this book helps authors to understand what publishers do. Chapter 6, 'The author', sets out the main elements of a book proposal made to a publisher, and a section on how to start out and self-publish. The growth of celebrity publishing has increased the use of ghost writers. Agents play an important part in supporting writers of general books and their business role is introduced here. The following chapters trace how a book goes through various stages until it reaches the bookshop shelf or internet store.

How are books commissioned and acquired? Hundreds of aspiring job seekers believe that becoming a commissioning editor is the ultimate dream job in publishing. Does it mean reading and editing an endless supply of manuscripts, and spending hours in fashionable restaurants with famous authors and their agents? Sometimes, but Chapter 7, 'Commissioning', dispels a few myths. You will find out that editors are responsible for coming up with marketable ideas and matching them to saleable authors. Successful publishing is founded on contracting good books that sell, and each new book is a business in its own right contributing to the business as a whole. The commissioning editor, holding an exposed and high-risk position, presents new book proposals to the senior management for approval. The editor has to make the business case for the investment. This chapter shows the way a new title is costed at the outset.

When a new book proposal has been given the green light, the publisher's editor (the buyer) issues the contract to the author (the seller). In most other kinds of business the seller writes the contract. The signature of the contract is a critical milestone for the author at which point their work acquires value: the publisher endorses their work. Furthermore, in trade publishing especially, the publisher pays the author (who may not yet have written the book) an advance sum of money which is set against their future royalty earnings, based on the publisher's prediction of sales. The big trade publishers compete fiercely to secure established bestselling authors, celebrities and new talent through the payment of large advances. Sometimes the sales of the book fall far short of expectations but the author keeps the money, which is written off by the publisher.

The first part of Chapter 8, 'The author contract and product development', covers the main elements of the contract and the impact authors' agents have on contractual relationships. Agents and UK and US publishers spend a lot of time arguing about in which countries (called 'territories') each publisher is to hold exclusive rights when publishing a book, even though books can be bought on the internet avoiding such territorial arrangements. Some US publishers do not seem to recognize the implications of the UK being part of the European Union and its single market. The contracts between authors (sometimes represented by agents) and publishers, and between publishers themselves, are the legal expression of the deals made. However, they include clauses that derive from practices of past eras which are increasingly challenged by market and technological change.

The second part of the chapter concentrates on editorial product development from contract through to publication. Books and their authors need different levels of care and attention during their development. Editors help authors to achieve their best work for the intended readership. The timing of publication can be critically important in maximizing sales. The publication of a book is a complex activity demanding flexibility and great attention to detail at every stage, and close liaison with many specialist staff in other departments. It requires planning and project management skills. Publishers find the management of authors quite vexing, since many run late in the handover of their manuscripts – these can also be incomplete or with unresolved loose-ends. In comparison to faster-moving industries such as music, video, software and consumer magazines, book publishers take a long time to produce a book from author's manuscript through to publication. Production schedules of four to nine months (or more) are typical – partly to allow adequate time for worldwide promotion and sales, described in later chapters.

Good design sells books. In Chapter 9, 'Design and production', we examine the ways books are designed, including the all important cover, and the ways in which books are produced and manufactured. Book production has not conceptually changed for hundreds of years. The author's raw manuscript is edited. The book is then typeset, proofread, made up into pages, and the book printed and bound in multiple copies. In the last decades of the twentieth century, computers were applied to typesetting and the pagination, but the end product remained the printed book.

A radical shift in the way books are prepared is now underway. Around the turn of the century, the publishers of learned journals, of professional content for lawyers and medical practitioners and of reference works appreciated that their customers, mainly institutional librarians in the case of journals and reference, wanted content in digital form for their users in addition to print. But the publishers face the technical problem that even when, and if, they locate the electronic files of the text used to produce their printed volumes, these files are of little help for digital delivery. Publishers have to break free of the fixed typographical world of Caxton's printed book. The text files now have to be prepared in a way which enables the content to be distributed in a variety of print formats (including large print for the reading impaired) and in digital formats (ebook, web, mobile and digital audio) which meet the needs of ever more demanding consumers.

Publishers have maintained their profitability by reducing their staff costs, for example by outsourcing the detailed editing of books and by reducing costs from their suppliers. The production costs of typesetting have fallen, and publishers have taken advantage of the competitive pressures on the UK printing industry from overseas firms offering lower manufacturing costs. Authors are suppliers as well and their cost, expressed in the form of royalty earnings they receive from publishers, has been cut back. Unfortunately for publishers, marketing and sales costs have risen significantly, especially in trade publishing.

How green and ethical is the book trade? Publishers source paper and printing from around the world, including the developing nations where labour costs are low and work practices possibly questionable. Such concerns are rising up the agenda and attention is being paid to the use of eco-friendly papers, the estimation of the carbon footprint resulting from the transportation of books from printers around the globe, to waste in the UK. For a high proportion of books, especially cheap paperbacks, if they are unsold within a matter of weeks of their publication they are pulped. Some titles are transported back and forth around the road network clocking up their book miles. Staple backlist books for which there is a continuing demand are returned by retailers to the publishers, only to be re-ordered and shipped out again.

In 2005 over 625,000 separate titles were sold in the UK market, and the top 500 titles accounted for 24 per cent of sales

Compared with other industries, book publishing launches a vast range of new products each year, many of which fail. Typically 20 per cent of a publisher's titles account for 80 per cent of its revenue but the uncertainties of estimating demand make the success of such books initially difficult to determine. Few new books could support the cost of retaining a market-research company to pre-test the market. Books like any commodity need a clear perception of the product and buyer and vigorous marketing to bring them together, but the marketing techniques deployed by other consumer goods industries are not wholly appropriate. Books are not a basic life necessity; the reader usually buys a single copy, only once, not repeatedly; author branding is important for sales, but company brand name identification, with some exceptions, is of little consequence to the reader (it can be of value to authors, agents, booksellers, the media and prospective employees). Readers are confronted by a multiplicity of choices to satisfy their interests. Books are borrowed free from libraries and from other sources, and used books are widely circulated, aided by internet selling and other means.

Around a third of adults in the UK do not buy a book at all – how can publishers reach this part of the population? The first part of Chapter 10, 'Marketing', gives a background to the market for books, the demographics of book buying and the way market segments may be targeted. The second part focuses on the marketing mix: product, price, place and promotion. Under 'product' we look at the use of branding by publishers to promote themselves and their authors. Book covers can give messages about a book's target audience, and they help to position the book in the mind of the consumer. The pricing of books exhibits unusual features. Trade publishers set high recommended retail prices on their potential bestselling new titles which are immediately slashed on launch by the major UK retailers in order to drive high sales volumes of hardbacks, which would have been unheard of in earlier times. Critics argue that publishers' pricing of popular books has become almost a fiction and that massive discounting to the consumer is undermining the value of books. The word 'place' covers the various sales channels through which books are promoted and sold. Some channels such as supermarkets and internet booksellers are growing in importance. Publishers' promotion of books can now extend to emarketing and the use of social networks to increase the visibility on the internet of books and authors as well as the engagement of readers. The main part of the chapter describes the promotion and publicity techniques deployed by different kinds of publisher to reach different market segments. The lead titles (i.e. the most important titles) consume most of the publishers' marketing expenditure. Nevertheless, publicists are adept at generating free media interest in a broader range of books, including those from smaller publishers.

Most publishers do not sell their books directly to readers. Publishers' main customers are the booksellers and others in the supply chain. The prime task of publishers' sales departments is to sell their new books in advance of publication and their backlist books to the intermediaries (retailers and wholesalers) in the UK and overseas, predominantly face to face.

Chapter 11, 'Sales and distribution', describes the different methods publishers use to sell at home and overseas. Publishers derive most of their sales revenue from a small number of customers, and a small revenue from a great number. The sales managers of the large trade publishers concentrate on selling their most important lead titles to the central buyers of the UK bookselling chains and supermarkets, which decide which books are going to be featured in their stores nine to 12 months later. A tiny number of people determine which books are going to be displayed to the bulk of the public. For smaller publishers, access to the main retail channels has become increasingly difficult and expensive, and they may look for alternative routes to market. Higher education textbook publishers promote their texts to lecturers, who determine which texts will be adopted and bought by students from campus stores and internet booksellers. The school textbook publishers sell their books directly to schools, although some sales go through intermediaries.

UK publishing is highly successful at exporting and more than matches the efforts of US publishing with its much larger home market. Exports overall are nearly double imports into the UK. Much of the industry depends on export markets for its survival and profitability. Around a third of UK publishers' sales are exports and additionally publishers receive royalties and other income from editions licensed abroad. In some sectors of publishing, such as English Language Teaching (ELT) and in some academic and STM areas, exports form the majority of sales. Sales to mainland Europe have grown and supplanted North America as the main export destination, and sales to Australasia have declined. Asian markets such as the fast-growing economies of India and China have attracted investment and sales effort. Piracy in developing countries is a considerable threat and is the enemy of UK publishers, legitimate indigenous publishers and authors alike. The trade body, The Publishers Association, is active in leading anti-piracy campaigns.

Most of a publisher's cash is tied up in stock. The turnover of a publisher's complete stock of all books commonly takes more than a year. Only the largest publishers can afford to have their own warehousing and distribution services. Smaller publishers use the large publishers to distribute their books, or independent distribution companies or wholesalers. It is not worth while for distributors to service the very small publishers, who may distribute their books from their back bedroom. In view of the high cost of storing books, publishers have to rid themselves of books which have ended their sales life, through selling them off at rock bottom prices to remainder dealers (who sell them to retailers at home and abroad), or by pulping.

It is thought that half the books that are in print sell less than 250 copies per year, many just a few copies. Hitherto, the economics of conventional printing precluded publishers from reprinting titles in small quantities for which there was a very small and continuing sale. Such titles were allowed to go 'out of print' once stock was exhausted, in effect meaning that orders from customers were rejected. However, the new printing technology called 'print on demand' (POD) enables the manufacture of tiny quantities, of say 50 copies, or even one copy at a time. The large academic publishers and the university presses with back catalogues of thousands of highly specialist titles sold at high prices were the first to take advantage of POD, but improvements in the technology and falling costs allow its use in other areas. It offers the prospect for publishers to reduce the amount of cash tied up in stock and the costs of storage. Indeed there are new publishers who hold no stock at all, who use their POD supplier (some are linked to wholesalers) to print copies in direct response to customer orders.

Chapter 12 examines the area of rights sales. The author–publisher contract sets out the scope of the publisher to license various kinds of rights to other firms

In 2007, through one leading wholesaler, only 70,000 titles sold seven or more copies

which enable them to exploit the author's work in different ways, media, territories and languages. Authors' agents, however, often retain some rights on behalf of their authors and license them directly. Examples of rights sales include selling to a book club, to a US publisher, to a foreign language publisher to translate the book (for example in mainland Europe, Russia, China, Japan, South Korea, Latin America), to a newspaper or magazine to serialize the book, to an audiobook publisher, to a film or TV company to dramatize the work, to a mobile phone company to bundle content with its information services, or to a digital content supplier offering a distinct service.

Since rights income usually attracts little in the way of direct costs, it cannot be compared directly to sales income on the print edition. More correctly, the revenue retained after paying the author their contracted share can be compared to the profit on print sales. To be compared directly to the sales income, rights revenue should be multiplied by a factor of six to eight.

Chapter 13, 'The sales channels for books in the UK', looks at the different kinds of retailers, wholesalers, library suppliers and the companies which sell directly to consumers, and the ways in which publishers conduct their business with them. Changes in the channels impact on the publishers and influence their publishing strategies. The last decades of the twentieth century were marked by the decline of small and independently owned bookshops and the rise of large bookselling chains. More recently the bookselling chains have themselves come under pressure from the rapid growth of internet bookselling and from supermarkets giving more space to highly marketable books. The larger the size of the retailer, the greater the leverage it has to extract better terms of business from its suppliers. When retailers buy goods from suppliers it is normal for retailers to take the risk of actually selling them on to consumers: if the goods do not sell it is the retailer's problem. The book business is different. Publishers trade with the retailers (and wholesalers) on a 'sale or return' basis. This effectively means that if the retailer is unable to sell the book it has stocked it returns the copies quickly to the publisher: the retailer's risk of stocking or over-ordering is borne by the publisher. Retail exposure is vital for trade book sales. But the cost to the publishers of securing that display in the powerful retailers is ever increasing. Publishers sell their books to the retailers at a discount, a percentage of the publisher's recommended retail price. On some bestselling trade books, the big retailers get a discount of 60 per cent of the recommended published price and ask the publisher for additional payments to promote the book. The retailers in turn offer the books at a large discount off the publisher's recommended published price, especially during the peak sales period running up to Christmas. The market is polarizing. The big books sell in huge quantities while other titles struggle to maintain a presence. For many kinds of books, the sales quantities have declined and their shelf life in terrestrial retailers has shortened. Large numbers of the more specialist titles, including academic and STM titles, are not stocked at all.

Some analysts foretell that two to three publishers will eventually come to dominate worldwide, the sales of books and related products in each field – consumer, education and high-level STM and professional publishing. Will the big publishers succeed or even want to cut out the intermediaries – their current main customers – from the supply chain from author to reader and supply end-users directly? This question relates to the question 'will publishers continue to exist?'

Businesses owe their existence to their ability to charge, at a profit, for the added value they give to a product or service in the supply chain. The learned journal publishers, albeit operating in a market of unique characteristics, were amongst the first to build platforms of their digital content to enable direct supply to their library customers. But the intermediaries serving libraries developed their own technological solutions and services. The big trade publishers are rapidly digitizing their books and building their own platforms. From a consumer's viewpoint (including librarians and other institutional purchasers) the ease of purchase is of great significance. However big the publishers get, there are thousands of publishers issuing books that people want to buy. The retailers, and the wholesalers supplying them, aggregate the content from virtually all publishers, then market and make it available to purchasers. Furthermore, being that much closer to the end-user, their level of service is orientated to consumer needs, to a greater extent than any one publisher can achieve, and thus they can outsell the publisher's direct route.

Throughout the chapters on the work of publishers, there are boxes on desirable skills relating to the particular job. Chapter 14, 'Getting into publishing', gives help and tips to secure the first job, advice on potential career paths, and stresses the importance of continuing professional development. It concludes with a section on diversity: the gender and ethnic imbalances in the UK publishing workforce. The survey of publishing provided in this book necessarily excludes much detail but we hope that it gives you an insight into what is for many in the industry an exciting and satisfying way of life.

The endmatter of the book includes a glossary (a simple look-up guide to UK publishing terms), a bibliography of key texts and resources, and a directory of publishing organisations. There follow lists of networking opportunities, training organisations, scholarships and grants, recruitment agencies and career advisers, and relevant university courses.

We believe that books still matter. To read *Cold Mountain* by Charles Frazier is a different experience to seeing the film. Reading a book can be a highly personal pleasure, or a sociable activity – just think of the success of reading groups in the UK. Digital resources have firmly taken hold in professional and educational spheres, but books should still be an important part of education at school or university. For the authors of this volume, the words of the novelist Margaret Drabble sum up our level of attachment to books and print: 'I need words and print . . . I need print like an addict. I could live without it, perhaps. But I hope I never have to try.'

CHAPTER 2

A short history of modern trade publishing

The aim of this chapter is to provide a brief overview of the development of modern trade publishing. In the 1950s book publishing was broadly based with around 50 medium-sized UK firms each employing around 50 staff and issuing several hundred titles per year, usually in hardback. The publishers were owned privately, usually by family members who held a majority share. They concentrated on fiction and non-fiction – termed 'general' or 'trade' or, more recently, 'consumer books' – although they also developed educational (school textbook) and academic lists subservient to the general side.

The 1960s brought great optimism as in other cultural industries such as music and fashion. Rayner Unwin of George Allen & Unwin talks of the 'informal, almost casual, publishing that was still possible during the sixties' (Unwin, page 238). For example, work on the travel writer Eric Newby's book, *Grain Race* (1968), took place in Unwin's flat in the evenings. Censorship was dealt a blow with the publication of the unexpurgated version of D. H. Lawrence's *Lady Chatterley's Lover* on 10 November 1961 – a victory for Penguin, which had won the right to publish the previously banned novel against a charge that it was obscene. The first print run of 200,000 sold out on the first day and within a year Penguin had sold 2 m copies. 'The trial was a turning-point, and after it was over previously forbidden works like *The Ginger Man* and *The Kama Sutra* were finally published in this country' (Lewis, page 333).

Throughout the 1960s and 1970s (apart from in the recession of the early to mid-1970s), much of the publishers' fast-growing prosperity was based on readers' affluence and increasing public expenditure (Table 2.1). Sales of hardback adult and children's books were underpinned by generous government funding of schools and libraries.

Mass-market paperback publishing grew substantially and was carried out by separate firms. In the main they acquired reprint paperback rights from the houses that originated titles in hardback. Literary agents, who increasingly began to represent the interests of fiction and non-fiction authors, were resented by some traditional publishers, who saw them as unwarranted intruders into the publisher–author relationship. New publishers arose producing in large quantities highly-illustrated non-fiction books in full colour at low and affordable prices – described by traditionalists as 'down-market' or as 'non-books'. Paul Hamlyn

> The judge in the *Lady Chatterley's Lover* trial asked the jury: 'Is it a book you would wish your wife or servants to read?'

Table 2.1 Number of titles published in the UK from 1950 to 1980 (source: Norrie, page 220)

Year	Number of titles and new editions
1950	17,072
1960	23,783
1970	33,489
1980	48,158

(1926–2001), the greatest exponent of affordable illustrated books, made a series of fortunes from illustrated book publishing. In turn he sold his Paul Hamlyn imprint to the magazine company IPC, founded Octopus by buying back the Paul Hamlyn imprint for a nominal sum, plus liabilities, and then sold his imprints to Reed Consumer Books for an enormous sum. In his lifetime, he founded the Paul Hamlyn Foundation to give greater access to the arts.

The publication of *The Reader's Digest Great World Atlas* (1961), which had double-page spreads displaying superb full-colour graphics, and extended captions not unlike those found in magazines, and the *Treasures of Tutankhamun*, tied-in to the British Museum exhibition (1972) were inspirational to some embryonic book packagers. The packagers went on to produce highly illustrated full-colour information books which they presold to publishers around the world to be marketed and distributed under the publishers' imprints. In the late 1970s, the highly illustrated publishers brought colour books into the supermarkets by producing own brand books for them at very low prices.

By the end of the 1970s the era of the 'gentleman publisher' was fast disappearing. The phrase had been used historically to describe grand publishers of literary fiction, typically derided as gentlemen who ran their companies by the seat of their pants, who adopted a paternalist management style, or who according to some literary agents exhibited ungentlemanly behaviour in their contractual arrangements with authors. Some of the foremost publishers, who had personally built great publishing companies, had reached the end of their careers. Some of their descendants, given senior management positions, were either incompetent or ill prepared for the changes to come.

The stable and expansionary publishing world of the 1960s and 1970s was rudely shattered by the recession of 1980 which forced publishers to cut their lists and overheads – by making redundant both older staff and the weaker staff sucked in during the era of fast growth. From then on progressive cuts in public expenditure throughout the English-speaking world would be the order of the day. Reductions in public funding adversely affected the publishing and availability of some kinds of books. These included hardback fiction from new and minor authors destined for public libraries, children's books supported by public and school libraries, high-priced academic monographs for university libraries, and textbooks produced for UK state schools. A further factor of the 1980s and early 1990s was high book-price inflation and the appreciation of sterling against the

EXPERT

Women's publishing

Jane Potter, Senior Lecturer, Oxford International Centre for Publishing Studies

The second wave of the feminist movement in the 1960s and the subsequent rise of women's studies courses in the 1970s and 1980s not only created a new market for books but also inspired the foundation of women-run, women-centred publishing houses whose range and diversity reflect the multiplicity of female experience and writing.

Of the many women's publishing ventures of the last decades of the twentieth century, perhaps the best known – and certainly the most commercially successful – is Virago. Unlike radical women's presses, Virago did not eschew the mainstream. Its founder Carmen Callil aimed for it to become 'the first mass-market publisher for 52 per cent of the population – women' and for its books to be enjoyed by both sexes. Founded in 1973, Virago's feminist agenda reflects the changing attitudes and roles of women in the 1970s and 1980s, while its business history reflects that of the industry as a whole in the same decades, when fluctuating markets, corporate mergers, and (often) hostile takeovers dominated British publishing. Having published its first 10 titles in association with Quartet Books, Virago was then run as an independently owned editorial imprint by Callil, Ursula Owen and Harriet Spicer. In 1976 with capital of £1,500 and a loan of £10,000, Virago became self-financing. By 1982 the firm was a wholly owned subsidiary of the Chatto, Virago, Bodley Head and Cape Group, but when this was bought by Random House in 1987, Callil, Owen, Spicer, Alexandra Pringle and Lennie Goodings succeeded in a management buy-out to make Virago independent once more. In 1995 the board voted to sell the company to Little, Brown, and Virago became an imprint under the direction of Lennie Goodings. The success of Margaret Atwood's novel *Alias Grace* in 1997 helped the firm to achieve its highest-ever trade turnover.

Virago's brand was established by its distinctive green covers and bitten-apple logo and inspired a devoted female readership. The Virago Reprint Library was founded in 1977 specifically to showcase women's history titles, while the Virago Modern Classics series, launched in 1978 with Antonia White's novel *Frost in May* (1933), was instrumental in the rediscovery of a forgotten female literary tradition. Virago Vs were launched in 1997 to cater to a new generation of readers, with titles such as Sarah Waters' hugely successful *Tipping the Velvet*.

Other, smaller presses also continue to foster women's writing. Founded in 1974, Onlywomen Press prioritizes the writing of lesbian authors, while the Women's Press (founded 1978) publishes feminist fiction and non-fiction. Sheba Feminist Press (founded 1980), a not-for-profit workers' co-operative, focuses on marginalized writing by lesbians, women of colour, and working-class women. The promotion of Welsh women's writing is the guiding principle of Honno (founded 1986), which is supported by a co-operative of shareholders and the Welsh Book Council. The independent publishing house, Persephone Books (founded 1999), reprints neglected 'middlebrow' twentieth-century fiction and non-fiction mainly, though not exclusively, by women.

currencies of countries to which UK publishers traditionally exported. This led to a continued decline in export sales to the benefit of US publishers. General books from America, particularly mass-market paperbacks, were more competitively priced in mainland Europe and Australia.

MERGERS AND ACQUISITIONS

The rise of European publishers through their purchase of US publishing began in the 1970s. The UK banking, investment and publishing group Pearson, owner of the *Financial Times*, bought the UK publisher Penguin in 1970, and the New York based Viking Press in 1975. The German family-owned media group Bertelsmann broke out of Europe through the purchase of the US publisher Bantam Books in 1980 and Doubleday in 1986. It became the world's largest trade publisher in 1998 when it purchased the US publisher Random House.

In the UK, the 1980s were the start of a period of mergers and acquisitions which restructured the publishing industry. A handful of large international publishing groups eventually came to control over half the home market: long-established, medium-sized firms were to become a rarity – today Faber & Faber is one of the few left. The deregulation of financial markets led to the increased availability of long and short-term equity and debt financing allowing the large players to take over medium-sized publishers, and small publishers to expand or start in business. Book publishing was attractive to investors who could see that the industry had consistently, that is until 1987, returned pre-tax profits and return on capital above the average level of all industries.

Unlike today, book publishing had traditionally been linked to printing. Some book publishers either owned printers or were owned by printers. The idea that general book publishing was part of the larger media leisure industry evolved slowly. At the end of the 1960s and into the 1970s, companies from a variety of industries, including TV and electronics, began to buy up and amass publishing companies. An example was RCA buying Random House in the USA (1965), and the purchase of Hutchinson by London Weekend Television (1978). They tended to keep such companies as separate, sometimes prestigious entities, rather than parts of an overall corporate industrial logic.

Throughout the 1990s, the international consolidation of the main English language publishers continued. But the boardroom strategies switched from acquiring publishers across the range of different market segments to focusing on the leadership of such segments.

The turn of the new century was marked by an increase in the gathering strategy of European-based publishers to acquire US publishers and the willingness of some of the giant US media corporations to sell off their book publishing interests. From the latter's perspective, book publishing represented a small fraction of their stock market capitalization and was seen as a mature and niche business in comparison to their faster growing and central media interests (television and the internet). By contrast, the smaller European-based media corporations, focused to a greater extent on book publishing, seized the opportunity. Their purchase of US publishers gave them access to the world's largest and richest nation and the ability to grow quickly their dominant market

Founded in 1929, Faber & Faber remains an independent publishing house. William Golding's *Lord of the Flies* was published by Faber in 1954

share of book publishing worldwide, including the UK. The steady earnings growth derived from book publishing in US and UK markets are more attractive to mainland European publishers, some with a strong history of family ownership; in France and Germany companies have historically been less exposed to the vagaries of the stock market.

The corporate strategy of leading international publishers is to achieve leading market shares (number 1 or 2) in their chosen sectors through their own organic growth and often the acquisition of other publishers. Though they publish books predominantly in the English language, their geographical spread allows them to publish in other languages.

THE CHANGING CHARACTER OF TRADE PUBLISHING

The restructuring of UK book publishing in the 1980s affected all types of publishing but its effects were most dramatic in consumer publishing, the fault lines having appeared in the 1970s. As mentioned above, ownership was traditionally divided between many hardback publishers and around a dozen separate mass-market paperback houses. In 1969 the top paperback houses were Penguin (selling 27 m copies), Fontana (13 m), Corgi (13 m) and Panther (9 m).

The publishing strategy was to establish a book in hardback at a high price and subsequently to reissue it, around a year later, in a paperback format at a lower price to a wider audience. Hardback fiction and non-fiction were published in half-yearly seasons (the spring/summer, and autumn/winter) headed by major 'lead titles' and sold to booksellers, libraries and book clubs. Mass-market paperbacks were fast-moving books published in monthly batches, with each month headed by lead fiction and non-fiction titles, with various category titles forming the remainder. Paperbacks were published in A format – 'pocket' or 'rack-sized' books. They were often straight reductions of the original hardbacks – pages of the hardback edition were, in a pre-digital age, photographically reduced to the size of the paperback edition. Printed in large quantities on cheap paper, they reached a wider retail market beyond bookshops and were sold in a way more similar to that of magazines.

The respective character of hardback and paperback publishers was very different. The hardback publishers inhabited their fine but slowly decaying Georgian houses in Bloomsbury, around Bedford Square, and in other high-class central London locations. The palatial former reception rooms, with Adam fireplaces and hung with chandeliers, were impressive settings for the managing director or the editorial director. When Tom Maschler decided to pursue a career in publishing in the 1950s, he went to see André Deutsch (1917–2000), who was to publish in hardback some of the most important names in post-war fiction, including John Updike, V. S. Naipaul, Philip Roth and Norman Mailer. When Deutsch told him that he had no openings, Maschler responded that the salary was not important. 'At that he asked when I could start. We settled for the following Monday' (page 39).

The editors were very much in control and women were in the majority in the publishing workforce. Diana Athill, who also worked with André Deutsch, writes in her memoir *Stet*: 'All publishing was run by many badly-paid women and a few much better-paid men: an imbalance that women were, of course, aware of, but which they seemed to take for granted' (page 56). The production staff, who hired the printers to produce the books, and the marketing and sales staff were crammed in smaller offices in the basement and the attics. The mass-market paperback reprinters occupied office blocks in cheaper London locations. Theirs was a sales driven operation.

The hardback publishers played their traditional role of nurturing new writing talent and working closely with authors on manuscripts. Their backlists were complete with great and loyal authors, and some enduring money-spinning books. Their formidable reputation ensured that new books were reviewed (literary review editors ignored paperbacks), that the public librarians would automatically order sufficient quantities, and that the compliant independent booksellers would display and stock their titles. The advent of book clubs supplied another outlet. The booksellers complained that the book clubs were undermining their business by offering their members new hardbacks at discounted prices by mail order. The publishers were pleasantly surprised by the paradoxical increased sales through bookshops stemming from a book club's large-scale consumer advertising campaigns. However, by the early to mid-1980s, hardback publishers found themselves making hardly any profit from selling copies themselves: the copy sales business model. They derived their profit and laid off risks by making rights and co-edition sales to others: to paperback publishers, book clubs, US publishers and foreign language publishers: the licensing business model. While the hardback publishers employed highly talented editors, they also had editors who favoured their pet projects and authors who produced books which few wanted to buy.

VERTICAL RESTRUCTURING

The false dichotomy between hardback and paperback publishing could not survive. The book market was rapidly changing, readers' expectations were altering, competition between publishers to secure bestselling authors was intensifying and literary agents were far more adept in extracting maximum advance payments for their authors from publishers. Bookshops had steadily increased the display space for paperbacks, and publishers such as Penguin had provided free paperback shelving for bookshops.

The hardback publishers were used to acquiring the exclusive right to publish an author's work for the full term of copyright in hardback and paperback, even though they had no mass-market paperback publishing capability; and similarly to acquiring US rights which they in turn licensed to US publishers. The hardback publisher would sublicense to a UK paperback publisher – for a fixed period (on average eight years) – the right to publish the paperback on which it would pay the hardback publisher a royalty of 7.5 per cent on the published price, rising to 10 per cent or more after specified large quantities had been sold. The hardback publisher would share the royalties received with the author. The paperback publisher would want to acquire its main titles two years ahead of paperback publication. The originating publisher would secure at that time a large advance payment from the paperback publisher, similarly shared with the author.

Paperback publishers facing escalating advances increased their output of

Stet (2000) by Diana Athill is a memoir of her fifty years in publishing

original titles, sometimes licensing rights to hardback publishers. Since authors derived most of their income from paperback sales (and sometimes US sales), it made sense for agents to cut out the hardback publisher's share of such sales. Agents looking to maximize income would license the book separately to an independent hardback publisher, a paperback publisher, and a US publisher, thereby obtaining advances from each party and full royalty rates for their authors (less the agent's commission). Eric de Bellaigue describes the expanding role of literary agents as 'one of the most arresting developments of the last thirty years in trade publishing' (page 204). The general publishers which owned both hardback and paperback firms (vertical integration) paid authors full royalty rates on each edition and were therefore better positioned to capture the leading authors. Paperback and hardback publishers without a hardback or paperback arm became increasingly desperate – sometimes they entered into alliances in order to bid for the big books jointly.

Another strand leading to the amalgamation of consumer book publishing, again reaching back to the late 1970s, was the weakening polarization between the traditional formats. The mass-market paperback houses, facing increasing competition in the industry and higher title output, recorded lower unit sales per title. Paperback prices rose and the ownership of paperback houses became more concentrated. Furthermore readers' expectations created a new market for certain books and authors to be published in the larger B format – quality or trade paperback. Peter Mayer, Chief Executive of Penguin from 1978 to 1996, had launched this concept when he was at Avon Books in New York in the 1970s. Literary fiction and a range of non-fiction could be published at higher prices in B format; and Mayer applied this idea to more commercial fiction, such as M. M. Kaye's *The Far Pavilions*, which was to sell 400,000 copies within six months of its publication in paperback in 1979. Such books could be reprints from hardbacks, reissues or originals. Both mass-market paperback and hardback houses started up trade paperback imprints and some hardback houses ventured into the A format field, usually with disastrous consequences. Over time, the use of the trade paperback to publish original fiction (including new writers) and non-fiction has grown apace as has the increased use of a range of paperback sizes.

Intellectual property rights

The main financial assets of a publishing company are its intellectual property rights (IPR). These are enshrined in the contracts it holds with suppliers (negotiated directly with authors or via their agents; book packagers, US and other international publishers) and with companies to which it has sold rights, such as book clubs, US publishers and foreign language publishers. The original IPR derives from the author – the publisher then adds value. Ultimately the value of the IPR depends on consumers buying the product.

By the end of the 1980s and early 1990s, most of the formerly independent hardback houses were part of the major publishing corporations. Each had the capability of publishing and acquiring rights in all formats: mass-market paperback, trade paperback and hardback. Their imprints were gathered together in modern London offices. The new owners combed through the old contracts entered into by their hardback houses with the paperback publishers and noted the titles which had, from other takeovers, fallen into the hands of rival paperback imprints and the termination dates of the licences. In due course they would claw back the paperback rights to those books for their own paperback imprints, much to the consternation of the bereft paperback houses, and some authors and agents.

Most of Graham Greene's novels were published from the 1920s by the hardback publisher Heinemann and from the 1960s by The Bodley Head, and sub-licensed in paperback to Penguin. Random House subsequently purchased these originating hardback publishers, reverted the paperback rights from Penguin and re-issued his major works from the beginning of the twenty-first century under the Vintage Classics imprint.

The pressure to control rights internationally prompted US general publishers to acquire UK imprints, and vice versa, and both UK and US publishers were attractive to the mainland European publishers, especially to the German media corporation Bertelsmann, and more recently to the French group Lagardère. However, although all the major consumer book publishers attained sister imprints on both sides of the Atlantic, their ability to acquire world English rights in the works of bestselling authors is still constrained by the US and UK literary agents, who continue to license UK and US editions to imprints in competing ownership.

A CHANGE IN CULTURE

The hardback general book publishers, which had developed valuable IPR over decades, held an increasing rarity value and at the peak of the merger boom commanded high prices. As for the staff of the newly taken-over general publishers, the outlook for many was bleak. If not made immediately redundant, they found themselves entering the world of corporate publishing. The editors especially had worked in a small company culture, where they had enjoyed considerable autonomy over the kinds of books they wanted to publish. They carried with them a set of values quite often at odds with those of their new employers, which emphasized sales and profit and sometimes demanded clean and tidy desks, clear of manuscripts and books, in an open plan environment.

Some editors blamed the accountants for preventing them from doing the books they wanted to publish. It was not the accountants per se: the whole culture had changed. The nature of consumer book publishing had changed from being *product-led* to being *market-driven*. As Alan Bartram noted at the end of the twentieth century,

> the practice of financing a potential poor-seller by profits from successful books, as a publisher such as Victor Gollancz would do because he, personally, believed it deserved publishing even if it cost him money, or as university presses considered it their duty to do – behaviour once considered normal practice – has almost disappeared. (Bartram, page 9)

Editorial individuality is still present in the large corporations. Some major publishing groups have attempted to regain some of the advantages of the smaller publisher by retaining or creating individual imprints. It is vital for innovation that they can lead the market by introducing new authors, publishing books in different formats, and marketing and selling them in different ways. Furthermore, while major publishers attract talented staff from smaller publishers, senior staff of major publishers leave to start up new companies or to reinvigorate smaller publishers.

THE RESHAPING OF RETAIL

While trade or consumer publishing was being restructured, the increased availability of finance in the 1980s also aided the transformation and concentration of UK bookselling. Traditionally, UK bookselling had meant the major chain WHSmith (which had its roots in station bookstalls and high street stationery outlets), small independently owned chains, and a large number of independent or small bookshops. But in the 1980s, new chains, principally Waterstone's and Dillons, brought a new kind of bookselling – large well-stocked bookshops, stocking up to 50,000 titles, three to four times the size of many independents. The enhanced professionalism in bookselling spread to the existing larger independents which had to compete. The small independents lost market share. The new chains expanded aggressively and argued that they needed higher discounts (the bookseller's percentage margin between the retail price of a book and the price bought from the publisher) and extended credit periods (the time to settle invoices). The consumer book publishers benefited from the well-stocked and branded bookshops displaying their books, and agreed to better discounts, easier credit and the continued right to return unsold books. The power relationship between publishers and booksellers, for so long weighted in the publisher's favour, began to tip towards the major retailers, as is common in most consumer goods industries. Furthermore by the mid-1990s, the major supermarkets were devoting more space to bestselling books and were intent on driving down book prices to the consumer, and their costs of supply.

> The first Waterstone's was opened in 1982 by Tim Waterstone in Old Brompton Road, London

Another factor impinging on the publishers' margins, pushing up the average discount on sales made to UK customers, was the rise of the trade wholesalers supplying the declining and fragmented independent bookshop sector. From the early 1980s to the early 1990s, the proportion of a publisher's sales passing through the wholesalers grew from around 10 per cent to over 20 per cent, at the expense of direct supply to bookshops. While the chains won discounts from the publishers of well above 40 per cent off the published price, the small independents were stuck with the traditional discounts of 33 to 35 per cent. The trade book wholesalers argued they needed at least a 15 per cent margin between the price they bought the books from the publisher and the price they sold them to a retailer, thus they pressed for a 50 per cent discount or more from the publisher. WHSmith and the bookseller chains, meanwhile, ratcheted up the publishers' discounts still further. Overall, from the mid-1980s to the late 1990s, the average trade discount given by the consumer publishers to their UK customers increased by 10 to 15 per cent.

The major publishers also locked themselves into a battle of paying rocketing levels of advances for lead titles in order to keep their share of the limited number of such titles available. Consumer expenditure on books peaked in 1993, and by the time many of those books with high advances were published, the consumer book market was in decline. The return of unsold books from booksellers, a long-time feature of consumer book publishing (especially of paperbacks, usually pulped), surpassed more than 25 per cent of the publishers' sales as booksellers destocked hardbacks and paperbacks. On some lead titles, the actual sales fell far short of the expected number on which the author's advance against royalties had been calculated – the advance was thus unearned. A publisher which may have budgeted an author's royalty rate of between 15–20 per cent of the publisher's revenue, may have paid an advance (in effect a non-returnable fee) which equated to an effective royalty rate of 30 per cent of sales income, or more in disastrous cases. The consumer book publishers emerged from the recession of the early 1990s leaner and fitter but with low levels of profitability.

In the immediate aftermath of the collapse of the Net Book Agreement (NBA) in 1995, under which minimum prices had been set for books, consumer spending on books bottomed out in the spring of 1996, and then staged a steady recovery to a new peak in 1998 – a vintage year for bestselling titles. Heavy discounting by retailers of the new, most popular titles became the norm. Publishers increased their recommended retail prices above the general rate of inflation to accommodate the higher discounts given to both retailers and the public.

PUBLISHING AFTER THE NBA

The low company valuations of the consumer book publishers in the 1990s were in marked contrast to the boom of the 1980s. While most of the owners persevered, Reed decided to sell its consumer imprints in order to concentrate on STM and professional publishing, recording a massive write-off in the process. Nevertheless, newer independent UK publishers, such as Bloomsbury, Fourth Estate, Orion and Piatkus grew strongly. Another source of new publishers were the book packagers, usually concentrating on illustrated non-fiction and reference, many of which decided to publish their books in English under their own imprints in the UK, and sometimes the US, rather than license them to publishers.

By the end of the century, the main consumer publishers had mostly recovered their levels of profitability, and WHSmith paid what was considered by some competitors to be a high price for the UK publisher Hodder Headline. The commercial logic of a retailer owning a publisher was to come under question.

It took nearly a decade for the full effects of the removal of resale price maintenance to work through the supply chain. Early gainers were the bookselling chains, which grew at the expense of the independents and expanded their number of branches. The chains came to compete on price and adopted the 'three for two' promotional offers at the front of their attractive and well-stocked stores. Losers in the post-NBA world were the businesses which benefited from pricing regulation: the bargain bookshops (a large number had to close); the book clubs (which were to lose sales to the internet and the major retailers); and independent booksellers (who could not compete on price). Latterly the chains have come under pressure themselves from the price cuts and expanding ranges of the supermarkets (led by Tesco), and from the ultimate range bookseller, Amazon. Supermarket and internet sales have increased in market share in relation to the faltering bookseller

F O C U S

Net Book Agreement

The Net Book Agreement (NBA) or the resale price maintenance (RPM) of books, which had endured throughout the twentieth century, collapsed in September 1995. Up to that date, the publishers set the retail prices of books (termed the 'net price'). Retailers were not allowed to sell net books to the public below the stated prices, and therefore could not use the price incentives commonly used for other kinds of products. In that virtually all the main consumer book publishers were members of their trade organization, The Publishers Association (PA), and were voluntary signatories of the NBA, the PA was highly successful in enforcing the NBA amongst retailers, and defending it against critics. The PA regulated the operation of the market in other ways, such as negotiating the rules governing the operation of book clubs, which offered books at discounted prices to their members by mail order. Also libraries, under a special licence, were allowed to purchase books at 10 per cent off the net price.

The purpose of the NBA was to create a well-ordered book market in which a large number of dedicated booksellers could afford to stock a wide range of new and backlist titles, and to offer free customer services, sure in the knowledge that they could not be undercut by predatory retailers taking the cream off the narrow range of current bestsellers and fast-selling backlist titles.

Prior to the demise of the NBA, consumer spending on books continued to fall, and pro and anti arguments concerning RPM raged amongst publishers and booksellers. By the 1990s opponents of the scheme argued that price was an important lever for generating sales. Some retailers, such as the bookselling chain Dillons and the supermarket chain Asda, presented themselves in the press as championing the consumer's right to low book prices, by selling books at deeply discounted prices from publishers who had abandoned the NBA – these retailers and publishers such as Hodder Headline and Reed Consumer Books appeared to be gaining a competitive advantage. The pro-NBA publishers and booksellers also faced expensive and uncertain legal proceedings to defend the NBA in the courts, threatened by the government's Office of Fair Trading and the European Commission. Then in September 1995, the announcement of a cut price promotion by major trade publishers Random House and HarperCollins with WHSmith triggered the collapse. With no consensus among publishers and booksellers, the NBA passed into UK trade history and was formally ended in 1997. Various forms of fixed pricing continue in some mainland European countries, including France and Germany; and in the USA the law ensures there is greater equality in the discounts offered to bookstores.

chains carrying excess stock and expensive retail space. The pressure on margins throughout the supply chain has forced the consolidation of the major book wholesalers and library suppliers.

Today readers are able to purchase heavily promoted bestsellers at large discounts off the publishers' recommended published prices from a wide range of retailers, which compete for consumers' attention primarily on price. Consumers have enjoyed a period of book price deflation. As the UK economy enjoyed continued growth from 1992 into the new century, publishers experienced a period of increasing book sales, albeit made at yet higher discounts to wholesalers and retailers.

Legacy practices of the NBA era endure. Consumer publishers still print the price on the book's cover, and author royalties are usually based on the recommended price, albeit with let-outs for sales at high discounts. The non-consumer book publishers have mainly abandoned these practices.

A CHANGE IN PUBLISHING STRATEGY

From the late 1990s, the major publishers reversed their former 'scatter-gun' strategy of publishing as many titles as possible in the hope that one or two would be hits. Facing increasing polarization in the market between the bestselling titles and the also-rans (the 'winner takes all' maxim common in the creative industries), they cut their new title output progressively to concentrate on books and authors considered marketable, especially those that would fit the retailers' promotional plans.

The so-called 'midlist' authors were casualties, not that publishers admit publicly to having a midlist. Writers whose works had been well received within the writing community, who were previously supported by publishers over a number

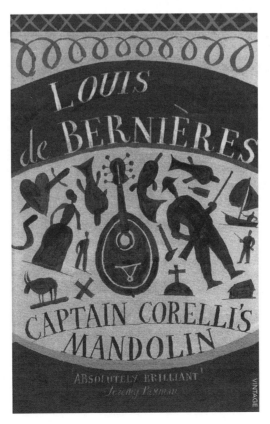

Few book covers have the iconic status of album covers. One example, however, is the 1995 design for Louis de Bernières' *Captain Corelli's Mandolin* (Minerva), which endured until its redesign in 2008

of books – awaiting their sales breakthrough – could be seen as on their way out much earlier and were rejected after only their first few books. Some moved to smaller and welcoming publishers while others were dropped by their agents too.

The major publishers' other strategies (apart from reducing the advances and royalty income of less-favoured authors), included giving greater emphasis to branded series and growing their audiobook lists. They also entered into 'licensed' partnerships with television and film companies to merchandise their properties, and marketing and sales partnerships with smaller publishers sometimes through equity stakes.

Some firms want to fulfil the traditional role of publishing fine literary works, but only a few authors and books become part of the perennial backlist alongside Austen, Dickens and Orwell. Publishers are opportunistic – they must respond fast if they want to capture a well-known author or personality, or take advantage of current fashions, media events or topical issues on which to hang a book's promotion. Books are firmly positioned in genres and categories, whether crime, fantasy or horror in fiction or home and garden, history, or popular science in non-fiction (see Table 2.2). This is reflected in the cover design and associated marketing. As Claire Squires remarks about literary publishing:

> By the turn of the twentieth and twenty-first centuries, the necessity of finding arrangements for the 100,000+ books produced yearly by the UK industry is readily apparent. The prolific and diverse nature of the marketplace demands it; the sheer number of individual product lines calls out for some sort of taxonomy. (page 71)

A new category may be initiated by smaller companies before being adopted by mainstream publishers. If the market then diminishes, the category is often left to specialist publishers to pursue.

Some publishers make a category their own. The Canadian-owned Harlequin Mills & Boon has over 70 per cent of the romantic fiction market in the UK and 3 m women regularly read one of their books. 'Mills & Boon' has entered the *Oxford English Dictionary*, with the definition 'romantic story book'.

The public libraries aid, but to a heavily diminished extent, the hardback publishing of fiction and non-fiction. Table 2.3 gives a list of the 10 most borrowed authors from public libraries.

Table 2.2 Top five book genres for men and women (*source*: 2006 data from Book Facts Online)

	Bought by men	Bought by women
1	Biography	Popular fiction
2	Adventure/thriller	Crime/mystery
3	Crime/mystery	Biography
4	Maps/atlases	Literary fiction
5	History	Cookery/food/drink

Table 2.3 The 10 most borrowed authors from public libraries 1996/7 to 2005/6. All had over 10 m borrowings in this period (*source*: www.plr.uk.com, accessed 10 September 2007)

Position	Author
1	Catherine Cookson
2	Danielle Steel
3	R. L. Stine
4	Josephine Cox
5	Jacqueline Wilson
6	Janet and Allan Ahlberg
7	Dick Francis
8	Roald Dahl
9	Agatha Christie
10	Jack Higgins

PUBLISHERS' MARKET SHARE

If the consolidation of the consumer book publishers in the last quarter of the twentieth century was about the vertical restructuring of an archaic industry, the current consolidation is about gaining market share in the face of ever more powerful retailers. The market shares of the leading publishing groups in 2007 are shown in Table 2.4 – the top four groups have 50 per cent of the market.

The long-time pole position of the Bertelsmann companies in the UK (Random House and Transworld, with strengths in fiction) was overtaken by the

Table 2.4 Market shares (percentages) of publishing groups for consumer sales 2007 (*source*: Nielsen BookScan)

Publishing group	Market share (%)
Hachette	16.6
Random House	14.7
Pearson (including Penguin and DK)	11.6
HarperCollins	7.9
Bloomsbury	4.2
Macmillan	3.4
Oxford University Press	1.8
Simon & Schuster	1.5
Egmont	1.4
Others	36.9

rapid growth of the French media group Hachette Livre, owned by Lagardère. Hachette had previously acquired Orion, Octopus, Watts and Chambers-Harrap; it then bought Hodder Headline from WHSmith in 2004. In 2006 it bought the book publishing businesses of the US company Time Warner (whose imprints included Little, Brown), taking the number one spot in the UK and for the first time giving it access to the US market. In 2007, Bertelsmann responded with its own purchase of BBC Books, which it merged into Ebury.

Both Bertelsmann and Hachette adopt a decentralized approach to the management of their publishing groups. While centralizing some functions to gain economies of scale in print and paper buying, the literary agents are encouraged to submit projects to editors across their imprints, even to the extent that their constituent publishing companies may be in direct competition against one another.

In a market increasingly dominated by powerful retailers and bestsellers, publisher size is crucial, especially in the largest market segment – fiction – which accounts for around a third of the domestic market by volume and a quarter in value. In 2006, the big four (Hachette, Random House, HarperCollins and Penguin) took over 80 per cent of the fiction market by value, and the top 10 over 95 per cent. Non-fiction publishing is less concentrated with many smaller publishers. In the adult non-fiction market, the same big four took 47 per cent by value and the top 10 nearly 60 per cent (Richardson, 122–4). It is likely that further concentration will occur.

There is a notable polarization between the big players and a large number of much smaller firms – in between is only a small number of medium-sized companies. The middle-ranking publishers lack the scale of operation and deep backlists of the large players and are sometimes too small to resist the pressures from the large retailers for improved terms of trade, at the expense of their margins. They also face greater risks in publishing brand-named authors on which they depend to give them access to the main retailers. If for example they are in competition to buy a potentially huge book, they may be outbid by an advance on royalties from a larger publisher. Alternatively if they won the book and its sales were disappointing, the failure of their prime investment would have severe consequences on their profitability. In contrast, a major publisher could afford to purchase six potentially huge books, of which the chances are that three or four turn out winners. The biggest authors migrate to the largest publishers – even those who achieve their early success with a smaller publisher are likely to be tempted away by larger advances.

Although consumer book publishing is dominated by the existing majors, there are other large publishers, including Bloomsbury, Macmillan (owned by Holtzbrinck), Simon & Schuster (owned by CBS Corporation), Oxford University Press, and Reader's Digest (mail-order and trade sales). Quarto is a sizeable player in the illustrated book field. Medium-sized independents include Faber & Faber, Atlantic, Quadrille, Canongate (in Edinburgh), Constable & Robinson, John Blake, Michael O'Mara, Mainstream and the art publishers Phaidon, Thames & Hudson and the Tate Gallery. There are also fast-growing recent entrants such as Profile and Quercus, and a host of smaller specialist publishers producing adult or children's books. The smaller publishers cannot compete against the large corporations in terms of advances paid to agented, established authors. Thus, for example, they concentrate on bringing forward new writers, or those overlooked writers who may not have agents or have been rejected by larger publishers. They may opt to build a stable of authors who will work for one-off fees instead of royalties – common in the field of highly illustrated books.

Faced with the power of the retailers, leading independent publishers responded in 2005 by forming the Independent Alliance of publishers. The Alliance offers more favourable terms to independent booksellers, comparable to those received by the chains, and has provided better access for the publishers into the major retailers. Andrew Franklin, Managing Director of Profile Books, one of the publishers in the Alliance, wrote:

> it is Faber's chief executive, Stephen Page, who has devised the inspired scheme that may now help bookshops and publishers compete more fairly and effectively with the chains. Like the French wine cooperatives, Page has established an alliance of independent bookshops and publishers. This is not exactly a union: there are no membership dues, no strike ballots and no secondary picketing outside Asda. But nor is it a mere talking-shop, of which there are far too many already. It's more like a 19th-century friendly society. And like those early cooperative organisations, it is completely new and feels very exciting. (*The Guardian*, 8 July 2006)

Founded in 2004 by Anthony Cheetham, formerly of Orion, Quercus won the Costa Book of the Year Award for 2006 with *The Tenderness of Wolves* by Stef Penney

CHILDREN'S PUBLISHING

By the late 1970s the outlook for publishers of children's books, especially those producing quality hardbacks, appeared grim. Many bookshops, other than WHSmith, were hardly enthusiastic buyers, public and school libraries (traditional major markets) were cutting back their expenditure, and the birth rate was forecast to fall. In that the vitality of children's publishing creates the book buyers of the future, there were serious worries about the demise of book reading, foreshadowing the end of publishing itself. Between 1981 and 1990 the population of 5- to 14-year-olds did indeed fall by 13 per cent but the inventiveness of authors and illustrators, of existing publishers, of new publishers, such as Walker Books, and book packagers transformed children's publishing during the 1980s into arguably the most dynamic sector of the industry. Retail sales per child rose by nearly three times, and the number of new titles doubled to around 6,000. Between 1985 and 1990, the sales of children's publishers rose in real terms by 26 per cent while their adult general publishing counterparts achieved growth of only 7 per cent.

The publishers found new ways of reaching the home market via supermarkets (from the mid-1980s titles appeared under a supermarket's own brand label), toyshops and direct sales – including book clubs and school book fairs. They sold international co-editions to US and European publishing partners, enabling picture books and highly-illustrated non-fiction or information books to be published at low and affordable prices worldwide. Paperback sales grew enormously and in volume terms came to dominate the market. Teenage fiction lists were established.

The recession of the early 1990s saw a reversal in sales of around 13 per cent

Mark Haddon's *The Curious Incident of the Dog in the Night-Time* was published in separate editions for adults (*left*) and children (*right*)

yet the publishers continued to increase their title output through to 1995 when it stabilized at around 8,000 titles. The UK market for children's books declined from 1990 through to 1997, as other new products competed for children's attention and parents' spending. However, in 1998–9 the market staged a substantial recovery. Government policy to give greater emphasis to literacy in primary schools was a fillip to some children's publishers, encouraging school and library sales. Some titles became more answerable to the needs of the National Curriculum, although this did create a tension between the book as entertainment and as a learning aid. In a multimedia age there has been a decline in the market for picture books and booksellers have reduced their range in this area. Publishers have to be more innovative in their pricing and combining the books with digital offerings.

By the end of the twentieth century an explosion in new children's fiction was apparent. This was led by J. K. Rowling's *Harry Potter* series, which not only rocketed the independent publisher Bloomsbury up the charts for retail sales in the UK, but also the books became international bestsellers and widely translated. They were attractive to a crossover market – read by children *and* adults – and stimulated consumer interest in children's books across the board (and interest from film companies in children's book properties). In fiction, the importance of the branding of authors, such as Jacqueline Wilson, Philip Pullman and Francesca Simon, strengthened. Publishers were keen to develop series based around the fictional characters, which could lead to sales of associated merchandise. In the early years

Table 2.5 Carnegie Medal winners 1998 to 2007. The medal is awarded by children's librarians for an outstanding book for children and young people

Year of award	Author	Title	Publisher
2007	Meg Rosoff	*Just in Case*	Penguin
2006	Mal Peet	*Tamar*	Walker Books
2005	Frank Cottrell Boyce	*Millions*	Macmillan
2004	Jennifer Donnelly	*A Gathering Light*	Bloomsbury
2003	Sharon Creech	*Ruby Holler*	Bloomsbury
2002	Terry Pratchett	*The Amazing Maurice and his Educated Rodents*	Doubleday
2001	Beverley Naidoo	*The Other Side of Truth*	Puffin
2000	Aidan Chambers	*Postcards from No Man's Land*	Bodley Head
1999	David Almond	*Skellig*	Hodder
1998	Tim Bowler	*River Boy*	OUP

of the new century, children's publishing became a vibrant sector with publishers willing to invest in both authors and marketing in search of the next bestseller.

The major children's publishers include the children's imprints of Puffin, Ladybird and Dorling Kindersley (all in the Penguin group) and of the other adult consumer publishers such as Hachette UK, HarperCollins, the Bertelsmann companies of Random House and Transworld, Pan Macmillan, Simon & Schuster and Oxford University Press. There are other specialist children's publishers, which are not part of adult book publishing groups. The magazine and book publisher Egmont (majoring in licensed character publishing) is in the top rank of children's publishing. Others include Scholastic, Templar, Usborne and Walker Books. Parragon, which began as a packager, has expanded rapidly by publishing books for supermarkets, and extended its reach into high street retail by becoming the licensed publishing partner of Disney. The rapid growth of Bloomsbury has depended largely on the *Harry Potter* series.

It is important to note that the children's publishers sell their books through many different distribution channels beyond booksellers, such as direct to schools (for example Scholastic and Troubadour).

AUDIO AND EBOOKS

At the time of writing the audio market in the UK is relatively undeveloped, with a survey on behalf of the Audiobook Publishing Association finding that only 8 per cent of consumers had listened to an audiobook in the last year (*The Bookseller*, 6 April 2007). Sales figures for 2006 showed the overall market in the UK to be worth £71.4 m – adult titles sold £50 m and children's titles the remaining £21.4 m. For adult titles three times as many units sold were for the abridged version compared to the unabridged, while it was fairly evenly split between abridged/unabridged in the children's market.

The launch of readers such as the Sony Portable Reader, Amazon Kindle and iRex Iliad has renewed interest in the consumer use of ebooks. The Sony Reader holds up to 80 books in its internal memory, and hundreds more with external memory. Andrew Marr writes: 'it's clear enough that after all the waiting and the over-hyping, the ebook is arriving. Before long you are going to see them being carried nonchalantly around. And after that some of you, at least, are going to buy one' (*The Guardian*, 11 May 2007).

The rise and collapse of multimedia publishing

F◉CUS

In consumer publishing, the first wave of new media excitement – the publishing of multimedia titles on CD-ROM – occurred in the early to mid-1990s. At that time there were large numbers of US imports. Analysts pointed to the rapid rise in the number of of computers with CD-ROM drives being purchased by UK households. This would lead, it was argued, to an exponential rise in the consumer purchase of content titles. Some of the major trade publishers, such as HarperCollins, Penguin and Reed, and the illustrated book reference publisher Dorling Kindersley, established new media divisions. The world's main encyclopedia publishers converted their works on to CD-ROM, Microsoft created *Encarta*, localized successfully around the world, and major entertainment companies such as Disney exploited their character properties on the new medium. UK start-up multimedia producers arose. But by 1996, most of the UK trade book publishers, with the exception of Dorling Kindersley, withdrew from the marketplace bearing large losses. No mass market appeared for these products and the publishers could not cover their high development costs. The US also proved resistant to imports. The booksellers did not stock the titles sufficiently and the publishers were left to compete in the computer stores, an alien and difficult setting for their business. By the late 1990s, the remainder dealers had extensive stocks of lifestyle titles from around the world to sell off for a few pounds per title. Nevertheless, the publishing of multimedia titles on disk has continued mainly in the educational (home and school), cartographic and text-based professional reference fields.

The failure of multimedia publishing reinforced many publishers' sceptical view of new media publishing and negatively coloured many senior managements' response to the news of ebook growth in the USA in the late 1990s. If the business model for multimedia publishing on disk was loss-making, they argued, what hope would there be for publishing on the internet, a generally free medium devaluing the price of information, with few viable business models for selling content? This view was confirmed by the internet dotcom bubble of the late 1990s, which saw investment pouring into many start-up companies that later became worthless. Yet publishers took little or no action to future proof their business for the digital age. Comforted by the oft-quoted mantra 'content is king', few foresaw that in the next century big money would be made from consumers searching for content on the internet, by the internet search engines, especially Google, a company that would turn its attention to book content.

The US book market is some years ahead of the UK in the uptake of ebooks. It is growing in double digits from a very low base (less than 1 per cent of sales in 2005), despite being bedevilled by baffling technical barriers confronting the consumer. There is a proliferation of proprietary ebook reader formats, such as Adobe, Microsoft and Mobipocket. The Open Ebook Format (OEBF) is designed to create a common reader standard but does not deal with the proprietary and incompatible digital rights management (DRM) systems designed to control reader's usage. The backlit and high-energy-consuming screens on computers are not conducive to easy reading. The development of low-energy-consuming e-ink technologies that are emerging on new hardware devices appear to offer a better reading solution.

An ebook can be read on a PC, PDA or dedicated reader

Ebook enthusiasts may download out-of-copyright classics provided for free, for example by Project Gutenberg (gutenberg.org), or copyright books from pirate websites. Some publishers sell copyright ebooks through a range of intermediaries or directly from their own ebook platforms. Unlike the leading academic and STM publishers, which at the turn of the century started to digitize their books (and journals) for institutional library markets, most consumer publishers avoided digitizing their books. The wake-up call for the consumer book publishers came from a surprise source. In December 2004 Google, as part of its Book Search tool, announced its plan to scan and index books in major libraries – a controversial issue for author groups and publishers. The publishers realized that unless they gave the search engine companies (Google, Microsoft and Yahoo!) access to their content for indexing they and their authors would face potential invisibility on the internet. During 2006 most of the major publishers embarked on their own digitization of their backlist books and began to create digital files of their new books, and many allowed Google and other search engines to index their digital archives for searching.

While consumer book publishers await the arrival of a mass-market ebook reading device with the reach of the iPod, the use by consumers of alternative digital sources of 'good enough' and free information is impinging on printed book sales, especially in travel and reference book publishing. The travel book publishers, for example Lonely Planet (part of BBC Worldwide), Dorling Kindersley (DK) and Rough Guides (both part of Penguin), are experimenting with new ways of delivering their content to travellers directly from their websites or via new intermediaries such as licensing content to mobile phone companies or through technology partners.

As will be seen later in this book, the advent of the internet and of epublishing affects every dimension of the publisher's business: markets, distribution channels, pricing, formats, production methods and the exploitation and control of rights.

Sources

Diana Athill, *Stet*, Granta, 2000.
Alan Bartram, *Making Books: Design in British publishing since 1945*, British Library, 1999.
Eric de Bellaigue, *British Book Publishing as a Business since the 1960s*, British Library Publishing, 2004.
Simon Eliot and Jonathan Rose, *A Companion to the History of the Book*, Blackwell, 2007.
Jason Epstein, *Book Business: Publishing Past, Present, and Future*, Norton, 2002.
John Hampson and Paul Richardson, *Kitchen Table to Laptop: Independent publishing in England*, Arts Council, 2004.
Jeremy Lewis, *Penguin Special: The life and times of Allen Lane*, Viking, 2005.
Tom Maschler, *Publisher*, Picador, 2005.
Ian Norrie, *Mumby's Publishing and Bookselling in the Twentieth Century*, 6th edition, Bell & Hyman, 1982.
Paul Richardson, *Publishing Market Profile: The United Kingdom*, The Publishers Association, 2007.
Claire Squires, *Marketing Literature: The making of contemporary writing in Britain*, Palgrave Macmillan, 2007.
Rayner Unwin, *George Allen & Unwin: A remembrancer*, Merlin Unwin Books, 1999.

Web resources

www.carnegiegreenaway.org.uk Carnegie and Kate Greenaway Children's Book Awards.
http://www.brookes.ac.uk/schools/apm/publishing/culture/feminist/femcont.html Feminist publishing resource at Oxford Brookes University.

CHAPTER 3

The consolidation of non-consumer publishing

Non-consumer publishing encompasses the educational, academic, STM (scientific, technical and medical), and professional publishing sectors, including the publication of learned journals. The major publishers strive to dominate the sectors in which they specialize, worldwide. The publishers producing high-level books and information services for professionals (for example in STM, business and law), and also learned journals, are highly profitable and strongly cash generative.

Increases in government funding for schools in the 1960s and 1970s aided the expansion of the educational publishers. The academic publishers similarly responded to the growth in higher education. Expansion in student numbers, and the ample funding of UK and US university libraries, stimulated the publishing of high-priced academic monographs and learned journals, produced especially by the STM book publishers. Many of the main educational, academic and STM publishers moved out of London to cheaper office space in Oxford and other locations.

The British publishers enjoyed their traditional export markets: the USA, Commonwealth and northern Europe. The American publishers had a much larger home market and so gave little emphasis to exports, the major exception being the college textbook publishers. The US government's Marshall Plan after the Second World War, designed to aid the reconstruction of post-war Europe, helped the US publishers to export college textbooks, which were sold in the UK at very low prices. The publishers opened subsidiaries in the UK and came to dominate college textbook adoption markets worldwide, Commonwealth countries included, by issuing international editions, not for sale in the US.

In terms of ownership, consolidation has continued apace into the twenty-first century and European publishers have acquired US publishers. Private equity groups have played a significant role in reassembling publishing imprints and assets, both by purchasing them and selling them on in new forms. A major driver for consolidation has been the migration to electronic formats and services, and the high costs involved in making the transition.

MERGERS AND ACQUISITIONS

The UK-owned Pearson, well known for its Longman imprint purchased in 1968, acquired the US publisher Addison-Wesley in 1988, and then in 1998 acquired Simon & Schuster's educational operations, including Prentice Hall, Allyn & Bacon, and the US Macmillan Publishing, from its parent Viacom. Pearson Education is the world's largest educational (i.e. textbook) publisher. It holds leading market shares in the US school market and the US college market. Two-thirds of Pearson's sales derive from the USA, and around one-quarter from Europe.

A further shake-up of publishers occurred around the turn of the century. In 1995 the Macmillan family had sold a majority stake in Macmillan Publishers (whose interests included the paperback publisher Pan and the journal *Nature*) to the German publisher Holtzbrinck. The remaining shares were purchased by Holtzbrinck in 1999. Taylor & Francis floated on the London Stock Exchange in 1998 and shortly after more than doubled in size with the acquisition of the Routledge group of publishers. It has continued to acquire numerous academic and STM publishers on both sides of the Atlantic.

In 1999, the German and family-owned Bertelsmann – primarily a consumer-focused media group – bought the German and family-owned STM publisher Springer. In 2003, British private equity bought Springer, and the academic and STM publishing operations of the Dutch publisher Kluwer. The companies were merged in 2004 and the enlarged Springer became the second largest STM publisher to the Anglo-Dutch leader Elsevier, and the largest STM book publisher.

In 2002, a private equity consortium bought the large US educational publisher Houghton Mifflin, which then in 2006 underwent a reverse takeover by the smaller Irish educational software company Riverdeep. In 2007 Reed Elsevier, the world's biggest publisher of information for professional users operating in the markets of science, medical and legal, having previously bought the US publisher Harcourt, decided to sell its school educational imprints (including Heinemann) to Pearson, while keeping the higher education and medical publishing businesses. Likewise the other major information and professional publishers decided to concentrate on providing content and services for professionals digitally, rather than compete in education against Pearson.

In 2007 the Dutch information and health publisher Wolters Kluwer sold its school publishing assets to private equity, in order to concentrate on its online businesses. In the same year, the Canadian family-owned Thomson Corporation sold Thomson Learning, a division focused on higher education (second only to Pearson in the US college market), again to private equity, and bought Reuters. This left McGraw-Hill as the last remaining major US publisher with significant shares in US school and college markets. Educational markets (school and college) have been slower than professional markets to take up digital content and services.

Running against the trend of European purchases of US publishers, in 2007 the US family-controlled STM, college textbook and journal publisher John Wiley purchased the family-owned Blackwell, based in Oxford, which published for STM, humanities and social science markets. In 2008 private equity combined Cengage Learning (formerly Thomson Learning) with the Houghton Mifflin College Division.

The migration to electronic formats drives consolidation, not least in the ability enabled by size to invest in technology. The big players can afford to make the necessary large investments in online scientific journals and accompanying tools to aid researchers, and in building ebook collections for libraries. The larger the publisher's content and the greater their control over the intellectual property, the greater is the leverage of the aggregation. It is argued by the large publishers that it easier for academic libraries and purchasing consortia to deal with just a few publishers and to use their platforms providing online content and services – rather than have to negotiate with dozens of publishers and intermediaries.

EDUCATIONAL PUBLISHING

Schools publishing

The educational market is subject to the influence of government perhaps more than any other. It is affected by National Curriculum strategies (most recently vocational subject reforms for the 14–19 age group), the vagaries of government expenditure, and occasional intervention from 'state publishing' – manifest by the BBC's proposal to use funding from its licence fee to provide free curriculum resources online.

In comparison to the consumer book publishers, the UK educational publishers (sometimes referred to as 'curriculum publishers') are less affected by the powerful retailers since many sales are direct to schools (typically more than 50 per cent; it can be more than 80 per cent in the case of primary schools). Their lists of books can take longer to build and their sales, though more steady and generally more profitable than in consumer publishing, are subject to periodic downturns.

Go Science! from Heinemann is aimed at 11- to 14-year-olds

The first overseas subsidiaries of UK companies were opened in the late nineteenth and early twentieth centuries in Australia and Canada, and in the 1960s the educational and academic houses opened subsidiaries in the newly formed African Commonwealth countries and exported large quantities of UK-based textbooks. The educational systems there were based on UK curricula or examinations.

The first wave of publisher consolidation occurred during the 1980s when school pupil rolls declined, and the number of significant educational publishers decreased from around 30 to 15. Sales volumes fell from 1986 to 1990 reflecting in part the underfunding of UK state schools. Export sales were affected by the poverty of some Commonwealth countries and a more nationalist approach around the world to the school curriculum. By the early 1990s, the top three publishers commanded 50 per cent of sales to schools; and the top seven over 75 per cent. The remaining publishers concentrated in specialist areas or subjects.

Consolidation amongst publishers proceeded more slowly until 2007, when Reed Elsevier decided to sell its UK education interests (Harcourt) to Pearson, and Wolters Kluwer decided to divest its educational publishing assets (Nelson Thornes) to private equity. The main players (in alphabetical order) are:

- Cambridge University Press,
- Collins Education (News Corporation),
- Hodder Education (Hachette),
- Nelson Thornes,
- Oxford University Press, and
- Pearson Education.

The other publishers tend to concentrate on specialisms, and a somewhat different range of publishers serve primary schools and the school library market, including children's publishers such as Scholastic.

Government

The home market used to be characterized by little central government intervention and a variety of examination boards setting curricula. A diversity of books and ancillary materials were published by a variety of publishers. The books were purchased through local education authorities and supplied to schools via specialist suppliers, local authority purchasing organizations and bookshops.

However, the effects of the 1988 Education Reform Act were profound. The new National Curriculum was far more prescriptive and defined, rendering many backlist textbooks (from which publishers earned most of their profits) largely redundant. The race was on to produce new materials, especially schemes or programmes of study in core subjects, quickly and at great cost. This favoured the large publishers. Speed and quality were of the essence as each school had to be locked into the publisher's programme ideally for say three to five years. Slow publishers risked being knocked out, as indeed some were.

Governments worldwide are increasingly regulating their school systems which have the effect of impeding if not curtailing the import of textbooks and other learning materials. The export of UK-originated schoolbooks still occurs,

Digital content in UK schools

Although the UK educational system was an early adopter of information and communication technologies (ICT), the development and take-up of digital content has proved difficult and slow.

From the early 1990s there were government initiatives to increase the use of ICT in schools in terms of hardware and software provision, teacher training and digitally delivered curriculum resources. At the start the market was filled by US imports which were not designed for UK curricula and cultural needs. Amongst UK multimedia publishers, many went bust or recorded severe losses. On its purchase of Dorling Kindersley, Pearson closed its multimedia division. The curriculum publishers restricted themselves to modest experiments, preferring the business model of book publishing. Granada Learning, acquired by private equity in 2006, endures but recorded a loss in that year.

In 2002, the government introduced elearning credits (eLCs) which ring-fenced funds for the purchase by schools of digital content. These were extended to at least 2008. However, such state pump-priming of the market does not guarantee future spending and use. The government's parallel idea for the BBC to use licence fee income to deliver parts of the curriculum free online, raised concerns by the publishers that this would undermine private sector investment, and not lead to a long-term sustainable model. Launched in 2006, the service BBC Jam was suspended only a year later as complaints by educational publishers were made to the European Commission. More general concerns about the use of digital resources are that teachers have so far proved less adept with using them than their students, and that learning outcomes and cost effectiveness do not match the use of print.

Spending on hardware meant that by 2007 the average number of interactive whiteboards in a school had reached 8 in primary schools and 22 in secondary schools. Half of primary schools and more than four-fifths of secondary schools made use of wireless technology (Becta, 2007). The main beneficiaries of school spending on digital resources have been newer companies such as Boardworks, Espresso, and 2Simple. The curriculum publishers which have developed digital resources, including self-learning and testing products, have adopted a range of models. For example, CD-ROMs are sold on a simple licensing model whereby the school buys the disk at a relatively high price and each subsequent disk at a very much lower price. Although the trend is towards online delivery, sometimes free to support textbook adoptions, or sold on a subscription model, teachers remain attached to CD-ROMs, which once bought do not necessarily require further expenditure. Online subscriptions are dependent on a reliable funding stream. The prevalence and reported success of interactive whiteboards in UK schools has enabled the curriculum publishers to produce digital resources for that medium to complement their textbooks.

FOCUS

mainly in the sciences, or in versioned form; and to sub-Saharan Africa, largely dependent on aid funding.

A further UK government reform was the weakening of the local education authorities and the transfer of local management to schools. This enabled state schools to order books directly from publishers rather than through their local education authorities. Many intermediaries in the former supply chain (specialist suppliers, local authority purchasing organizations and bookshops), which were receiving discounts of 17–20 per cent from the publishers, were cut out.

In the late 1990s, there were successive changes to the National Curriculum, and the examination boards in England were merged down to three: the treatment of subjects narrowed further. The boards, which receive a fee per candidate, compete vigorously to secure schools' choice of their syllabus and accreditation (secondary schools usually pay a greater sum to the boards than they spend on textbooks). In the USA, Pearson took the strategic step of acquiring service companies which provided testing and other software for schools. In the UK, the company controversially bought the examination board Edexcel in 2003. This was seen by some as creating a conflict of interest for the board, which lends its endorsement to textbooks.

In the UK, government underfunding of textbook provision in state education is a perennial problem. Although overall expenditure on education rose in real terms from 1997 into the new century, there was little or no benefit to publishers. The Educational Publishers Council (EPC), a division of The Publishers Association, lobbies actively for increased school funding. Slumps in school spending occurred in the late 1980s and then again in 2003, when the EPC estimated that spending on books in primary schools fell back 12 per cent, to the same level in cash terms as 10 years previously, and spending in secondary schools fell back 7 per cent to 2000 levels. Publishers laid off staff, up to 20 per cent in some cases, especially in their sales teams selling directly to schools. Book purchases represent a small part – less than 1 per cent – of overall school budgets.

FOCUS

Trade education

An important subsector of educational publishing is referred to as 'trade' or 'consumer' education. This area embraces study and revision guides aimed at students and the parental anxiety market. It is referred to as 'trade' since historically such product lines were purchased by parents through booksellers and not by schools for class use, although more recently they have been used in schools.

Specialist publishers occupy the field, such as the long-established Letts (Huveaux Education), which was overtaken as market leader in 2007 by the independent Cumbria-based publisher Coordination Group Publications. The curriculum publishers are also strongly represented, such as Hodder Education (including *Teach Yourself*); Pearson Education (*York Notes*) further strengthened its position through the purchase of the BBC's educational division (BBC Worldwide Learning) which was sold off by BBC Worldwide.

ELT publishing

The publishing of English Language Teaching (ELT) course materials engages very large investments and a worldwide marketing strength for this predominantly export-orientated field. The publishers enjoyed strong growth from export sales through the 1990s but in 1997 it began to falter. Though the quantity of books exported rose, prices fell in sterling terms and the real value of turnover decreased. The strength of sterling, the Asian economic crisis, and the problems in Brazil and Argentina (important ELT markets) took their toll. ELT publishing continued to consolidate. By 2000, four publishers (in alphabetical order) came to lead the global ELT market:

- Cambridge University Press,
- Macmillan,
- Oxford University Press, and
- Pearson.

Oxford University Press (OUP) is the largest international ELT publisher and this part of the business accounts for a significant part of its profits. It maintains a market leadership in British English (especially in Europe) while also publishing in American English. Pearson is the biggest player in the American English market. It added the important American English lists of Addison Wesley (in 1988) and of Prentice Hall (1998) – thereby leading the markets in Latin America and Asia – to its original mainly British English Longman imprint. Cambridge University Press (CUP) has built its business without acquisition and benefits from its close association with the University of Cambridge Local Examination Syndicate (UCLES), which operates the internationally recognized examination English for Speakers of Other Languages (ESOL). Macmillan developed its ELT business through the purchase of Heinemann ELT in 1998. There are smaller UK ELT publishers, which specialize in niches, and packagers also offer editorial, design and production services to the major players – often their former employers. Some overseas ELT publishers have taken advantage of UK expertise and have established UK operations, for example Richmond Publishing owned by the Spanish publisher Santillana.

From the standpoint of the major players, ELT publishing is a distinct field of publishing needing its own publishing operations, typically based in the UK and the US to produce British and American English materials; plus other publishing centres such as those in Spain, the Far East, Latin America and Eastern Europe to fulfil national or regional markets; and marketing sales offices elsewhere. The strategic importance of ELT is that as a growing market worldwide it provides the publisher with a local or regional foothold in non-English areas of the world, through the opening of local companies or marketing offices, or through the acquisition of local publishers. Although the major publishers dominate the international provision of teaching materials, they face increasing competition from indigenous local publishers (which in many European countries are the national market leaders in schools); private language school chains with publishing operations; newer entrants such as Disney; and online providers.

Vocational publishing

In the UK many students carry on in vocational education after they leave school for a range of careers such as catering, hairdressing or engineering. This is a separate path from going on to university. Imprints such as Cengage Learning (formerly Thomson Learning), Heinemann (part of Pearson Education) and Hodder Arnold provide both books and electronic resources.

ACADEMIC, STM AND PROFESSIONAL PUBLISHING

The internationalization of academic, STM and professional book publishing occurred earlier than in consumer book publishing, and is far more extensive. High-level books and journals in English, especially in STM, have an international currency throughout the developed world. Such publishers do not have to contend with literary agents' retention of territorial and other rights: they invariably acquire all rights in authors' works worldwide.

The fortunes of academic publishers and the kinds of books and other products they produce are inextricably linked to institutional spending on research, especially in relation to library budgets in the developed world, to the numbers and wealth of full-time and part-time students (particularly in UK higher education), and to the behaviour of librarians, researchers, teachers and students.

Professional publishing in the areas of law or finance has traditionally been highly profitable. The trend has been towards online content and services and, for example, Lexis-Nexis, part of Reed Elsevier, offers access to '5 billion searchable documents from more than 32,000 legal, news and business sources' (lexisnexis. com, accessed 1 October 2007).

Overview of publishers

Major publishers dominate these fields on a world scale. The market sectors are diverse in respect of the character of the publishing operations. Two giant publishers occupy either end of the spectrum. Pearson Education (part of the UK listed company Pearson) is the world's leading higher education publisher, primarily focused on teaching and learning (i.e. textbook publishing with technology support). Elsevier (part of the Anglo-Dutch listed company Reed Elsevier) is the world's leading STM publisher, with a focus on scientific journals and the supply of information to health and pharma markets, with associated book businesses, including some textbook, academic and professional book publishing, and law.

Other leading publishers are arguably more diverse in their discipline span and the character of their operations. Wiley-Blackwell, another leading STM publisher, with important journals, encompasses the humanities and social sciences, along with significant book publishing operations covering textbook, academic and professional book publishing. Taylor & Francis (part of Informa, and including the imprints of Routledge, CRC Press, and Garland) has a not dissimilar spread of journal and book publishing and a large book title output. Springer, which includes the former Kluwer academic publishing businesses, majors on STM journals and books.

The global STM market is led by four big players, and between them they have over 50 per cent of the market:

- Elsevier,
- Springer,
- Taylor & Francis, and
- Wiley-Blackwell.

Other important academic publishers commissioning in the UK include Palgrave Macmillan (associated through ownership with the prestigious journal *Nature*), and the US privately owned Sage Publications (which began as a social science publisher but has since diversified). Big US players with some UK commissioning are represented by McGraw-Hill (which includes the Open University Press, previously the subject of a management buy-out from the university), and Cengage Learning (formerly Thomson Learning). Smaller companies include Ashgate, Continuum, Earthscan, I. B. Tauris, Pluto and other specialists.

The university presses are very significant book and journal publishers. Oxford University Press is by far the largest university press in the world and competes alongside the leading private-sector publishers. OUP spans most academic disciplines at the higher level of academic and scholarly publishing, and includes textbook, reference and journals publishing. Its annual turnover (including trade, reference, educational and ELT publishing) exceeds the combined turnover of the UK and US university presses, and is more than three times the size of the other leading university press, Cambridge University Press, with a similar spread of activities. The other UK university presses operate on a very much smaller scale and are far more specialist, and include the presses of Manchester and Edinburgh. The Policy Press is based at the University of Bristol. The US university presses are also represented in the UK, notably Yale University Press specialising in art, architecture and humanities books commissioned out of the UK. Other US publishers may have UK marketing and sales offices to import their books, usually into Europe, the Middle East and Africa (EMEA or EMA).

All publishers specialize in publishing books or journals in particular academic disciplines or groups of allied disciplines. Not even the largest would claim to publish in all disciplines. Their output can be divided into three broad categories:

- textbooks,
- academic and professional, and
- journals.

Textbooks

UK teaching differs from US practices. However, the US core textbook model best exemplified by Pearson, McGraw-Hill, Cengage Learning, Wiley (and Elsevier in health science) is instructive and offers pointers as to the way publishing is changing. This model is applied to the arguably more defined and quantifiable subjects: mainly the hard sciences, maths, psychology, business and economics. The very high cost of the model limits it to a very small number of major existing titles and new lead titles of expected high saleability, mainly at the first and second year levels. Such subjects are international. The publisher's aim is to create scalable learning and teaching solutions worldwide.

In the US, textbook publishers analyse and synthesize curriculum needs across the continent, and create printed textbooks of up to 1,000 pages with high design values and special learning features. The US professors adopt one book per course, from which they, or their instructors, usually teach chapter by chapter. In view of the large class sizes and the high value of adoptions, US core textbook publishing became a very large and competitive business. The publishers invest millions of dollars in such texts, priced highly in the US market but cheaper overseas. The worldwide annual revenue from some of these bestselling titles may dwarf the annual turnover of some medium-sized UK publishers.

The publishers became engaged in a virtual arms race. In order to secure adoptions of their books they compete to offer the instructors additional and free supplementary material to help them teach the course, such as an instructor's guide. This material started out as a marketing device to persuade the instructor to use the publisher's book. It grew in scale and complexity. As part of these supplements, the publishers built test banks of thousands of multiple choice questions to support their big texts. The delivery of the supplementary packages has gone through every development of technology: print, video tape to disk, overhead projectors to PowerPoint slides. With the advent of online delivery and connectivity, the supplements were renamed 'resources' or 'bonus content' and from around the turn of the century they came to embrace publisher technology support.

Textbook publishers have moved beyond their provision of teaching content to the supply of services and the prospect of personalized learning. For example, by building on their archives of question test banks, they have developed assessment software, held on their servers. It enables instructors to set and customize assessments for their students. These are marked automatically and downloaded into their students' gradebooks. It saves time for the instructor and lowers the university's cost of delivering teaching. The assessment software has become more sophisticated and has developed beyond simplistic multiple choice. It is sensitive to the students' responses and offers them help (for example links to the pertinent section in the ebook of the textbook, sometimes enhanced with animations and video) and at the top end automated tutorial support. Publishers claim that their online packages aid student performance and retention. Institutions use a variety of Virtual Learning Environments (VLEs) or Learning Management Systems (LMS), such as Angel Learning and Blackboard or the open source Moodle. Some publishers offer institutions their own LMS.

A long-term problem facing the US textbook publishers, increasingly affecting the UK, has been the used book market. A high proportion of US students typically invest in the purchase of the textbook and then sell it at the end of their course, affecting the income of publishers and their authors. To counter this trend, publishers have issued new editions at all too frequent intervals, sometimes irritating the lecturers, who are forced to check the extent of the changes, and the students who complain about high new book prices. The provision of passworded online resources provides the publisher with another counter measure.

Although some of the online resources are available freely on companion websites for marketing purposes, the rich material is restricted to password or unique pin code access. The instructor is initially given time limited access to review the book's adoption potential. Once adopted, the instructor is given access to their area, and each student is supplied with a pin code on purchase of the book, giving them access to their area on the publisher's server, but only for the duration of the course. The publishers for so long separated from the students by the intermediaries (for example campus bookstores), can now make the direct link. Students may be offered access to additional content and services beyond the textbook itself. Publishers are trying to make the transition from the free supply of online content and services (on condition of textbook adoption) to charging for premium content and services.

In the UK the teaching tradition differs, and lecturers are far less likely to adopt only one book for a course, or even if they do, to teach from it chapter by chapter. The blockbuster textbooks may be criticized as being too long, exhaustive and expensive. Lecturers do not expect, as of right, the free provision by the publisher of extensive teacher resources. Students have not bothered much with publishers' websites. However, the US-originated core texts are still used extensively. Texts in management studies and the social sciences are usually versioned or localized in the UK for the European or EMEA market, and by other publishing centres elsewhere. The uptake of custom publishing and of associated technology enabling instructors to tailor a publisher's content for their specific teaching is growing in the UK and mainland Europe. The reselling of textbooks by students is more noticeable. Publishers originating UK textbooks are increasing their online support, and it would be unthinkable to publish a mainstream textbook without a high level of associated resources for both lecturers and students.

An example of a higher education textbook from Palgrave Macmillan

From the 1990s, textbook sales did not rise in line with the great expansion of UK student numbers. From 2003 to 2006, textbook purchasing by students was at best flat (at around £150 m per year), and while 'students find textbooks helpful, they are no longer the lynchpin of university learning materials; they are now part of a wider mix of learning resources that include on-line journals, VLEs, and custom published materials' (Carpenter et al., page 1). Nevertheless 'the student survey [in 2005] found emphatically that they do value textbooks. 91 per cent described them as important in their learning' (ibid., page 2).

UK-originated publishing largely avoids competing directly against the US core textbooks, but nonetheless is extensive in title output. It covers a variety of subjects, takes account of the different approaches of UK academia, and extends up through the undergraduate levels to the very specialist graduate courses. Although rarely finding a significant US market, some UK-originated textbooks are highly exportable elsewhere. There is innovation and enormous diversity in UK teaching that finds expression through publishers.

Academic and professional publishing

This embraces all kinds of books used in academic institutions for teaching and research and by practitioners in the workplace. These include edited volumes, reference works, conference proceedings, and the publication of academic monographs of original research published in hardback at high prices and destined for the libraries mainly in the UK and US, and in other research centres. Books with some trade sale may be categorized as academic trade. Since the 1980s, the economic viability of publishing monographs – for so long a corner-stone of commercial academic publishing and of the university presses briefed to disseminate works of scholarship – has been questioned. Library cutbacks and their changing purchasing behaviour, such as the switching of printed book budgets to the subscription of journals and other electronic resources, has progressively reduced sales quantities to very low numbers, from 1,500 copies in the 1980s down to 300 or 400 copies. Some of the commercial academic publishers have now abandoned monograph publishing. However, the remaining publishers (for example OUP, CUP, Palgrave and Taylor & Francis, and some of the STM publishers) have maintained their publication by reducing the costs of production (including author royalties, sometimes to zero). The advent of print on demand (POD) which enables even single copies to be manufactured economically, and the advent of online ebook collections (such as the pioneering initiatives of OUP, Springer, Taylor & Francis) has aided the continuance of the publication of highly specialist titles. UK university libraries purchase books through the library suppliers such as Blackwell, Coutts and Dawsons.

While the uptake of ebooks has been slow in consumer markets, academic librarians have been keen to extend their collections by offering ebooks to their users: academics and students. In the UK, the Joint Information Systems Committee (JISC) has been influential in facilitating uptake. For librarians facing cuts or static funding by their institutions, ebooks save shelving, storage and maintenance costs; and ebook services can be paid for out of budgets for digital resources. Ebook collections are licensed to institutional libraries by the academic and STM publishers either directly from their own platforms or through

Research Assessment Exercise

In the UK, the Research Assessment Exercise (RAE) determines the allocation of more than £1 bn of state funding to research in the universities. The sixth exercise took place in 2008. Essentially, the RAE examines the research output and its quality carried out by researchers working within defined subjects in each institution. Their individual publication record in quantity and its grading are key determinants. As a result, the departments rated by the RAE as international centres of excellence (mainly within the top universities) receive most of the money, and those in big science the lion's share. In view of the weight given to research publications, especially journals, the RAE buttresses an alliance between authors and publishers. But it also has adverse side-effects, especially the risk that teaching quality is given less importance. For instance, in the years running up to the RAE, it is very difficult for publishers to commission academics to write textbooks when their management is directing them to concentrate on research. It also creates peaks in primary research publication.

FOCUS

intermediaries. New companies have arisen, such as OCLC NetLibrary, ebrary and Questia, and existing library suppliers have reinvented themselves such as Coutts, owned by the major US wholesaler Ingram. They are sometimes called *content aggregators*. Generally speaking, the publishers license a selection of their specialist titles, usually backlist academic, STM and professional titles (not major textbooks), to the aggregators, which in turn create ebook libraries or collections which are licensed to libraries on a subscription basis. Generally speaking the larger the institution in terms of staff and student numbers the higher its subscription. Users gain free access to the ebook collection via the library, protected by the institution's password access. The business model of such ebook collections usually reflects the library loan practice of printed books: for instance, the number of concurrent users accessing each copy of a title may be limited and the 'loan' time period set.

Journals

The publishing of refereed or peer-reviewed learned journals (or serials), sold on subscription to libraries, is a major adjunct to academic book publishing. In STM publishing the revenues may far outweigh the publishers' subject-related book operations. Historically, the higher profits (25–30 per cent) and higher gross margins (well over 80 per cent) derived from journals have in effect cross-subsidized their book publishing, which earned lower profits (of say 10–15 per cent). The learned societies and associations also publish their own journals (for example in the US major players such as the American Chemical Society and in the UK the Institute of Physics), or may have their journals produced and marketed for them under contract by the publishers. For many societies, journal publishing keeps them afloat.

In STM, there are at least 20,000 journals published worldwide, and the major publishers are Elsevier, Springer, Taylor & Francis, and Wiley-Blackwell. The main markets are North America, Europe and Asia Pacific. The constant rise in scientific and other kinds of research (for example in China) is putting great pressure on the peer review process and on library budgets.

The journal publishers, especially in STM, have been at the forefront of driving their businesses online. Throughout the 1990s, the printed journals became increasingly available in electronic format. At first, the journal publishers tried to charge extra for the electronic version in an effort to recoup their additional costs. However, subscription rates to the printed journal came to include the e-format for free, mainly because of the UK Value Added Tax (VAT) anomaly whereby electronic materials attract VAT and printed materials do not. More recently some publishers offer discounts on electronic only subscriptions.

The major publishers have developed their own e-platforms. For instance, in 1997 Elsevier launched the first large-scale e-platform, ScienceDirect, which allowed the STM community full online access to its journals and other databases (for example abstracts). In 2007 ScienceDirect offered 'more than a quarter of the world's scientific, medical and technical information online', including 2,000 journals and 4,000 ebooks (sciencedirect.com, accessed 10 September 2007). In 2001 it had introduced the first online peer review system and by 2003 had completed the digitization of its back issues, the first back file collection to be made available online. Wiley's InterScience had a similar programme, due for completion in 2007. The major publishers are large enough to deal directly with the institutional librarians or purchasing consortia (some at state or nation state level), through which the institution's subscriptions to journals (and ebook collections) are negotiated.

Platforms such as ScienceDirect are brands. The publishers compete on the usability of their platforms, such as reliability, speed, and ease of use and browsing. However, the strength of the platform is based on the brand value of the individual journals. Publishers without their own platforms may use companies like Ingenta or HighWire. The smaller publishers, in the main, use subscription agents, such as Blackwell's Information Services and Swets, through which libraries obtain their journals from a vast number of publishers. The US aggregators of journals and content databases, such as EBSCO and ProQuest, provide library access to the output of publishers. The subscription agents are developing their businesses in many directions.

Online access offers additional functionality over the printed page (such as search facilities or click-throughs to other articles via references). In many cases, the concept of the journal itself is being eroded and the unit of currency is becoming the individual paper – papers may be released when ready rather than waiting for a complete issue. Services have also been developed to serve discrete subject areas (known as portals or communities), drawing material from different journals and publishers.

The brand value of many journals is reflected in their *impact factor*, a measure of the citations to journals, calculated by the Institute for Scientific Information (ISI), which is part of of the major US publisher Thomson. It should be appreciated that different disciplines use citations in different ways. Some of the highest-rated journals are published by societies and associations in the UK and US, not by commercial publishers. Nevertheless, a major strength of a commercial publisher's business is expressed by the number of leading journals they have created over long periods and own outright. Since researchers' careers are often

Robert Maxwell (1923–91) made a fortune in publishing from learned journals through his Pergamon Press, which he later sold to Elsevier. After his death, having fallen overboard from his yacht, his company Maxwell Communications was found to have substantial debts

evaluated on their publication record, they try to be published in the highest ranked journals in their subject they can attain. Academics from the world's top research universities mainly populate the leading journals.

Open access

The advent of the internet gave rise to electronic journals and also to the concept of open access (OA): the free and unrestricted online access to peer-reviewed research articles in journals. It has several manifestations. Authors who publish articles in a peer-reviewed, subscription journal can make them freely available as a digital draft *preprint* (prior to peer review) or as a *postprint* (sometimes the same as the published version) depending on the policy of the publisher; usually by depositing them in an institutional repository, perhaps run by their university, or a central repository such as PubMed Central. They can publish them in OA, subscription-free journals (for example from the publisher BioMed Central). Or they can submit them to some of the commercial publishers' hybrid subscription/OA journals, in which they can elect OA from the publisher, once the article has been accepted for publication through peer review (to avoid corruption). The author (or their institution or funding agency) pays the publisher a one off-fee to make it OA. It is sometimes called the 'author-pays' model. Some funding agencies, notably the Wellcome Trust, financially support and insist on some form of OA on research it has funded. The effects of OA are most felt in medical publishing. For academics in the humanities and social sciences, who have little access to funds, the prospect of paying for OA publication seems problematic.

The long-term sustainability of OA publishers (mostly subsidized either directly by funding agencies or indirectly by institutions, while trying to secure other more reliable sources of income), and the impacts of OA on scholarly research, libraries and institutions, the learned societies and publishers are not yet clear.

> A collaboration amongst the publishers in 1999 and the Digital Object Identifier Foundation created CrossRef, a system that enables citations to articles in other journals to link through directly

---

Sources

Becta, *Harnessing Technology Schools Survey*, 2007.
Eric de Bellaigue, 'British Publishing 1970–2000: How deregulation and access to capital changed the rules', *Logos*, 17/3, 2006.
Philip Carpenter, Adrian Bullock and Jane Potter, 'Textbooks in Teaching and Learning: The views of students and their teachers', *Brookes eJournal of Learning and Teaching*, 2:1 (2007).
Paul Richardson, *Publishing Market Profile: The United Kingdom*, The Publishers Association, 2007.
John B. Thompson, *Books in the Digital Age*, Polity Press, 2005.
UK Serials Group (UKSG), *The E-Resources Management Handbook*, 2007.

Web resources

www.direct.gov.uk/en/EducationAndLearning/index.htm UK government information on education and the National Curriculum.

CHAPTER 4

The characteristics of the main publishing sectors

The last two chapters have traced the development of the book publishing industry across its various sectors. Common themes can be identified but there remain differences in the ways books are published for different markets. Publishers specialize in reaching particular markets, and each market has a separate dynamic. The skills of their staff, the activities they perform and the structure of the business are aligned accordingly.

UK PUBLISHING

Table 4.1, using figures from The Publishers Association, gives the scale of the UK publishing industry in 2006 based on publishers' sales. The size of the domestic market was estimated at £3.3 bn in terms of *end-purchaser prices* (see the pie chart opposite), an increase of 3 per cent on the previous year. There were around 2,300 book publishers registered for VAT, plus thousands more individuals and organizations publishing a narrow range of titles (publishers.org.uk).

The number of titles published in the UK in 2006 – 115,522 – was around the level of 10 years previously. In 2005 over 625,000 separate titles were sold in the UK market, and the top 500 titles accounted for 24 per cent of sales (OFT).

All kinds of publishers can be described as serving niche markets. Attaining a critical mass in a particular field, right down to a list of books on the narrowest subject area, is vital to publishers of every size. It allows the employment of editors who understand and have contact with authors and associates in a particular field, and who can shape projects for their intended markets. A respected list attracts

Table 4.1 UK publishers' sales in 2006 (*source*: The Publishers Association)

	Home	Export	Total
Volume of books sold (m)	472	314	786
Sales (£m)	1,814	999	2,813

Table 4.2 Number of titles published in the UK 1996 to 2006 (*source*: Nielsen BookData)

Year	Number of titles and new editions
1996	114,153
1997	112,916
1998	123,580
1999	130,053
2000	124,941
2001	123,679
2002	125,449
2003	131,271
2004	124,027
2005	110,925
2006	115,522

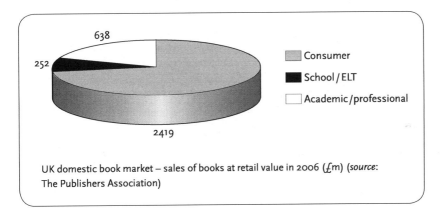

UK domestic book market – sales of books at retail value in 2006 (£m) (*source*: The Publishers Association)

authors. Furthermore, a list of books needs to generate sufficient turnover to allow effective marketing and selling, which in turn feeds new publishing.

Books in the UK are zero rated for VAT alongside newspapers, magazines published at regular intervals (more than once a year), and printed music. VAT is charged on digital products such as CD-ROMs and online content.

Themes shared across publishing sectors include the growth of digital publishing, changes in publishing processes, and the search for new talent, sometimes from outside the industry. The larger companies have shown an increased interest in corporate social responsibility (CSR). Pearson is 'guided by the UN Global Compact's 10 principles on labour standards, human rights, business ethics and the environment', and aims to review the performance of its suppliers against the Global Compact (pearson.com). In the area of environmental impact, HarperCollins set itself the target of achieving carbon neutral status by the end of 2007, and all its 4th Estate titles are now printed on recycled paper.

CONSUMER PUBLISHING

The consumer or trade publishers are the most visible part of the industry. Their hardback and paperback titles are displayed prominently in high street bookshops and other outlets, receive considerable mass-media coverage and are aimed mainly at the indefinable 'general reader', and sometimes at the enthusiast or specialist reader. They form the mainstay of public libraries and book clubs, and in some cases penetrate academic markets. In 2006 Nielsen BookScan, which tracks nearly all retail book sales, reported consumer sales in the UK market of £1.7 bn and 225 m books. That is an average selling price (not cover price) of £7.56 per copy.

Most trade publishers are in London, giving them ready access to authors, agents, other publishers, social venues, journalists and producers of the mass media, and other influential people who decisively affect the life of the nation. The remaining publishers are spread around the country, with concentrations in Oxford and Edinburgh, and tend to be more specialized.

Consumer book publishing is the high-risk end of the business: book failures are frequent but the rewards from 'bestsellers' – some of which are quite unexpected – can be great. At the top end of the spectrum is the *Harry Potter* series. The potential readers are varied, spread thinly through the population, expensive to reach, difficult to identify, and have tastes and interests that can be described generally but are not easily matched to a particular book. Publishers bet to a great extent on their judgement of public taste and interests – notoriously unpredictable. Sometimes the publication of a book creates its own market. And the authors

The seventh volume in the Harry Potter series, *Harry Potter and the Deathly Hallows*, was published in 2007

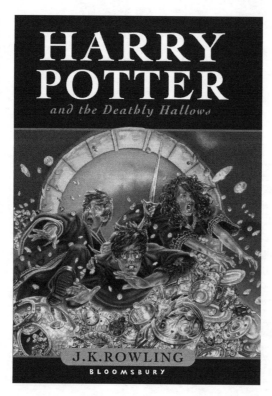

whose work arouses growing interest can develop a personal readership, thereby creating their own markets – perhaps attaining a 'brand name' following, especially in fiction. Publishers compete fiercely for their books.

Few other consumer goods industries market products with such a short sales life. Generally speaking for a book to flourish, it is vital for the publisher to secure advance or *subscription* orders from booksellers before publication and for the response to the book to be good in the opening few weeks post-publication. The peak sales of most new books occur well within a year of publication. Most adult hardback fiction and paperback titles are dead within three months or just weeks, while hardback non-fiction and paperback fiction written by famous authors may endure longer. Compared to the non-consumer book publishers, the trade publishers earn a higher proportion of their revenues from their frontlist publishing. With the increasing focus on the lead titles that are part of bookseller promotions and which receive supermarket exposure, frontlist revenues are increasing in proportion to backlist revenues. Some publishers' lists are very frontlist weighted (such as television and film tie-in publishers), while others keep strong backlists alive from their new book programme and by relaunching old books in new covers, reissuing them in different sizes and bindings, adding new introductions or revising them. An energetically promoted backlist provides retailers with staple and more predictable stock, should earn good profits for the publisher, and keeps authors in print.

Many readers mistakenly believe that the large price differential between hardbacks and paperbacks is due to the extra cost of binding a book in hardback. The considerable price gap does not represent that cost (which is low); rather it reflects the ways in which publishers try to maximize the revenue from a title by segmenting the market through the use of different formats and price points, often sequentially. For example, a fiction title could be launched first in hardback at a high price to satisfy eager readers, then subsequently at a lower price to reach a new and wider market of readers in trade or mass-market paperback; or it might be published as a paperback original. Furthermore some titles of minority appeal would not recover their investment if first published in a lower paperback price range – meant for books with higher sales potential. Over time it has become harder to sell some categories of book in hardback editions. In 2007 Picador announced that it would launch most of its literary fiction in paperback, with only a few authors appearing in hardback editions.

> Richard and Judy's Book Club on Channel 4 has been credited with hastening the end for the hardback by insisting a new book is out in paperback before it is added to its influential list. Libraries, which used to in effect underwrite the hardback market by guaranteeing to buy almost every new literary novel, have diverted resources to music, computers and DVDs. (*The Guardian*, 17 November 2007)

The key characteristics of consumer publishing are illustrated on the next page.

High risk

The business is high risk with large print runs and large sums invested in new books. The cash return, however, can also be large, and the large publishing groups can afford to gamble on a variety of new projects.

When *Harry Potter and the Deathly Hallows* was published on 21 July 2007, it sold 2.6 m copies in the UK on that day alone

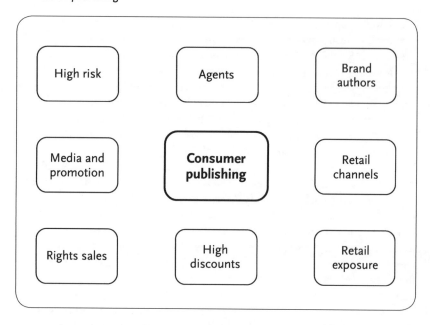

Agents

Publishers are squeezed to a far greater extent by agents (on behalf of their authors), who look to negotiate higher royalty rates and advances. The major trade houses may pay out 30 per cent of their sales revenue to authors (more than twice the percentage paid out by non-consumer publishers).

Brand authors

Consumer publishers give greater emphasis to top authors in terms of promotional expenditure, sales effort and high-profile publication dates – author brands help to sell books.

Variety of retail channels

The main customers and channels to market are diverse, including the bookselling chains, independent bookshops, supermarkets, internet retailers such as Amazon, wholesalers, book club and direct distribution channels.

Retail exposure

Publishers depend to a great extent on retail exposure to sell their books, and on gift buying for adult and children's books (the pre-Christmas period is of immense importance).

High discounts

Publishers are also squeezed by the large retailers ratcheting up the discounts granted to them. The discounts granted to the book trade, essential to gain exposure in the shops, can reach 60 per cent of the published price of a book, at least 10–20 per cent higher than those granted by the non-consumer publishers. Trade publishers suffer from high returns of unsold books from retailers and wholesalers.

Rights sales

There is usually greater scope in consumer publishing to sell rights in the author's work to other firms, and to set up co-edition deals with book clubs and overseas publishers.

Media and promotion

Media exposure makes an enormous difference to sales. Promotional efforts will boost a book's profile in the retail trade and amongst consumers. A large promotional spend may have to be promised in order to secure large orders from key retailers.

Children's publishing

Children's books accounted for 29 per cent – by volume – of consumer sales in the UK in 2006 (Richardson, page 13). Children's books are published by the specialist children's divisions of the major consumer book publishers and independent publishers. The vitality of children's publishing creates the book buyers of the future. The text and illustrations of children's books must excite and appeal to children of different age groups, and at different levels of reading skill and comprehension. They must also appeal to adults in the supply chain (the major non-book and book retailers, wholesalers, book clubs) and to adults who buy or influence choice (parents, relations, librarians and teachers). Many titles are in full colour yet have to be published at low prices, and these often need co-edition partners in the USA, in Europe and elsewhere in order to attain economies in printing.

   The books are usually aimed at age bands reflecting the development of reading skill. The bibliographic information supplied by publishers to the book trade is formalized through the Book Industry Communication (BIC) Children's Book Marketing Categories standard which denotes amongst other things, the title's intended age range (bic.org.uk). These are divided up as follows:

A   0 to 5
B   5 to 7
C   7 to 9
D   9 to 11
E   12 upwards.

The 0–5 age group from babies to toddlers may be described as the *parent pointing* stage. Included here are the so-called 'novelty books' (which extend above the age group), a category of ever-widening inventiveness, such as board books and bath books (introducing page turning), sound story books with electronic panels, colouring and activity books, question and answer books, pop-ups; and the lower end of picture books. Books for the very young need to be durable and often use cloth, plastic or hardback binding. The production departments of children's publishers are particularly concerned with product safety.

   The 5–7 age group may be described as the starting to read, as well as reading to children stage. Picture books figure prominently. These books, invariably in full colour, tend to be 32 pages long (12–14 double-page spreads), display strong

The *Horrid Henry* stories by Francesca Simon are popular with the age group 5 to 9

narrative and may include just a few words up to possibly several thousand. They may be created by an illustrator or writer (or one controlling mind), and invariably need co-edition partners. Story books for younger fiction tend to have more text, say 2,000–7,500 words, and may be published in paperback in smaller formats, with black and white, or colour illustrations; and are designed for children reading their first whole novels. There are major series produced by many of the main trade publishers as well as reading schemes by the educational publishers. Moving up, and through, the 9–12 age group, longer length novels of up to 35,000 words come into play as well as the more recent mass-market genre series. Above 11–12, there are the teenage or young adult, fiction titles. Much middle and young adult fiction is published straight into paperback.

Some teenage fiction has aroused controversy for its adult content. For example, when *Doing It* by Melvin Burgess was published in the children's imprint Puffin in 2003, the children's laureate Anne Fine attacked the decision:

> All of the publishers who have touched this novel should be deeply ashamed of themselves. Astonishingly, they are almost all female. It's time they sat round a table, took a good long look at themselves and decided that it was an indefensible decision to take this book on. They should pulp their own copies now. (*The Guardian*, 29 March 2003)

Non-fiction, sometimes highly illustrated, spans the age groups as do home learning series, reference titles (for example dictionaries), anthologies and character books (some which are tie-ins to films).

Children's books (but not *Harry Potter*) receive less window or promotional space in general bookshops; and children's publishers of quality books earn a higher proportion from backlist sales. The children's and young adult (YA) market is subject to huge – often advertising- or character-led – crazes and recently to overseas publishing phenomena, notably the irresistible rise of manga.

Echoing developments in adult publishing, children's publishers have little time to build authors slowly. The focus is on promotable first-time authors, established adult authors or celebrities writing for children, and media tie-ins. Author branding and the development of branded series are notable features of children's publishing. As in adult publishing, the gender differentiation of books for male and female markets is evident, in part influenced by consumer advertising of other products to children.

Children's publishing in the UK continues to push out the frontiers of book availability into a wide range of retail outlets, including grocery, toy and garden centres reached via the wholesalers. Such retailers, and some of the book clubs, tend to concentrate on books for the younger age groups. Internationally, the Bologna Book Fair held in the spring is the world's meeting-place of children's publishing. The UK publishers and packagers have for long dominated the international trade in the selling of overseas co-edition rights and, like their adult counterparts, they import far less.

Reference publishing

Reference works (spanning words, pictures, numbers and maps) are sold by all kinds of publisher from consumer book to professional. Although some are ephemeral, reference publishing is usually for the long-term backlist. Major works can take years to compile and can involve investments of millions. *The Oxford Dictionary of National Biography* was published in 2004, both in an online edition and 60 print volumes. Formed in 1992 as a research project of Oxford University, the Dictionary was funded by a £3.5 m subvention from the British Academy and by £22 m from OUP.

Reference publishing is most amenable to the application of new technologies in terms of aiding the product development and the publishing of a family of products in different media (for example as a paper product or online), of different sizes and prices for various markets. The *Oxford English Dictionary* could never have been revised as a complete entity without computerization. Dictionary lexicographers (and in bilingual works, translators) no longer have to rely on the manual identification and retrieval of words in primary sources. Typically they use electronic text corpora holding a vast range of primary and diverse sources from which evidence of word meaning and sentence contextual meaning can be retrieved, manipulated and to an increasing extent analysed electronically. Once the main dictionary database has been built and coded, spin-off shorter or special purpose dictionaries can be subsequently published. Generally speaking, the publishers of online databases, such as in law, try continually to enhance their functionality, for example, by improving their web browser interfaces and analytical research tools for users.

FOCUS

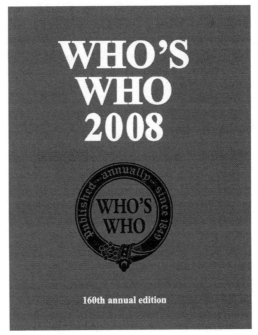

The reference work *Who's Who* is available both in print and online. It has been published annually by A & C Black since 1849

NON-CONSUMER PUBLISHING

The educational, academic, scientific, technical and medical (STM) book publishers have a number of advantages by comparison to firms operating in consumer markets:

- Their markets are more defined.
- Their authors and advisers are largely drawn from the same peer groups as their customers.
- Customers can be reached through their place of work.
- Backlist sales, especially if textbook and reference, account for a major proportion of their business.
- Institutional and business purchasers are far more amenable to buying digital formats.

Schools publishing

The total value of the UK educational market (i.e. school related) in 2005/6 was thought to total £287–340 m (the precise figure is difficult to establish), of which £176–214 m was accounted for by core textbooks, around £34–39 m on school libraries, and £65–75 m on digital resources and software. There is additional provision for schools via local libraries – around £12 m in 2005. The market for trade education was worth £42 m (Richardson, page 8). In 2006 school and ELT books together represented 38 per cent of all book exports from the UK, and 25 per cent by value (ibid., page 10).

Educational publishers provide materials for schools: chiefly textbooks bought in multiple copies, sometimes supported by ancillary printed materials for class use or for teachers (and where appropriate audio, CD-ROM, websites), published individually or as a series (for example representing a progressive course of study). Publishers concentrate on the big subject areas. The main publishers are located mainly outside London.

The key characteristics of schools publishing are shown opposite.

Long term

Compared with consumer book publishing, educational publishing is for the long term. Publishers derive most of their sales revenue from established backlist books. Schools can ill afford to dump adopted texts frequently. New books are published in the hope that they will be reprinted and revised in following years, but in practice they may fail. Curriculum publishing calls for a large amount of working capital – the liquid assets of a company – invested over a long time. The development costs of digital resources are also very high.

Defined curriculum

The books are market-specific (i.e. precisely tailored to the National Curriculum, examinations, academic levels and age groups). While to some extent the broad content is predetermined, curriculum publishers and their external advisers and authors give great attention to the pedagogy, and also cater for more conservative teachers. They help raise the quality of teaching.

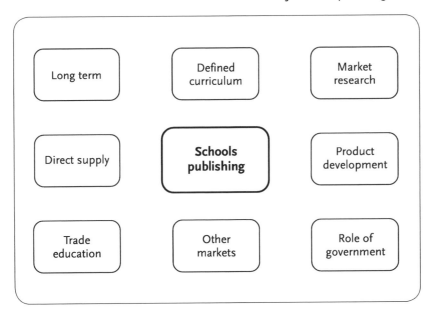

Market research

Understanding the market is vital to the creation of a new textbook course for schools. Primary research may include sending out questionnaires to teachers or the use of focus groups.

Product development

Many books are highly illustrated, printed in colour, and involve a publisher in much development work. Yet they must be published at very low prices. Furthermore, the costs of developing accompanying digital materials are very high.

Role of government

The educational sector is dependent on school budgets. Book provision in state schools is always underfunded; and the government has given money to schools for digital resources.

Other markets

Some educational publishers produce books for further education (especially for vocational qualifications) and reference (for home or school library use). UK-orientated school textbooks will have reduced export potential (other than to the international schools) though there can be scope, for example, to produce specially prepared textbooks, such as in science and mathematics.

Trade education

There is a growing trade market for self-study and revision books, sold mainly through bookshops to parents and pupils. Teachers can influence this market through their recommendations.

Direct supply

New and backlist titles are promoted by mail directly to teachers and by publishers' sales representatives in schools and at exhibitions. Teachers scrutinize bound copies before adopting a book. Textbooks are mainly supplied directly to schools, or via booksellers, specialist school contractors and local authority direct purchasing organizations, and may be stocked by booksellers for parental purchase. The direct supply route to schools provides valuable marketing information to publishers.

ELT publishing

In 2006, 600,000 foreign students came to the UK for study and spent around £24 m on publishers' materials (Richardson, 2007). However, the publishing of English language teaching (ELT) or English as a foreign language (EFL) course materials is export-orientated (say above 90 per cent of sales) to better-off countries and has to some extent offset the overall decline in exports of UK school books. The main markets are in Southern Europe (Spain, France, Italy, Greece, Turkey), Eastern Europe, Japan, the Far East and South East Asia (China, Taiwan, Korea, Thailand), Latin America (Argentina, Brazil and Mexico) and the Middle East. The ELT publishers have set up companies, opened offices or acquired publishers in such areas, or have copublishing links with local publishers, or local marketing arrangements.

> One estimate is that by 2010 there will be 2 bn learners of English worldwide

The mixed media ELT courses are major investments and may be orientated or versioned to regional cultural distinctiveness and are sometimes produced for ministries. The courses serving primary, secondary and adult sectors are backed up with supplementary materials (such as reading books, dictionaries and grammars) with a broad international appeal. They are sold to the Private Language Schools (PLS) (from primary to adult), primary and secondary state schools, and sometimes to universities. In the UK there are specialist booksellers that supply the local and export markets.

Whereas previously UK publishers could rely on the same course to sell well around the world, there are now separate needs for different markets, which raise the costs of product development. The big change has been the growth of the state school market – for example in Italy, Spain, Argentina and Eastern Europe – which has probably overtaken the PLS market. A state syllabus has its own demands, specific to the country, and offers an opportunity for local publishers to enter the market. A key competence in ELT publishing is the ability to network with local schools and educational authorities.

ACADEMIC AND PROFESSIONAL BOOK PUBLISHING

The terms 'academic' or 'professional' publishing are used loosely and interchangeably. Professional books usually have an applied focus to aid practitioners directly in their work, for example schoolteachers, health care workers, engineers, architects, managers, and those working in law and finance. STM, reference and information books usually fall into the professional book publishing area. Some academic/professional titles may be designed for vocational or continuing professional development courses and be adopted. Their pricing level varies widely, depending on the target audience's ability to pay and whether they are purchased by the individual or the employer.

The business model is changing. The publisher's traditional role of quality assurance and accuracy in the supply of information (for example peer review of learned journals) – to become a trusted brand – is supplemented by the direct provision of services and tools to end-users. A key added value is to provide users with access tools to the content they need quickly, and in a form they want, at the point they need it *in their workflow*, be they researchers or lawyers in their offices or at home, or medical practitioners on the move. A good example is the delivery of information to doctors on personal digital assistants (PDAs).

Not even the largest publisher could claim to be equally strong in all disciplines, or even those in science alone. Publishers concentrate on particular subjects, and vary in the emphasis given to different categories of book. The books for professional or practitioner use which have a wider market beyond teaching institutions tend to be those in the applied sciences for researchers or practitioners in industry and government agencies; and those serving professional sectors (for example law, medicine, management, accounting, finance, architecture). Such high-priced titles are bought by the wealthy (offices, commercial libraries and individuals). Special sales channels include booksellers or training companies serving corporations, agencies and individuals; dedicated business, computer and medical book distributors or book clubs reaching end-users directly; conference and exhibition organizers; and companies which take bulk orders of titles as promotional items.

The legal and financial publishers, especially, traditionally used loose-leaf publishing for some of their reference titles. The purchaser, having bought the initial volume, received updated pages. Such publishers, as well as those producing books for business, sell a high proportion of their materials by mail order to end-users, not via booksellers. Sometimes, reference products (including directories, sometimes dependent on advertising revenue) are written in-house. Publishers have migrated their businesses to digital information services, either alongside printed products or in lieu of print. Their products may be available on disk or online, and are usually licensed directly to libraries and businesses on subscription or by site licences governing usage on intranets. Key abilities of such publishers are to identify information needs and the way that information is used in the workplace, and to translate that knowledge into the creation of products, tools and services using the appropriate media and technologies.

The total value of higher education sales in 2006 was estimated at around £400 m, with a total market of £600 m if imports are included (Richardson, page 11). Western Europe and North America account for more than 50 per cent of export sales, followed by the Far East and Southeast Asia, and Australia. For many publishers, mainland Europe is the single most important market but one which is diverse and growing. The Scandinavian and Benelux countries can be significant markets for English language textbook adoptions, and for professional lists. Holland in terms of sales often ranks third after the USA and Australia, and is dominated by a few major bookselling chains, while Germany, another large market, is served by a variety of regional and local chains. Southern Europe, for example Spain and Italy, is a market for high-level professional texts, especially in STM; undergraduate texts exist in translation or are published locally. The sale of translation rights to Eastern Europe and more recently to China and Korea, for example, has grown.

High-level textbooks and professional titles are sold to the USA, the largest and richest market, via a sister company. A UK firm without a US presence may develop a copublishing link with a US firm, or license rights to a variety of publishers, or sell through importers. Sales to less developed countries tend to be dependent on aid agency funding. Publishers may on their own account arrange for special low-priced editions of some of their textbooks to be published in less developed countries, either through their own local companies or through sublicensing editions to local publishers. At the minimum, such editions have different covers in order to reduce the possibility of their penetrating developed markets through conventional and internet traders.

Academic and STM publishers are mostly outside central London with a high concentration in Oxford, and their output includes major textbooks (often the preserve of the larger publishers); higher-level textbooks for more advanced students through to graduate; edited volumes of reprinted or commissioned articles for students or academics; research monographs; books for professional use; reference titles (mostly online) and learned journals (print and online). These broad categories are not clear cut (for example high-level 'textbooks' may incorporate original research).

Textbooks

There is no commonly accepted definition of what constitutes a 'textbook'. Indeed there are plenty of examples of books of different kinds that are never written or intended as textbooks but which subsequently become adopted by lecturers for teaching and bought by their students (such as this book from 1988). However, from a publishing standpoint, a higher education or 'college' textbook is commissioned, designed, timed and priced at the outset to meet teaching and learning needs in a defined area and at a particular level, and is marketed to lecturers with the intention that they adopt the book for use on a course, resulting in the purchase of multiple copies by students.

There are many factors affecting textbook purchasing in the UK, including student use of the internet, competing financial demands, the rise in published prices above the rate of inflation, changing behaviours about the sharing of books, and the rise of the used book market.

Broadly speaking textbooks are published in paperback, though some for professional training (for example medicine, law) may be hardback. The high-level supplementary texts occasionally have a short high-priced print run for libraries, issued simultaneously with the paperback. Conversely, textbooks, printed in larger quantities, may become established and are reprinted for annual student intakes and revised through new editions when appropriate. Competitors constantly attack the market share of successful books. Many of the campus bookshops are owned by the bookselling chains. Nevertheless, publishers have been more successful than the consumer book publishers in resisting booksellers' demands for higher discounts, and in containing author royalty rates and advances. Trade wholesalers find it difficult to enter the supply chain.

Publishers promote (and sometimes sell directly) their books to lecturers, researchers and practitioners (mainly by mail, email and telephone) and compared with consumer book publishers usually have smaller sales forces calling on a limited range of booksellers, and sometimes campuses, or attending exhibitions. However, some firms publish titles of wider general interest and of bookshop appeal in which case booksellers may be granted higher 'trade' discounts. These include more titles in the humanities, especially history, than the social sciences, some technical books (for example on computing) and medical works (for example personal health) supplied through specialist wholesalers. They are sometimes bought by specialist book clubs.

Other titles, sometimes referred to as 'supplementary texts', may include the author's original research or commissioned edited collections. These can be priced for student and individual academic purchase, and can be published economically in small quantities – from around 1,500 copies in paperback. Paradoxically, if an author's primary research were to appear in a textbook it could seriously damage saleability through being seen as idiosyncratic or too advanced. The highly saleable textbooks usually reflect a mainstream view of current teaching and assessment. Other kinds of books, such as course readers and anthologies, may be bought by students and academics. Some publishers continue the practice of publishing dual paperback and hardback editions. Their new books are issued in paperback for personal purchase, and simultaneously as a short-run hardback, say 150 copies, priced at around three times the paperback price, for sale to academic libraries worldwide.

The figure below shows the key characteristics of textbook publishing.

Long term

Initiating and developing a textbook list requires planning and sufficient attention to product development. Textbooks require development editors to control the authoring, schedule and budget.

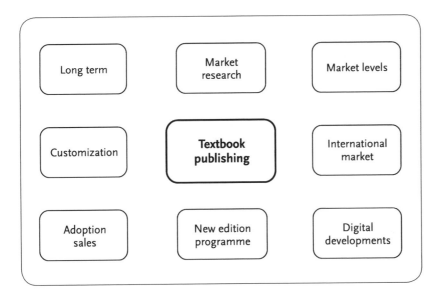

Market research

Just as in educational publishing, a major investment in a new textbook requires comprehensive research into the market and competition.

Market levels

There will be different levels in the market, from first-year undergraduate through to graduate. More introductory texts may have a larger potential sale but will encounter fiercer competition.

International market

For some subjects there may be a large international market. For example, a business textbook may be used around the world, and some business schools in non-English-speaking countries may teach in English. Successful textbooks may be localized in different markets. For example, Kotler et al.'s *Principles of Marketing* is available in a European edition. The adaptation of textbooks for particular regions of the world aids local sales and inhibits their exportation to other higher-priced regions.

Digital developments

Publishers producing major textbooks for subjects with high student intakes adopt US practices, such as higher design and production standards, with possibly a CD-ROM in the back of the book, or increasingly, a periodically updated companion website carrying data, activities and website links, and lecturers' guides.

New edition programme

In order to ensure that texts are up to date, and also to minimize lost sales from the used book market, textbooks regularly go into new editions.

Adoption sales

The successful sale of a textbook entails persuading the lecturer to adopt it, the bookseller to stock it and the student to buy it. Students and lecturers are becoming far more demanding.

Customization

The large publishers offer lecturers the ability *to customize* – to personalize – the book content to meet their specific teaching needs. If the teacher wants a book shortened, or to use an old edition, for example, the publisher will produce it specifically for that course (assuming sufficient numbers of students). Or the teacher may want to compile their own book by slicing and dicing content from the publisher's other books, to insert their own material, or include articles or case-studies. The publisher will undertake the production (and any third-party rights clearance, if possible), usually within three months. The teacher sees their name on the cover of the custom book. The publisher creates a unique product for the particular institution.

Monographs

Monographs are usually high-priced hardbacks published mainly for libraries. They are printed in small quantities once only, though a few are reissued in paperback. Short-run publishing is not risk free – the profit may come from the sale of the last 50 copies. Such books can live on through print on demand and as part of ebook collections. For academics in the humanities and social sciences, the publication of their primary research in full-length monograph form by highly respected publishers, which maintain a thorough peer review process, is still important to their research rating and hence career.

> As the competition for academic jobs and promotion to senior posts intensifies, the pressure on academics and prospective academics to publish scholarly work grows, and academic publishers find themselves faced with an ever growing avalanche of scholarly book projects. And yet the expansion in the supply of scholarly content . . . has occurred at the same time as the market for scholarly books has collapsed. (Thompson, page 175)

As we saw in the previous chapter, the average sale of a monograph has been in steady decline. Could the answer be publication in electronic form? Print will remain important but there are predictions that by 2020 around 40 per cent of research monographs will appear in digital format only (British Library). For scientists, the publication of their primary research as articles in prestigious peer-reviewed learned journals is far more critical.

Journal publishing

The total value of the global journals market was around £7 bn in 2006, with UK publishers controlling one-third of the market and three-quarters of their sales in export markets (Richardson, page 12). The value of global sales for the STM segment was estimated at around £5 bn in 2004 (EPS, page 14). The content of learned journals, as distinct from magazines, is not predetermined (commissioned or written in-house), and contributors submit papers of original research to an academic editor for refereeing and inclusion. Refereed journal articles are a primary information source and serve the research community. Generally speaking, learned journals are not dependent on advertising for their viability; their revenue is derived from subscriptions. Some publishers produce magazines for professional use that are supported by advertising.

Journals are published by not-for-profit societies and research institutes (a few of which run substantial journal and book publishing operations), and by divisions of academic and STM publishers including the university presses. The commercial journal publishers initiate journals, or produce and market journals for societies and others under contract. The provision of such services to societies can be a significant proportion of some publishers' business.

The key people in a journal publisher are the commissioning editors who bring in new journals, the production editors who organize and produce them, direct marketing specialists, and sales staff who negotiate subscription packages directly with librarians and purchasing consortia, or with intermediaries; plus, where appropriate, advertising sales staff. Publishers provide advice to the academic editor and the editorial board (say 20–30 experts), fund their office costs, editorial meetings (say once per year) and expenses; maintain peer review management, submission and tracking systems; undertake the production workflow; market each journal directly to readers both to attract authors and subscriptions via their libraries; sell them to intermediaries in print and electronic formats; and manage subscription and distribution systems, including websites.

There are more STM journals than in other academic areas. They are promoted by mail and at academic conferences, supplied on subscription, sold mainly to academic libraries worldwide (either directly from the publisher's platform or through intermediaries) and to a lesser extent sold direct to individuals (more so in the USA). Journals of applied science, management, economics and law also sell to industrial and commercial libraries. Members of societies may receive a journal free as part of their membership fee, or at a reduced rate. Journal academic editors may be paid – some only expenses, some handsomely – but contributors and referees are not. Many authors assign their copyright to the journal publisher or society, although this model is changing.

Journal publishing, unlike book publishing, does not require a complex network of overseas agents. The discounts granted to intermediary subscription agents may be from 0 to 10 per cent. The credit risk is low, and the return of unsolds rare. Other income can arise from advertisements and inserts (especially in STM), from copyright fees from commercial document suppliers and from subscription list rental. The lists and journals can be used to advertise and sell the publisher's books. There is cross-fertilization of contacts and ideas between book and journal publishers.

Most journals are still available in print for archival reasons. Some librarians believe that print on paper is the only guaranteed form of proven technology which lasts. Print also conveys status and pleases authors. However, researchers, students and industry practitioners mostly access journals online away from the library. It is estimated that 90 per cent of English language journals from publishers in the UK and US are available online (EPS, page 20). Librarians are able to check the value for money of a subscription from user statistics on articles downloaded.

The key characteristics of journal publishing are shown opposite.

Subscription model

Whereas book publishers operate a business model based on the sales of individual copies, journal publishers have the advantage that annual subscriptions are received in advance of production. The profit margins in journals publishing are generally higher than in book publishing. Historically, there have been higher profits (25–30 per cent) and higher gross margins (well over 80 per cent).

Brand

Long-established and successful journals, such as *Nature*, become established as brands, attracting the best submissions from authors. They are essential purchases in their relevant communities.

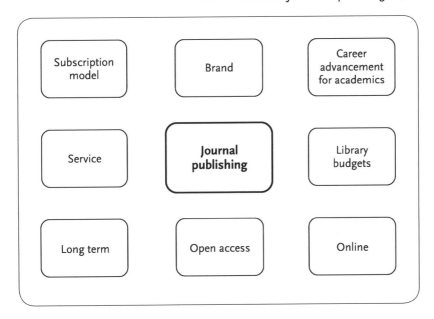

Career advancement for academics

Publication in high-ranking journals can establish or enhance the academic standing of authors – counting towards their personal and institutional research funding and their promotion prospects.

Library budgets

Journals sales are dependent on library budgets in universities and other institutions. The tendency for publishers to offer the 'Big Deal' – large collections of journals bundled together – has been attractive to libraries after better value. But some librarians have expressed concern about being tied into longer-term contracts and the price increases applied by publishers to these packages.

Online

Journals publishing has been at the forefront of online publishing. The large players have invested huge sums in online platforms, which enable them to sell direct to their customers.

Open access

The open access movement argues that access to journal articles should be free to the end-user. There are a number of OA models in existence, from 'author pays' to the institutional repository.

Long term

New journals take a long time to break even – up to 5 or 7 years for some STM journals – and may involve enormous investment. The older titles tend to be much more profitable. Once a journal is established, the sales pattern is more predictable than books, the demand for capital lower (as are staff overheads), and the value of sales per employee is higher.

Service

The migration to electronic publishing has meant the transition from a physical product industry to an electronic service information industry. Journal publishers constantly strive to improve the service they offer their customers – including access, search facilities, and product range. For example, the cross-industry initiative CrossRef is a system that enables journal citations to link through directly.

Now read this

Paul Richardson and Graham Taylor, *A Guide to the Publishing Industry*, The
  Publishers Association, 2008.

Sources

British Library, 'British Library Predicts "Switch to Digital by 2020"',
  press release, 29 June 2005 (available at http://www.bl.uk/news/
  pressreleases2005.html; accessed 10 September, 2007).
EPS (Electronic Publishing Services), *UK Scholarly Journals: 2006 baseline report*,
  12 September 2006.
David Graddol, *English Next*, British Council, 2007.
OFT (Office of Fair Trading), report into completed acquisition by Woolworths
  Group plc of Bertram Group plc, 16 April 2007.
Paul Richardson, *Publishing Market Profile: The United Kingdom*, The Publishers
  Association, 2007.
John B. Thompson, *Books in the Digital Age*, Polity Press, 2005.

CHAPTER 5

Creating and protecting value

THE PUBLISHING VALUE CHAIN

The aim of a book publisher is to publish and sell at a profit. Even not-for-profit publishers will want to at least break even, covering their costs, unless they receive a subsidy from their parent organization. A publisher might previously have cross-subsidized less popular titles from the profits of its top sellers, but that approach has largely been abandoned. Of course a book may acquire value as a collectable object or a great literary work to be admired and studied by future generations, but this chapter will concentrate on the creation of monetary value by publishers as commercial enterprises.

Taking the raw material – the author's text – the publisher aims to add sufficient value so that it sells the final product at a higher value than the costs that have been incurred. A number of activities are undertaken in order to take the author's text and make it available as an attractive product that consumers will want to buy. These activities are shown below. Each of the publishing functions is described in more detail in the relevant chapter.

Once a book is acquired from an author, it has to be edited, designed, produced, marketed to the book trade and readers, and sold to bookshops or the end-purchaser. Once the book has been printed, it has to be stored, orders are taken from retailers or consumers, and the book is then dispatched from the warehouse.

Publishers can choose which elements of the value chain they undertake themselves, and which are outsourced to third parties. For example, while

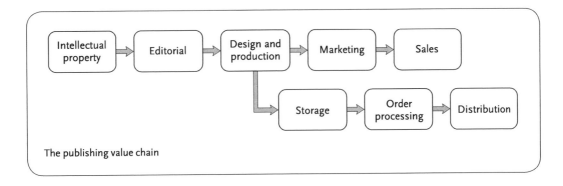

The publishing value chain

commissioning new titles is usually done in-house, copy-editing and proofreading are typically carried out by freelance editors. The key elements of the value chain are the acquisition of intellectual property, editorial, design and production, marketing, and sales, and most publishers will control these functions directly. Publishers can look to combine stages of the value chain and, for example, editorial, design and production may be combined into one function, and the post of production editor is increasingly common.

Publishers seek to gain competitive advantage in the market, and this is done through acquiring and controlling the best intellectual property. Having the best possible people in the commissioning roles will be the key to many publishers' success. There is also value to be found in other parts of the value chain. For example, a larger publisher will be able to negotiate from a stronger position with printers and paper suppliers, and with key retailers and wholesalers. 'In the experience of two independent trade publishers, on absorption into large groups they found their print bills reduced by more than 25%' (de Bellaigue, page 192). Some publishers like Dorling Kindersley build up expertise in the area of design. Everyman's Library, now owned by Random House, offers editions of literary classics in hardback editions with high production values that contrast with the predominant cheap paperback. Giving away high discounts to the bookshop chains has the aim of ensuring that a publisher's stock is widely available, and should increase sales, but it also squeezes a publisher's profit margins. Selling direct, rather than through intermediaries, enables a publisher to keep more of the product's final value. There are economies of scale in production if co-edition orders can be added to the print run. Using print on demand to print smaller quantities, or selling ebooks, may minimize or eradicate investment in stock. Smaller publishers can gain benefit from speed to market – commissioning and publishing faster than larger rivals.

There is less competitive advantage to be found for a publisher in the physical distribution of books, since the levels of service are now high across the industry. Nevertheless a larger publisher benefits from economies of scale in distribution in such areas as investment in IT systems, the size of orders, negotiation over carriage costs with shippers, and the collection of money from customers. In electronic distribution the larger publisher benefits from the greater aggregation of its intellectual property.

Adding value

Publishers add value to an author's work in a variety of ways – these reflect both creativity and business acumen. Embedded throughout the book, they are summarized in the figure on the next page.

Brand

By lending their brand or imprint, the publisher is making a statement about the value of the author's work – it is worth publication by an investor, i.e. the publisher. The brand (or imprint) adds value and endorsement. In consumer book publishing, the character of an imprint is understood by author's agents (this influences the supply of similar books and authors), informed sections of the media (affecting the attention and coverage given to the book), trade buyers in

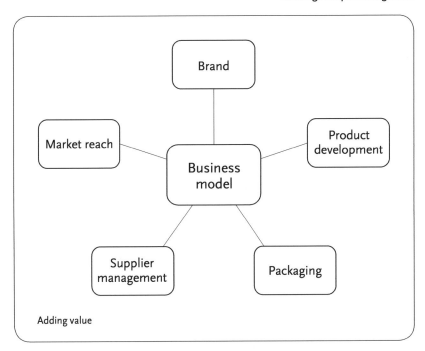

Adding value

the supply chain in the UK and overseas (affecting access to channels to market and order quantities), and by other media companies and overseas publishers (affecting rights sales). In non-consumer book publishing, an imprint's status is recognized by associated peer groups (for example teachers) and those in the supply chain, including institutional and corporate purchasers. Major textbook brands offer authors a platform to show their approach to teaching is better than existing texts, and the advantage of online support services. Highly rated academic and professional publishing brands (including learned journals) offer authors peer group recognition worldwide and personal career advancement.

Product development

The publisher's knowledge and judgement of current markets and future trends adds value to those authors who are commissioned and selected by the publisher. They are helped through the creative development of the proposal to match market and user needs, including filling gaps in the market (also of course imitating the competition) and realizing opportunities, and through the provision of other guidance and advice.

Packaging

Another creative expertise of the publisher is to design and present the author's work to best effect in a saleable printed book: length, size, format, usability, fitness for purpose, quality and accuracy of content, feel and look (design and production values), especially the cover to sell it. A hardback art book, for example, will be produced to a very high standard and sold at a high price. An inexpensive paperback will be produced with lower production values. The publisher organizes and manages the workflow to deliver the book. Electronic distribution breaks the link between the contents and the physical packaging – for example the download of a book chapter or journal article.

Supplier management

The publisher orchestrates the production of the book or journal through the procurement of a range of external services from individuals – freelance editors, designers – and companies – typesetters, printers, paper suppliers, technology companies. The outsourcing and procurement of services extends to marketing, sales and distribution worldwide. From a publisher's perspective, authors are critical suppliers and their 'management' is arguably the most vexing.

Market reach

The publisher sets the time of publication of the author's work in order to maximize sales. It may be related to a specific marketing and sales opportunity or need, to the publication of the publisher's other books, to competitors' publishing schedules, or be subject to the demands of the retailers.

The realization of the author's sales and readership depends largely on the effectiveness of the publisher to promote and publicize the work, to sell it through the numerous channels to market (home and export, including sales of rights), to distribute it, and to collect the money and to account to the author.

By way of the author contract, the publisher acquires from the author an exclusive licence to exploit the intellectual property rights in the author's work. The publisher's responsibility and expertise are to exploit the rights granted to the fullest in print and electronic forms (and when available to license others to do so), and to protect the author's rights against infringement by others using technical and legal means.

Business model

Ultimately a publisher has to operate a profitable business model – there may be more than one – that delivers sufficient return to enable the publication of authors' works and which offers authors remuneration in terms of readership, money and status.

The potential financial worth of the author's work is assessed by the publisher at the outset. The publisher envisages in advance the product package, its price, the potential demand over a time period and the projected sales income, balanced against the estimated costs of production and the payments to the author, resulting in the publisher's forecast profit. The publisher takes the risk decision based on multiple factors as to whether to invest in the author's work or not. When the publisher issues the contract to the author, it confers financial value on the author's work.

Impact of the internet

The internet offers publishers opportunities for value creation. It has speeded up communication and encouraged a global market in design, typesetting and print, which has led to lower costs. It provides a means of marketing books – both promoting them and identifying individual consumers. For Victoria Barnsley, Chief Executive of HarperCollins, this means:

We've got to embrace the fact that we're becoming a direct consumer business. We have a website and we can have a direct dialogue with our readers. We can capture your name and ultimately sell you something. That's a complete change. (*Independent*, 19 November 2007)

Providers of digital content can create extra value by adding the element of service. Electronic services can be created using a wide range of content, offering users on demand up-to-date and searchable content (including pictures, video and animation) from a range of different sources. Such services may be highly profitable once established, but the initial costs can be significant. If ebooks become popular, publishers would be able to save on the costs of distributing the physical book, and perhaps avoid the large discounts they give to intermediaries such as the bookshops.

The internet also offers a new set of issues. Firstly, there is a vast range of information for free. This has impacted on reference book publishing, for example. Can consumers see the value of publishers' products when there are free sources of 'good enough' information on the web? The coming of Web 2.0 has highlighted the mechanisms available for user-generated content, such as blogs and wikis. Stephen Fry has described Web 2.0 as

> an idea in people's heads rather than a reality . . . It's an idea that the reciprocity between the user and the provider is what's emphasized . . . People can upload as well as download. (videojug.com, accessed 21 August 2007)

In a relatively short space of time, Wikipedia has come to dominate online searches for information. Founded in 2001, users can write entries and edit the content. In 2007 the English Wikipedia contained over 600 m words. By comparison the 32-volume print set of the *Encyclopaedia Britannica* (2007) had 44 m words. User-generated content also covers video (for example YouTube) and images (Flickr).

In 2007 Wikipedia contained around 2 m articles

It becomes difficult to price electronic products if there is an expectation that content on the internet should be free. As Andrew Keen writes, 'the more self-created content that gets dumped onto the internet, the harder it becomes to distinguish the good from the bad – and to make money on any of it' (Keen, page 31). Publishers have developed good business models for online services sold to an institutional market of companies and libraries, and have developed strong brands, but how do you sell to consumers reluctant to pay for content? If the advertising market is buoyant, this can provide one model. Publishers can also create additional revenue streams by encouraging click-throughs to companies selling related products – they then receive a percentage on the products' sales. A further issue is how to price ebooks – the same as the print version or cheaper? If cheaper, by how much?

If there is a strong market for a particular author, what is to stop the author themselves capturing the market? For example, the wine writer Jancis Robinson runs her own subscription site, offering 'thousands of articles including insider tips, nearly 20,000 fine wine tasting notes with brand new search, the recently upgraded and hugely civilized member's forum, and the world's only online version of *The Oxford Companion to Wine*' (jancisrobinson.com, accessed 21 August 2007). There are other issues connected to online publication. Transferring print

Web 2.0 and publishing: a time of change, challenge, and opportunity

Allen Noren, Vice President, Online and Digital Initiatives, O'Reilly Media

E★PERT

In the summer of 2007 I had the opportunity to visit a colleague who works at a major New York publishing house. The building is a landmark in the industry, tall and glass faced, with a cavernous lobby lined with glass cases displaying first editions of well-known classics that have sold millions of copies. Several thousand people work in this building, all of them feeding this integral machine and scrupulously tending the increasingly antiquated processes that have defined publishing in much of the world as we know it. My visit was fascinating, and not unlike similar visits to other publishing houses. What was similar was the worry and fear at the rapid pace of profound change in the industry and society at large, changes similar to those that have rocked the music industry, and nobody is quite sure how to navigate a way forward.

This is due in large part to the internet and the phenomenon known as Web 2.0. More than anything else, Web 2.0 typifies the ease with which old and established business models can be challenged by ones that are simple to create, easy to deploy, and are nimble. This is especially evident in the publishing and media sectors where sites like craigslist, with a staff of just 28, has been accused of bringing the US newspaper industry to its knees; where Wikipedia, the non-profit and user-generated content site, has decimated the $650 m a year business once dominated by the venerable *Encyclopaedia Britannica*; where any number of filesharing websites make downloading the latest songs, movies and books as easy as downloading one's email; where YouTube, the video sharing website, is drawing more viewers than several TV networks combined.

Dale Dougherty of O'Reilly Media coined the term Web 2.0 – popularized by Tim O'Reilly

At O'Reilly, our own business is being similarly affected, and I think we are on the leading edge of where the changes are taking publishers. This is because of the nature of our content (we publish computer and technology books), and because our customers are the most adept when it comes to using the internet.

But this is not a unique phenomenon. Someone once said that the responsibility of the young is to destroy the past, and a stroll through history is a walk past once seemingly unshakable, and now quaint, industries that succumbed to innovative ideas. The trouble is that too many of the captains of the publishing industry are working harder to defend their existing business models than they are on creating new ones. In the mean time, some kid, sitting in his room or at a café, is creating the future.

Which means that the future is bright for those interested in creating the next generation of publishing models. The need for good content in all its forms is not diminishing. What is changing is the means of production and exchange, the business models and rules of the game. It is an exciting time.

I would like to conclude with one piece of advice: think like a beginner. As the great Zen master Shunryu Suzuki said, 'In the beginner's mind there are many possibilities. In the expert's mind there are few.'

brands to the internet is not straightforward, which has led some publishers to create new brands for the Web. One example is the EFL teacher's resource onestopenglish operated by Macmillan (onestopenglish.com). Many publishers do not control the full rights to their books, and this can hinder the transfer of illustrations, for example, into digital products and services.

In the world of the printed book, authors and publishers devote a great deal of thought and effort to the creation of a physical entity – the bound volume which is sold as a complete package of information. Readers usually have to buy the entire book, even if they only want part of it. In the digital world, the focus has shifted. As John Thompson writes, publishers have increasingly realized that it is the 'content, and the control of the copyrights that governed what they could do with the content, which was in some respects their key assets, not the books themselves' (Thompson, page 9). Innovation in style and content is encouraged by digital publishing, from the use of sound and video to new ways of structuring texts.

The search for information through Google, Microsoft and Amazon unravels the content packaged in printed books. In the digital world, content may be purchased at different levels of *granularity*. Consumers may wish to purchase by the chapter or even in smaller chunks such as by the page or illustration. Alongside the fear that consumers will cherry pick the best chapters and sales of the complete work will be cannibalized, there are the potential benefits for publishers – additional purchases may come from those who are not considering buying the whole book. The implications of the digital world for the control of intellectual property are discussed in detail later in the chapter.

Risk

In the traditional business model for book publishing – where transactions are based around the physical copy – there are issues around risk, the power of retailers to ask for high discounts, and the fact that returns of unsold books can take some months to materialize. There are different risk levels according to the publishing sector, and for example consumer publishing is riskier than academic publishing. Paying a large advance to a celebrity whose star may not be shining so brightly when the book is published is a risky venture. The investment in a large print run bears the associated risk that the book will simply not sell. In order to secure the book's availability in the shops, cash will need to be spent on promotion and high discounts will have to be given to retailers. Money is paid out and only recouped some weeks after publication – retailers will demand a period of grace (the credit period) before they have to pay for the stock. By contrast journals publishing has a more secure and profitable model. Subscribers pay money up front to receive a journal, and the evidence is that the market is price inelastic – demand does not drop significantly if prices are raised.

Booksellers have sought a higher share of the value created for trade books, asking for higher discounts off the recommended price. But at the same time price competition has lowered the prices paid for books. With books sold at up to 50 per cent discount, profit margins have either been squeezed or have disappeared. Just as publishers try to capture more value by selling direct, retailers have been investigating their own publishing operations. The US bookstore Barnes & Noble has done this for a number of years.

Publishers have attempted to alter the traditional book publishing model, and one example is Macmillan New Writing. Under the scheme, launched in 2006, new fiction authors can approach Macmillan directly with their manuscripts. Previously Macmillan tended to buy first novels from agents, and to secure good authors would have to pay an advance on royalties. If authors want to go ahead and publish under the New Writing scheme, the terms are not negotiable. In return for a generous royalty rate, authors forgo any advance. The scheme caused quite a stir and no little controversy. 'Hari Kunzru, author of *The Impressionist*, has described the initiative, in which writers receive no advance and may have to bear editing costs, as "the Ryanair of publishing; it's like having to pay for your own uniforms". Natasha Fairweather, an agent, calls it "an exercise in futility". Macmillan, by contrast, describes its newly launched New Writing fiction list as offering a lifeline to thousands of writers who struggle to get their work seen by an agent, let alone an editor' (*The Guardian*, 30 April 2005).

Financial performance

From a financial viewpoint, a publisher strives to increase the rate of return on the company's capital, and to improve the profit margin to finance expansion and pay a dividend to the owners. The management aims to:

- Maximize the income and minimize the production costs.
- Contain royalty rates while keeping competitive. In consumer book publishing it is important to monitor the amount of money and level of risk tied up in authors' advances.
- Control stock levels by selling a high proportion of a print number on publication or soon after, and storing only adequate stock of backlist titles. Print on demand is changing the management of the backlist.
- Re-price the backlist titles regularly (usually upwards) in line with current prices.
- Exercise tight control over the firm's overheads (for example, staff and office costs) while maintaining effective management. If profits fall, overheads have to be reduced and output increased.
- Take all available credit from suppliers, whether paying printers after a certain period or deferring royalty payments to authors.
- Keep discounts as low as possible and minimize returns while maintaining stock levels in retail outlets.
- Collect debts quickly from customers.
- Obtain the best terms from capital providers such as banks.
- Invest in fixed assets (warehouses, IT systems) only if a favourable return can be shown in comparison with subcontracting or leasing.
- Sell off underused or underperforming assets, whether buildings or publishing lists.
- Buy complementary businesses at home and abroad.
- Forecast regularly the cashflow (the flow of money payments to, from, or within the firm) over time; even a profitable publisher can exceed its borrowing requirement before profits are earned and go bust.

One key aspect is the compilation, at least six months ahead, of a financial plan showing a profit target for the forthcoming year (or longer). It is built up partly from the historic costs of running the business and from forecasts – the estimated costs of producing the new titles and the revenue from estimated sales of new and backlist titles made through various channels at home and abroad. Departmental managers will prepare budgets for carrying out their activities. Actual performance can be compared with the plan at monthly intervals, and with the performance of the previous year; and the plan itself is updated. Some publishers compile rolling plans for up to five years ahead. The annual profit and loss statement of a publisher reveals the cost profile of the business as a whole. This will differ according to the publisher and the publishing sector. The following figures give an impression.

The total sales revenue is the sum of money the publisher receives from home and export sales after discounts have been deducted from the recommended prices. Taking the revenue as 100 per cent and subtracting from that the production costs of the books (around 30 per cent, plus or minus 5 per cent) plus the write-off of stock unsold (2–10 per cent) and the cost of royalties (10–15 per cent), leaves the publisher with a gross margin of 45–55 per cent. A consumer book publisher may suffer from the write-off of unrecoverable authors' advances, but it may benefit from greater rights sales income. From the gross margin, the publisher's overhead costs are deducted (percentages):

Editorial	5–7
Production and design	2–4
Marketing and sales staff	5–10
Advertising and promotion	3–6
Order processing and distribution	8–11
General and administrative expenses	7–12

These overheads and expenses roughly total 30–50 per cent. When deducted from the gross margin, this leaves the publisher with a net profit (before interest charges on borrowing and tax are deducted) of 9–12 per cent. After interest and tax, a dividend may be paid to shareholders and the remaining profit re-invested in the business.

Valuing a company

The worth of a publisher can be measured in terms of its physical assets – buildings and stock – but more importantly by the intellectual property it controls. Valuations of publishing companies – how much they are bought and sold for – tend to be based on the revenues of the companies and the sector in which they operate. This is partly because the balance sheets of companies, which show their assets, can be difficult to interpret. Debts owing to the company may include advance payments to authors which will never be earned out, and the value of stock may be inflated by books in the warehouse that will never be sold. Hidden liabilities could include an overseas distributor having the right to return tens of thousands of books for credit. Companies with interests in legal, STM and electronic publishing are likely to be bought for a higher multiple of sales than

E★PERT

How publishing companies are valued

Eric de Bellaigue, author of *British Book Publishing as a Business since the 1960s*

The valuation of publishing companies takes centre stage under a number of different circumstances, where they are subject to differing pricing pressures:

- On the death of a major shareholder, often in a private company, for inheritance tax purposes.
- When a publishing business is sold to another company; this can involve an independent private firm – say a founder who wishes to realize his investment – or, within a company, a division or merely a list that has come to be judged surplus to requirements.
- When a business secures a quotation on the stock exchange, sometimes raising money for the company at the same time.
- When a publishing company receives a bid from another company – or a financial group, such as a private equity firm. Such bids may be agreed between the parties concerned. They may be unsolicited and viewed as hostile. If several bidders enter the fray, the process can convert into an auction.

The variety of occasions that call for valuations is matched by the diversity of sectors within the industry, the main categories being trade, education, scientific-technical-medical (STM), and legal. At the same time the interests of many publishing groups extend over several of these fields.

Faced with this kaleidoscope, there is general agreement on a common denominator – namely sales – in relation to which publishing businesses are valued. This may appear a pretty crude measure, but sales have the merit of being relatively clear cut in the way that profits are not, given accounting differences from one firm to another, the dissimilar reporting practices between private companies and public companies, and uncertainties over how overheads are allocated to publishing activities within the larger groups.

The sales figure is then related to the amount being paid and this is expressed as a multiple of sales. At a price of £1.5 m, a business with sales of £1 m is consequently said to have been sold on a sales multiple of 1.5 times. A refinement is to add any debt in the balance sheet of the business that is being bought to the price being paid; in this example, were such debt to amount to £250,000, the consideration would be raised to £1.75 m and the exit multiple comes out at 1.75 times sales.

Application of this measure to transactions across the full range of publishing sectors has given rise to a variety of results over the last 15 years or so. The range of multiples is shown below. Within the broad sectors, a pattern can be discerned, with legal publishing attracting the highest valuations, followed by STM and then education, while trade publishing, notwithstanding its high public profile, brings up the rear.

Publishing valuations as a multiple of sales

Trade	0.7 to 1.8
Education	1.7 to 2.5
STM	1.8 to 4.0
Law	2.5 to 4.2
Diversified	2.0 to 3.4

consumer companies. This reflects the varying degree of control over intellectual property – higher in legal and STM publishing with, for example, the easier acquisition of world and subsidiary rights – and the lower levels of risk. There tend also to be higher levels of profitability.

Publishers create value through innovation, coming up with new ideas and variations on existing titles. Larger publishers strive to maintain innovation with the maintenance of small imprints with their own distinctive profile. Smaller publishers may be more likely to try out new authors and formats. Innovation is encouraged by the system of copyright, which creates value in intellectual property and provides a mechanism to protect that value. Reflected in a company's value are the intangible assets, such as their publishing licences and goodwill. Goodwill is the term for those elements which contribute to the company's competitive advantage, including its brand and employees. It is given a monetary value if the company is taken over. The goodwill then appears on the balance sheet of the acquiring company. The publisher's licences and brand will be protected by intellectual property rights.

INTELLECTUAL PROPERTY

The intellectual property (IP) owned or controlled by a publisher includes its copyrights and licences. The publisher may own some copyrights outright, for example in the case of reference works, or have acquired licences from their authors. Other IP may be brands which could be registered as trade marks. Trade marks can cover words, logos, or pictures used as identifiers for goods and services.

It is important to examine on what basis publishers control their copyrights and licences. Book publishing today rests on copyright. In general terms, copyright is a form of protection, giving authors and other creative artists legal ownership of their work – that is, it establishes their work as their personal, exclusive property; and because it is their property they have the absolute right to sell or license it to others.

It is these exclusive rights that make an author's works attractive to publishers. What the publisher wants from authors is the sole, exclusive right to publish their work and sell it as widely as possible. Without the protection of copyright, authors would not be able to grant this exclusive right and could not demand payment for their efforts; and publishers would not risk issuing a book which, if successful, could be instantly copied or plundered by competitors. Copyright stimulates innovation in a market economy, protects the author's reputation and is the common foundation for publishing and the other cultural industries.

For copyright to subsist in a literary work (one which is written, spoken or

Although copyrights need not be registered in the UK, trade marks need to be protected by registration

There is no
copyright in
ideas, or in the
title of a work

sung) it must be 'original', i.e. some effort, skill or judgement needs to have been exercised to attract copyright protection, and it must be recorded in writing or otherwise. Copyright exists in the concrete form of expression, the arrangement of the words.

Copyright protection in the UK endures for the author's life plus 70 years from the year end of the author's death. After that period the work enters the public domain. If, for example, an author died on 11 January 1928, their work came out of copyright on 31 December 1998. This is the case with the novelist Thomas Hardy. The previous period for copyright was 50 years and under that system the works of Hardy had already come into the public domain at the end of 1978. When, in 1995, following an EU directive, the period in the UK was increased to 70 years, Hardy came briefly back into copyright until the end of 1998. Publishers compete fiercely on the pricing of public domain classics, such as Jane Austen, on which no royalties need be paid. The period of copyright in the European Union and the USA is also 70 years.

Works created by employees in working hours – and covered, as a further safeguard, by their terms and conditions of service – are the copyright of the employer. Publishers who commission freelance editors, technical illustrators, indexers and software engineers ensure that copyright is assigned in writing to the publisher through an agreement. The publisher's typographical layout of the page is the copyright of the publisher and that lasts for 25 years from publication. Copyright in an index belongs to the compiler, unless assigned to the publisher; copyright in a translation belongs to the translator. Copyright exists in compilations, such as databases, provided that there is an adequate degree of originality in the selection and arrangement of the information.

Moral rights

Under the 1988 Copyright, Designs and Patents Act, authors were given additional statutory rights, called moral rights. Deriving from the practice in mainland Europe, they are as follows:

Paternity

The moral right
of paternity
must be
asserted by
the author

Firstly, there is the moral right of *paternity*, which gives the author the right to be credited as the author of the work. This must be asserted by the author before it can be enforced. Often this can be seen on the title verso of a book – the reverse of the title page: 'The right of Giles Clark and Angus Phillips to be identified as the Authors of this Work has been asserted by them in accordance with the Copyright, Designs and Patents Act 1988.'

Integrity

Second is the right of *integrity*, which is the author's right to be protected from editorial distortion of the work.

False attribution

Third is the right to prevent *false attribution*, which prevents an author from being credited with something that they did not write.

Privacy

A final right gives privacy to individuals in the case of photographs they have commissioned, perhaps for a wedding, from a photographer who owns the copyright.

Moral rights are likely to grow in importance in the age of electronic publications, which frequently involve substantial adaptation of the work of authors and illustrators. Such uses greatly ease the manipulation of authors' works and facilitate the risks of non-attribution and of plagiarism. Moral rights can be waived by an author, and if a publisher owns the copyright in a book, it will probably want to ensure that such a waiver is contained in the contract. The moral rights of paternity and integrity have the same duration as copyright; the right to prevent false attribution lasts for life plus 20 years.

Copyright or licence?

Should a publisher be content to negotiate a licence with an author, or should it take outright the copyright? Theoretically the latter will give it more control over the work. Journal publishers, for example, used to take the copyright in all the articles that they published. But increasingly book publishers regard a licence as giving them the necessary protection that they require. The licence is a grant by the author of the rights to publish and sell a work, and also the right to stop others from copying the work. If a licence is in place which grants the publisher all the necessary rights, there is usually no need to take the copyright from the author. Hugh Jones and Christopher Benson write:

> a sole and exclusive publishing licence, drafted in wide terms if necessary (including a very robust clause allowing the publisher to take legal action if necessary), will probably meet most publishers' needs. It has been likened by a number of commentators to taking a lease of a house rather than buying the freehold – a long lease for all practical purposes will probably be just as valuable. (Jones and Benson, page 74)

The civil law protects copyright holders in the UK, and cases can be brought by them or the exclusive licence holder against individuals or institutions who copy texts without the necessary permission. Under a set of international treaties and conventions, UK copyright works are also protected around the world. These include the Berne Convention, which dates from 1886, and the WIPO Copyright Treaty signed in 1996. Under the Universal Copyright Convention (1952), all copies of a book should carry a copyright notice, and again on the title verso you will find the standard wording – © Giles Clark & Angus Phillips 2008. The date given is the year of publication, and a new edition attracts a new date in the copyright line. Copyright can be held jointly, as is the case with the present book.

The copyright symbol © is required under the Universal Copyright Convention

Permissions

An author seeking to quote from a work by another author should seek permission from the publisher of the work, which usually holds the anthology and quotation rights on behalf of the author. It is not necessary to ask for permission if the quotation is used for 'criticism or review', allowable as 'fair dealing' under the 1988 Copyright, Designs and Patents Act. The Society of Authors and The Publishers Association have stated that they would usually regard as 'fair dealing' the use of:

- a single extract of up to 400 words,
- a series of extracts (of which none exceeds 300 words) to a total of 800 words from a prose work, or
- a series of extracts to a total of 40 lines from a poem, provided that this did not exceed a quarter of the poem.

The words must be quoted in the context of 'criticism or review' (societyofauthors. net, accessed 21 August 2007).

In order to use an illustration contained in another book, permission should be sought from the publisher or original source of the illustration (this could be a library or gallery). Obtaining permission to use material from websites is fraught with difficulty, since there may not be a satisfactory paper trail to prove who owns the original copyright.

Digital rights management

Digitization has reduced the costs of copying and distribution to next to nothing. Yet the production of ideas and information by authors and publishers is very expensive in time and money. Publishers earn their living from selling ideas and information and make efforts to protect it from illicit copying. They are fearful that their work will escape into the wild on the internet from which they receive no payment. The technical means of controlling usage is broadly referred to as Digital Rights Management (DRM). As Hugh Jones and Christopher Benson write, DRM is more than just encryption:

> it enables rights owners to identify their intellectual property via metadata identifiers such as DOI, the Digital Object Identifier, increasingly being developed for the publishing world . . . and giving the opportunity to describe the rights on offer, fees and access conditions for potential users in a reliable licensing environment. It can also track usage and collect appropriate revenues. (page 134)

The software for DRM is problematic. DRM systems are frequently broken into by hackers – not least because of the weakness that each time a proprietary system gives someone a locked item, a secret hidden key is provided to unlock it. Hackers around the world work on discovering such secrets – they may then publish them on the internet for others to access the content. DRM can also be sidestepped by a user scanning a printed book and posting it for free on the internet.

When a reader buys a printed book, under the 'first use doctrine' there are few restrictions on its further uses.

> If you read a book, that act is not regulated by copyright law. If you resell a book, that act is not regulated . . . If you sleep on the book or use it to hold up

a lamp or let your puppy chew it up, those acts are not regulated by copyright law, because those acts do not make a copy. (Lessig, page 141)

There can, however, be restrictions on the use of an ebook – the reader buys the book under a licence. By accessing the book over the internet, a copy is made and copyright law comes into the picture. There may be controls on the number of times the book can be read, whether it can be printed out, or on its transfer to other devices.

Since the use by consumers of digital materials is defined by a licence, it may be sufficient in some cases for publishers to take the risk that they are sufficiently honest and trustworthy not to abuse their rights. A good example is the way publishers license materials to universities, via their libraries. The user group is clearly defined – staff and students of the institution – and they are authenticated through the use of a password system giving controlled access to the institutional site. Authentication reassures publishers that any points of leakage outside the user group may be identified and halted, and helps universities to limit their liability in the case of defamation, obscenity or copyright infringement.

Future of copyright

Without the copyright regime, publishers would be unable to prevent works being copied at will. Books would be photocopied or even printed and sold without a return for the copyright holder and their licensee. Publishers are naturally anxious about any threats to the stability of the copyright regime. They can see what is happening in the music industry, for example, and the tendency for music to be downloaded and shared for free, and have become concerned that a change in public attitudes and the digitization of books could lead to a similar situation. If a device like the iPod takes off for books, will consumers be sharing content and how will authors and publishers receive a fair return?

Major digitization projects are carried out by commercial publishers, libraries, or technology companies such as Google. The latter is in the process of digitizing out-of-copyright works in the collections of major institutions including the New York Public Library and the Bodleian Library in Oxford. Google Print is also digitizing books in print from a variety of publishers, enabling searches within the titles. Links then offer ways of purchasing either the printed book or online access. Such developments have divided the publishing industry. Some welcome a new way of marketing their books while others fear the 'napsterization' of book publishing – the growth of free downloads as in the music industry.

There is also the issue of authors who would like to see their work – text or pictures – more widely disseminated and feel that the present system of copyright does not adequately meet their needs. If publishers are only selling a few copies each year, and the author is receiving little by way of income, could there be a better way? Founded in 2001, Creative Commons is an initiative to enable authors to offer their work on different terms to the usual publisher's licence. 'Offering your work under a Creative Commons license does not mean giving up your copyright. It means offering some of your rights to any member of the public but only on certain conditions' (creativecommons.org, accessed 21 August 2007). For example, a photographer may choose to publish their work with a Creative Commons licence

E★PERT

Open content licensing

Richard McCracken, Director, eech, an organization promoting the case method of learning with the largest collection of management case studies and journal article reprints

The online distribution of content via the internet and other digital networks brings many individual users into direct contact with copyright regulation and practice for the first time and many, particularly academics, accessing or sharing research work or seeking teaching materials, find the traditional copyright licensing and clearing models time consuming and frustrating. Out of that frustration has grown the concept of 'open content' – using a range of licensing models that make it easy to share and access digital content without negotiating sophisticated copyright management and licensing.

The terms 'open source' and 'open content' are used almost interchangeably but 'open source' is generally taken to apply to the release and exchange of open software, while 'open content' refers to other forms of media content. Under open content licences text, moving images and sound, or a mix of them, are made available easily and simply for copying and reuse.

A number of standard open licences are available of which the most common are the Creative Commons, AEShareNet and GNU licences. Each licence may vary in its drafting and may be more suitable for some forms of content than others. There are a number of common characteristics:

- Users may copy, distribute, display, make available digitally, and make facsimile copies of the work in any format.
- The licences are global and are not territorial.
- Digital rights management systems (DRMs) cannot be used to restrict access to the work.
- The copyright notice must be retained in or attached to the work.
- Authors must be attributed.

Perhaps the most commonly used open content licensing system is the Creative Commons (CC). Lawrence Lessig, a law professor at Stanford University, is widely credited as one of the chief proponents of the Creative Commons, an organization or movement intended to promote the wide uptake of open content around the world. Work released under CC licences is intended to be used and reworked easily and quickly without the delays associated with copyright clearance. Instead of individual negotiation, the CC licences are standardized and linked to each piece of content so that users may easily see and recognize the licensing terms. There are a number of CC licences, each sharing the common characteristics outlined above but with some variation between each. These variations allow CC licensors to add further information about how their work may be used according to their response to very simple questions:

- Is commercial use permitted or not?
- Are derivative works permitted or must the work remain in its original form?

If derivative works are allowed, then the derivative work must itself be released under the same licence as the original work. This is called share-alike.

The Creative Commons website lists instances of work released under CC licences by both individuals and organizations. Some major media institutions have chosen to release some content under CC or similar licences. The BBC and Channel 4, for example, have used an amended version of the CC model to release archive material in their Creative Archive, the Flickr photo-sharing site uses a CC licence, and The Open University uses a CC licence to release educational materials through its OpenLearn site.

It is easy to imagine why an individual or a public-sector institution may choose to release content openly. The open ideology may coincide with government policies on accessing public information, for example, or with the collaborative nature of some educational research. The difficulty for commercial publishers is in assessing the extent to which open digital content models present a threat or an opportunity. Some analysts argue that commercial markets may be built on the back of open release. Making some content available openly may generate publicity or marketing benefits, enhance brand reputation or lead to the commercialization of added benefit services such as advisory services or enhanced, paid-for content.

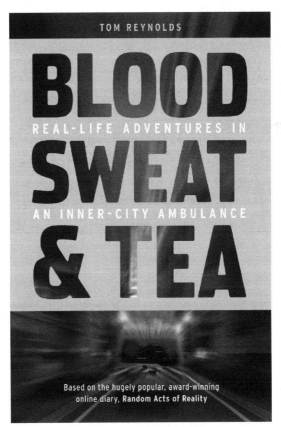

Blood, Sweat and Tea by Tom Reynolds was published by The Friday Project in 2006 under a Creative Commons licence. Under the terms of this licence users can make copies of all or part of this work for their own personal use and for other non-commercial use. They can also republish online with the correct acknowledgement that enables others to copy, distribute or display the photographs, provided that the work is attributed to them. The objective is for more people to have the opportunity to view their work.

In the area of journals publishing, the open access movement has gathered pace, which argues that publicly funded research, notably in the area of science and medicine, should be freely available. Some mainstream publishers now offer an open access option for authors. If the author, their institution or, more usually, the research body that funded the research, provides payment, the article will be freely available from first publication. The 'author pays' model has yet to prove its sustainability. Open access has also stimulated self-archiving. Journal publishers will usually allow an author to self-archive the preprint of an article on their homepage – the preprint is the unpublished version of the article before it is refereed – and sometimes the final published version in their institutional repository. Even open content models rely upon the retention of copyright. The initial decision to release open content licences is made by the copyright holder.

> An institutional repository is a digital collection of research papers by members of an institution

If digital publication becomes the norm for books as well as journals, will there be further shifts to come in the copyright regime? Printed books continue to offer a model of publishing that publishers understand and know how to make work. They are comfortable with the book: the sale of a physical item yields a return against a predictable cost. Digital publishing adds considerable uncertainty as to *who* will control intellectual property – publishers or technology players such as Google – and *how* it will be controlled.

Sources

Eric de Bellaigue, *British Book Publishing as a Business since the 1960s*, British Library Publishing, 2004.

Bill Cope and Angus Phillips, *The Future of the Book in the Digital Age*, Chandos, 2006.

Hugh Jones and Christopher Benson, *Publishing Law*, 3rd edition, Routledge, 2006.

Andrew Keen, *The Cult of the Amateur*, Nicholas Brealey, 2007.

Lawrence Lessig, *Free Culture*, Penguin, 2004.

Nicholas Negroponte, *Being Digital*, Hodder and Stoughton, 1995.

Tim O'Reilly, 'What is Web 2.0?', 30 September 2005, www.oreillynet.com, accessed 3 September 2007.

Lynette Owen, *Selling Rights*, 5th edition, Routledge, 2006.

Angus Phillips, 'Does the Book Have a Future?', in Simon Eliot and Jonathan Rose (editors), *A Companion to the History of the Book*, Blackwell, 2007.

Michael E. Porter, *Competitive Advantage: Creating and sustaining superior performance*, Free Press, 1985.

Michael E. Porter, 'Strategy and the Internet', *Harvard Business Review*, March 2001, pages 63–78.

John B. Thompson, *Books in the Digital Age*, Polity Press, 2005.

Web resources

www.jisc.ac.uk Joint Information Systems Committee – the website provides a briefing paper on open access.

www.creativecommons.org Creative Commons.

CHAPTER 6

The author

Authors have different motivations for writing, according to the type of book and the individual. Writers of poetry and fiction may be driven to write by an inner force – they just have to write. Academics have to be published in order to advance their career. Professional authors may earn their living from their books, and writing is what they do.

The reality for many authors is that the financial returns are low. A survey published in 2007 by the Authors' Licensing and Collecting Society revealed that the average earnings for authors in the UK were £16,531 and the median (or typical) earnings were only £4,000. For those who are successful, the rewards can be very high – the top 10 per cent of authors earned more than 50 per cent of the total income earned by authors – but only 20 per cent of those surveyed earned all their income from writing.

Authors such as Dan Brown are highly organized in their approach. In his witness statement for the 2006 case in the High Court regarding *The Da Vinci Code*, he said:

> Writing is a discipline, much like playing a musical instrument; it requires constant practice and honing of skills. For this reason, I write seven days a week. So, my routine begins at around 4 am every morning, when there are no distractions. By making writing my first order of business every day, I am giving it enormous symbolic importance in my life, which helps keep me motivated. If I'm not at my desk by sunrise, I feel like I'm missing my most productive hours. In addition to starting early, I keep an antique hour glass on my desk and every hour break briefly to do push-ups, sit-ups, and some quick stretches. I find this helps keep the blood (and ideas) flowing. (*The Bookseller*, 31 March 2006)

The Da Vinci Code sold around 40 m copies in its first year, and has made Dan Brown a fortune. Yet for many authors, the income earned is of secondary importance, and the pleasure of making it into print is a reward in itself. There is no shortage of authors who would like to be published. How then do authors set about getting published? The traditional method was to send your manuscript to a number of publishers, and hope that it catches the eye of the relevant editor.

The novelist Jeanette Winterson says about writing: 'It is what I'm for'

After all, J. K. Rowling was rejected by a number of publishers before being picked up by Bloomsbury. What is known as the slush pile is still a system operated by some publishers but has become far less common. In consumer publishing it is becoming more important to be signed up by an agent first and many publishers do not accept unsolicited material. Agents can receive hundreds of submissions each month and the chances of being taken on are slim, but first-time authors are still discovered through this route. Robert McCrum writes:

> there's a vigorous trade in new writing in a new arena – the email queues of literary agents, scouts and publishers. Here, sample chapters, outlines, book proposals, synopses and heroic first drafts whiz about the marketplace as email attachments looking for likely buyers. (*The Observer*, 14 November 2004)

Most academic theses that are sent direct to editors are unpublishable as they stand, but a fraction can be turned into monographs. It is very unlikely that an unsolicited textbook manuscript would have the right structure to be commercial, but occasionally unsolicited ideas can be developed. In areas such as non-fiction and textbook publishing, publishers will want to see a proposal from the author as the first stage. This is an outline of the proposed book, which sets out the content and gives the publisher a sense of the book's commercial potential. The advantage of this system is that the author need not take the risk of writing the whole book until they have a contract in place.

Book proposal

The following are the main elements of a book proposal.

Title

This must be eye catching and can be crucial to the book's success.

Introduction

This gives a summary of the idea for the book and its likely market.

Contents

This provides an outline of the structure of the book, fleshed out to show what each chapter will cover.

Readership

Who will buy the book and what is the market? The danger here is to rely on the mythical general reader, and avoid the difficult task of saying who is likely to need, or be interested, in the title. (An equivalent danger is trying to reach too many markets with one book.) For a book on tennis, will it help someone to learn how to play the game? What is the readership for a business textbook – first-year undergraduate or graduate students?

Competition

Successful authors know the market for which they are writing – not just the readership but also competing titles. How will the book differ and improve upon the titles presently available? Existing titles on the same subject may not be a disadvantage, since they can help prove there is a market.

Marketing ideas

How can the book be marketed? Ideas can include forthcoming events or anniversaries, hooks to arouse media interest, public appearances and connections with influential people.

Author details

This means biographical details of the author with relevant information such as previous publications. For non-fiction books it is important for the author to prove their credentials as an expert in the subject area of the book. Publishers may be interested in whether the author is promotable to the media, for example in the case of a first-time novelist. An author can also display a talent for self-promotion, and they might have their own website or blog. Simon Flynn of Icon Books stresses the importance of the background of the author:

> Unless the idea sells itself completely, it's important to look at how useful the author is in terms of how we're going to get publicity and stories; it's extra hooks from which to hang the book. If the author is a recognised expert, that helps. (*The Guardian*, 6 October 2007)

Additional material may also be attached, such as sample sections or chapters. There should be no spelling or grammatical mistakes in the sample material.

Once completed by the author, or with the help of an agent, the proposal is sent to the relevant in-house editor. If they are interested in taking the project forward, suggestions for changes may be made before the proposal is circulated to key decision-makers in sales and marketing. The final decision on a proposal is taken at an editorial meeting attended by the relevant staff.

A poll in 2007 found that 'almost 10 per cent of Britons aspire to being an author, followed by sports personality, pilot, astronaut, and event organiser on the list of most coveted jobs' (*The Guardian*, 21 August 2007)

STARTING OUT AND SELF-PUBLISHING

It can be tough to get your work published. It is common for authors to begin their published career with smaller publishing houses, which may be less conservative in their approach to commissioning titles. The difficulty for smaller houses is that they may not have the funds to keep authors who have become successful.

There are trends in publishing which may affect what types of books publishers would like to acquire. For example, of the 'top bestselling paperbacks in 2006, 11 were misery memoirs; with combined sales of 1.9 m copies, this lucrative sub-genre accounted for 8.8 per cent of unit sales across the Hot 100 bestselling paperbacks' (*The Bookseller*, 23 February 2007). The genre of misery memoirs – or 'mis lit' – is a recent hit, especially popular amongst supermarket consumers, and publishers have responded with more confessional tales from those who have experienced terrible traumas, whether child abuse, addiction or a dysfunctional family. Celebrity memoirs are also popular, and many are ghostwritten by professional writers. A further refinement is the celebrity mis memoir.

Ghostwriting

Claire Squires, author of *Marketing Literature: The Making of Contemporary Writing in Britain* and Senior Lecturer in Publishing, Oxford International Centre for Publishing Studies

The practice of ghostwriting is no longer the shadowy process it once was. The increasing demand for books 'by' sports figures, pop stars and people famous just for being famous has meant that ghostwriters are teaming up with celebrities to help them find their words (as David Beckham put it in his passing reference to his ghost). Whether the ghostwriter is tucked away in the acknowledgements, credited on the title page, or coupled in the formation 'x with y', ghosts are a vital part of the contemporary publishing industry.

Some ghostwriting partnerships are matches made in heaven. The dream ticket of sports writer Hugh McIlvanney and football manager Alex Ferguson is one example. The ghost Hunter Davies, who has worked with footballers Paul Gascoigne and Wayne Rooney, and politician John Prescott, has become a very visible ghostwriter, adding prestige and marketing focus to the books he pens on behalf of others. Occasionally, ghostwriters have regretted that celebrities do not always take the time to read the book purportedly written by them, and there are instances of ghosts rather too creatively putting words in authors' mouths.

In a book market awash not only with celebrity autobiographies, but also with misery memoirs and politicians' diaries, ghostwriters take on a variety of roles from reshaping and restructuring existing manuscripts to the wholesale creation of the author's narrative. Even novels are ghosted, including Naomi Campbell's *Swan* and Katie Price's *Angel*. Price (aka the glamour model Jordan) has been particularly controversial, with sales figures for her subsequent novel *Crystal* in excess of those of the combined Booker shortlist in 2007. Jennie Erdal's memoir *Ghosting* tells the tale of her fictional creations on behalf of 'Tiger', the publisher Naim Attallah. The fascination surrounding ghostwriting extends to fictional depictions, with Robert Harris's novel *The Ghost* portraying the man tasked to pull an ex-prime minister's narrative into shape.

Many ghosts also have careers as editors, journalists and authors in their own right alongside their ghostwriting activities. The financial arrangements between authors and their ghosts vary. Ghosts may take a cut of the royalties and the advance, or agree to a flat fee. Some ghosts approach publishers to pitch projects, while at other times, publishers seek out ghosts (sometimes via their literary agents). The process of ghostwriting is an editorial function, part of a continuum of activity that ranges from proofreading and copy-editing, via larger textual interventions, to the complete creation of texts. Although some cultural commentators lament the ubiquity of ghostwriters, seeing their presence as indicative of a decline in literary standards, for most in the publishing industry ghostwriting is perceived as a legitimate and necessary activity, and a way of harnessing busy public figures (or figures not capable of writing their own story) to the production and promotion of their books.

First-time novelists may be offered a two or three-book deal, which ensures that they are already signed up should their first book prove to be a winner. If an author does hit the big time straight away, this can prove to be a mixed blessing, increasing the pressure on them to deliver another bestseller. An author with several modestly successful titles in print runs the risk that they are dropped by their publisher in favour of new authors, perhaps seen as more 'promotable' (viewed by some to mean young and good looking).

Other routes to publication are now open to authors, including self-publishing which is inexpensive on the web and increasingly cheap in print form. The internet has given a route for all kinds of self-publishing. For example, in the area of fan fiction – new works written by fans of original fiction – there are now hundreds of thousands of stories available online based on the characters from the *Harry Potter* books. For print publishing, the growth of print on demand using digital printing means that print runs can be as low as a few or single copies. Companies such as CreateSpace (owned by Amazon), AuthorHouse and Lulu offer authors a low-cost route to publication. Only when a book is ordered from Lulu's website is it then printed and sent to the purchaser. The company was founded by the digital entrepreneur, Bob Young, who saw the need for a way to help authors publish niche items such as poetry or technical manuals: 'We think Lulu offers a better way for bringing these works to market than the very narrow channel that currently exists, through the few major publishers there are' (*The Independent*, 12 December

2005). However, self-published authors usually find that booksellers will not stock their titles.

Publishers are looking to pick up titles that have originated in blogs or from the large number of creative writing courses that are now available. The Blooker Prize was started in 2006, to be awarded to the best book originating in a blog. The first prize went to *Julie and Julia* (2005) by Julie Powell. Sales had reached more than 100,000 copes before the book scooped the prize. Julie Powell recounted in her blog and then the book how she cooked all 524 recipes in Julia Child's *Mastering the Art of French Cooking*. Day 1, recipe 1 is entitled 'The Road to Hell is Paved with Leeks and Potatoes'. The chair of the judging panel, Cory Doctorow, described Powell's book as a 'heartfelt, funny and occasionally obscene tell-all about her journey of self-discovery and cholesterol'. Blogs offer publishers market testing as to which writers can attract and keep an audience. There are also peer-review websites on which authors can post chapters or short stories.

Creative writing courses have proliferated in the UK and famously Ian McEwan was the first writer on the MA course at the University of East Anglia, run by Malcolm Bradbury and Angus Wilson. More recently, Marina Lewycka's first novel, *A Short History of Tractors in Ukrainian* (2005), was picked up by an agent when she joined the course at Sheffield Hallam University, and published in 2005 when she was 58.

> I have two complete unpublished novels in my drawer, along with a pile of rejection slips, and a number of false starts, so it feels as though I've been at it forever. In fact I've been writing poems, plays and stories for as long as I can remember – my first poem was written when I was four – so you could say I'm a very late developer. I started writing the Tractors book about ten years ago, just doing a bit now and then in the evening after work. It was the decision to go on an MA Creative Writing Course that galvanised me to finish. After that, I had it ready in about eighteen months. (loadedshelf.com, accessed 16 May 2007)

New consultancies have developed in the UK offering writers' services. For a fee, the company offers to give the author an assessment of your manuscript, both the writing and the likely market, and editorial services. Based on a survey of writers in 2005, the literary consultancy WritersServices offered the following advice on getting published (writersservices.com, accessed 24 February 2008):

- become a journalist – or write articles (this will provide a network of contacts),
- be prepared to write what people want,
- be prepared to contact up to 10 agents or publishers, and
- do not ignore self-publishing.

AGENTS

Literary agents, now called authors' agents (reflecting the broad range of writers they represent), are mostly located in the London region giving them close proximity to their main customers – fiction and non-fiction editors, mainly in adult

In 2007 there were over 80 m blogs active worldwide

but also in children's book publishers and other media industries. Their business is selling and licensing rights to a variety of media (not just book publishers) at home and abroad on behalf of their client authors with whom they have a contract on each book for the full term of copyright. Agents receive a commission on authors' earnings, typically 10 to 15 per cent on earnings from home sales but rising to 20 per cent on deals made abroad. Owing to increased administrative and sales costs, the minimum commission on UK earnings has crept upwards from the historic figure of 10 per cent. The commission on film and TV deals tends to be from 15 to 20 per cent. The prevalence, power and influence of agents are very much a feature of the Anglo-American media worlds – in mainland Europe and elsewhere there are few agents, and they are usually 'sub-agents' of English language agents or publishers, not of local authors. Sub-agents may earn half of the 20 per cent commission received by the UK agent. Some Anglo-American agents sell directly into foreign language markets. There are also literary scouts, who tip off agents and publishers about new authors – or established authors in other territories – in return for a fee.

Agents operate in an increasingly polarized market in which a small number of top-selling authors secure advances against royalties of more than £100,000, compared to the majority of authors receiving advances below £10,000. An agent may spend equal amounts of time on both types of author, but with a very different financial return. For example, if an agent secures an advance of £6,000 and charges 15 per cent commission, their share is just £900.

Agents represent many of the established professional writers, i.e. those who derive much of their income from writing. While some agents are prepared to review unsolicited manuscripts from aspiring novelists for which they may charge a reading fee, others discourage this practice and take on new clients only on personal recommendations from credited sources, such as media contacts and their other clients. Agents manage lists of authors and taking on a new writer may mean dropping an established client. Rarely is it worth while for an agent to represent academics unless their work appeals to a wide readership. Authors can make multiple submissions – to several agents at once – but this method should be used with caution. Agent Andrew Lownie says:

> Agents understand that authors need to make multiple submissions to agencies but dislike 'beauty parades'. It is not flattering nor encouraging to be told one is simply one of a hundred approaches. Time is limited and if one suspects the author may go elsewhere then one simply says no at the beginning. Keep quiet about multiple submissions and only send a few at a time so one can adapt the submission in the light of responses. (andrewlownie.co.uk, accessed 22 February 2008)

Once an agent has taken on an author, it is their job to pitch the book to the right editor in the most suitable publishing house. The literary publishing house Jonathan Cape was rarely offered more commercial books, and in his memoir *Publisher*, Tom Maschler recalls being sent the manuscript for *Not a Penny More, Not a Penny Less* by the literary agent Deborah Owen. The author, unknown at the time, was Jeffrey Archer.

In 2003 Michelle Paver, author of *Wolf Brother*, secured an advance of £1.8 m for a six-book deal

She did not actually say it was a first submission but, in the manner of certain agents content to mislead, this was the implication. The aspect of Archer's book which especially intrigued me was that he himself had been involved in a con and had lost a great deal of money, both his own and others'. And now he had written a thriller about a man similar to himself, and furthermore was doing so in order to earn a large sum so that the money could be repaid . . . I found the conceit intriguing, and although the style was indifferent, decided to offer a contract. I must admit I was motivated, in part, by the feeling that Jeffrey was so obviously ambitious that he would be likely to succeed in almost anything to which he put his mind. (page 200)

An agent manages a writer's career primarily from a commercial viewpoint, for example by placing the author's work with the right publisher or fuelling competition between publishers (on major books by holding auctions); negotiating deals to secure the best terms; by submitting their own contracts to licensors weighted in the authors' favour; checking or querying both publishers' advance payments against royalties, and royalty statements, and chasing debts.

The example of the author–publisher contract summarized in Chapter 8, and weighted in the publisher's favour, shows the author granting various world rights to the publisher. Because most authors are unable to market the rights on their work worldwide they mainly allow publishers to do so on their behalf. But an agent representing an author may limit the rights granted to a publisher, and their territorial extent, and license the rights retained on behalf of the author to other firms at home and abroad. For instance, the UK publisher's licence may apply to the English language only, and the territory (the countries) in which it has the exclusive right to publish (e.g. the Commonwealth and Europe) are listed, as well as those from which it could be excluded (e.g. the USA, including/excluding Canada). An agent could then license the book in the English language to a US publisher directly. A UK publisher, within its exclusive territory, could for instance be granted the following rights: the right to publish in hardback and paperback; an audiobook and ebook; and to license to others – book club, reprints, second and subsequent serial (i.e. extracts appearing in newspapers after the book's publication), quotation and anthology, mechanical and reproduction, broadcast reading rights, etc. An agent would then retain, for example, foreign language translation, first serial rights (extracts appearing before book publication thereby giving a newspaper a scoop), stage/radio/television/film dramatization, merchandising, and other electronic rights.

However, there is no clear-cut division of rights or territories covered – each book differs. A publisher which has the idea for the book and contributes much editorial and design effort, or which is investing a large amount, for instance in a new writer on a two-book deal, has a strong case for acquiring wide territorial rights and the sharing of other rights. Adult and children's publishers and packagers producing highly illustrated books for the international market need world rights in all languages. A wider set of rights is needed in order to recoup the initial high costs of these books. Book packagers and some highly illustrated book publishers often try to acquire the copyright outright from authors, enabling subsequent repackaging and recycling of authors' material without further payment or author contract.

UK agents retaining rights may sell them directly to US publishers, film and TV companies, or mainland European publishers, or use overseas agents with whom they have arrangements. Conversely, UK agents may represent well-known American authors on behalf of US agents, and sometimes US publishers via their rights sales managers. The selling of rights from a publisher's viewpoint is described in Chapter 12; an agent's work is similar except that an agent solely represents the author.

The additional dimension of agents' work falls under an editorial heading. For instance, agents send out synopses and manuscripts for external review, comment on manuscripts and advise authors on what they might write and the media they might write for, and develop ideas with them. Agents might be asked by publishers to supply authors; or they might initiate projects themselves for sale to publishers. In such ways, some agents increasingly take on roles which were once the province of publishers' editors. They can reflect trade realities back to authors, and arbitrate on arguments between their authors and publishers.

Agents can provide a degree of continuity in the face of changing publishers and editors. However, some authors decide to change agents or are poached by them. This famously happened when Martin Amis changed agents to Andrew Wylie, known as 'the Jackal', when selling the rights in his novel *The Information* (1995). The former agent may continue to receive commission on contracts which they negotiated. The long-established agencies manage the literary estates of classic authors whose work remains in copyright.

Agents usually specialize in particular genres, such as adult fiction or non-fiction, or children's books. Many operate from home as single-person companies. There are medium-sized agencies consisting of several agents plus assistants, and major agencies such as Curtis Brown and AP Watt. A large agency has a range of agents, each of whom specializes in broad areas of books or the selling of particular rights, though each agent usually looks after a particular primary group of authors. A specialism is film and TV rights, which involves selecting books for screen adaptation, and submitting them to producers. Some of their assistants show sufficient aptitude to develop their own list of authors, and new agents come from rights and editorial staff of the publishers. The larger agencies usually have agencies on both sides of the Atlantic, and good connections in Hollywood. There are also agencies which specialize in selling particular rights, such as translation, or film and television, on behalf of publishers and authors' agents. Sometimes a package of talent (book, star and director) is offered to a film studio.

Now read this

Chapter 7, Commissioning.
Carole Blake, *From Pitch to Publication*, Pan, 1999.

Sources

Julia Bell (editor), *The Creative Writing Coursebook*, Pan, 2001.
Alexander Gordon Smith, *Writing Bestselling Children's Books*, Infinite Ideas, 2007.
Tom Maschler, *Publisher*, Picador, 2005.
Publishing Scotland Yearbook, Publishing Scotland, 2008.
Rachael Stock, *The Insider's Guide to Getting Your Book Published*, White Ladder Press, 2005.

Published annually, the following guides contain useful information about publishers and literary agents:

The Writers' and Artists' Yearbook, A & C Black.
The Writer's Handbook, Bramley Books.
Writer's Market UK, David and Charles.

Web resources

www.fanfiction.net This includes thousands of examples of fan fiction, from *Harry Potter* to *The Lord of the Rings*.
www.freakonomics.com/blog/ An example of an author blog – for *Freakonomics* by Steven D. Levitt and Stephen J. Dubner.
www.jeanettewinterson.com This includes a Flash movie profiling her books.
www.societyofauthors.net Society of Authors.
www.youwriteon.com A peer-review website sponsored by the Arts Council.

Commissioning

The commissioning editor in a publishing house is responsible for coming up with marketable ideas and matching them to good authors. Working for the editorial director or publisher, who manages the editorial team, the editor is a key player in the publishing process. The more senior commissioning editors will take a strategic view of their list or imprint – called *list-building* – while junior editors may commission within a set brief.

EDITORIAL COMMISSIONING

In consumer books, editors may cover adult fiction, or specialize in hardback or paperback lists, non-fiction areas or children's books. In educational, academic and STM houses, an editor may concentrate on several subjects, spanning a variety of academic levels and markets, or on product types, such as journals or textbooks. The style and identity of each list are the outcome of the editor's attitudes and effort.

A publisher depends on these editors to provide a sufficient flow of publishable projects to maintain the planned level of activity, for example 15 to 30 new books annually per editor, sometimes far less or three times more. Editors are assessed on the revenue they bring in or the overall profit, or contribution, of their books. They are seen by some publishers as business managers. Publishers may have electronic systems in which editors record their output in terms of titles commissioned and forecast revenue. Editors out of tune with senior management regarding the character of the books, or who fail to produce a profit, leave voluntarily or are fired. The job is high risk and exposed.

With some exceptions, such as in the area of fiction, editors do not assess titles for publication on their thorough reading of complete manuscripts. Most books (including some fiction) are commissioned from authors on the basis of a proposal or specimen material, or are bought from agents. Editors generally do not edit the author's work in detail – that is done by freelancers or junior in-house staff. However, the senior editors may structurally edit by giving authors substantive criticisms and suggestions to help them produce their best work and to shape it for the intended market.

A distinction can be made between books acquired from agents or authors, where the idea often comes from the author, and those books that are commissioned from scratch by the editor. In the case of the latter books, the idea comes from the editor, who then goes in search of a suitable author. In textbook publishing, for example, this is the typical process for commissioning.

List-building

Publishing lists have their own identity and even within the larger groups there has been a conscious decision to keep separate imprints, each with their own distinctive flavour. In consumer publishing, imprints assist the trade to make sense of the large number of new and existing titles. Lists may be built around authors (in fiction, for example), subjects (the Yellow Jersey list of sports books), or brands (the *Teach Yourself* and *For Dummies* titles span a large range of subjects), or design character (text only or illustrated). List-builders may be asked to create a new imprint from scratch – reflecting changes in the market or strategic ambition – or to expand and strengthen an existing list. They will be on the look-out for new authors and projects, bearing in mind their list's identity and future direction.

A programme of new editions may be important in non-fiction and essential in textbook publishing, in order to refresh the list and keep titles up to date. Rebranding the list in new covers can also achieve this. A strategic view includes planning digital developments, for example in the areas of travel or textbook publishing.

Editorial contacts and market research

Good personal contacts are paramount for commissioning. An editor's in-house contacts are the members of senior management who accept or veto projects; the people who produce the books; and those who market and sell them. But more significant are the editor's external contacts. Prime sources of new books are the firm's previously published authors. They often have new ideas, or editors suggest ideas to them which are developed jointly.

Consumer books

In consumer book publishing, editors try to establish a mutual trust with authors and their agents (often over lunch). Agents may send fiction manuscripts or non-fiction proposals to selected editors one at a time, or sometimes conduct auctions amongst several publishers on highly saleable titles. Conversely an editor may contact an agent if they are after one of their stable of authors, or have an idea and want the agent to find an author. Fiction editors may find new talent by spotting people who can write well, not necessarily fiction. They may be journalists or writers who are being published poorly or in an uncommercial medium.

Non-fiction editors develop contacts in a variety of fields, constantly keep an ear to the ground, notice people's enthusiasms, or review the media for topical subjects. They try to predict trends or events which will be in the public's interest, monitor successful book categories and authors by understanding what makes them good and why are they selling, and either avoid the competition, imitate it, or attempt to find unfilled niches by developing a new twist. They write speculatively to people who have the potential to capture the public's imagination – as do the agents. Specialist fields, clubs and societies and their magazines and websites can

Yellow Jersey Press, an imprint of Random House, was founded in 1998 by Rachel Cugnoni: 'Then followed the two most terrifying years of my life. I'd never commissioned a book before, let alone edited one, but somehow or other it was successful, and hallelujah'

EXPERT

Working with authors

Sue Freestone, Publisher at Quercus Publishing

For any book editor, certainly for me, the best thing in the world has to be when you are invited into an author's imagination to observe and sometimes even take part in the writing process as it happens.

When Douglas Adams (author of *The Hitchhiker's Guide to the Galaxy*) rang me up and asked 'How would you feel if you were a Norse thunder god and therefore immortal but nobody believed in you any more, and you woke up to find yourself super-glued to the floor of a warehouse in South London?' my heart soared. As I answered 'I think that's one for you, Douglas', I knew we were off on another mad, glorious, infuriating adventure. This time it was *The Long Dark Tea-Time of the Soul*, perhaps his most autobiographical novel. The thing about Douglas was that when he wrote the radio scripts of *Hitchhiker* (they came first) he had worked with a team of people and therefore wanted the same instant feedback he had back then. That meant he could work only if I was actually there with him. He would thrash out his ideas with me then go and write a page or so and loom over me as I read them. He was six foot five and a half and very good at looming. When things went well it was the most exhilarating time in the world. When they did not it was hell, with Douglas in the pit of despair. Then my job was to tease him out of it, throwing ideas and challenges at him until he got so maddened by them he got going again with his own.

Not all writers want that degree of involvement from their editor, thank

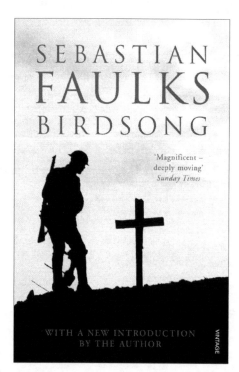

'Magnificent –
deeply moving'
Sunday Times

goodness. Sebastian Faulks would tell me only that he was working on a story about the First World War, nothing else at all, until he delivered *Birdsong* to me fully polished. Every writer is different and your job is first to try to figure out their needs and then to take care of them. First base, you have to love their writing. Without that you will get nowhere. Second, you have to be able to feel where they are going with a story, so that if they get lost, you can point them back in the right direction. Crucially, you have to be their champion in the publishing house. Sometimes, surprisingly, it gets forgotten that in trade publishing the author is the most important person. Without them there is nothing. I always try to make sure that writers feel there is a whole team there for them, from production through to sales, by introducing them to everyone. It lessens the writer's sense of isolation and reminds us all of why we are doing what we do.

If all this sounds like hard work, it is not the job for you. If it sounds the best job in the world, then go for it, you will love it too.

be sources of ideas and authors, and indicate level of interest. Editors interested in television and film tie-ins keep abreast of new productions and monitor audience ratings.

Editors forge links with other firms from whom they might buy or sell to, for example at the Frankfurt Book Fair or, in the case of highly illustrated books, with packagers. UK editors are in contact with US editors and rights sales managers in order to gather market intelligence on new projects. Children's book editors have contact with agents, packagers, teachers and librarians, and if producing illustrated colour books know US and foreign language publishers with whom they might trade.

Non-consumer publishing

The educational, academic, STM and professional book editors publish for more defined markets about which more statistical information is available. This includes student enrolments, and the numbers of researchers or professionals working in specific fields. These editors, apart from reading school and college syllabuses, and the relevant journals, are engaged in direct market research and product development, especially in textbook publishing. Quantitative research can include:

- student numbers,
- number of courses in a subject,
- sales figures of similar titles, and
- market share of the leading titles and publishers (indicated by data from Amazon).

Qualitative research covers:

- trends in the subject area,
- analysis of competing titles – their extent, features, authors, strengths and weaknesses,
- questionnaire results on products used and future needs,
- focus group data – from students, teachers or librarians, and
- visiting schools or universities.

The academic and STM publishers may retain for each discipline exclusive advisers who direct new writers to their publishers. They could be senior academics or professionals with worldwide contacts. Expert general or series editors may be employed by publishers, especially in non-consumer sectors. Their task is to help editors develop and edit the books, and they usually receive a small royalty.

It is vital for editors to understand the current and future market on the ground. Educational editors see local education subject advisers, inspectors, examiners and lecturers on teacher training courses; school heads, and teachers using the materials in the classroom, and attend conferences. ELT editors, in addition to using UK contacts, will travel abroad and visit Ministries and Institutes of Education, private language schools, offices of the British Council, and local publishers and distributors to meet key contacts and decision-makers. College textbook editors spend several days a week visiting universities and will meet teaching staff in order to discover subject trends, find out their views on the books currently available, and to flush

Nielsen BookScan provides the publishers with sales data on their own and competitors' titles

EXPERT

The editor in educational publishing

Brenda Stones, author, editor and lecturer on educational publishing

What is special about educational publishing?

Because both the content and the size of market are fixed, UK educational publishing is fiercely competitive, and the areas in which publishers can compete are often less to do with the products and more to do with the services offered to the customer. The content is prescribed by the National Curriculum and exam syllabuses, with little opportunity for different interpretations. The size of the market is fixed in terms of the number of students in a year group or for a particular subject or syllabus, and of the funding delivered to schools by the government. So the only opportunities for expanding the market are, for example, in export territories and from parental spending. The publisher usually sells directly to teachers, rather than through the intermediary of bookshops or distributors, and this gives the opportunity for direct contact with the purchasers.

What are the key tasks of the educational editor?

The editor has to research their markets thoroughly, in order to gain familiarity with the curriculum and anticipate its future changes. They have to study their competitors – their market shares, and how their products compete – and their audience, meaning both the teachers who make the purchasing decisions and the students who are the ultimate consumers. Each editor has to make a forward plan of books and multimedia products to be published in a range of subjects and levels, to meet the revenue targets expected by the company. Appropriate authors or author teams are commissioned to write materials to the editor's specification, and the editor has to maintain communication with the authors throughout the development of the project.

Additional tasks include briefing the design of the products, so that they are easy to teach from, easy to read, and appealing to teachers and students. There is still hands-on editing in educational publishing, to ensure that the text covers the curriculum requirements, is factually accurate, and is at an appropriate language level for the particular students. The editor writes promotional copy and briefs the promotion and sales staff on the benefits of the new publications. Finally the editor monitors the sales of their educational list against targets for revenue, profitability and market share.

What experience and skills do educational editors need?

- Teaching experience, especially if this involved writing teaching materials.
- The ability to write and edit to different language levels.
- A sense of accuracy and eye for detail.
- Numeracy, and the ability to interpret numerical data.
- Visual awareness, and the ability to organize visual information
- Sympathy for children and their interests at different ages.
- A deep interest in the importance of education and how children learn.

out ideas and contacts they have and to sell the firm's books. Academic editors may forge links with institutions, societies, and industry organizations for which they could publish or distribute books or journals. They will visit academic conferences to network and become known amongst the relevant academic communities. When large US sales are anticipated, editors shape the material in conjunction with their US counterparts and visit their sister companies. All editors receive in-house feedback from the marketing and sales departments.

The decision to publish

Many factors influence an editor's decision to pursue a new project.

Suitability for list

A title has to fit the style and aims of the list it will join, so that it is compatible with the firm's particular marketing systems and its sales channels to market. Taking on a book in a new subject area has implications for marketing and sales, not just editorial. Editors assessing new titles are also concerned with the list's overall balance, direction and degree of innovation.

Author assessment

This covers the author's qualifications, writing ability, motivation and time available to write the book, public standing, reliability to deliver on time, and responsiveness to suggestions. Whether the author is 'promotable' is a key question for some types of consumer books. This can be interpreted as – is the author personable? – although the more cynical will say it is also a question about age and looks.

Unique sales proposition (USP)

What will make this book different from others, or what makes it special – the quality of the author, a new treatment of the subject, or some differentiation by price or format? What are the special marketing opportunities through which the book could be promoted? This could be a tie-in with a TV series, taking advantage of a special sporting event for a sports autobiography, or the author's status and celebrity.

> The USP defines what makes a book stand out from competing titles

Market

Understanding the main audience for which the book is intended, who would buy it, and the possible take-up at home and overseas. The sales records for the author's previous books or those of similar books may be used as a guide. Sometimes the rights sales potential is assessed, such as likely book club, translation and co-edition sales. This is most relevant to trade titles.

Competition

The title's features and benefits compared with competing titles are evaluated. This is important for textbooks and reference titles, and for a variety of non-fiction. The strengths of competing titles should be acknowledged, not just their weaknesses.

> New titles are the frontlist; established titles the backlist

Frontlist/backlist potential

Is the book expected to have a short life on the frontlist, or does it have the potential to backlist for a long period?

Investment and return

How much time and money needs to be expended on acquiring the book, such as the size of advance expected by the agent, and on developing and marketing it through to publication, in relation to its expected earnings and profitability? Would its earning power justify its place on the list?

Risk and innovation

What are the external factors at play affecting the risk investment, such as the timing of publication in relation to the optimum time to publish, the link to topical events and their perceived popularity, and the actions of competitors? What is the downside if the expectations are not realized? To what extent is the project experimental in terms of taking on a new author, or publishing in a new area or format (print or electronic), or price? Without taking risks and innovating, the publisher is overtaken by competitors.

Content

The editor's judgement of the quality and appropriateness of the content is aided by others. Fiction editors may use junior editors, or external readers, to supply plot synopses or to offer first or second opinions. Non-fiction editors may ask specialist external readers to comment on specialist titles. Other publishers rely heavily on experts – teachers, academics, professionals – sometimes worldwide to comment on material. All these external readers are paid small fees and remain mostly anonymous to the author. The management of the peer review process is critically important in academic and journals publishing.

Physical appearance and price

The editor envisages a proposed title's desirable physical packaging and price. This covers word length, illustration content, size, binding style and production quality, the likely cost and the price range within which it could be sold.

Approval process

Some ideas are rejected by the editor, especially after unfavourable reports. Some authors are asked to resubmit in the light of the editor's suggestions. If an editor wants to take forward a project, they cannot offer a contract without the agreement of the senior management. Editors sound out and lobby senior colleagues, such as the marketing and sales managers, over possible prices and sales forecasts, and the production manager over production costs. For a major investment, such as a large advance, the finance director will be consulted. The editor prepares a publishing proposal form, which covers the scope of the book, its format, its market and competition, readers' reports, publication date, and the reasons for publication. A costing or financial statement sets out the expected sales revenue, the costs of producing the book and the proposed royalties to the author, in order to show the hoped-for profit margin – provided the book sells out. For standard formats there may be a set of production scales that feeds into the costing form. Different combinations of prices and sales forecasts, and of production costs and royalties may be tried – they will reveal differing margins.

Many publishers hold formal editorial meetings at which the senior management hear editors' proposals – most get through, but some are referred back or rejected. Editors have to be prepared to defend their proposal and demonstrate their wholehearted commitment. Tom Maschler writes: 'To publish well the publisher must be passionate about the book for its own sake. . . . Once the choice is made the task begins. It is to transmit one's conviction first within the publishing house and then to the outside world' (page 282).

If given the green light, the editor negotiates the contract with the author or agent (see the next chapter), agrees or invents the book's title, and on commissioned books ensures that the author appreciates what is expected (for example content, length, deadline). Titling is an important skill. In a crowded book market, unusual titles can attract attention, for example the novel *Salmon Fishing in the Yemen* (2007) by Paul Torday. Internet searches drive the need for clear and explanatory titles for specialist titles. Sometimes the book 'does exactly what is says on the tin', such as Andrew Marr's *A History of Modern Britain* (2007). Some titles work at more than one level. The footballer Frank Lampard's autobiography was called *Totally Frank* (2006); Steven Norris, the former Conservative transport minister, used the title *Changing Trains* (1996).

When signing up a new fiction writer, the editor may decide on a two- or three-book deal – if the first novel is a hit, the author is already safely under contract for the second novel. There may be an optimum publication date which would maximize sales. The book may be topical or need to be published for the Christmas market. In the case of textbooks, bound copies will be needed for inspection by teachers in time for the details to be added to the relevant reading lists – ideally they should be published around the turn of the year, and by March at the latest.

The Bookseller's Diagram Prize is awarded each year to the oddest title for a book. Past winners include *Reusing Old Graves*, *Greek Rural Postmen and their Cancellation Numbers*, and *The Joy of Chickens*

NEW TITLE COSTING

Successful publishing is founded on contracting good books that sell, and each new book is a business in its own right contributing to the business as a whole. The decision to publish is the crux of the whole enterprise. If mistakes are made here, all efforts of management to control overheads will come to nothing. Books which fail to achieve their target sales and profitability must be counterbalanced by equal profits from other books which exceed their target.

We said earlier that in order to gain approval for a project, editors must prepare a costing – a profit and loss form – to prove the book's profitability. There are varying degrees of sophistication in this process, and electronic templates are now in widespread use. What is important, however, is to understand the principles behind a new title costing. The editor is not simply finding out a cost for the book, but comparing revenue and costs to maximize profitability, while working within the price constraints of the market and the format chosen.

Net sales revenue

The publisher's *net sales revenue* (NSR) – also called the *net receipts* – is the sum of money the publisher receives after the trade discounts have been deducted. For example, a book with a recommended price of £20.00 may be sold to bookshops by the publisher at an average discount of 50 per cent. The bookshop will pay the publisher £10.00 for the book, and this is the net sales revenue for one copy.

Price:	£20.00
Average discount:	50 per cent
Net sales revenue:	£10.00

In order to calculate the *total revenue* for a book, a sales forecast needs to be made. If a book is overpriced, few copies will be sold and the total revenue will be low. If a book is priced too low, the opportunity will be missed to maximize the income for a title. The art is to price the book competitively within the market, thereby maximizing sales and the total revenue. There is a more detailed discussion of pricing in Chapter 10.

The sales forecast is related to a time period. Publishers print stock sufficient for a limited period only (six to 12 months, or for mass-market paperbacks only a few months) in order to minimize the cash outlay, costs of storage and the risk of overprinting. The planned life of a hardback may only be one sales season before the book goes into paperback – it will simply stop selling when the paperback appears. Judging the print run is a difficult art. Keeping the run low may lead to lost sales if a title is selling fast; raising the run may lead to overstocks which cannot be sold. The latter approach runs the higher risk.

While each book is sold at many discounts, according to the customer and sales channel, an average discount can be derived by working out the likely orders from different types of customer or territory. Estimates may be gathered from the sales departments or overseas branches.

The ways in which international publishers trade within the constituent parts of the group vary and depend upon in which territory it is advantageous to declare profits for taxation and shareholder benefit. For instance, by transfer pricing they may sell internally a UK-originated book to their sister US firm at a very high discount thereby increasing the profit in the US.

Costs

The costs of producing a book usually come under two headings. The *fixed costs* are incurred before the printing presses roll and do not change whatever the quantity of books ordered. They may include:

- sums paid to external readers, translators, or contributors,
- legal fees – for example, if the book needs to be read for libel,
- permission fees for the use of third-party copyright material (text and illustrations), unless paid for by the author,
- payments to freelance copy-editors, proofreaders, illustrators, and designers (for both text and the cover),
- indexing, if not done by the author, although this charge may be put against the author's royalties, and
- payments to suppliers for typesetting, origination of illustrations, proofing, corrections.

The *variable costs* occur after the presses start to roll and depend on the quantity of books ordered. They include the costs of printing and binding, and the paper consumed. The quantity ordered would be the sales estimate plus an allowance for copies wasted or gratis copies given away, for example for review purposes. The total production costs are the sum of the fixed costs and the variable costs.

The average cost of producing each copy, the *unit cost*, is calculated by dividing the total costs by the print quantity. The unit cost diminishes with increasing print quantities, falling rapidly on short printings of between, say, 500 to 2,500 copies and then more slowly. The rapid decline in unit cost results from the fixed costs being spread over larger quantities. Although the per copy cost of producing the book becomes progressively lower with increasing quantities, the total cost still increases. Therein lies the danger for editors preparing a costing. The temptation is to reduce the unit cost by increasing the print quantity – but if the books are not sold the publisher has sunk an even greater amount of cash into the book's production.

The author's royalties are calculated by applying the different royalty rates to the sales forecasts for home and export markets. A costing prepared before a contract has been signed with the author will show suggested royalty rates for the title. The royalty may be based on the book's price or on the net sales revenue – the sums actually received by the publisher. To carry on with the earlier example:

In the late 1990s Dorling Kindersley printed 13 m copies of its *Star Wars* titles – sales only reached around 3 m

> Recommended price: £20.00
> Average discount: 50 per cent
> Net sales revenue: £10.00

If the royalty is 10 per cent of the published price, the author would receive 10 per cent of £20.00: £2.00 on each copy sold. If the royalty is 10 per cent of the net sales revenue, the author would receive 10 per cent of £10.00: £1.00 on each copy sold. A publisher looking to reduce their costs would work with royalties based on the net sales revenue. The author may not necessarily agree with this approach or even understand the difference. A good agent would push hard for the best deal.

Gross and net profit

The *gross profit* is what is left after the unit cost and royalty have been deducted from the net sales revenue.

Net sales revenue:	£10.00
Unit cost:	£4.00
Royalty to the author (10 per cent of NSR):	£1.00
Gross profit:	£5.00
Gross margin:	50 per cent

The *gross margin* is the percentage of the net sales revenue that forms the gross profit. In the above example, the gross profit forms 50 per cent of the revenue.

The management may say to their editors, 'We want to see each publishing proposal attaining a minimum gross margin of 55 to 60 per cent'. That percentage represents the sum of money the publisher would have left after the production costs and royalties have been deducted from the NSR, provided all the copies were sold. The sum would, in theory, be sufficient to recover the overheads and expenses and to provide a net profit. The publisher's overall net profit is the sum left after all the costs of running the business have been deducted. Overheads for a publisher would include the costs of salaries, marketing and sales, warehouse and fulfilment, general administration, office space, heating, lighting, and other items such as bank interest and bad debt.

The editor strives to balance the income and costs so that the desired gross profit is attained. This is called *value engineering*. If the gross profit is too low, the production costs could be reduced (fewer pages, fewer illustrations, cheaper paper) or the author's proposed royalties cut. Conversely the price and sales estimate could be increased. But while the publisher worries about costs and margins, the end-user is concerned with price and perceived value, and does not care about the costs, the number printed or the author's effort. Reducing the production values on a book, for example by using cheaper paper or fewer colours for the cover, may harm the book's sales. It will depend on the type of publishing and the expectations of the market – which are high in some markets like art or cookery books. For an editor publishing a book with a limited market, there remains the fatal temptation to imagine a non-existent larger market and to increase the print-run in order to lower the unit cost.

When the publisher takes the final decision on fixing the price and print quantity, the fixed costs have already been incurred and cannot be changed. On account of the uncertainties of estimating demand, a prudent publisher favours a higher price and a lower quantity rather than a lower price and a higher quantity. If the actual demand for the book is less than expected, a price on the high side may still return a profit, whereas too low a price could lead to substantial loss. The great dangers are underestimating costs, overestimating demand, and underpricing. This leads not only to a loss on the individual book, but also can wipe out the profit on others. Successful books can always be reprinted, but at a price and quantity which again are chosen to avoid loss. If a book is likely to be added to the backlist, there may be an argument for accepting a lower than usual gross margin on the first printing, on the grounds that a reprint will have a much healthier margin. The first printing of a school textbook may attain no profit, but the hoped-for second and subsequent printings should move it into profitability. Also hardbacks can perhaps tolerate a lower gross margin, since the follow-on paperback will not have the production fixed costs to bear. A quirky trade title, such as *101 Uses for a Dead Cat*, has to make its money straight away.

Other factors affecting the pre-publication decision concern the level of investment at risk, for example very high authors' advances or a large investment in a major textbook, and its duration. Several combinations of price and print run may be tried out, including 'worst case scenarios', and the break-even may be calculated. A project's *break-even point* is the minimum quantity that must be sold to cover the production costs and the author's advance or royalty. Also included might be a proportion of the company's overheads. On some proposals, if the break-even is considered attainable, that may inspire sufficient confidence to go ahead. Some publishers calculate a project's cashflow and the interest incurred over time. From the outset to after publication, the publisher usually endures a net loss before the income surpasses the outlay. The estimated income is derived from the sales forecasts broken down over time (for example, monthly, quarterly and yearly).

Possible rights sales income, other than that from co-edition deals, usually does not enter into the early costings and thus can be regarded as extra profit. However, it may be included, especially when needed to justify paying the author a large advance.

Some publishers stop their calculations at the gross profit line while others continue and deduct direct overheads expressed as overall percentages (for example for editorial and marketing or sales and distribution) to reach the net profit. The way in which overheads are apportioned, either as actual sums or percentages, varies. To continue with our example:

Net sales revenue:	£10.00
Unit cost:	£4.00
Royalty to the author:	£1.00
Gross profit:	£5.00
Gross margin:	50 per cent
Editorial and marketing overheads (15%):	£1.50
Sales and distribution overheads (15%):	£1.50
Net profit (Gross profit less overheads):	£2.00
Net profit margin (as percentage of NSR):	20 per cent

The problems with the method as outlined above are that titles are allocated overheads in proportion to expected revenue (which may not accord with reality).

It also focuses attention on a desired percentage rather than money – for example a title with a 25 per cent gross margin may yet deliver much more cash than one with a 55 per cent gross margin. It is important therefore to look at the total sums involved, and not just concentrate on the percentages. A costing should also include a column showing the totals received and paid out: revenue, costs and royalties.

Recommended price:	£20.00
Average discount:	50 per cent
Net sales revenue:	£10.00
Unit cost:	£4.00
Royalty to the author:	£1.00
Gross profit:	£5.00
Gross margin:	50 per cent

Print run:	10,000
Copies sold:	9,500
Total NSR:	£95,000
Total production costs:	£40,000
Royalties due to the author:	£9,500
Gross profit:	£45,500

In the above example, the royalties are calculated on the sales, but in order to secure the book a much larger advance might have to be paid to the author. This sum is paid even if the book's sales are disappointing. If the advance paid to the author against royalties was £15,000, the overall cash surplus would be reduced by £5,500. A fuller costing would show income from the paperback edition and projected rights income.

Mark-up method

An alternative costing approach is the mark-up method. This traditional and simple method is severely criticized but can be used as a ready-reckoner. The unit cost is derived from dividing the quantity of books to be ordered into the total production costs. This is then multiplied by a factor (say 5–8 for a trade title) to arrive at the published price. The accounts department calculate for editors the factors pertaining to different kinds of books (for example consumer or academic) with different royalty rates and discounts. Provided the copies sell out, the factor accommodates the firm's costs and profit. But if the published price is thought too high, the editor is tempted to increase the print run to lower the unit cost in order to arrive, by multiplication, at a reasonable price. Conversely, the publisher may print the number it believes it can sell but fixes the price too high to absorb that number. Unless careful the publisher ends up with unsold copies or loss-makers. The method, based on a predetermined level of activity, disregards the fact that costs do not act alike as output increases or decreases. It encourages rigid pricing and conceals assumptions. Worse, it focuses attention on the unit cost and away from the market and price elasticities.

The method can be used in reverse. The gross retail value (price multiplied by sales estimate) is divided by the factor to arrive at the desired unit cost. The book's specification could then be adjusted to match.

The use of a mark-up factor often occurs when consumer book publishers buy books from packagers. A mark-up factor (say 6 to 7) is applied to the packager's all-in, royalty-inclusive, price per copy to arrive at a published price. If the publisher is translating and resetting a title, the mark-up could be 5 or 6.

Case study: *Inside Book Publishing*

Publishers rarely show their confidential costing of a book to authors. But Routledge, part of Taylor & Francis (T&F), provides here their preliminary estimate for this book which was compiled by the development editor for signing off by the publisher. Prepared in advance of the authors' handover of the typescript to the publisher, it is revised during the course of production to take account of the inevitable changes to the book's specification and sales prospects.

The preliminary estimate is reproduced here (pp. 110–12) in three parts:

- product specification,
- estimated production costs (for the paperback edition), and
- income and expenditure showing the book's estimated gross and net profit.

There are other costing spreadsheets lying behind these figures which are not reproduced here.

The publishing proposal is for a new edition of a 'small' textbook (meaning a specialist student text), the sales history of which stretches back 20 years. It is, however, costed as a new book with the advantage that the likely demand can be informed from its past history. Seven years after the publication of the 3rd edition, annual paperback sales are around 450 copies. An active used book market for all three editions is all too evident on the internet. Its medium is classified as a 'printed product', based on a copy sales business model. The various other ways it may be sold or licensed, for example as an ebook or in translation, are not shown.

The printed product is published simultaneously in two editions: paperback and hardback, each of which is allocated an ISBN. The plan is to print 1,200 copies of the paperback edition to meet the sales expectation over the first 18 months, and to reprint 500 copies to meet demand from 18–36 months. The life-cycle calculation is thus three years, typical for a textbook adopted annually on courses. Major textbooks are usually maintained on a three-year revision/new edition cycle. The paperback is priced at £19.99 in the UK, and at $35.98 in the US – a parity dollar price on the exchange rate at the time of estimate: 1 : 1.80. The hardback edition is priced at £65 in the UK and $117 in the US, and the 100 copies to be printed are destined for libraries (mainly academic) in the first 18 months.

The estimate starts by locating the product within the organization, part of the international group of T&F. It summarizes the book's paperback specification (for brevity details of the hardback edition have been deleted here). Its 'extent' is stated at 224 pages (this was to increase to 320). This is an even working of seven 32-page

Preliminary estimate – INSIDE BOOK PUBLISHING ED4   Created on 28/11/2007
ISBN: 978-0-415-44157-5

Extent: 224	**Pages per sheet:** 1	**Total sheets:** 224	**Lifecycle calculation** ☑

Production project/Product

Publisher:	Humanities
Division:	Media & Cultural Studies
Medium:	Printed product
Version type:	Paperback
Binding style:	Limp
MS type:	Disk
Reprint type:	
Original editing language:	
Copy-editing level:	Simple
Pages Roman:	
Pages Arabic:	224
Production method:	Litho
Binding method:	Notch
Format:	Pinched Crown Quarto
Interior colours:	1 colour
Print file format:	PDF
Typesetting difficulty:	Medium
Font:	Scala
Typesetting format:	MSWord

Binding	**Finishing**	**Paper quality**	**Colours exterior**	**Colours interior**
New design	Matt laminate	240 gsm 1-sided	CMYK	

Sections	**Whole sheet**	**Oddment**	**Paper quality**	**Colours**	**Bleed**	**Paper weight**	**Paper size**
TEXT	224	No oddment	Matt Blade 90 gsm	1 colour	No	90 gsm	716 x 1008

Illustrations	**Colours**	**Qty**	**Tables**		**Formulas**	
Positioning only	1 colour	41	**B/w**	17	**Math.:**	
Redraw (line)	1 colour	8	**Colour:**		**Chem.:**	
			Difficulty:	Basic	**Difficulty:**	

Paperback edition

Cost element		1st printing	2nd printing
Currency: GBP		**1,200**	**500**
F	Author/series editor fee	0.00	0.00
F	Contributors' fees	46.15	46.15	0.00
F	Subsidies and grants	0.00	0.00
F	Illustrations permissions	369.23	369.23	0.00
F	Legal fees	0.00	0.00
F	Translation fees	0.00	0.00
F	Text permissions	0.00	0.00
F	Cover design	350.00	350.00	0.00
F	Illustration fee	0.00	0.00
F	Additional design fee	150.00	150.00	0.00
F	Copy-editing	543.46	543.46	0.00
F	Proofreading	255.45	255.45	0.00
F	In-house	220.39	220.39	0.00
F	Typesetting	820.38	820.38	0.00
F	Typesetting corrections	143.69	143.69	0.00
F	Proof sets	60.92	60.92	0.00
F	Tables	69.23	69.23	0.00
F	Relabelling a/w	0.00	0.00
F	Redraw line a/w	59.08	59.08	0.00
F	Redraw maps	0.00	0.00
F	Artist drawings	0.00	0.00
F	A/w positioning	68.31	68.31	0.00
F	Retouch a/w	0.00	0.00
F	A/w origination	0.00	0.00
F	Scan line	30.00	30.00	0.00
F	Cover origination	36.93	36.93	0.00
F	Digital proofing	24.00	24.00	24.00
V	Cover printing	0.23	276.00	188.66
V	Binding	0.21	252.00	157.88
V	Text paper	0.32	384.04	160.01
V	Litho printing	0.45	540.95	532.58
F	Other manufacturing contingency		99.41	100.00
	Prod. costs total fixed		3,346.62	124.00
	Prod. costs (total) variable		1,452.99	1,039.12
	Prod. costs (total)		4,799.61	1,163.12
	Prod. costs fixed per unit		2.79	0.25
	Prod. costs variable per unit		1.21	2.08
	Production costs per unit		4.00	2.33

(exchange rate £1:$1.80)

Version type	ISBN	Project no.	Prod. project no.	Calc. no.		Price UK£	Price US$	
Hardback	978-0-415-44156-8	13094		59538		£65.00	$117.00	
Paperback	978-0-415-44157-5	13855		59539		£19.99	$35.98	

Small text

3-YEAR SALES PROJECTION

1st printing sales (18 months)				2nd printing sales (18–36 months)			3-year sales projection		
	Qty	£	% sale	Qty	£	% sale	Qty	£	% sale
Hardback	100	3,894	20.00%				100	3,894	20.00%
Paperback	1,200	14,273	80.00%	500	6,487	100.00%	1,700	20,760	80.00%
Total NSR	1,300	18,166	100.00%	500	6,487	100.00%	1,800	24,653	100.00%

GROSS PROFIT	10,305	56.7%	4,385	67.6%	14,689	59.6%

DIRECT VARIABLE COSTS

	£	% sale	£	% sale	£	% sale
Manufacturing	5,298	29.16%	1,164	17.94%	6,462	26.21%
Royalty	1,656	9.11%	614	9.46%	2,269	9.21%
Contingency	908	5.00%	324	5.00%	1,233	5.00%
Total	7,862	43.28%	2,102	32.40%	9,964	40.42%

OVERHEADS

	£	% sale	£	% sale	£	% sale
Distribution	1,998	11.00%	714	11.00%	2,712	11.00%
Allocated costs	6,800	37.43%			6,800	27.58%
Total	8,798	48.43%	714	11.00%	9,512	38.58%

	£	% sale	£	% sale	£	% sale
CONTRIBUTION	1,506	8.29%	3,671	56.60%	5,177	21.00%

	% sale	% sale	% sale
RETURN ON INVESTMENT	9.04%	130.39%	26.58%

BREAK EVEN POINT

Hardback	83		83
Paperback	1,000		1,000
Total sales to b/e	1,084	113	1,084

% of print run to b/e	83.36%	22.56%	60.21%

CONTRIBUTION

	1st printing	2nd printing	Total
	£	£	£
Revenue	18,166.36	6,486.76	24,653.12
Manufacturing	−5,297.80	−1,164.00	−6,461.80
Royalties	−1,655.67	−613.69	−2,269.36
Contingency (stock w/o)	−908.32	−324.34	−1,232.66
Distribution	−1,998.30	−713.54	−2,711.84
Allocated costs	−6,800.00		−6,800.00
Net profit	**1,506.27**	**3,671.18**	**5,177.46**
Net profit %	**8.29%**	**56.60%**	**21.00%**

Authorized by

28/11/07

(Editor)　　　　　　　　　　Date

(Publisher)

printed sections, with no 'oddment': a printed section of less than 32 pages which would increase the costs every time the book is litho printed. The *format* (or page size) is pinched crown quarto; the *interior* (the text) is printed in one colour (black) by litho printing on 90 gsm paper from a PDF file. The *binding* (or cover) is a new design, printed in CMYK (four colours) on a heavier paper of 240 gsm, with a matt laminated finish. The binding is *notch* – the spine folds are glued together but not cut off. The numbers of illustrations and tables are estimated. An assessment is made of the amount of work required – copy-editing is classified as 'simple' – or of the difficulty in typesetting tables ('basic'). The automated costing system applies the current costs of T&F suppliers to the specification.

Costing

Lying behind the estimated figures is a mass of actual cost information built up by a publisher producing more than 1,600 new books per year in the UK alone. The page extent is an important factor in determining costs and for some production headings, the publisher would have worked out a set per page cost. Following the product specification is a table of estimated production costs for the *paperback edition*, stated in GBP (Great Britain pounds). Each row has the prefix F (fixed costs which do not depend on the quantity produced) or V (variable costs which change with the quantity produced). The costs given for the F rows leading down to *cover origination* are set against the first printing of 1,200 paperback copies, and are not carried over to the second printing, the straight reprint of 500 copies. The variable costs of cover printing, binding, text paper, and litho printing relate to the quantities of the first and second printings. The fixed costs represent 70 per cent of the total production cost of producing 1,200 paperback copies. The impact of setting the fixed costs against the first printing becomes very evident in the totalled production costs:

- £4,799 for the first printing of 1,200 paperback copies – unit cost of £4
- £1,163 for the second printing of 500 copies – unit cost of £2.33

The estimates above are called *direct* costs in that the publisher can identify the labour and materials related to the production of this book, payable to external suppliers. For under £5,000 the publisher can produce this book economically.

Sales

We now turn to the all important forecast of sales over the first 18 months of the hardback (HB) and paperback (PB) editions, broken down by territory, as follows:

	HB	PB
UK	20	700
US	40	100
Rest of world	30	300
Frees	10	100
Total	100	1,200

Exports of the book – predicted here at 36 per cent of sales – have been increasing over the years owing to the greater international marketing and sales strength of T&F and the growth in publishing studies, especially in fast-developing book markets. *Frees* are copies given to the authors and contributors and for review. Teachers considering adopting the book for student purchase now receive an e-inspection copy instead of a printed copy.

The copy sales forecasts are converted to sales revenue in the section headed '3-year sales projection: first printing sales (18 months)'. The hardback edition (100 copies printed; 90 to sell) is forecast to deliver a net sales revenue (NSR) of £3,894 (or 20 per cent of the total NSR £18,166). The paperback edition (1,200 copies printed; 1,100 to sell) is forecast to deliver a NSR of £14,273 (or 80 per cent of the total NSR £18,166). How has the publisher arrived at these NSR figures? The system, using the sales forecasts, has deducted the average book trade discounts from the local published price in the given territories (overall the average discount for the paperback is around 40 per cent) and taken account of the frees from which no revenue is received.

The revenue from the hardback edition accounts for 20 per cent of sales, an apparently disproportionate amount in view of a sale of just 90 copies. The argument here is that the libraries buy one copy at triple the price in a more durable binding for multiple and free use by readers. There is also an element of cross-subsidy. If there were no hardback edition, the price of the paperback (sold mainly to students) would increase. The hardback is printed once only and is intended to sell out within 18 months.

Gross profit

Beneath the total NSR of £18,166 is the gross profit line. The gross profit of the first printing is calculated by first summing the direct variable costs paid out to suppliers and listed here under *manufacturing* (the total production costs of both the hardback and paperback editions: £5,298) and the authors' royalty of £1,656 (calculated by applying the authors' royalty percentage to the publisher's net receipts). A contingency budget of £908 is included for stock write-off, such as books too damaged to dispatch again after returning unsold from booksellers. These direct variable costs totalling £7,862 are deducted from the total NSR of £18,166, to give the *gross profit* of £10,305, which when expressed as a percentage of the NSR, gives a *gross margin* of 56.7 per cent:

$$£10,305/£18,166 = 56.7 \text{ per cent}$$

The gross profit on the second printing of 500 paperback copies for the period 18–36 months, reflecting the expected decline in the rate of sales, is £4,385. However, when expressed as a percentage of NSR, the gross margin jumps to 67.6 per cent because the fixed costs of developing the book were only applied to the first printing. On the three-year view, the gross profit totals £14,689, which at 59.6 per cent achieves the gross margin target of 60 per cent so often set to editors by their senior management.

Contribution

To reach the *net profit* or *contribution* (the so-called bottom line), the publisher's overheads have to be deducted. These are sometimes referred to as indirect costs because they cannot easily be attributed directly to the individual book.

The overheads of operating different areas in the company are aggregated and expressed as overall percentages. These percentages are applied to the NSR and then deducted from the NSR. Publishers treat overheads in different ways. In this particular example, T&F applies two areas of direct overheads to the title:

- distribution at 11 per cent of NSR and
- allocated costs at 37 per cent of NSR.

Distribution includes storage, order fulfilment and shipping costs. The allocated costs or direct overheads cover editorial and marketing. The general or *indirect* overheads of other parts of the business, such as IT and human resources, are excluded from the estimate. The distribution costs are incurred for as long as the book remains in print. But the allocated costs are set against the first printing only and once again are not carried over to subsequent printings of a book, which may never occur. In reality, much of the staff time devoted to developing and marketing the book occurs in the 12-month period before and around publication.

The contribution line shown here is calculated by deducting the direct overheads from the gross profit. Thus on the first printing, the total overheads – set at 48 per cent on sales of £18,166 – work out at £8,798, which when deducted from the gross profit of £10,305, leaves a contribution or net profit of £1,506. When expressed as a percentage of NSR this gives:

£1,506/£18,166 = 8.29 per cent

The publisher's net profit from the first printing is below the amount paid out in royalties to the authors. If sales of the book struggle to get through the first printing, the publisher would incur a potential loss or at best record a very low level of profitability. But on the second printing, the contribution rises dramatically to £3,671 and leaps to 56 per cent. On the three-year view, it is estimated that the contribution would be £5,177: a 21 per cent net profit. If the sales forecast is cautious, not least to avoid tying up too much cash in stock and storage, and sales exceed expectations, the net profit would nudge up further and be attained earlier.

Return on investment

There is another percentage measure to assess the book. The return on investment (ROI) line in the estimate shows the ratio of money gained, expressed as a percentage, on the publisher's investment in the book for the first and second printings over the given time periods, and over the three-year view. For instance, if a publisher invested £10,000 in a book and got back £15,000 in revenue, the ROI would be 50 per cent. This is calculated by expressing the profit of £5,000 as a percentage of the investment:

£5,000/£10,000 = 50 per cent

For *Inside Book Publishing*, on the first printing, the publisher's investment is the direct variable costs of £7,862 and the direct overheads of £8,798. These total £16,660. The NSR is £18,166 from which is deducted the total costs of £16,660

S K I L L S

Commissioning

No editor can simply sit back and expect marketable ideas and authors to flow in. Editors need to be creative in that they encourage and develop received ideas or initiate ideas themselves and match them to authors. Inevitably these lead to false trails, so editors have to be agile enough to hunt the front-runners, ruthless enough to weed out the wrong projects, and tough enough to withstand their exposed position within the publishing house.

Publishing is a business, and it is vital that editors have financial acumen. Profitable publishing also depends on a perception of trends in markets and timing. Good editors pre-empt competitors – in textbook publishing the lead time can easily be three years. In specialist fields the work involves asking experts the right questions and being able to talk to them intelligently. The skill lies in choosing the right advisers and readers. The consumer book editors, who face great difficulty in ascertaining market needs, base their judgements on a combination of experience of what sells, having a finger on the pulse, and intuition. Backing one's own hunches takes considerable audacity and confidence.

Fundamental to book and author selection is the editor's ability to assess the quality of the proposal and of the author's writing and purpose. This critical faculty is underpinned by skills in speed reading and sampling sections of writing. Most editors will be able to assess a manuscript from the first few pages, and this skill develops with experience. Editors should be able to contribute to structural improvements, and in specialist areas appear to the author not merely as a cipher for expert readers' comments.

Authors are engaged in long spells of isolation when writing with little else to draw on but experience, knowledge and imagination. In their books rest their dreams and hopes. In their eyes the editor is exclusive to them; to the editor an author is one of many. Authors expect editors to represent their interests in-house, to get things done and so judge editors on their in-house clout. Conversely editors must represent the best interests of the publisher to authors – at times a fine juggling act. Good editors persuade authors to write, often plead with them to deliver, and foster author loyalty to the house. Authors need encouragement, reassurance and praise – that, and the editor's diplomacy, are vital. Those authors who rely on their books for income (unlike teachers, academics etc.) centre their whole life around their writing. To some, an editor becomes inseparable from their private lives.

Editors need a knowledge of production methods (limitations and costs), digital opportunities, and contracts, and the skill to negotiate with authors, agents and others. As the book's champion, the editor must display infectious enthusiasm and superb persuasive skills.

leaving a net profit of £1,506. Expressing £1,506 as a percentage of the investment of £16,660 gives the ROI of 9.04 per cent:

£1,506/£16,660 = 9.04 per cent

However, on the three-year view, the ROI is 26.58 per cent:

£5,177/£19,479 = 26.58 per cent

which nearly approaches the ROI target set at 30 per cent, sufficient to cover all the overheads of the publisher and to provide a reasonable profit.

Break-even

The break-even point is the number of copies the publisher would need to sell to surpass the total costs (the direct variable costs and direct overheads). For *Inside Book Publishing*, on the first printing, the publisher would need to sell 83 hardback copies (of the 90 to sell) and 1,000 paperback copies (of the 1,100 to sell) to break even. Taken together, the break-even point is reached at 83 per cent of the total sales on the first printing. This feeds into the publisher's risk judgement.

The preliminary estimate ends with a table headed 'contribution' which provides a summary of the figures above, and spaces for the editor and publisher to sign and date.

Successes and failures

If a book reprints and the publisher has recovered all its development and marketing costs from the first printing, the gross margin dramatically increases because such costs do not recur. But substantially revised new editions incur renewed fixed costs and relaunch overheads. Publishing is a high margin business and can be immensely profitable. But for numerous publishers, those profits are a mirage – they make just too many mistakes.

Some authors either fail to deliver manuscripts or submit unacceptable material. The consumer book publishers which pay significant sums on signature of contract, can find them difficult to recover if the author does not deliver. If a proposed book is not published, its estimated contribution to overheads needs to be recouped from elsewhere. It is relatively easier for a consumer book publisher to fill its list more quickly, for example by buying from agents or from US firms, than a school textbook publisher. All the decisions regarding the quality of a book, its market, price and sales potential are based on advance subjective judgements. Amongst the new books there inevitably lurk those that fail to recover their production costs or the author's advance, let alone make a contribution to overheads. Generally speaking, publishers make very little net profit from their new book publishing programme over the first year. Their profits stem from the surviving titles that reprint. That said, a Christmas bestseller can still make a large sum of money, as can a title timed to coincide with a sporting event or anniversary.

A vigorous and profitable publisher is in a strong position to publish books which, it is estimated at the outset, will not show a profit; indeed there may be good publishing reasons for doing so. A book could be published for prestige purposes.

With the growth of print on demand, small numbers can be reprinted much more easily and this model is spreading across many sectors of book publishing

A fiction publisher may believe in a novelist's long-term ultimate success, or want the author's next more desirable book. A textbook publisher may want to enter a new area and undercut competitors. A university press may be obliged to publish a great scholarly work – sometimes supported by a subvention. Some publishers keep titles in print even though the storage costs exceed their revenue. For example a fiction publisher may keep in print an author's body of work, and a university press may keep scholarly titles in print for years.

Now read this

Gill Davies, *Book Commissioning and Acquisition*, 2nd edition, Routledge, 2004.

Sources

Diana Athill, *Stet*, Granta, 2000.
Eric de Bellaigue, *British Book Publishing as a Business since the 1960s*, British
    Library Publishing, 2004.
Ros Jay, *The White Ladder Diaries*, White Ladder Press, 2004.
Tom Maschler, *Publisher*, Picador, 2005.
Angus Phillips, Mark Saunders, Sue Pandit and Deshini Chetty, 'The Nature
    of the Relationship between Authors and Editors', *Publishing Research
    Quarterly*, 21:2 (Summer 2005).
Christopher Potter, 'Evolving into Something', *Publishing Research Quarterly*,
    16:1 (2000), pages 20–5.
'Refreshing that Vintage Appeal', interview with Rachel Cugnoni, *The Bookseller*,
    24 May 2007.

CHAPTER 8

The author contract and product development

Once the costing for a new title has been agreed and the book receives the green light, a contract is drawn up with the author. This chapter examines the author contract and the editor's continuing role in shaping and developing the project.

AUTHOR CONTRACT

Each publisher – as the buyer of rights from an author – draws up its own contract, also called the agreement. The contract differs according to the book and the author, but most publishers operate with standard contracts. Commissioning editors negotiate contracts with authors or their agents, and can then adjust the standard contract to fit the final terms agreed. The publisher is usually in a position to weight the contract in their favour. Some authors sign the contract that is offered; others, or their agents, will try to improve the royalty rates and advance offered, or ask for changes to particular clauses, which may have to be reviewed by the publisher's legal department.

The contract formally defines the relationship between author and publisher. Today's publishing contract can be a lengthy document as the publisher seeks to secure as many rights as possible, and the obligations of both parties are set out in detail. The full acquisition of rights will prevent problems that may occur whether in selling a book around the world or its exploitation as an electronic product. It will also maximize the income from licensing a range of rights to third parties. Although it is unlikely that a book will be turned into merchandised goods such as tea towels and duvet covers, it did happen with Edith Holden's *The Country Diary of an Edwardian Lady* and Flora Thompson's *Lark Rise to Candleford* – many years after they were first written or published.

A contract is usually a legal document signed by both parties – the author and the representative of the publisher. The requirements seen as important for an enforceable contract (Jones and Benson, page 62) are:

- a clear agreement,
- an intention to be legally bound by it, and
- some valuable consideration to seal the bargain.

The first page of the
contract signed for
this edition of *Inside
Book Publishing*

AN AGREEMENT

dated 22nd January 2007

between

(1)   **Giles Clark & Angus Phillips**

of

(the 'Author', which expression shall, where the context admits, include the
Author's executors, administrators and assigns or successors in title as the case
may be)

and

(2)   **Routledge, an imprint of Taylor and Francis Books Ltd**

of   2 Park Square, Milton Park
         Abingdon,
         Oxfordshire OX14 4RN

(the 'Publishers', which expression shall, where the context admits, include any
publishing imprint subsidiary to or associated with the Publishers and the
Publishers' administrators and assigns or successors in business as the case may
be).

Recital/   The Author is writing, compiling or editing an original work at present entitled
Background

         Inside Book Publishing, 4th Edition

consisting of approximately 110,000 words inclusive of all references,
bibliography, appendices and index, together with figures and illustrations
(hereinafter called 'the Work').

If these requirements are in place, a verbal agreement may be enough to form
a contract. This was highlighted by the case of Malcolm v. OUP (1991), when an
editor offered assurances over the telephone to the author that he would publish
his book. The book was later turned down by the publisher, but in court it was
revealed that the author was tape recording the conversations. The court ruled in
favour of the author, who was awarded significant compensation. Since that case,
editors have been cautious about giving verbal agreement to publish, and most
companies have tightened up their procedures so that deals are subject to a final
written contract. It is rare, however, for disputes between the author and their
publisher to reach court, and there is little case law in existence.

> **A verbal
> agreement can
> be sufficient to
> form a contract**

Main elements of the contract

The following are the items covered in a typical contract between the author and
the publisher. Of main interest to the author will be the level of the royalty and any

advance. Other clauses that can cause dispute include any option on the author's next work, royalties for new editions (should they be increased?), payment for illustrations (does the author or publisher bear the cost?), and the number of free copies for the author.

Preamble

The date, names of the parties (their assigns and successors in business) to the contract, and the book's title are stated.

Author's grant

The author usually grants to the publisher the sole and exclusive licence and right to publish the book (the 'Work') in volume form (print and electronic), in all languages, for the full term of copyright (author's life plus 70 years), throughout the world. By granting a licence, the author retains ownership of the copyright. Sometimes authors, such as contributors to multi-authored books or to highly illustrated general books, assign their copyright, thereby passing ownership and all control to the publisher. The grant of electronic rights may include 'in any media not yet invented', or other similar phrase, to cover the publisher against future technological developments.

Author's warranty

The author warrants that they control the rights granted, that the work is original (not a plagiarism), does not contain defamatory, libellous or unlawful matter; and will indemnify the publisher for any loss or damages.

Competing works

The author agrees not to write a directly competing work for another publisher.

Manuscript

The contract will detail the length of the manuscript (preferably in words not pages), the delivery date and form (disk plus two hard copies, double spaced). It will also cover the author's responsibility for supplying illustrations and the index, and for obtaining and paying for third-party copyright material (unless otherwise agreed). The publisher reserves the right not to publish if the delivered manuscript is overdue or does not conform to a previously agreed brief.

Corrections

The author is constrained from making extensive corrections to the proofs – other than those attributable to the publisher or printer – and is charged if author's corrections exceed a specified percentage (say 15 per cent) of the cost of typesetting. The author must return proofs within a certain period, usually two to three weeks.

Publication

The publisher solely controls the publication – production, design, publicity, price, methods and conditions of sale. In practice authors may be consulted on matters such as the cover design. The author is given a number of free or gratis copies (typically six) and may purchase more at a discount.

Payments to the author

On the publisher's own editions, the author is normally paid a royalty expressed either as a percentage of an edition's recommended published price on all copies sold; or as a percentage of the publisher's net receipts, i.e. the sum of money received by the publisher after discounts have been deducted. The author's earnings are thus proportional to price (or net receipts) and sales. Royalty rates are quoted for each of the publisher's own-produced editions: hardback; paperback (generally lower); sales made in the traditional home market (the UK and Ireland), and in export markets. Export rates are usually lower to take account of the higher discounts involved. Royalty rates on the publisher's own electronic editions are also given.

A scale of royalties rising by steps of 2 to 2.5 per cent when certain quantities have been sold may be included, especially on home market sales. Royalty rates on the published price can range from 5 to 15 per cent (many authors never surpass the lower base rates). If an author has reached a higher rate on a scale (whether based on the published price or net receipts), and a new edition is produced, the royalty reverts to the base rate. When the book is remaindered, no royalties may be paid. Other provisos where lower royalties apply are stated. If royalties are based on the published price, for example, the rate applied may be reduced or based on net receipts if the publisher sells the book to a large retail chain at a high discount of say 52.5 per cent or above. A lower royalty rate may also apply to small reprints.

Subsidiary rights

The contract lists further rights granted to the publisher, which it could license to other firms, and the percentages payable (from 50 up to 90 per cent) to the author on the publisher's net receipts from the sales of those subsidiary rights. If the publisher is granted, for example, US, book club and translation rights, the firms to which these rights could be licensed may print their own editions and pay royalties to the publisher to be shared with the author. However, the publisher may print bulk quantities, for example for a co-edition partner. The publisher sells such copies at a high discount (up to 80 per cent) and the author's royalty may be based on the actual sums received (a common rate is 10 per cent). There are many other rights such as serial and extract rights; dramatization rights on stage, film, television and radio; broadcast reading rights; audiobook; quotation and anthology; large print; digest condensation; mechanical reproduction rights (for example on CD); and electronic publishing rights. There is a fuller discussion of rights in Chapter 12.

Accounting

The publisher's accounting period to the author is usually six months for general books and a year for educational and academic books, with settlement up to three to four months after. Consumer book publishers normally withhold a proportion of royalties payable in an accounting period as a reserve against subsequent returns of unsold books from retailers.

Revisions and new editions

The author agrees to revise the book when requested or to permit others to do so at the author's expense.

Reversion

The rights may revert to the author if on request the publisher fails to keep the
work in print. The reversion of rights has become more complicated – print on
demand and the ebook mean that a book need never go out of print. Some agents
now argue that the rate of sale should be the determinant of whether rights can
be reverted. By contrast many academic authors are only too pleased to have their
works available indefinitely.

Arbitration

Arbitration may be necessary in the case of a dispute between the author and the
publisher.

Option

The author may give the publisher the right of first refusal on their next book.

Moral rights

These are covered in Chapter 5.

Advance

An advance, if paid, is set against the author's future royalties. It is important
to note that the advance has to be earned out before the author receives further
payments for the book. Most authors receive either a small advance – up to
£12,000 for a two-book deal in the case of a first-time novelist – or none at all.
Big advances tend to make the headlines in the trade and sometimes the national
press, for example the reported advance to the England footballer Wayne Rooney:
'Manchester United and England striker Wayne Rooney has signed the biggest
sports book deal in publishing history. The 20-year-old has agreed a 12-year
contract with HarperCollins to write a minimum of five books for an advance of
£5 m' (bbc.co.uk, 10 March 2006). Advance payments may be staged, with separate
payments on signature of the contract, delivery of an acceptable manuscript, and
on publication.

In 1996 Random House in New York sued Joan Collins in an attempt
to retrieve an advance paid to her of $1.3 m for two novels. It alleged that the
manuscripts she delivered were unpublishable. The star of *Dynasty* won the case
since the original contract only said that the manuscript should be 'complete' not
satisfactory.

Signatures of the parties

The author and the nominated representative of the publisher will sign at least two
copies of the agreement, and one copy will be kept by the author.

The signature of the contract is the trigger for allocating an ISBN to the title,
and the editor's dispatch to the author of the author questionnaire for marketing
purposes.

Electronic rights

In the above example, under author's grant, the publisher's 'volume rights'
or 'primary rights' encompass print and electronic. Some of the far-sighted

educational, academic and STM book publishers included electronic rights in their contracts with authors during the 1990s, even in the 1980s. By 2007 many of the main publishers had secured electronic rights from authors on tens of thousands of old contracts which had made no previous provision for electronic rights. The learned journal publishers are also free to publish electronically since the contributing authors usually assign their rights to the publisher, or society. Similarly, many of the book packagers and highly illustrated publishers own the copyright in the text, and in the commissioned artwork and photography, through assignments.

The trade publishers, however, do not generally hold electronic rights in their backlist books. Agents have withheld them. Agents do not agree with the publisher's view that the publisher's volume rights must include ebooks, and license them separately, possibly to another publisher, as well as licensing other kinds of electronic rights, such as turning the book into an interactive game. The royalties paid on ebook sales range from the rate payable on the printed book to as high as 30 per cent of net receipts.

The exploitation of electronic rights in trade publishing is in flux. This issue was highlighted in the USA by the case of Random House, Inc. v. Rosetta Books 2001, in which it was ruled that the publisher did not automatically hold ebook rights, even if it was granted the right to publish a work in book form, and if the rights were not specifically granted in the contract they were retained by the author.

The inclusion of third-party material – text extracts and photographs – in many books across most sectors of publishing is another impediment to the epublishing of the backlist and of new books. The rights holders, both printed book publishers and picture agencies, can be resistant to granting electronic rights or charge exorbitant fees – in effect a refusal. Thus ebooks may be devoid of third-party material, and epublishing is likely to benefit most publishers and rights owners who control very pure products, comparatively free of third-party content.

Impact of agents

The agent's contract typically is shorter than one from a publisher, reflecting the more limited grant of rights by the author

Where the author has an agent, the contract used may be provided by the agent weighted in their client's favour. So-called *boilerplate* agreements – standard contracts – may be used with the leading publishers, avoiding wrangles over the wording of standard clauses. Agents may opt to withhold many of the subsidiary rights (to them they are not subsidiary), such as serial and translation, preferring to either sell the rights themselves or to negotiate if the publisher proposes a deal later. The decision may also be taken to divide up the English language territories, selling UK and US rights separately. For sought-after books this should yield a higher income for the author.

Territorial rights

Traditionally, the UK and US publishers (especially consumer) have been in separate ownership and have divided the world English book market between them. For books published on both sides of the Atlantic, the UK and US publishers seek exclusive market areas (closed markets) from which the other's competing editions of the same book are excluded. The US publisher's exclusive territory was essentially the USA; the UK publisher's the Commonwealth, Ireland and South

Africa and a few others. The remaining areas are then non-exclusive to either –
called the open market, such as mainland Europe – where UK and US editions of
the same book are in direct competition. Canadian rights were exclusively retained
by UK publishers on their own originated books, and by US publishers on theirs.
For some books this broad division still persists and can affect the way agents and
packagers grant rights to publishers, and the way publishers trade books between
themselves. For example, a UK publisher holding world rights could either sell
its own edition to the USA through its related US firm, or license the rights to
a US publisher, in which case the US publisher's exclusive, non-exclusive, and
excluded territories would be negotiated. Conversely a UK publisher may buy a
US-originated book from a US publisher or author represented by an agent, and its
rights and territories would also be carefully defined.

This traditional territorial split in English language publishing of exclusive,
non-exclusive (open market) and excluded territories is threatened by actions of
governments, consumer pressure groups and internet traders. By the late 1960s,
India became an unofficial open market. Singapore legislated itself into the open
market in the mid-1980s. In 1991 Australia required local publication (for example
by UK publishers) to occur within 30 days of first publication, in effect from the
publication date of the US edition, if the UK publisher was to maintain its exclusive
rights. In 1998 New Zealand declared itself an open market.

EU single market

Nearer home, the advent in 1993 of the EU single market principle of free
movement of goods is in conflict with the traditional UK/US publishers' contracts
whereby the UK is an exclusive territory and mainland Europe is open. The
greatest fear of UK publishers is that the UK itself might potentially become
flooded with cheaper US editions imported from mainland Europe, negating
the UK publishers' exclusive contractual and territorial rights. Such 'parallel'
importation is unlikely to occur from direct breaches of contracts by US publishers,
and instead at the hands of third-party traders in the USA or mainland Europe.
UK publishers argue that the European Union and additional countries joining
it should be treated as a single market and that it should be the exclusive territory
of UK publishers, in the same way as the US unified market is treated. Projects
originated in the UK tend to be sold by agents with exclusive rights in Europe;
and UK publishers may offer Canadian rights to US publishers in exchange for
exclusivity in Europe. Stephen Page, President of The Publishers Association, said
'there is a fundamental principle at stake here. We need to own Europe exclusively
to know we own the UK exclusively' (*The Bookseller*, 23 June 2006).

The development of internet bookselling in the late 1990s enabled UK
consumers to purchase easily a US edition from US-based internet booksellers.
Some of the major internet booksellers in the UK have agreed to list only the
UK edition, based on territorial rights information provided by the bibliographic
database supplied by Nielsen BookData.

One answer to the thorny issue of territorial rights is for the publisher to
acquire world rights from the author. This is easier to do in some sectors of
publishing, such as educational and academic. Most of the major UK and US
consumer book publishers are in common ownership and aim to be strong enough

to acquire exclusive world English language rights in authors' works. This enables them to overcome legislative difficulties anywhere in the world and ameliorates any 'buying around' practices of third-party traders. However, the authors' agents may still believe that they can secure better offers from different international publishers by dividing exclusive territorial rights amongst competing publishers.

The collapse of territorial rights is not a foregone conclusion. If they are in the interests of the US media corporations, the US government would defend their continuance. The major power blocks of the USA and European Union also have to grapple with the related issue of the potential loss of tax revenues from off-shore internet traders escaping the conventional tax nets. On the internet, the consumers' choice of bookseller is affected by the cost of shipping the physical book and the timing. If a book is available online – say as an ebook – those factors will be removed: the world publication date would need to be instantaneous.

Apart from price differentials between competing editions (which are influenced by £–$ exchange rates with the Euro and other currencies), the time of the release of different editions of the same title is another factor. US and UK consumer book publishers deploy the strategy of maximizing earnings through the sequential publication of a particular book in different formats and prices. For example, first publication would be in a higher priced hardback, followed by a trade paperback and a smaller-format, mass-market paperback edition. In export markets, especially the growing mainland European market, UK and US publishers attempt to pre-empt the other's competing edition in paperback while maintaining their home markets for a period exclusively in hardback. Hence UK export editions of paperbacks are available earlier on mainland Europe than in the UK, and can be bought on the air-side of UK airports. Mainland European paperback importers may hedge their bets by simultaneously ordering their stock from both US and UK publishers to ensure they receive stock from whichever is the earliest. Importers also compare the prices of competing editions, and scout around for bargain-priced editions.

The major college textbook and academic publishers holding world rights face a related problem of maintaining differential prices across territories. Third-party traders may look to transfer products from low-priced territories, such as parts of Asia, to high-priced territories, such as the USA.

> **In the UK printed books do not attract VAT, whereas digital products, such as ebooks, do**

PRODUCT DEVELOPMENT

Once a book has been commissioned from an author and the contract has been signed, it needs to be monitored while it is being written, and planning begins for the editing, design and production stages that are interlinked with the book's marketing.

Books need differing levels of care and attention during their development. Commissioning editors may await the completed text of a novel or biography. Some authors would like editors to read chapter drafts while the writing is in progress. For textbook and reference titles especially, attention will be paid to word length, any co-ordination necessary if there are a number of contributors, and the use of templates during the writing process, which can help with the tagging vital for electronic editions. Authors may deliver the complete manuscript on time or later, an inherent trait of many authors. The non-deliverer may have their contract cancelled. The delivered manuscript is checked for length, completeness and quality. It may be returned for revision, or accepted and passed on for production. The author may be reminded to complete the author's questionnaire which is used for marketing purposes.

Commissioning editors brief and liaise with junior editors, designers, production, promotion and sales staff. Editors may write the blurb for the cover and catalogue entry. The copy may also be used as the basis for the book's AI – advance information sheet – which is needed six to nine months ahead of publication. Although editors have no managerial control over other departments, they endeavour to ensure their books receive due attention. Commissioning editors may present their books to the publisher's sales force at the regular sales conferences.

Some editors, especially those involved with complex and highly illustrated books, or major textbook projects involving online resources, get very involved in the product research and development stages. Some textbook publishers have introduced development editors who directly support the commissioning editors on major textbook projects. Such an editor carries out survey research in association with the marketing department, organizes the external reviewing of drafts, and helps shape the project with the authorial team from conception to completion.

At the page-proof stage, the book's published price is fixed, as well as the number of copies to be printed and bound. The number printed may differ from the number envisaged at the outset, and changes may have been made to its format and pricing. This may reflect feedback from the major retailers, changes in the market or a new view of the best way to publish the book. Editors may also make decisions on reprints and have to manage stock for their lists. In some larger companies this work is handled by sales and inventory control specialists.

Commissioning editors may undertake development work themselves, or hand on the work to junior editors, whose job titles could be Editor, Development Editor, Production Editor, Assistant Editor, or Editorial Assistant. Those working across print and electronic products are sometimes called Content Managers or Editors. The editor maintains contact with the author so as to plan backwards from the proposed publication date, trying to ensure that the manuscript is delivered in good time to make smooth progress through the production process.

Particular times of year can be good for publication of trade books, and the publisher has to make sure the book appears at the time of the relevant sporting event, anniversary (for the subject of a biography), or the relevant season (Christmas for cookery, Spring for gardening titles). Publicity opportunities such as media exposure or festivals (for example Valentine's Day) may influence the date of publication. The New Year, and its associated resolutions, offers opportunities for publishers of health and personal improvement titles; beach reads are out for the summer months. Hardbacks tend to get the most media coverage in the spring (around the time of most of the literary festivals) and autumn (in the run-up to Christmas).

The New Year is a good time to publish self-improvement titles

Illustrations can add value and this continues to be reviewed during product development. Are illustrations necessary to aid the explanation in the text – for example in a school textbook? Are they essential in a particular market – art publishing or cookery? Can you charge more if there are many illustrations – will you sell more copies? A balance needs to be struck between the cost of illustrations and their likely added value.

Editorial project management

Planning tasks as part of the product development process include:

- a schedule for the editing, design and production stages,
- the necessary clearance for permissions for both text and illustrations,
- a brief for the text and cover design,
- copy written for the cover, and
- a budget.

Schedule

This is preferably drawn up in advance of the delivery of the typescript from the author. A copy-editor can be booked in advance, and the design and production stages can be planned around the proposed publication date. Schedules can be more or less complicated, and can be done using software or simply a single sheet of A4. There may be a standard set of weeks allowed for different stages, but there is no formula set in stone. If a competing title is to be beaten to market, or if revenue is required within a particular financial year, the schedule may be severely shortened. If this was done with every title, however, there would be the risk that quality would suffer and there would be tremendous pressure on the staff involved. Here is a sample schedule.

June to December	Picture research/clearance of permissions
January	Delivery of the manuscript
	Copy-editing (six weeks)
	Cover copy written
March	Handover of typescript/illustrations to design department
	Cover proofs
April	Typesetting
May	First page proofs (three weeks for checking)
	Index preparation
June	Revised proofs and index proofs (one week for checking)
	Passed for press
July	Advance copies from the printer
	Copies into warehouse (six weeks before publication)
September	Publication

Permissions

Permission may need to be sought for the use of text and illustrations in the book. Longer quotations not covered by fair usage will need to be cleared, and for anthologies of poetry or prose some detective work may be required to track down the relevant copyright holders. A freelancer may take on the work of clearing permissions for an anthology. Usually the first approach is to the originating publisher, who may control subsidiary rights. Occasionally you will see a line in a book saying that 'every effort has been made to contact the copyright holder', and the extract will appear without permission having been granted. The publisher has made a rights risk assessment.

Under the contract the author may have to clear and pay for the permissions. The publisher may still have to undertake picture research or brief a researcher, putting the cost of the permissions against the author's royalty. If the publisher is responsible for obtaining copyright permission, the editor or researcher writes to the copyright holders. Each illustration or table is labelled and compared against the accompanying text and caption. Caption and source copy are prepared.

Drawn illustrations are prepared from copies of those previously published, if suitably amended, or from the author's original line work, roughs or ideas. They are edited for sense and consistency before being passed to the designer or illustrator. The desired position of the illustrations is indicated in the text.

Design brief

Standard forms or memos may be used to brief the cover and page designers. The cover designer will be briefed on the market for the book and its contents. For the page design, the brief may be to follow the design of another title (copy enclosed) or to create something new and distinctive. A sample chapter or two enables the design to be started on before the book's delivery. For key titles, sample spreads may be needed to help sell rights or to assist the author in writing to the correct length.

A design brief may contain the following elements:

- *the market for the book* – in the case of fiction, age and sex,
- *the content* – synopsis or contents list,
- *some text elements* – with sample text (to show content, heading structure) and illustrations,
- *single or double column format* – double column format can accommodate smaller type and is often used for reference works,
- the style of the running heads – chapter heads are more informative than simply the book title, and
- *a similar title* – if the book is to follow that more or less closely in style.

Cover copy

The cover is needed well in advance of the printed book for promotion and sales purposes. Cover copy (for example title, author, blurb and ISBN) may be prepared before the book's delivery by the author. Blurb writing is an important skill. In the case of fiction, it must grip the potential reader without giving away too much of the plot. Review quotes or advance puffs from prominent names may be used. Editors may ask sales or marketing to review the blurb copy for important titles.

Short sentences can be highly effective in a blurb

Budget

The title costing will have estimates for the first costs of the book, including editorial and design work, and permission costs. The budget may be reviewed in the light of real costs or any change in the book's specification – page extent, number and type of illustrations.

EXPERT

Writing a blurb

Cathy Douglas, word doctor

The blurb is what publishers call the copy printed on the book – on the back cover of a paperback and usually on the front flap of the jacket of a hardback. Many people believe it is unimportant, almost an afterthought. This is very far from the truth. For most books – those that don't command huge publicity budgets – it is the only piece of selling copy the consumer will ever see, and independent research by two major publishers, Penguin and Orion, in the 1990s, identified it as the key factor in the decision whether or not to buy, so it is enormously important. It is also hard to write well.

The first thing to consider is practicality. People reading blurbs have very little time or attention to spare – it usually happens in a crowded space, full of people with rucksacks and carrycots, often listening for announcements about trains or planes, so probably less than 40 per cent of the potential buyer's attention is on the product. The modern trend for ever-fatter books also makes the automatic response to being attracted by the front cover – to pick the book up in one hand and flip it over to read the blurb – actually quite uncomfortable. So no blurb should be longer than 120 words – fiction blurbs probably no more than 100 – and must be:

- impactful,
- intriguing,
- relevant, and
- short.

Paperbacks may make generous use of review quotes. Non-fiction blurbs need to be concise but complete – in other words, answer all the questions you would want to ask a salesperson if you were buying the product in a shop. Bullet points can help put across the key benefits of the book; short sentences can be very effective; jargon should be avoided, and time taken to choose the right word.

Fiction blurbs are more emotional: so you must think yourself into the story. Try to draw potential readers in with the first few sentences. The first line for Anne Tyler's *The Accidental Tourist* was: 'How does a man addicted to routine – a man who flosses his teeth before love-making – cope with the chaos of everyday life?', which pretty much drew everyone in. Any shoutline should sell the atmosphere rather than try to tell the story. Think film and perfume ads – a grainy black-and-white photo of a perfect couple sells you the mood, not the content, and the ever-memorable shoutline for *Alien* was 'In space, no one can hear you scream', not 'An epic battle with aliens that invade your body and warp your personality'.

Editorial work

Although a commissioning editor or junior editor may copy-edit manuscripts in detail, this work is usually done by freelance copy-editors. There are also project management companies and packagers which undertake the entire production process up to the delivery to the publisher of the final digital file of the book ready for manufacturing and electronic publication, although the publisher still retains direct control of the cover. High technology companies based in India, focused on digital file processing and paginating books, at first undertook editorial and production work for journal publishers, then extended their services to high-level academic titles and textbooks. Such companies do work previously undertaken by UK freelance workers and production companies.

Junior editors supervise the progress of books from manuscripts to bound copies, working closely with the production/design department, and giving information to marketing and sales people. They may copy-edit manuscripts and organize illustrations themselves; they may edit manuscripts for overall clarity and pass them to freelance copy-editors for the detailed work. They subsequently send proofs to authors and to freelance proofreaders, collate corrections and generally oversee the book's production from an editorial standpoint. Some academic book and journal publishers employ production editors, who are also responsible for the design and production stages, and the management of suppliers. The production department may organize freelance editing and proofreading. In illustrated book publishers and packagers, editors work alongside designers to create the book spread by spread.

Only in firms where job demarcations are drawn not too tightly, and where junior editors work specifically for sympathetic commissioning editors, is there the likelihood of commissioning experience, usually without responsibility. This may depend on the size of the company. A common job role is that of editorial assistant, whose work ranges from administrative support to editorial work under supervision, such as proofreading, collating corrections, finding pictures for the text, applying for the clearance of third-party copyright material, and handling reprints. In consumer book publishing, junior editorial staff may write reports on new book proposals. In textbook publishing, development editors may look after the commissioning of new editions.

Copy-editing

The aim of the copy-editor, who may be the only person other than the author who reads the book before publication, is to ensure that the text and illustrations are clear, correct and consistent for both the printer and the ultimate readers. 'Good copy-editing is invisible: it aims to present the book the author would have written if he or she had had more time or experience – not, as some new copy-editors think, their own improved version' (Butcher et al., page 32).

The copy-editor is also usually expected to look out for passages that may be libellous.

> Any statement in a book or journal or newspaper, or any other published matter (an advertisement, e-mail or website, for example), runs the risk of being defamatory if it contains an untrue allegation or imputation which disparages the reputation of another. (Jones and Benson, page 163)

In the case of an unauthorized biography of a leading celebrity, a read by a lawyer may be required alongside evidence from the author to back up any controversial

The novelist Iris Murdoch (1919–99) refused to have her work edited, even resisting changes to her punctuation

SKILLS

Editorial

Getting on with authors, senior editors and other in-house staff, and briefing them are crucial editorial skills. Agreeing changes with authors and getting them to return proofs on time takes tact, self-confidence, persuasion, tenacity and negotiation. Editing manuscripts and proofreading demands a meticulous eye for detail, a retentive memory, sustained concentration, patience, commonsense detective work and an ability to check one's own and others' work consistently. Authors often have great loyalty to both commissioning and more junior editors, and this loyalty binds them to the company. They may pay tribute to their editors in the acknowledgements at the front of the book.

Copy-editing and proofreading skills can to some extent be learnt from books, but added to that must be an editor's sound grasp of grammar and spelling, and preparedness to look things up. Editors should be able to place themselves in the reader's mind whatever subject knowledge they themselves hold. Good copy-editors and proofreaders are prized and valued.

The enhancement of an author's work involves not only a knowledge of current stylistic conventions and language, but also judgement on the desirability and extent of their application, recognizing when it is necessary or unnecessary to make changes. Breaking the rules for effect is not restricted to fiction. Appreciating the intangible quality of the author's voice can be important, especially in children's books.

Although an editor needs an enormous capacity to soak up detail, the ability to examine the text's overall sense is equally important. Visual awareness is valuable, especially in highly illustrated adult and children's publishing and packaging, and low-level textbook publishing. Knowledge and understanding of production processes and ways of minimizing costs at all stages are essential, as is clear marking of the text. An understanding of publishing software is also important as the range of editorial duties expands.

A publisher's office is hardly conducive to concentration. Editors dealing with many books (all at different stages of production) are pressed by the production office to meet deadlines, and are constantly interrupted by colleagues wanting instant information. Good editors are unflappable, they set priorities, manage time efficiently, juggle projects, switch quickly from one activity to another, and expect crises.

claims. Investigative reporting and publishing were given a boost in 2007 with the case of Graeme McLagan's book *Bent Coppers* (2003) – 'The inside story of Scotland Yard's battle against police corruption'. The court of appeal decided that the author had acted responsibly when writing and researching the book. 'The court upheld the so-called "Reynolds defence" of qualified privilege, under which journalists can claim the right to publish material in the public interest even if they cannot prove its accuracy or it turns out to be untrue' (*The Guardian*, 11 October 2007). This was the first time the Reynolds defence had been applied to a book.

The copy-editor, who is briefed on the nature and market of the book, first needs to check that all the manuscript items handed over are indeed present and that they have been clearly labelled and numbered by the author. The author is asked for any outstanding items, otherwise the book will be held up.

The work of copy-editing falls into three related processes:

- consistency,
- substantive editing, and
- structural mark-up.

Consistency

The most basic task is to ensure that the author's text is consistent in such matters as spelling, hyphenation, capitalization, agreement of verbs and subjects, beginning and ending of quotation marks and parentheses, and many other points sometimes included in the firm's editorial house style. The house style may be based on a particular reference work, for example *The Oxford Style Manual*, or may have been developed internally. In the USA most editors use *The Chicago Manual of Style*. One advantage of following a house style is that proofreaders and other staff working on the text will have a set policy to help resolve problems later on in the production process.

If the editor is working on-screen, tools such as the search facility can help with the enforcement of consistency in spelling and hyphenation. The danger is that some words, such as in quotations or references, are also changed by mistake. The editor must check the accuracy and relationship of parts of the text to others, such as in-text cross-references to illustrations, captions, chapters and notes; the matching of headings on the contents page to those in the text; and of citations to the reference list. The arrangement and preparation of pages about which authors may be unsure (for example the preliminary pages) are also the editor's concern. Each new book presents its own problems in the detailed handling of stylistic points, and decisions have to be made in regard to alternative ways of applying the rules.

Substantive editing

While some publishers restrict copy-editing to work on consistency, others expect editors to engage in the second parallel editorial process, which may be termed substantive or content editing. This calls for clear perception of the author's intent and sometimes restraint from the copy-editor. Where appropriate, attention is paid to discordant notes, such as obscure, incoherent, misleading or ambiguous sentences, or non sequiturs in factual passages; unintentional use of mixed metaphors or of repetition; unusual punctuation in sentence construction; paragraphing; and over or under use of headings. Furthermore, errors of fact, and inconsistencies, omissions, contradictions and illogicality in the argument or plot may be found. Substantive editing may entail the rewriting of sentences, reorganization, or suggesting other ways to present material. It is important, however, not to annoy the author by making unnecessary changes.

Editors look out for abbreviations and terms unfamiliar to readers. The avoidance of parochialisms or culturally specific UK examples is especially important in books aimed for overseas markets. Books can be edited in British English, American English or even mid-Atlantic English. The avoidance of offensive – for example, sexist or racist – language or values and of corresponding stereotypes are issues which confront editors, designers and illustrators,

House style

R. M. Ritter, author of *The Oxford Style Manual*

E★PERT

In its broadest sense, 'house style' is the way a publisher or printer typically produces its work: it encompasses every aspect of how a publication is presented, including its spelling, grammar, punctuation, typography, hyphenation, references, and layout. This definition can extend beyond print to such physical features as uniform bindings, paper, format, or dust jackets, and even specific colours and presentation of logos or colophons. In practical terms, the purpose of house style is to establish guidelines for everyone involved in creating a publication to follow, in order to ensure accuracy and consistency. Nowadays it is usually imposed by a publisher's copy-editors and proofreaders as part of the editing process.

While the vast majority of these guidelines are unremarkable – good grammar, standard spelling, sensible punctuation – people who are not involved in producing texts (and some who are) tend to think of house style as concentrating on those elements that are either contentious or arbitrary. For example,

"She said she liked the colors 'red, white and blue.'"

is nearly identical to

'She said she liked the colours "red, white, and blue".'

and the minor differences in spelling, punctuation, and quotation marks do not affect its meaning. So why go to all the trouble to impose such seemingly whimsical alterations?

Since the birth of printing, printers recognized that authors are notoriously inconsistent. This is hardly surprising: when writing we are concerned for the most part with *what* we are saying, not *how* we are saying it, or what it looks like thereafter. And a text of any length is likely to have variations in style that are inconsequential to the writer, who is concentrating on substance over style. Nevertheless, readers do pick up on irregularities, though they might not be looking for them. Even if such variations do not actually muddle the sense, they can diminish the ease or pleasure of reading; and if there are enough of them, they can actually cast doubt on the quality or reliability of the writer or publisher.

One might think the most sensible course is simply to mirror a writer's preferred usage, and iron out the differences. Unfortunately, such a task is time-consuming, expensive, and inexact, since it is by no means certain that a writer's usage on page 1 will reflect the style that carries through – barring lapses – to the end. To do this accurately would require compiling a list of all style preferences as they crop up, deciding which are most common, and then starting over to impose them properly – a process that would need to begin afresh for each work. So, to avoid the effort of reinventing the wheel with each text, publishers impose their own styles, which are familiar to them, to ensure that consistency is followed from the very first.

These days, publishers rely on style guides that are considered to reflect established standards in their own countries or, in the case of academic work, their own disciplines or fields. They might disagree with those guides in some respects: variations are often listed on a publisher's website. If a work is to be published quickly, or is to be collected with similar works, or is non-fiction, a publisher's house style is more likely to be imposed unilaterally during editing. In the case of fiction or larger works, publishers tend to seek authors' preferences, and establish a happy medium.

particularly those in educational and children's publishing. These staff also try to ensure that the level of language and the illustrations are appropriate for the intended age group.

Structural mark-up

The parallel editorial process carried out, whether the second substantive form is done or not, is to indicate to the designer or typesetter the structural elements of the text. Items so tagged or coded include the heading hierarchy (chapter headings, section and sub-section headings) and other elements (long quotations, lists, notes, captions, tables). The following shows Extensible Markup Language (XML) tagging for a chapter opening. Each opening tag must be completed with a closing tag.

```
<ch>40  Does the Book Have a Future?<chx>
<au>Angus Phillips<aux>
<epig>Old media don't die; they just have to grow old gracefully. (Douglas
Adams 2001)<epigx>
```

Text that is structurally tagged is platform independent and can be published in different formats (ebook, online) or readily licensed to third parties. A further impetus on publishers (especially educational firms) to make books available in structured, digital formats is the Disability Discrimination Act (1995). There is demand from the reading impaired (not just the visually impaired) and their institutions. Text in digital form can be adjusted by the user in size, style and colour contrasts. Functionality also includes the ability to have the text read out loud using a screen reader, or the provision of extra navigational information – such as whether a line is a heading or a short sentence. Publishers can also produce audio files for download.

Working method

Individuals differ in their approach to copy-editing. A common method involves the editor quickly looking through the manuscript to gain a measure of the author and the book. Ideally, decisions regarding the handling of stylistic points (for example spelling, hyphenation, capitalization, terminology) are taken at the outset. A style sheet is developed to aid consistency and memory, and helps the proofreading, which will be done by a separate freelancer.

To a varying extent, house style editing and substantive editing conflict, in that concentration on one may lead to neglect of the other. Good editors may go through the copy several times at different speeds, focusing attention at various levels,

impulse is a short signal comprising a single value followed by zeroes. The nature of the filter's

response, called the *impulse response* will characterise the filter. The simplest form of filter is

called a Finite Impulse Response FIR filter, in which 'taps' are taken from successive samples,

which are then multiplied by a coefficient (a multiplicative factor) and the results are added

together to form the output of the filter. This is called 'finite because there are a fixed number of

taps. An IIR filter, by contrast, allows feedback between the output and the input, which can

create some long-lasting results, including growth of decay over time. This is particularly useful

for effects such as reverberation. Where the impulse-response of a physical space may be

recorded by, for example, firing a gun or bursting a balloon, the IIR filter may be used to model

the same digitally. However, IIR filters are often unstable and somewhat inaccurate, owing to the

complexity of their operation and can easily produce feedback and other such unwanted results.

This makes digital reverberation one of the most difficult things to achieve sucessfully, and the

range of commercially available solutions can be quite variable in quality.

Creative uses of such filters include interpolation, in which sounds of two different types are

apparently fused together over time and convolution, which combines two soundfiles / an input

and an impulse response by multiplying their spectra together to produce a new sound file.

Frequencies that are common both sound files will tend to be reinforced and resonate together.

The filter will try to match bin content across the two spectrum. Where there is a match, the data

is preserved. Where there is no match, it is discarded (or, strictly, multiplied by 0). Among other

things, this enables the application of the reverberant properties of resonance to FFT windows

over time and thus the superimposition of the reverberant characteristics of one sound upon

another.

Where digital filters find the most direct parallel with analogue equipment is in the field of EQ,

or Equalisation. Both analogue and digital EQ are designed to make the final recorded sound

equal to the original source, by correcting inadequacies of both equipment and the recording

environment. However, it can also be a highly creative tool when used skilfully. EQ adjusts the

please give in full

A sample page from a copy-edited typescript

moving back and forth during each examination. Editors may work on hard copy – a typical example is shown opposite – or on screen (using software tools), or both.

> Skilled on-screen copy-editors, making good use of their computer's tools such as find and replace and macros, can work quickly and efficiently; and if they are able to present the typesetter with fully corrected and coded files that can be simply passed through the typesetting system and run out as pages, there can be genuine savings in the schedule. (Butcher et al., page 15)

Publishers may provide macros to editors that will help incorporate basic elements of house style.

During each examination editors make alterations on matters – especially those of house style – they believe to be right and defensible, but even so authors may disagree. Queries to the author are marked on the copy in the electronic file using track changes, listed separately or scanned to make a portable document format (PDF) file. Those that affect the design or production of the book are addressed to the design or production department.

If the author is contacted by telephone, email or in writing, editors need to be particularly tactful, explaining the kind of editing that has been done – perhaps by mentioning representative samples – raising matters needing assistance, and reaching agreement on matters of concern. It is vital that the edited copy is returned to the author for checking. This reduces costly and time-consuming changes at proof stage. Sometimes a meeting is held with the author. By adopting the reader's viewpoint, and suggesting solutions, the editor sets out to persuade the author to make necessary changes. If the text has been edited on-screen, the edited copy forms an early proof.

Prelims and end-matter

The editor usually drafts the preliminary material – *prelims* or *front matter* – the first few pages of the book. These include the pages giving the book title and author, the name of the publishing house, the copyright notice, and the International Standard Book Number (ISBN) – a unique number identifying the book. Other pages are the contents page, list of illustrations, and acknowledgements – for advice and support to the author, or for copyright material used. The author writes a Preface; a third party provides a Foreword. The cataloguing in publication (CIP) data (supplied by the British Library and Library of Congress) has to be applied for.

The usual order of the prelim pages is as follows, with variations according to the book. A right-hand facing page is called a *recto*; a left-hand facing page a *verso*. Recto pages are visually more important.

> *Half-title page (recto)* – the main title without the subtitle and author's name
> *Half-title verso* – often blank, or a list of the author's previous works
> *Title page (recto)* – full title and author's name, with the publisher's imprint
> *Title verso* – copyright page with the publication history and ISBN

The other prelim pages follow. These include the dedication, acknowledgements, preface, contents page, and the list of illustrations. The prelim pages are paginated using roman numbers, switching to Arabic numerals for the introduction or the first chapter. The advantage of this system is that changes can be made to the prelims at proof stage without affecting the main pagination (which could have knock-on effects for the index). If pages need to be saved to achieve a set extent, the prelim pages can be adjusted. The pages at the end of the book, or *end-matter*, can include appendices, notes, bibliography and the index.

Proofreading

Most unillustrated books, or those with only a few illustrations which are easily placed, go straight to page proofs. The typesetter arranges the page breaks, inserts any illustrations, and returns proofs of pages numbered as they will finally appear. Proofs may arrive as paper or be sent as PDF files by email. Proofs are normally read by the author and publisher (most commonly by a freelancer). They can be checked against the original copy, which is more expensive, or simply read by eye for obvious errors. The corrections and improvements are collated by the editor and inserted using standard symbols – proof marks are set by the British Standards Institution – on one master set (the marked set) or can be marked in the electronic file. Correction marks have traditionally been colour-coded (red for typesetter's errors, blue or black for author's and publisher's) so that costs can be apportioned, but this practice is not always followed. Publishers may charge authors for excessive corrections. The marked set or file is returned to the typesetter for correction, and second page or revised page proofs are produced to check the author's and proofreader's corrections have been correctly implemented. Books with many illustrations integrated with the text may follow a different path. The designer may supply a page layout to the typesetter or work on the pages themselves. A sequence of page proofs is checked by the author and publisher.

Most manuscripts arrive on disk or by email, and there is no necessity to have them rekeyed. This minimizes errors at proof and if the copy-editor works on screen a high-quality version of the text is passed to the typesetter. In some companies production editors and designers prepare the digital file from which the book is printed. Publishers also use typesetters to rekey hard copy or to reset new editions of books for which the publisher has lost the electronic files; and the typesetters themselves have redefined their roles, for example, by extending their typographic and pagination services to include editing, artwork preparation, and

A sample piece of text showing proofreading corrections

Singapore – City of Contracts

Odd and new, East and West meet in Singapore Arriving at the super efficient Changi Airport you drive in along a brand-new highway lined with the bautiful maintained gardens learn Singapore the name the 'Garden city'. But a block from the towering skyscrappers of the centre, the crumbling, bustling shops of Chinatown epitomize exotic asia. On night you'll dine at a ultrasophisticated gormet French restaurant the next you'll be eating an equaly delicious rice and curry disk with your fingers of a banana-leaf plate in the street

even design. Some publishers use project managers or 'full service suppliers' to coordinate all work between copy-editing and the delivery of files to the printer – as with this book. Typesetters also carry out structural tagging and return files to the publisher for reuse in other formats or digital licensing.

Index

Serious non-fiction books should have reliable indexes that anticipate readers' needs and expectations. The author is often responsible for index preparation and the cost, and either compiles it themselves or is supplied with a freelance indexer, found by the editor sometimes from the Society of Indexers. Typesetters can prepare simple indexes using standard software. Indexes are prepared from a page proof and have to be edited and typeset at great speed because the publication date is close. The professional indexers have usually passed their Society's course exams, use specialist indexing software, and may wish to retain copyright.

Now read this

Judith Butcher, Caroline Drake and Maureen Leach, *Copy-Editing: The Cambridge handbook for editors, copy-editors and proofreaders*, 4th edition, 2006.
Hugh Jones and Christopher Benson, *Publishing Law*, 3rd edition, Routledge, 2006.

Sources

Alison Bone, 'Tug of Rights', *The Bookseller*, 13 July 2007.
Barbara Horn, *Editorial Project Management*, Horn Editorial Books, 2006.
Barbara Horn, *Copy-editing*, Horn Editorial Books and Publishing Training Centre, 2008.
Blake Morrison, 'Black Day for the Blue Pencil', *The Observer*, 6 August 2005.
The Chicago Manual of Style, 15th edition, University of Chicago Press, 2003.
Lynette Owen (editor), *Clark's Publishing Agreements: A book of precedents*, Tottel Publishing, 2007.
R. M. Ritter, *The Oxford Style Manual*, 2003.
R. M. Ritter, Angus Stevenson and Lesley Brown, *New Oxford Dictionary for Writers and Editors*, 2005.
Katharine Rushton, 'A Time to Publish', *The Bookseller*, 29 June 2007.

Web resources

www.indexers.org.uk Society of Indexers.
www.sfep.org.uk Society for Editors and Proofreaders.

CHAPTER 9

Design and production

Alongside the work of the editor in product development, the contributions from the design and production departments are equally critical. Good design sells books – whether it is the cover of a novel attracting an impulse buyer in a shop, or the effective use of typography and illustrations in a school textbook. Some publishers, especially in the highly illustrated book and art book markets are actively design-led. Their design standards are used as a marketing and sales tool internationally. Production managers make crucial decisions about quality which affect how a book is perceived in the market. Through effective project management they ensure that work is kept to budget and schedule.

The previous boundaries in the design and production process have been

A typical digital workflow

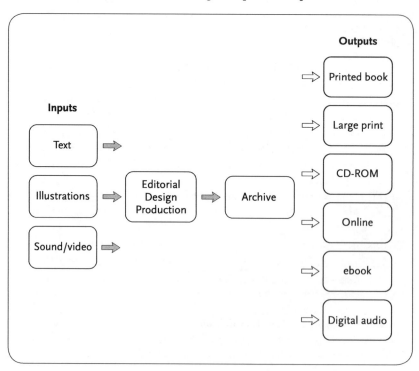

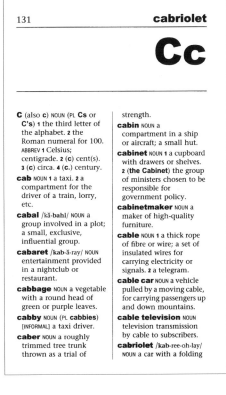

For the *Paperback Oxford Large Print Dictionary*, the text was based on the *Oxford English Mini Dictionary* (left). As well as the use of larger type and generous spacing, the text was rewritten and entries were denested – subentries became separate entries. By permission of Oxford University Press

broken down so that authors, editors and designers are much more involved in producing the final text. Designers, not typesetters, may produce the final file for the printer. Conversely, the increasing sophistication of the typesetters' automated pagination software reduces the need to employ designers to layout illustrated texts which used to be hand crafted by them. At the same time the requirements of digital publishing mean that the file of the printed book can be rendered to several outputs, and there is now an imperative to hold a properly archived version of a book so that it can be published in other formats. There is growing use of XML (Extensible Markup Language) for tagging and archiving text. Publishers making the transition to digital publishing have to re-engineer the workflow.

DESIGN

With regard to the text design, the basis of the book designer's job is visual planning. They operate within technical, cost and time constraints, and take into account the views of the editor, and the production and sales departments. Their task is to transform and enhance the author's raw material, text and illustrations. The printed book should have aesthetical appeal and meet the practical needs of its users – whether for leisure, information or education. The drawing element of the job, if any, usually extends to providing blueprints or rough visuals for others (technical illustrators, artists, typesetters, image originators or printers) to execute. Design work can very greatly according to the nature of the content.

The use of freelancers or agencies to design books or websites is widespread. They are commonly commissioned by editors or production staff, and by in-house designers. Small publishers, without in-house staff, may ask a good printer to help with the design; and in some large firms issuing relatively straightforward books, editors or production controllers may design the books while commissioning freelance designers for covers. Many titles – for example fiction, lightly or unillustrated non-fiction, academic and professional books – follow pre-set typographic templates.

In-house staff tend to be employed by medium to large houses, designing covers or more complex illustrated books (from illustrated adult and children's non-fiction to textbooks), and by the more established book packagers. They will work in a design or production department, reporting directly to the manager. The design manager, responsible for the overall brand of all the firm's books, is concerned with the deployment of in-house and external services, budgets, scheduling and administration. Senior designers may coordinate the work of junior designers; there may be design assistants; and some in-house designers specialize in particular lists. The design of book covers for most kinds of books, other than the most utilitarian, requires specific design attention which is carried out by in-house cover designers, or freelancers under the supervision of the art director.

> The cover design is usually carried out separately from the text design

The design of promotional material may be the responsibility of in-house book designers, or solely of designers attached to the promotion department; or freelance designers or agencies commissioned by that department. The preparation of artwork is mainly done externally. Only a few large publishers (such as those publishing atlases and guidebooks) have in-house technical illustrators or cartographers. Some publishers and packagers employ illustrators and designers on short-term contracts. Photography is normally commissioned.

Design brief

The point at which a designer is first involved with a new book varies. It may occur before or after the author has completed the manuscript, the designer receiving either an edited or unedited copy. By then the book's overall parameters (for example format, extent, illustrations, binding, paper) have been planned.

In some firms editors personally brief designers while in others design meetings are organized, attended by the production team and sometimes the sales staff. The outcome may be a production specification, a budget, and the schedule. It is vital for the designer to be given a clear brief by the editor at the outset. A designer may be able to suggest alternative ideas to save money or to improve sales potential. Assuming the book is not part of a fixed format series or that a pre-existing design cannot be adapted to suit it, the designer's opening tasks are to prepare the type specification and page layout which are supplementary to the book's overall production specification.

Type specification and page layout

The type specification sets out how the main text elements should be typeset in respect of typefaces, sizes, and line lengths, and of the positioning and spacing of the elements. The elements include:

- body text,
- headings – the hierarchy of chapter heads, subheadings, etc.,
- displayed quotations – broken off from the main text,
- tables,
- captions for illustrations,
- running heads at the top of the page, and
- page numbers.

The page layout is a graphic representation of the printed page – invariably of two facing pages. Layouts are based on a grid – the underlying framework within which text and illustrations are placed on the page.

> A grid is the graphic design equivalent of a building's foundations. As we read from left to right and top to bottom, a grid is generally a series of vertical and horizontal lines. The vertical lines will relate to the column widths, while the horizontal will be determined by the space that a line of type occupies. (Roberts and Thrift, page 18)

Layout and typographic style considerably affect the readers' perception of a book. The two are interdependent and should, if well designed, allow the author's work to be presented consistently and flexibly, taking into account the content, aims, character, market, and technical and cost constraints of the book. Book typography has four main functions (Mitchell and Wightman, 2005):

- *readability* – the text should be comfortable to read,
- *organization* – the structure of the text should be clearly communicated,
- *navigation* – information in the book should be easy to find, and
- *consistency* – the overall effect is to create a unified whole.

The main text of this book is typeset in Scala and is unjustified (i.e. it has no fixed margin on the right-hand side); the boxed panels are in Scala Sans

A double-page spread from the *Rapid* reading programme from Heinemann

Adobe Caslon Pro

abcdefghijklmnopqrstuvwxyz 1234567890 1234567890

ABCDEFGHIJKLMNOPQRSTUVWXYZ fiflffiffl ½ ¼ ¾

At endre magna faccum velessis ad eu feuguercin henit lore et, vulla at, sequat,
consenibh et wisl iustie erosto odolessequat in vel utatue duis aliquam, quatem exeriure
vel ullam. Con utate te velit illumsan ullandre corperat alit nonsenim adit lutatie dunt
utpatie conse facipit at velesse quismol orperci tisi. Pit veliquate dolortie molutatem
ipsum vel do consenqu ipsustisi. El doloborem velis autet ad te ter luptatue ming estrud
esse modit laor aci tin hent dolortissi.

Adobe Garamond Pro

abcdefghijklmnopqrstuvwxyz 1234567890 1234567890

ABCDEFGHIJKLMNOPQRSTUVWXYZ fiflffiffl ½ ¼ ¾

At endre magna faccum velessis ad eu feuguercin henit lore et, vulla at, sequat, consenibh
et wisl iustie erosto odolessequat in vel utatue duis aliquam, quatem exeriure vel ullam.
Con utate te velit illumsan ullandre corperat alit nonsenim adit lutatie dunt utpatie conse
facipit at velesse quismol orperci tisi. Pit veliquate dolortie molutatem ipsum vel do
consenqu ipsustisi. El doloborem velis autet ad te ter luptatue ming estrud esse modit laor
aci tin hent dolortissi.

Adobe Jenson Pro

abcdefghijklmnopqrstuvwxyz 1234567890 1234567890

ABCDEFGHIJKLMNOPQRSTUVWXYZ fiflffiffl ½ ¼ ¾

At endre magna faccum velessis ad eu feuguercin henit lore et, vulla at, sequat, consenibh et
wisl iustie erosto odolessequat in vel utatue duis aliquam, quatem exeriure vel ullam. Con
utate te velit illumsan ullandre corperat alit nonsenim adit lutatie dunt utpatie conse facipit
at velesse quismol orperci tisi. Pit veliquate dolortie molutatem ipsum vel do consenqu
ipsustisi. El doloborem velis autet ad te ter luptatue ming estrud esse modit laor aci tin hent
dolortissi.

Typefaces
popular for
blogs and
web pages are
Georgia and
Verdana

Factors that should be taken into account are the fitting of the author's manuscript
into the desired extent; the ability of certain typefaces to cope with mathematics
or foreign languages, or to ease reading by early or poor-sighted readers; their
suitability for reduction if the book is to be reprinted subsequently in a reduced
paperback format; and the typefaces available from a supplier. The designer
presents one or more designs in the form of mock-ups to the editorial and
production staff for their comments and approval – usually specimen pages are
produced.

There are a variety of typefaces commonly used in books, ranging from
traditional faces, such as Bembo or Garamond, to *sans serif* fonts (without the
finishing strokes at the ends of letters) including Frutiger, Helvetica and Univers.

Typographic mark-up

Once the complete manuscript is edited, the designer may carry out the typographic mark-up, that is the addition of typesetting instructions to the manuscript or disk. Some instructions, such as the mark-up of the heading hierarchy and use of italic or bold within the text, may have been marked in copy-editing. The copy-editor may have implemented a system of coding to mark the different text elements. The designer checks, for instance, the editor's hierarchy of headings to ensure they conform to the agreed type specification, and may want them modified. The typesetter follows the specification or style coding. However, depending on the complexity of the material, the designer may indicate the design treatment of recurring text matter which, though covered by the specification, may still need to be marked by using abbreviations or codes. Complex text (including tables) as well as displayed text, such as that of the prelims, may require specific mark-up.

Design

Designers have technical proficiency and usually a vocational qualification. Underpinning design is a thorough knowledge of typography and the ways in which books and covers are put together. Mastery of software such as Adobe InDesign and Photoshop is essential. Designers need perception, clarity of thought, an ability to take a raw manuscript (perhaps badly presented), to analyse it, and come up with an effective design within financial and technical constraints. They should be able to anticipate the problems of readers. It calls for a combination of imagination, knowledge and understanding of current technical processes and current software, awareness of the work of leading freelancers and of trends and fashions in book design. For cover design a creative mind is pre-eminent, combined with a gut feeling of what sells.

Designers must develop the ability to extract a brief – tactfully overcoming some editors' quirks and preconceptions. They must be able to explain to authors, editors and sales staff, who rarely think in shape, colour and form, how they arrived at a solution, and why it is the best. They must be able to give clear and unambiguous briefs and instructions to other designers, illustrators, production staff and printers.

Highly illustrated work requires designers to get under the skin of a subject, to undertake research if necessary, to ask probing questions of experts and to pay due regard to ethnic or cultural sensitivities. The establishment of the all-important rapport with in-house staff and external suppliers takes time and experience to develop. The handling of artists, illustrators and photographers, some of whom can be awkward, calls for a special mixture of tact, pleading or coercion to induce them to produce their best work.

Most designers work on many books simultaneously, all at different stages in production. Thus, like editors, they need to be flexible and self-organizing.

SKILLS

Illustrations

The illustrations may reach the designer before the author has handed over the manuscript to the publisher. The designer may have briefed the author or supplied the editor with guidelines to help the author prepare drawn illustrations. Designers are usually responsible for commissioning the technical illustrators or artists who execute the final artwork – often prepared on-screen in software such as Adobe Illustrator. In children's books, more traditional techniques of illustration may still be used.

When many complex diagrams need to be drawn, the designer prepares an artwork specification to serve as a technical reference for illustrators.

Chosen freelance illustrators or artists are contacted directly, or are recruited from artist's agents or commercial studios. The designer, who may have developed or sometimes revisualized the author's roughs, briefs the contact about the purpose of each illustration and the style of execution (including the final size) and gives a deadline for completion; the cost is estimated in advance.

The finished artwork returns. The designer checks that the brief has been followed and that the technical standard of the artwork is suitable for processing and reproduction by the printer. Correction cycles follow. The designer ensures that mistakes attributable to the illustrator are not charged to the publisher.

Proofing stages

The page layout for this book was done by the designer using InDesign

With unillustrated books that go straight to page proofs, the edited and coded file (together with the type specification and grid) is sent off to the typesetter. For a book with illustrations grouped on pages, the designer provides a layout. When illustrations are interspersed with the text, the sized artwork and photographs are sent off with the text, or the designer instructs the typesetter to leave specified spaces for the illustrations to be inserted later. The designer may fine-tune the typography and correct any bad page breaks or layouts at page-proof stage.

With more complex illustrated books, the designer controls and plans completely the book's layout by means of a manual layout on screen, using Adobe InDesign or QuarkXPress. The designer may be involved with the final selection of photographs and advises whether they will reproduce well. The layout of a page can affect the choice, and the integration of text and illustration influences the sizes of photographs – these may need to be adjusted or cropped. At this stage the designer may work with low-resolution scans of the images, which enables proofs to be generated showing the illustrations. The designer tunes the ensuing page proofs and any illustration proofs, spotting visual errors which authors, editors and proofreaders may fail to recognize.

When the book is correct and ready for printing, the typesetter produces the digital file of the book in one or more formats such as a high-resolution portable document format (PDF) file used by the printer, a low-resolution PDF file and an XML file. There may be further stages undertaken by the printer to ensure the supplied PDF is reproducible by their system (a *pre-flight* check), and on colour books various kinds of proofs to verify the colour reproduction.

InDesign: software competition and change

Sally Hughes, Senior Lecturer, Oxford International Centre for
Publishing Studies, and freelance software trainer

E★PERT

'I would never go back.' This comment is from a senior designer with a magazine
publisher on their recent change from QuarkXPress to Adobe InDesign. It is not
only in magazine publishing where this comment is heard. InDesign is taking
over from QuarkXPress for design and page layout tasks in book publishing.
When faced with the need to make such a change, most designers have a
genuine concern for efficiency. Will there be an effect on their knowledge of
short cuts, their mental map of how to construct documents, or how they use
typography? But those designers provided with some training support have
experienced little difficulty in transferring skills to the new software.

Why change? Users have mentioned difficulties obtaining technical support
from QuarkXPress, and price is also a factor. While QuarkXPress and InDesign
are similar in price if purchased individually, InDesign is available with additional
software, such as Photoshop and Acrobat, in the Adobe Creative Suite package.
These are industry standard products for image editing and PDF (portable
document format) creation and manipulation. Adobe Illustrator (drawing
software), and Adobe Bridge (file management software) are also part of Creative
Suite. Add to this Adobe Dreamweaver, the website creation and management
software, and you have an attractive and difficult-to-resist package in Creative
Suite 3.

InDesign offers powerful publishing-oriented features for everyone working
on print projects. Editors enjoy the text-based Story Editor view of the file which
presents the text in a scrolling window instead of broken into pages. Designers
like the easy access to text and object features from the panels and their menus,
while production enjoy the pre-flight support.

Many publishing companies, Penguin, OUP, Elsevier, Taylor & Francis and
Usborne Books among them, have transferred new projects to InDesign in recent
years. They are still running QuarkXPress to ensure access to the electronic files
for completed projects when needed for new editions or reprints. The changeover
process is not without its problems. Felicity Brooks, Editorial Director of Usborne
Books at Home, comments: 'We trialled InDesign in a small department to
test the use of the new software "in theory". The designers all love it. However,
rolling out the software in a useful and commercial way requires a considerable
investment in training as well as in the software itself. In the long term it will be
fantastic, but there are issues around making sure everyone is able to work at the
same rate as with the old software.'

Aldus PageMaker (InDesign's predecessor) was quickly overtaken by
QuarkXPress in the mid-1980s as Quark's superior accuracy and keyboard
short cuts found favour with designers. While it is unlikely that Quark will be
completely replaced, the publishing industry is changing over to InDesign. The
positive reception for the application and the difficulties posed by any change
in the publishing workflow make it unlikely that Quark will regain its supreme
position.

Highly illustrated colour books

Some books are sold on the quality of their design and pictorial content, such as illustrated non-fiction and textbooks. The approach to the design of these titles is closer to that of quality magazine and partwork publishing – the designer's role is more central. Fundamentally, the interrelationship of the word extent and illustrations, and the positioning of colour within the book is planned and controlled, page by page, right from the outset. Sample spreads are produced to aid the writing by the authors or contributors. Moreover, such material (supplemented with the cover and a dummy) may be used to interest book clubs and overseas publishers in copublication. The designer normally has a greater say over the format, appearance, art direction and creation of the book, which allows more scope to vary its grid and pace, and to provide surprise elements. Some books, including school and ELT texts, use double-page spreads on topics. The strong headlines, dramatic illustrations and extended captions (often read first) capture the interest of a bookshop browser, mail-order buyer, or learner.

Books for international copublication have special design needs. To gain economies in coprinting (printing two or more editions simultaneously), the colour illustrations should remain unaltered in position, whereas the translations of the text are changed on the presses. The typographic design allows for the greater length of translations (into German, for example); chosen typefaces have the full range of accents; type is only printed in black; type running around illustrations is avoided; type is not reversed out of blocks or colour or illustrations; and illustrations are not culturally specific to the UK.

Cover design

The cover or jacket protects the book, identifies the author and title, and carries the blurb. The ISBN and bar code enable ordering. The cover's main purpose is to sell. The design should inform as well as attract, be true to the contents, and be tuned to the market. The sales objective of the image is more significant in consumer book publishing (especially paperbacks) than other areas because of the importance of impulse purchase; and covers are used by the sales department to sell books well in advance of publication to wholesalers and retailers. The image must be powerful enough to attract a browser to pick the book up within a few seconds, and be clear enough to be reproduced in catalogues of the publisher, of a book club, and of overseas publishers or agents, and on the websites of the publisher and booksellers.

Cover images are usually needed at least six months ahead of publication. The designer is briefed by the commissioning editor and generates rough visuals for approval by the editorial, marketing and sales departments. The chosen treatment is developed, and illustrators, photographers and picture researchers commissioned as necessary. Designers will typeset the copy and the cover will be proofed. The author may be consulted over the cover, or need to be persuaded by the editor of the merits of the publisher's choice. Covers arouse strong passions amongst all participants, and at worst may be revised right up to publication.

PICTURE RESEARCH

Picture research is the selection, procurement and collection of illustrations of
all kinds. The number of in-house picture researchers is very small. They are
concentrated in some of the highly illustrated, non-fiction, adult and children's
book publishers (where they may create a picture library), and the large educational
houses. Some commission photographers. A publisher or packager may, however,
use expert freelance researchers, who specialize in particular subjects and serve a
range of media. Otherwise, picture research for the text or cover may be just part of
an assistant's work in an editorial or covers department.

A general working specification for a book is drawn up in the editorial
department. This covers the title, author, publication date, print run, book's
market and its territorial extent, number of pictures required, ratio of colour to
black and white, page size and picture budget. The picture researcher will be
briefed by the editor or designer usually before the author has completed the
manuscript, to ensure that the pictures are ready for the design stage. The brief can
range from being very specific (the author or editor supplying a complete picture
list citing most sources), less specific (just listing the subjects), to very vague
(requesting pictures to fit the manuscript). It is vital for the researcher to clarify the
brief.

The researcher may read the outline or manuscript in order to generate a list
of ideas for approval by the editor and the author, or amend the picture list supplied
by the author to something more feasible. An estimate of cost is produced, based
on the researcher's experience, and the researcher advises whether the time and
budget allocated are realistic; and potential sources are listed.

The researcher cannot progress quickly with selection without knowing where
to look for an image, and without a relevant set of contacts.

Sourcing pictures

The possible sources, both home and abroad, are varied and include:

- museums,
- libraries,
- archives,
- commercial picture agencies,
- photographers,
- PR departments,
- professional and tourist organizations,
- charities, and
- private individuals.

Some major collections are accessible on the web in low resolution, and there
are low-cost banks of images which can be obtained on disk. Researchers consult
directories and picture source books, museum and library catalogues, guide books,
brochures, magazines, acknowledgement lists in books, and forage in reference
libraries. They build up personal contacts with picture libraries and agencies,
interview photographers, visit photographic exhibitions, and form contacts abroad.

They compile their own records, indexes and address books. Their knowledge accumulates with each assignment.

Photographs can be specially commissioned from photographers. Working to a brief, they will set up a shoot specially for the publisher. This can be expensive, with fees sometimes payable to the subject as well, but it should provide high-quality images. Often the relatives or friends of staff are called upon to act as subjects. Images may be put online during the shoot to ensure the right images have been taken.

The criteria for selecting picture sources include the nature of the material required, such as the subject range, type of material, quality, and the service offered – accessibility, speed and reliability, terms and conditions restricting borrowing or use of material, and cost. Researchers will know which picture libraries are more expensive and from which ones special terms may be sought, perhaps when selecting a number from the same source. Linda Royles, CEO of the British Association of Picture Libraries and Agencies (BAPLA), says:

> If you are doing a book about a specific subject, you are advised to go to an expert – a professor or someone with the world's largest collection on that subject. But if you are just looking for a picture of someone taking a phone call for a design brochure, a search on the web may be sufficient. (*The Bookseller*, 25 August 2006)

With the list of potential sources compiled, the next task is to request and collect the pictures by telephoning, emailing or visiting. The web has made it much

Picture research

SKILLS

While a degree level of education is not essential, some picture researchers have a fine arts degree, helpful in that this develops an appreciation of composition. Knowledge of foreign languages eases contact with overseas sources; and ICT skills are essential.

Picture researchers are only as good as their source address books and accurate visual memories. They must keep up to date and use imagination in research, not just in visualizing fresh uses for remembered pictures but almost instinctively knowing where to start looking for pictures on any subject. Also necessary are methodical thinking, the knack of finding cheap sources, and a dogged persistence to get into new areas, getting behind closed doors. It is vital to forge good relations with sources – on the telephone, in writing and face-to-face. Researchers need the ability to interpret the message the book is trying to convey and, during selection, to make critical judgements on technical possibilities and costs as well as on aesthetic values. An understanding of the complexities of copyright and permission fees backs up their knowledge of sources; and allied to budget consciousness are the skills of negotiation especially with commercial picture agencies. Researchers must be highly organized in their work. As one art director puts it, 'It's a fascinating job – creative as well as administrative and business-like.'

easier to view sample images, and today most images are received from agencies electronically. Under a limited licence, digital files can be used to prepare sample pages, but a full licence must be agreed in order to include the images in the final publication. For non-digital images, replies are reviewed, and the incoming material is logged and labelled with sources' names. The researcher is responsible for the good care of the material, so they select suitable items and quickly return the rejects to avoid paying holding fees and reduce the risk of loss.

The researcher does the initial selection and rejection of the pictures from a large assortment. The criteria for selection include the picture's editorial content – for example does the picture make the points or convey the impression or mood the author intended? Also important are the picture's composition, which should give the content clarity and impact, and reproducibility (tonal range, colour range and definition), bearing in mind the quality of paper and reproduction method to be used. The costs are assessed – reproduction fees, fees for digital use, print fees if buying prints, and search and loss/damage fees. Some pictures may be rejected on the grounds of cost.

Once the researcher has sufficient suitable illustrations, the cost is estimated again and a meeting held with the editor and designer to make the next selection. It might be that the researcher has to find more pictures very quickly before the final selection is made. Photographs must be ready by first proof stage to enable the designer to start the page layout. The researcher organizes the pictures for handover to the designer, and supplies the picture credit copy and information for the captions (provided by the sources of the photographs) to the editor.

The next task is to write to the sources for copyright permission to reproduce pictures, and to negotiate the fees. These will depend upon the territories and languages required, the print run, and the size (whole page, half page or quarter page), whether the image is for a cover/jacket or the inside of the book and whether electronic publication is also proposed. The researcher passes the suppliers' invoices for payment and calculates the total picture costs. After checking the page proofs (some sources want copies), the book is printed, and the final responsibility is to return the pictures to the sources when they come back from the printer.

PRODUCTION

The publisher's production department is the link between editors and designers and external suppliers. As the publisher's big spender, it buys raw materials and the services of the suppliers who manufacture the books. As publishers move further into digital publishing, the department increasingly deals with new technology developers and has the responsibility for reorganizing workflows. The production department manages the electronic prepress technologies and the digital archive of the publisher's products for print and electronic publication.

Production and book design go hand in hand. Production staff may design the books or hire freelance designers, or in-house book designers report to the head of production – if there is not a separate design department. The production department gives the accounts department information on anticipated costs and their likely timing, details of work in progress, and materials held in stock.

In a small firm an editor may carry out production duties or use freelancers or external companies which provide a project management/production service; but with increasing size a firm will employ production specialists.

In some publishers, production activities are split. One section deals with the prepress process: essentially concerned with originating the products with external suppliers, or creating them in-house; and with the maintenance of the digital archive and its internal and external connections. Another section organizes and purchases the manufacturing of books and journals: essentially from printers and paper suppliers; and sometimes of other non-print items, such as CD-ROMs and DVDs and their packaging.

Provisional estimates

The production manager, or an automated costing system, supplies the commissioning editor with estimates of the costs of producing a proposed new title, and may suggest alternative production options. The book is envisaged in broad terms, for example its format, extent, illustrative content, the quality of paper desired, and the binding style. The estimate itemizes the costs across different print runs. Some costs, such as for editorial and design work, will not change with the length of the run, and overall the unit cost will decrease as these fixed costs are spread over a longer print run. They include:

- the origination of illustrations,
- illustration permissions,
- design costs,
- editorial costs (including copy-editing and proofreading),
- typesetting,
- printing and binding,
- paper, and
- cover printing.

Once the author has signed the contract, production may advise the author, directly or via the editor, on how the text should be keyed – some publishers issue authors with style sheets or templates. The production controller, who gathers information from the editor or from preproduction meetings, prepares a specification – a detailed technical description of the book.

The book's desired physical attributes, the amount of money and time available for its production, and any special market needs (particular typefaces, a subsequent paperback edition or co-edition) are taken into account, and the choice of production processes and materials is made. In children's publishing, ensuring product safety is vital.

Print and paper buying

The specification is sent to one or more suppliers so that they submit an estimate or quotation. Although there are printers that carry out all the processes, they may not do all economically or well. The typesetting and printing specifications may be sent to different specialist firms, known as trade suppliers.

A publisher deals with a core of regular and trusted suppliers whose technology, machinery, staff, strengths and weaknesses are known; but new ones are tried. Sometimes price schedules are negotiated with major print suppliers for standard types of work, which reduces the need for quotations and simplifies estimating. Suppliers may offer discounts on titles processed in batches or during slack periods. Moreover, the long time (for example six to 18 months) books take to produce gives publishers and packagers the option of using overseas suppliers (for example in Europe, the Far East or the USA). Most colour book printing now goes abroad. The competitiveness of overseas suppliers is affected greatly by exchange rates, but other factors such as freight and communication costs, longer timescales, and the book's final destination are considered.

> While monochrome paperback novels remain, almost without fail, the exclusive domain of UK book printers, an increasing number of high-end print jobs end up on the continent, in places including Italy, Spain and France. And as membership of the European Union blossoms, this is presenting even more opportunities for publishers to place their work overseas. (*The Bookseller*, 23 March 2007)

Suppliers are assessed on five main criteria:

- *price,*
- *quality of work,*
- *service* – the ability to keep to dates, or to make up for slippage, and communication,
- *capability* – skills and machinery, and
- *capacity* – the ability to handle larger jobs/reprint quickly.

The priority given to each varies according to the type of work. For example, a small saving from the cheapest source may be outweighed if that supplier produces inferior work or misses dates. Cost savings can be achieved by sending work abroad, but if there are time sensitivities – for example the possible need for a quick reprint – the more prudent approach is to print in the UK. The environmental impact of shipping finished copies is being studied by some publishers.

The quotations are assessed, prices sometimes negotiated downwards and the work awarded. From the quoted prices, another in-house estimate is prepared. Paper is a major cost item and is bought either by the printer, or by the publisher from a paper merchant or directly from a mill. Pulp and paper is a world commodity subject to exchange rates and to price instability. During periods of price fluctuations or of real or imagined shortages, publishers may peg the price by buying forward, or store paper as an insurance against non-availability for quick reprints, even though that ties up the publisher's cash and incurs storage costs. Some publishers are responsive to environmental concerns, for example by choosing to purchase paper derived from sustainable forests and made with minimum pollutants; others use acid-free materials to ensure that their books and journals will last. The print run for the final Harry Potter volume, *Harry Potter and the Deathly Hallows* (2007), was printed on recycled paper, blended with virgin

Paper

Adrian Bullock, Principal Lecturer, Oxford International Centre for Publishing Studies

E★PERT

Paper is a versatile material which is strong enough to be used in a car, and soft enough to wipe your mouth with.

It can trace its origins back to China at the beginning of the second century (105 AD), when it was made from rags, hemp and old fishing nets. However, since the 1860s, most paper has been made from wood pulp, predominantly from softwood: coniferous trees, such as pine and spruce. These trees are used because of their longer fibres, which give paper its strength; and, because they grow best in temperate climates, most of the world's wood pulp is produced in northern countries like Canada or Finland. Pulp can be produced from broad-leaved, hard wood trees like oak or beech, but this is not generally done – their fibres are too short. This is also true of tropical hardwoods which grow in the rainforests of South America and Africa. The threat here does not come from papermaking: the rainforests are being cleared, and the trees burned, to make way for cattle ranching, agriculture and mining.

Trees for papermaking are planted as a crop, just like rice or wheat; and, like a crop, they are harvested at a later date – perhaps 25 to 30 years later, or sometimes even longer. Only part of the felled tree ends up as paper: the trunk, for example, is usually turned into timber for the furniture and construction industries. For every tree cut down, at least three seedlings are planted to ensure that the paper and the timber industries do not run out of their basic raw material – wood.

Despite the predictions of a paperless world, paper consumption has, if anything, increased over the past 15 years, bringing with it growing pressure on the forests as the need for pulp intensifies.

In 1993 the Forest Stewardship Council (FSC) was established 'to promote environmentally appropriate, socially beneficial, and economically viable management of the world's forests' (fsc.org).

Publishers, as major consumers of printing papers, are increasingly aware of the need to source their paper responsibly; and more and more books now carry the FSC logo with the statement that the publisher 'makes every effort to ensure that the paper used in its books is made from trees that are legally sourced from well managed and credibly certified forests'. Publishers also use recycled papers to print their books on, though evidence indicates that they still prefer papers made from virgin rather than waste pulp.

Paper comes in many qualities, from newsprint to coated art paper. The product determines the quality of the paper, as much as the paper determines the quality of the product. The publisher's skill lies in being able to match the paper to the product.

Paper, as a natural product, has properties which are critical to the publisher, as well as the printer, and binder. In addition to a paper's colour (shade), roughness/smoothness (finish), and the quality of the pulp used to make it (furnish), the publisher needs to give careful thought to the following:

Weight: measured in grams per square metre (gsm/gm²); in the US, paper is measured in pounds per 500 sheets of a certain size. Heavy papers make heavy books. This can be a problem for the reader, who might get tired of holding it; and for the publisher, because heavy books cost more to distribute than light ones. Book papers range between 70 and 115 gsm.

Bulk: the thickness of a sheet of paper, measured in microns. A more useful way of measuring bulk is by volume basis, which makes it possible to calculate the bulk of a complete book, and not just one sheet of paper. Bulky papers are thick, and can be relatively light: for example, a tissue.

Opacity: a paper's lack of transparency. Matter printed on high opacity paper (90 per cent plus) cannot be seen from the other side of the sheet. Opacity is not really an issue in work where lines of text are printed back to back on each side of the sheet, such as a novel. However, in highly illustrated work, like an art book, with pictures appearing anywhere on the page, high opacity paper is essential. Opacity comes more from the paper's finish and its furnish, than from its weight or thickness. Increasing a paper's weight does not necessarily make it more opaque.

Grain direction: the direction in which the fibres lie as they are made into paper. Good bookmaking requires the grain direction to run parallel with the spine (right grain), though this is not always possible, especially with books printed on a web press. Books bound with the grain running from side to side (wrong grain) handle less well, and may develop a wave along the foredge. Covers printed wrong grain often bow.

Getting the paper right is the first step to getting the product right.

---

pulp from forests certified by the Forest Stewardship Council. There is debate over which is preferable from an environmental point of view, recycled or FSC-certified paper.

Paper has both weight and thickness (or bulk). Short books can be bulked out with a thicker paper; long books may need to have thinner paper. Recycled paper tends to be thinner than virgin papers. Paper may also be judged on its opacity – the degree to which image or text shows through to the other side of the page – and its colour or shade – from white through to cream or ivory. Coated papers are used for highly illustrated titles such as art books. Acid-free papers have a longer life.

There is also a range of sizes in which books can be printed. A trade paperback is 198 × 129 mm (also called B format) and the mass-market paperback size is 178 × 110 mm (A format). Popular formats for hardbacks are demy octavo (216 × 138 mm) and royal octavo (234 × 156 mm). The dimension head to tail is given first in the UK, but in the rest of Europe and the USA the convention is to give the width dimension first.

Table 9.1 Standard book formats

Format	Dimensions
A4	297 × 210 mm
Demy quarto	276 × 219 mm
Crown quarto	246 × 189 mm
Pinched crown quarto	Up to 248 × 175 mm
Royal octavo	234 × 156 mm
Demy octavo (C format)	216 × 138 mm
A5	210 × 148 mm
B format	196 × 129 mm
A format	178 × 110 mm

The format of *Inside Book Publishing* is pinched crown quarto

Scheduling and project management

The production controller draws up the schedule of the internal and external operations that end with the delivery of bound copies to the warehouse a few weeks ahead of the publication date. The schedule, related to those of other books, takes account of any optimum publication date, cashflow demands, the time needed for the tasks and to route material to and from suppliers.

Production staff monitor progress and chase editors, designers and external suppliers to keep to agreed dates. As all the book's material passes between editor and designer, and between publisher and suppliers it is handled by production at every stage, as are any problems with suppliers. Outgoing material is accompanied by documentation and orders; incoming material is logged, sent on to editors and designers, and return dates agreed. If the return dates are not adhered to, the machine time booked at the printers will be missed and the book unduly delayed.

Content management systems

In some publishers, the prepress processes are carried out in-house and the documents progress through the stages and staff entirely in digital form. Content management systems (CMS) were first used by journal and reference publishers faced with processing and reusing large amounts of text data. They are designed to manage the creation, handling, storage and delivery of content for publication, and subsequent revision. Content is stored without print-specific formatting, and typically XML is used to tag the content using standardized templates. As digital publishing becomes more important, workflows are adapted to hold content in properly archived files, which can then be used to publish products on different platforms. Journals publishers have led the way in creating a production route that enables articles to be published rapidly online.

Additional functionality includes workflow management and access control. Such systems monitor the movement of jobs through the stages, and the workloads and performance of staff. Automated alerts track the progress of files as manual or automated sequences are applied. Users of the system are given differing levels of access. Authors may be part of the process – for example journal authors may be asked to write using a template supplied by the publisher; they can also track their articles online through the production process.

Monitoring costs and quality

Many books, especially if illustrated, may change from their original concept during the writing and design stages. A new format may be chosen or the number of illustrations varied. Deviations from the original estimate and specification are monitored and costed. There is a constant risk that the estimate of costs made at the outset will be exceeded. Substantial proof corrections quickly erode a title's profitability. Costs incurred to date are recorded and revised estimates of total costs produced, particularly at the page-proof stage. Then the publisher normally fixes the book's price and the number to be printed, influenced, for example, by the actual advance subscription orders from booksellers. Suppliers' invoices are subsequently checked, passed for payment, or queried.

The production controller checks the completeness of material at every stage as well as the accuracy of the instructions from the editor and designer, the quality of illustration originals sent to suppliers, and the quality of material returned. Technical advice is given to editors and designers to help them in their work. Constant contact with suppliers' representatives, and visits to suppliers maintain relationships.

Highly illustrated quality colour books may involve the production manager or controller in approving the sheets of each section run off the press – whether in the UK or abroad – and taking responsibility for the quality on behalf of the publisher/packager. The printing is compared against the final proof to ensure that corrections have been made, and that the colour quality matches the values agreed at the contract proof stage.

Advance copies of the bound stock are checked to ensure that the specified materials have been used, and that the binding, as well as the overall quality of the product, meets the publisher's standards. Exceptionally if a major error is discovered, an enquiry is held to determine who is responsible and has to pay. Finally, all the costs of producing the book are compiled.

Controllers also cost and organize reprints and new editions; some large publishers employ staff solely for this task. The publisher or packager owning the digital file does not always use the original printer in which case the job is moved to the new supplier.

Electronic prepress technologies are changing fast as are the opportunities for epublishing in various forms. Production plays a key role in their introduction and in ensuring that the publisher's titles are archived in suitable digital form to facilitate their exploitation.

The printing of editions for other firms (for example English and foreign language co-editions) involves supplying the rights department with estimates of costs. The costs will include printing the bulk order – or if the buyer does the printing, the cost of supplying digital files – and costs of imprint changes – for example, the name of the co-publisher will have to appear on the title page instead of the original publisher's and the details on the copyright page will change; all of this makes a halt in the printing and costs money. When the publisher or packager prints foreign language editions, the overseas publishers supply the file of the translated text which is checked by production to ensure it fits the layout of the

> The contract proof is the final colour proof and represents an agreement between the publisher and the printer

colour illustrations. Production staff may also be concerned with the purchasing of the manufacturing of non-print items and their special retail or mail-order packaging requirements.

Suppliers are chosen according to cost, technology, and quality. Significant cost savings can be achieved by outsourcing typesetting and printing to countries in the Far East or Europe. Companies in India, for example, not only offer typesetting but also IT services (digitization and tagging) and editorial and design work. It is now possible to outsource the whole process from receipt of the author's text through to the digital file for the printer.

Organization of the production department

Within a production department, there are commonly three main levels of job.

SKILLS

Production

Most production staff have a vocational qualification or equivalent professional background. Fundamental to production is a thorough understanding of current technical processes, of machinery and of materials and, in international buying, of freight systems and methods of payment. Knowledge of languages is useful in a department handling international co-editions. Numeracy, computer literacy skills, the ability to see alternative options and the consideration of all components are necessary in costing titles. Project management skills cover planning and progress chasing skills – ascertaining and clarifying objectives, setting priorities, assessing strengths and weaknesses of colleagues/suppliers, foreseeing crunch points, and the development of specifications and schedules. Strong negotiations skills are required to deal with a range of suppliers.

Effective and fluent communication with in-house staff and external suppliers is crucial. Production staff must be able to work with editors and designers as a team even though their priorities of tight cost control and the maintenance of dates may conflict with those of editors and designers.

Much of the work is highly administrative, requiring a good memory and meticulous attention to detail and record keeping. While friendly working relationships are formed with suppliers, production staff must never get too close to suppliers otherwise the negotiating edge is lost. Sometimes they have to be very tough, and they must have the integrity to reject any bribes offered by suppliers.

Production staff come under great pressure. As the buffer between publisher and suppliers they receive kicks from all sides. They must buy competitively, conserve the cash, meet the deadlines, and not make mistakes, which can be expensive to correct. Much time is spent troubleshooting and trying to keep everyone happy. They need to resolve problems, to think laterally and find the best solution, to switch quickly from one thing to another, and thrive under the strain; and to have the constitution of an ox to withstand suppliers' hospitality – still generous.

Production manager or director

They are responsible for the purchasing policy on sources of supply; establishing standard book sizes and papers; controlling the flow of work and maintaining quality standards; contributing to the preparation of the publishing programme by planning schedules and cost budgets for forthcoming books; and responding to major technical changes such as managing the electronic prepress services. This manager contributes to the firm's profitability by buying materials and services at the most economic cost, by conserving the firm's cash by influencing the timing of major items of expenditure and by obtaining the longest possible credit periods from suppliers. The manager also handles the production of certain important books.

Production controller

This role is responsible for seeing books through the production stages from manuscript to receipt of bound copies. They may specialize in part of the list, for example working alongside certain editors.

Production assistant

Some people start their production careers at this level. The production assistant gives clerical or administrative support to the department. They monitor proofs and production schedules, chase editors and suppliers, and record production costings.

PRODUCTION PROCESSES

Typesetting

The core business of a typesetter is text processing. This could mean rekeying manuscripts at very low rates or taking the disks supplied by the authors and incorporating editorial corrections from the marked-up hard copy. They may simply produce typeset pages from fully coded disks supplied by the publisher, or convert the publisher's file to XML after a book is printed; or they may digitize the backlist.

There is a diminished role for typesetters in a world where designers supply the finished files.

> The typesetters that remain specialize in the larger, more complex jobs, such as legal and science or medical reference books, and, being labor intensive, much of this work is carried out in countries such as India. Some publishers supply authors with templates, however, and so for text books the authors essentially typeset the book as they write. (Bann, page 48)

Some firms offer additional editorial and design services while others concentrate on highly technical material or text database management. The vast number of titles with no or minimal illustrations do not require designers to layout the pages – the typesetters' largely automated pagination systems do it for the publishers. They can generally take a 100,000-word manuscript and submit page proofs to a publisher within two weeks – much faster if supplied with coded disks.

Typesetters use a variety of applications, such as QuarkXPress and Adobe InDesign. Only typesetters who have specialist-trained staff operate the very expensive and sophisticated programs designed especially for academic books and journals (such as Arbortext Advanced Print Publisher – formerly 3B2). LaTeX, pronounced 'laytek', is an open source program with many variants, designed by mathematicians in Chicago for authors of physics and mathematics to present their papers and books full of equations in an attractive way.

The typesetter will supply paper proofs or PDF files for checking by the publisher and author. The publisher will usually ask the typesetter to convert the output of its pagination systems into PostScript (PS) files or PDF files. Where PostScript is a page description language, a programming language, PDF is a particular file format – it can 'contain fonts, images, printing instructions, keywords for searching and indexing, interactive hyperlinks, and movies' (adobe.com). From such files printers are able to output text and graphics straight to plate.

Reproduction of illustrations

Illustrations may be prepared or sourced in digital form and can be provided to the typesetter as EPS (encapsulated PostScript) files – from a drawing program – or as TIFFs (tagged image file format) or JPEGs (joint photographic experts group) – for half-tones. Non-digital originals of illustrations are converted to digital form. This can be done in-house, using an application such as Adobe Photoshop – or by a professional repro (reproduction) house, the typesetter or the printer – to sizes specified by the designer.

Book printing presses cannot reproduce directly the continuous shades or tones of colour appearing in photographs or pencil drawings, thus 'the half-tone

A Heidelberg colour press with printed output

process' is used. The image of the black and white or colour original is screened, i.e. broken into a series of dots of varying size with larger, closer or adjoining dots in dark areas; and smaller, further apart, or no dots at all in light areas. When printed, the dots create the illusion of continuous shades.

Printing a full colour image requires a four-colour process. The image needs to be broken down into four basic colours: cyan (blue), magenta (red), yellow, and black (known as key). These colours, used to put ink on to paper, are called 'CMYK', or *process colours*, and are *subtractive primaries*. Red, green and blue (RGB) are the *additive primaries*, used in TV screens and computer monitors. They cannot be used in printing. Colour separation can be done using a scanner, or a digital image can be saved as CMYK in an application such as Adobe Photoshop. In order to print a four-colour image, you ideally need a four-colour press, capable of printing all four colours in one impression. It is possible to print a four-colour image on a two-colour press, but this is less efficient way and can cause quality problems. Various kinds of proofs are submitted to the publisher before the final digital file of the illustrations is accepted. If necessary, books can be printed in six colours. This process was used, for example, for Kevin McCloud's *Choosing Colours* (2007), where orange and green inks were printed after the CMYK to create a six-colour job.

Imposition and platemaking

The printing plates on a press do not print one page at a time. Rather each sheet of paper, printed both sides, carries 8, 16 or 32 pages (or multiples of these), and is subsequently folded several times and cut to make a section (or signature) of the bound book. Since printers have different sized presses and different binding machinery, each printer is responsible for its own imposition: the arrangement of the pages that will be printed on each side of the sheet so that once the sheet is printed and folded the pages will be in the right sequence and position. The publisher will supply the printer with PS or PDF files that have been prepared by the designer or typesetter. The printer then imposes the pages on to each plate – this is called computer to plate (CTP).

Online content

Low-resolution PDF files can be conveniently put on the web for either downloading or viewing within a browser. The user sees a replica of the final printed page. Journal articles are often presented in PDF for the ease of librarians and others wanting a common standard, and for publishers who are working with print-designed documents. 'PDF files can offer most of the attributes of paper documents – page structure, elaborate graphics, and meticulous design – along with a host of extra features that can only work electronically' (Kasdorf, page 226).

Content may also be originated as, or converted into XML data. Structured mark-up of the text using XML, independent of any typographic mark-up, allows the text to be published in different ways. From a source XML file, the content can be published as a book, an ebook, an HTML (HyperText Markup Language) file for the web, or on a handheld device. Publishers also find it easier to sell XML data to third parties for electronic publication. Its use facilitates the online linking of elements such as bibliographic references and illustrations. The growing use of

A sample of XML
for *Business: The
Ultimate Resource*
(A & C Black, 2006)

```
<?xml version="1.0" encoding="UTF-8"?>
<!DOCTYPE many.htmls SYSTEM 'g:\dtd\busessay.dtd'>
<many.htmls>
    <html id="ID81C13E24-1D4B-4367-ADF9-A30840F5F0BD"
class="ACTIONLIST">
        <head>
          <title>Building a Cross-functional Team</title>
        </head>
        <body>
          <h1>Building a Cross-functional Team</h1>
          <h2 id="IDDB8B2581-D938-46E0-BB70-7BEEC9B8A8D8"
class="ACTIONLIST-GETTING.STARTED">Getting Started</h2>
            <p>Most projects require a wide variety of skills to complete the work
involved, so if you're managing a project of any type, it's likely that you'll have
to work with a group of people from different backgrounds. They may be
drawn from different parts of your organ<UK>isa</UK>
            <US>iza</US>tion; they may come from a number of separate
organ<UK>isa</UK>
            <US>iza</US>tions—wherever they're from, when they come
together, they're known as a <CIT>cross-functional team</CIT>.</p>
            <p>It's the project manager's job to bring cross-functional team
members together and form them into an effective group which operates as
one to achieve the overall goals of the project. Unsurprisingly, this can
sometimes be tricky. However, there are a number of rules which, if followed,
can make team building much easier and more likely to succeed. This
actionlist lays out the basics.</p>
```

XML – what it is and what publishers use it for

Meg Barton, Project Manager, Electronic Products in the Medical
books division, Wiley-Blackwell

E★PERT

XML (extensible markup language) is a method of tagging text so that it can
be used not just by typesetting systems but also by the programs used to build
electronic products like ebooks. Tagging is a way of adding invisible labels to
words in your text. For example, HTML tags are used to impose some basic
formatting on the web. The example below shows the tags for italic in HTML:

> Did you enjoy the film of <i>Pride and Prejudice</i> yesterday?
> Yes, but I liked the version with Colin Firth <i>much</i> better.

The opening tag switches on the italic and the closing one switches it off. HTML
has a single set of tag names.

Here is the same sentence tagged in XML:

<question>Did you enjoy the film of <filmtitle>Pride and Prejudice</filmtitle>
yesterday?</question>

<answer>Yes, but I liked the version with <forename>Colin</forename>
<surname>Firth</surname> <emphasis>much</emphasis> better.
</answer>

There are some important differences to note:

- XML tags identify items according to their *meaning*, rather than just specifying typography or layout.
- Unlike HTML, which has a single set of tag names, the naming for XML tags is not standard or universal. For example it would be equally valid to have named your tag <movietitle> rather than <filmtitle> or <query> rather than <question>.

Anyone can make up their own XML tag names (depending on the sort of items they want to tag), and can devise and use any number of them – which is why XML is called extensible. In the above example you could add more tags to Colin Firth, for example <namegroup> to identify his two names as a group, and maybe <filmstar> to distinguish him further: <filmstar><namegroup><forename >Colin</forename> <surname>Firth</surname></namegroup></filmstar> Apart from a few basic rules about consistency – for example each opening tag must have a closing tag – the only other requirement is to keep a reference list of the tags you have used – this list is called a DTD (Document Type Definition). Any piece of text that obeys these rules is a 'valid' XML document. Different publishers (and other industries) have different names for their tags and develop their own DTDs.

XML tagging of the text can be done by the typesetter as part of the typesetting process. The typesetter just needs to be supplied with a copy of the publisher's DTD. The typesetter can also supply the publisher with XML files either at the same time as the print files for the book ('XML first'), or can run off the XML files at some later date when requested by the publisher.

Publishers are able to use the tagged XML text for a variety of electronic products: ebooks on the web, text on CD, DVD, or PDA, extracts in databases or textbook question banks. Most importantly, the XML-tagged text can also be stored by the publisher to use not just for these things, but for any other electronic medium that might be invented in the future. Commissioning editors and production editors need to have some background knowledge of XML (just as they need to know the typesetting process without having hands-on experience of it). In-house programmers and technical staff will have a detailed knowledge of XML.

It is hoped that XML is the solution that publishers have long been looking for – a way of storing and reusing future-proof content. Unlike its predecessors, this system is likely to survive because of its simplicity and flexibility.

Adobe InDesign by publishers facilitates the origination of XML: 'For those that are working with more complex digital workflows it can also turn layouts into XML . . . preparing content for cross-media publishing' (Martin, page 7).

Publishers or content aggregators look to add value online by generating keywords for content, enabling online searches, and also by identifying text elements or chunks by metadata. For example, a journal publisher can use a DOI (digital object identifier) to identify an article or an illustration within the article.

A DOI name can apply to any form of intellectual property expressed in any digital environment. DOI names have been called 'the bar code for intellectual property': like the physical bar code, they are enabling tools for use all through the supply chain to add value and save cost (doi.org, accessed 20 February 2008). Industry-wide initiatives such as CrossRef enable the linking from references in online journals to the cited article (crossref.org).

Publishers with websites or online services which need regular updating or additions may opt to use a content management system (CMS) – software for managing websites. For some publishers the web is a different medium needing different design approaches, which are not based on linear textual organization and print-derived typographic design. Web pages may be prepared using HTML and supplementary content, such as animations, video clips, and sound recordings. Tricia Austin and Richard Doust write:

> there is no reason why a website should look like the printed page, and a new generation of new-media designers are seizing the opportunity to throw away the rule book and break new ground . . . Designers can introduce sound and movement into their new-media designs. (pages 89–90)

Printing

Most books are printed by offset lithography (abbreviated to *offset* or *litho*). Offset metal plates have a flat surface which is treated so that the areas to be printed attract grease (ink) and repel water; and the non-printing areas attract water and repel ink. A plate is clamped around a cylinder on the press, dampened and inked by rollers. The plate rotates against a rubber coated cylinder (or *blanket*) on to which the inked image is offset and from which the ink is transferred to the paper.

Many offset presses are sheet-fed and vary in plate size and in capabilities. There are also offset presses – known as *web presses* – that print on to a reel of paper. Sheetfed presses would be the usual choice for standard printings of black-and-white books. Web presses produce a folded signature at the end of the operation. This, and their high running speeds, make them attractive for long print runs.

Digital printing

High-speed digital printing has begun to challenge litho printing, particularly for very short runs. Digital printers do not use printing plates – instead they create the impression on the paper with an ink jet or by using toner and electrostatic charge (like in a photocopier). A number of single copy orders can be printed one after the other without the disruption of having to set up the press each time – the computer lines up the next titles. The quality of digital printing has been variable, but is now perfectly acceptable for most monochrome books and much colour work.

The choice of litho or digital printing comes down to economics. Manfred Breede writes: 'Conventional printing processes remain unsurpassed in their ability to reproduce large print runs cost effectively . . . In comparison, the cost per unit of operating a digital printing device is always the same regardless of the run length' (Cope and Phillips, page 35). For runs above 3,000 there are definite cost advantages of litho printing, whereas for runs below 1,000 digital printing makes economic sense. For runs in between, other factors may come into play such as

A Nipson VaryPress 400 web-fed digital book press at Hobbs the Printers, Totton, Hampshire. The web of paper can be seen on the left

the quality or format required. Digital printing facilitates the viability of printing a book with a very short run – for example 50 copies – but also genuine print on demand – where just one copy is ordered by a customer.

Digital printing was first used from the late 1990s by some of the high-level academic and STM publishers issuing titles such as monographs in standard sizes. After the initial printing (probably litho printed), such publishers would face a small but continuing demand. They could reprint a short run by litho or digital printing (whichever gives the lower unit cost), or a very short run by digital printing to hold in stock, or digitally print one copy in response to a firm order. Once the title moves to 'on-demand' status it need never go out of print.

Digital printing offers new ways of working. Wholesalers can use it to produce copies for end-users from digital files supplied by publishers. The printing of hard copies becomes 'distributed' as opposed to being centralized by publishers through their own print suppliers. Publishers can customize for a teacher a pack of teaching resources drawn from a variety of titles for student purchase. Smaller digital presses are now commercially available, and these have the potential to be placed anywhere in the world, in bookshops, libraries and universities, with access to an unlimited catalogue of titles over the internet. The Espresso Book Machine, which can print and bind a 300-page paperback in three minutes, was launched in 2006.

Binding

After printing, the sheets are folded by the printer or possibly by a trade binder. The folded 8-, 16- or 32-page sections are collated in sequence to make up every book. Some hardbacks and some quality paperbacks, especially those printed on coated papers (including some textbooks) have their sections sewn together. With quality hardbacks, the sewn sections are trimmed on three sides (leaving the sewn spine folds intact), end papers are glued to the first and last sections (unless the text paper is sufficiently strong), any decorative head or tail bands added, strong

material glued to the spine to reinforce the hinge with the case, and the spine
sometimes rounded. Meanwhile the case is made by gluing the front and back
boards (and paper backstrip of the spine) to the 'cloth' which in turn is blocked with
the title, author and imprint in gold, silver or a range of different colours. The outer
sides of the end papers are pasted, the finished case dropped over the book (spine-
side up), and the book squeezed. The jacket is printed on a small colour press,
sometimes by another firm. This is often laminated with clear plastic film and
wraps the finished book. Sometimes the printed cover is glued to the case before
binding to produce a *printed paper case* (PPC) or *cover to board* book.

Sewn bindings are stronger but more expensive. Adhesive binding methods
are commonly used for paperbacks and some hardbacks. *Perfect binding* is used
typically for cheap paperbacks – the spine folds of the sections are cut off and the
spine edge of the now individual leaves roughened. Glue is applied to hold the
leaves together and to stick the printed cover to the book, which is then trimmed
on three sides. The cover may have been varnished (on a printing press or special
machine) or laminated. Another method, cheaper than sewing but stronger and
more expensive than perfect binding, is known variously as *slotted, notch* or *burst*
binding. The spine folds of the sections are not cut off. Instead they are perforated
during sheet folding. The binding machine merely injects the adhesive to hold
together the folded sections, applies the cover and trims the book.

Packing and distribution

The printer/binder packs quantities of the book by shrink wrapping, parcelling
or in cartons and delivers them on pallets to the publisher's specified warehouse.
Printers have traditionally delivered the bulk stock of new titles to the publisher's
warehouse, which in turn ships them out to the main retailers and wholesalers.
However, UK printers, competing on service against foreign printers, may deliver
stock directly to some key customers. In the case of print journals, they may deliver
to subscribers.

Now read this

David Bann, *The All New Print Production Handbook*, RotoVision, 2006.
Keith Martin, *Creative Suite 3 Integration*, Focal Press, 2007.

Sources

Tricia Austin and Richard Doust, *New Media Design*, Laurence King, 2007.
Alan Bartram, *Making Books: Design in British publishing since 1945*, British Library and Oak Knoll Press, 1999.
Phil Baines and Andrew Haslam, *Type and Typography*, Laurence King, 2005.
Manfred Breede, 'Plus ça change: Print on demand reverts book publishing to its pre-industrial beginnings', in Bill Cope and Angus Phillips (editors), *The Future of the Book in the Digital Age*, 2006.
Robert Bringhurst, *The Elements of Typographic Style*, version 3.1, Hartley & Marks, 2005.
Simon Creasey, 'Europe is Closer than You Think', *The Bookseller*, 23 March 2007.
Harriet Dennys, 'Picture This', *The Bookseller*, 25 August 2006.
Andrew Dillon, *Designing Usable Electronic Text*, CRC Press, 2004.
David Evans, 'Postscript vs PDF', available from http://www.adobe.com/print/features/psvspdf/
William Kasdorf (editor), *The Columbia Guide to Digital Publishing*, Columbia University Press, 2003.
Marshall Lee, *Bookmaking*, 3rd edition, Norton, 2004.
Ruari McLean, *The Thames and Hudson Manual of Typography*, Thames and Hudson, 1980.
Michael Mitchell and Susan Wightman, *Book Typography: A designer's manual*, Libanus Press, 2005.
Lucienne Roberts and Julia Thrift, *The Designer and the Grid*, RotoVision, 2002.

Web resources

www.bapla.org British Association of Picture Libraries and Agencies.
www.crossref.org CrossRef operates a cross-publisher citation linking system.
www.doi.org International DOI Foundation.
www.tasi.org.uk Technical Advisory Service for Images.
www.worldbank.org/infoshop A video shows the Espresso Book Machine in use at the InfoShop at the World Bank in Washington DC.

CHAPTER 10

Marketing

Marketing within the publishing industry used to be regarded as simply the promotion of new books. In trade publishing, this would involve talking to the literary editors on the national newspapers, securing review coverage, and placing relevant advertisements. Today marketing has a much broader role and marketers play a pivotal role in many aspects of a book's publication. The expansion of the internet has given a prominent role to emarketing, which is a cost-effective method of reaching potential audiences and offers a way for publishers to find out more about their customers.

Marketing staff in large publishing groups may be attached to particular companies, imprints or lists in the group. Many marketing departments consist of just one or two people who do everything, but in medium to large firms there are usually at least three levels: marketing director; marketing or product manager, or promotion controller; and marketing executive or assistant.

Marketing encompasses numerous, diverse activities. The marketing manager may first become involved at the publishing proposal stage or immediately post-contract. They may advise on product development, especially when the project is a large investment. They may be involved in a range of discussions about the book's pricing, its cover, and its target market. From discussions with editors and sales staff, each book is evaluated and decisions made on the promotional material required – to support sales and for the target readership – and what publicity and media coverage should be sought. The marketing budget set may be proportional to the expected sales revenue. It is impossible to promote all books equally and, especially in consumer book and textbook publishing, the lead titles receive by far the largest budgets. The key judgement for every title is deciding how much to spend to generate profitable sales that more than recoup the outlay.

THE MARKET FOR BOOKS

The first step in marketing a product is to understand the nature of the market. A range of data is available on the purchasing behaviour and demographics of the consumer book market. Table 10.1 reveals the factors that influence book purchases. For marketers it shows the importance of having a book in stock in

Table 10.1 Purchase prompts for UK consumers (*source*: 2006 data from Book Facts Online)

Purchase prompt	Percentage of books bought
Saw in shop	35
Read other by author	14
Special information contained	13
Hobby information contained	12
Recommendation	10
Read other in series	5
Saw review in magazine/catalogue	4
Saw review in newspaper	3
On course list	3
Saw film/play on TV	2
Mentioned on TV/radio	1

a shop, the value of building author brands, and the impact of recommendation on a book's sales. Reviews and mentions in the media are by contrast much less important.

There is variation across the population in terms of the number of books bought. The bar chart below shows the distribution amongst adults. Some key features emerge from this. Firstly, 33 per cent of adults do not buy a book at all – how can publishers reach this part of the population? Generic initiatives to encourage reading are important for the industry. A prominent example is World

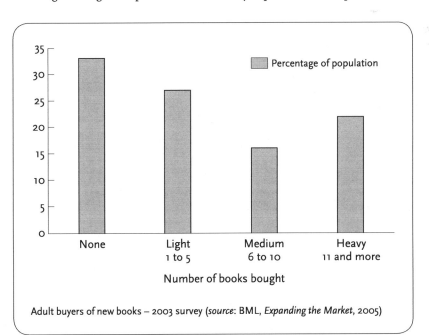

Adult buyers of new books – 2003 survey (*source*: BML, *Expanding the Market*, 2005)

Book Day, and in 2007 schoolchildren received a £1 book token to spend on a specially created £1 book; or they could put it towards the cost of any book. Quick Reads was launched on World Book Day in 2006 to provide 'fast-paced, bite-sized books by bestselling writers for emergent readers, anyone who had lost the reading habit or simply wanted a short, fast read' (niace.org.uk). 2008 was declared the National Year of Reading with the aim of building a greater national love of reading. Other initiatives include City Reads, which began in Seattle in 1998, where a whole city is encouraged to read the same book. In the spring of 2007, the centenary of the birth of Daphne du Maurier, everyone in Brighton was invited to read her novel *Rebecca*. In 2007 the Books for All promotion highlighted black and minority ethnic writers.

Organizations such as the National Literacy Trust and Booktrust are involved in the promotion of reading and literacy (an example of their work is on the facing page). There has been some concern, and mixed evidence, as to whether there has been a decline in reading for pleasure amongst children, but publishers consistently talk of the challenge of getting teenage boys interested in books, especially fiction. Publishers are certainly seeing growth in the sales of graphic novels, including manga, which appeal to a broad readership amongst both children and adults.

Puffin's website for teenage readers (spinebreakers. co.uk) has an editorial board of teenagers

Most publishers point to the changing face of the modern world as a prime mover behind the trend. Today's children are the first generation to grow up more accustomed to digital screens than the printed page; as wireless devices proliferate, kids increasingly understand and appreciate data that is transmitted to them in visual form. (*Publishers Weekly*, 19 February 2007)

This poster showing the England cricketer Monty Panesar was part of a campaign by the National Literacy Trust, using role models to encourage reading amongst boys and men

Libraries play an important part in promoting reading and the use of books, and librarians promote books in a variety of ways, from personal recommendations to working with children and schools to champion reading. Despite this, there has been a noticeable decline in library borrowings, falling from 534.6 m in 1994/5 to 330 m in 2004/5, a drop of 38 per cent (LISU, *Annual Library Statistics*, 2006).

The temptation for publishers is to concentrate on selling to the heavy book buyers, those who purchase a lot of books. They tend to be regular visitors to bookshops and so can be reached by ensuring that the books are in stock and promoted there.

Demographics

Table 10.2 (next page) shows book buying by gender, age and socio-economic group.

The overall picture is that book purchasing tends to increase with age and income. Although it might be assumed that those aged 60 plus would have more time to read, book buying declines at that stage in people's lives. Travelling by public transport encourages reading, as can most readily be seen on the Underground in London. One in five adults read a book when commuting or travelling (Mintel, 2007). Women buy more books than men. Children's books accounted for 25 per cent of purchases. For teenagers there is a lot of competition for their time, including the web and video games, but a BBC survey in 2007 showed that there are 650,000 teenagers who read more than 15 books each year (*The Bookseller*, 6 April 2007). They also mostly visit bookshops rather than buy

In 2006 in the UK, women bought 188 m books and men 128 m

Table 10.2 Book buying in the UK – demographics (*source*: Mintel, *Books*, 2005)

	Visited bookshop in last 3 months	Bought one book or more in last month
All	49	36
Men	46	31
Women	53	40
15–24	44	32
25–34	54	38
35–44	54	39
45–54	55	40
55–64	50	37
65+	41	30
AB	71	53
C1	55	40
C2	39	27
D	32	22
E	30	22

online. The age at which the person left education is also an important factor – those who leave later are bigger consumers of books.

Targeting

With a clear view of the market segments amongst book consumers, publishers can decide whether to target a particular audience. This will have implications for the cover design, where any advertising is placed, and what type of media coverage is planned. Other ways of segmenting the market include by retail channel: there are different demographics for those purchasing books at Waterstone's or in supermarkets. A book may be seen as ideal for promotion through a particular channel.

When HarperCollins published *Blood of Angels* by Michael Marshall in 2005, the target audience was mainly female, ABC1, and 'serious crime aficionados'. The hardback was promoted in the press – there is a link between reading crime and newspaper readership – but not with outdoor advertising – travellers tend to read paperbacks (*The Bookseller*, 10 June 2005).

MARKETING MIX

Marketing activities can be placed under the four general headings of what is known as the marketing mix:

- product,
- price,
- place, and
- promotion.

For lead titles, marketers will prepare full marketing plans which assess the target market for the title and lay out strategies for reaching that market.

Product

The marketing department plays a full role in the development of new projects, from coming up with new ideas and commenting on editors' proposals to market testing new projects during their development. Marketing will also be involved in commenting on the book's cover design and whether it fits the needs of the perceived target market.

Market research can inform decisions about new projects, covers and marketing ideas. Wayne Winstone, children's category manager at Waterstone's, says:

> There is a lot of cynicism around consumer research, but it's so important to talk to your customers and find out what will excite them. Magazines seem to have very interesting detailed data on who buys what, which competitions will work and so forth. (*The Bookseller*, 17 August 2007)

Research into the book market can be commissioned from specialist organizations such as BML (Book Marketing Limited). Regular data on the sales of individual titles, their demand curves, and books by category is available from Nielsen BookScan. Sales rankings on Amazon are a free alternative.

Publishers of educational titles have less interest in consumer sales information, but when developing a new textbook they will certainly want to assess market trends in terms of student numbers in that subject, and evaluate the competition. They will also conduct primary research in schools, and major new textbooks will be concept tested using focus groups. An academic publisher may seek the views of librarians to a proposed online database of key texts and journal articles.

Brand

It used to be said that the brand names of publishers and those of their imprints have little impact on sales – readers do not select books on the name of the publisher. It is true that the general public's recognition of publishers is generally weak, apart from notable exceptions such as Penguin. Brand names are, however, important to publishers' business connections – to agents, authors and to the book trade intermediaries – and to media relations. The success of *Eats, Shoots and Leaves* (see page 175) by Lynne Truss (2003), which sold half a million copies within six months of publication, will have persuaded bookshops to take seriously future titles from Profile Books. Teachers in schools recognize publisher brands and this may influence their purchasing decisions or recommendations. Branding is used to good effect for book series, for instance in language learning, reference, travel

Palgrave Macmillan is a noteworthy example of branding in academic publishing – the brand helps attract new authors to the publisher

E ★ P E R T

Market research

Guy Plowman, Director of Three23

The decision whether or not to use market research can split a nation, let alone a publishing team. Why is there so much disagreement about such a common practice? The most common arguments against market research are:

- It only confirms what we already know.
- No matter what selection procedure you use for your target responses, you are excluding some of your relevant demographic.
- Respondents to questionnaires tell you what they think they want rather than what they actually want.

None of these criticisms is without substance, but does this render the exercise 'completely pointless' as some of the more extreme opponents would say? Absolutely not!

First, confirmation of existing beliefs is not a bad thing. It suggests there have not been any substantial oversights. Second, these criticisms do not take into account the full scope of market research. Most people would agree that assessing the size of the market and doing competitor analysis are essential activities. Agreeing on what aspects of market research are being discussed first can obviously avoid this misunderstanding. Finally, it is important to understand that market research through mechanisms such as questionnaires, interviews and user groups, whether it gives definitive answers or not, does give a valuable insight into the collective mind of the target audience. This facilitates flexible and informed responses to the unpredictable variables, occurrences and information that may come to light during the life of the project.

Launched in 2003, Oxford Scholarship Online is a cross-searchable library containing the full text of a range of OUP academic books. John Campbell, Product Manager, recalls how the initial market research confirmed their choice of two from four of the potential subject areas most suitable for launch. The same research also challenged them to consider changing the other two launch subjects – almost certainly helping to account for the ensuing success of the project.

Further, the research showed that the preferred global sales model was likely to be subscription-based. However, despite the model being well received in the UK, the US library market in fact had bureaucratic problems spending subscription budgets on a book-based product. This kind of thing should not be unexpected even when a comprehensive research of the market has been carried out. However, if the original research is designed to understand the 'hearts behind the answers' as well as the answers themselves, even the unpredictable becomes manageable. OUP were ready to implement a second business model – the purchase of perpetual access – allowing the fruits of the US market to be realized.

Market research is a good way to clarify thoughts, understand target audiences, avoid oversights and spot golden opportunities. Although not perfect, it remains a powerful tool.

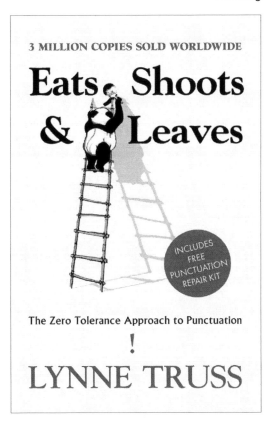

3 MILLION COPIES SOLD WORLDWIDE

Eats Shoots & Leaves

INCLUDES FREE PUNCTUATION REPAIR KIT

The Zero Tolerance Approach to Punctuation

!

LYNNE TRUSS

Eats, Shoots and Leaves by Lynne Truss (Profile Books) is an example of a title that sold by word of mouth

and computing guides, and in children's publishing especially. In ELT publishing, publisher brands will be an important guarantee of quality in overseas markets. In an internet world that is oversupplied with information of uncertain provenance, publisher branding should assume greater significance in conveying quality assured products and services. The risk for publishers is that users will head for the content that is free – perceived as 'good enough'.

Author branding and the cover

Since one of the factors that influences purchases is familiarity with the author, much attention is paid to the branding of authors, especially through their covers. Jonathan Hubbard of the branding consultancy, Interbrand, says:

> The first 20 to 30 feet of the book store is where most of the sales are . . . The jacket is stirring up for you an experience that you've possibly already enjoyed or you've heard from someone else that you will enjoy. (*The Bookseller*, 22 April 2005)

All the covers for an author may receive a similar treatment, encouraging the reader to look out for and buy the next book by one of their favourite authors. Brands also affect gift purchases. David Cooke, a category manager at Tesco, says of women's purchasing behaviour: 'If you're thinking of buying a book for your husband you go for a safe name' (*The Bookseller*, 17 August 2007).

Brands and travel publishing

Stephen Mesquita, travel publishing consultant

A strong brand encourages us as consumers to develop loyalty. This loyalty can become so strong that we buy without question because we know that the brand will deliver what we want. With the growth of the internet, where we are often buying products and services almost unseen, a strong brand is a 'must'.

It has been argued that brands do not really exist in publishing in the same way that they exist elsewhere on the high street and in the virtual shopping mall. The brand in trade publishing has tended to be the author or even one of their characters: Michael Palin is better known than Orion; Harry Potter than Bloomsbury; and *The Da Vinci Code* than Corgi.

But in reference publishing, brand can be vital to success. Take travel guide publishing. Historically, this has been a fragmented sector where local brands flourish without being successfully exported. Within the last few years, two publishers have succeeded in creating global brands – and success and profits have followed.

In the UK market, 66 per cent of the market is in the hands of three publishers: Lonely Planet (purchased by BBC Worldwide in 2007), Penguin (DK Eyewitness and Rough Guides) and the AA.* Two of these brands are mainly

local: the Rough Guides brand is strong in the UK, but has not been a major international success. The AA is a very strong brand in the UK – but its roadside assistance business means that, in publishing terms, it works better for maps than guides.

It is the same in many major markets. In the USA, Fodor and Frommer are strong local brands that do not really work outside North America. In France, there are Routard and Michelin. Michelin guides are published worldwide but generally have a small market share outside France. In Germany, Baedeker and Polyglott have not travelled in translation.

Yet Lonely Planet and DK Eyewitness guides have established global brands and global sales. Lonely

Travel publishers develop their brands in order to encourage repeat purchasing and wide stocking of their destination guides. Lonely Planet has developed from the backpacker's guide to a global brand

Planet has evolved from the backpacker's guide to the world's most successful mainstream travel brand. And DK has delivered a visual approach to travel guides which has enabled their look to become their brand.

Both these brands pass the global 'airport bookshop' test – you would pick up and buy one of these guides in an airport bookshop when your flight has been called and you do not have the time to browse. Wherever you are in the world, these two brands are available.

Can these brands resist the challenge of the global online information providers such as Google and Yahoo? To succeed in the arena of electronic information, publishing brands will need to find new ways to deliver their product to a new audience. They will also need to keep the standard of their information at the highest level.

* 2006 figures from Nielsen BookScan, *Travel Publishing Year Book* (2007)

Research may be commissioned into the readers of an author and a new cover look may reflect the results. For example, research by Anita Shreve's publisher, Time Warner, found that readers associated her books with emotions and human feelings. They then made sure that a new cover design put people on her covers.

Covers can give off messages about a book's target audience, and they help to position the book in the mind of the consumer. Research carried out for the Orange Prize for Fiction in 2000 found that the front cover and title of a book are taken by readers to be strong indicators of the kind of fiction, and whether the book is intended to be a male or female read. A novel was regarded as a female read based on the author's gender, the colour and general look of the cover, and its title. Women are far more likely to read books regarded as male reads (40 per cent of the women in the survey), with only a quarter of men interested in a book if they regarded it as a female read. Ian McEwan's *Enduring Love* was seen as a book which sent out signals from the look of its cover (including the use of pink) and from its title (using the word love) that it was a female read.

A good cover will encourage the consumer to pick up a book, and the consumer is then five times more likely to buy (Phillips, page 28). Mostly publishers target heavy buyers, who provide the bulk of their sales, and design the covers accordingly. Women are more likely to be heavy buyers of books, purchasing for their children, gifts, or themselves. Purchases can be classified by occasion – when the book will be read – and benefits – what the book offers to the reader. Covers can suggest a light read for the beach, an air of mystery, or a mood of passion. In general, hardback novels, which may become collectables, have elegant and restrained jackets, aimed at older groups. Fiction aimed at younger readers may go straight into paperback.

Sometimes a book is issued with two cover designs to capture different market segments. This happened with the Harry Potter books when it was found that they had a crossover adult market. Four designs were produced for Mark Haddon's *The Curious Incident of the Dog in the Night-Time*: adult and children's editions in both hardback and paperback. When Bloomsbury first published *The Little Friend* by Donna Tartt, it appeared with a disturbing image on the cover of a doll's face with a cutout eye. Two years later the book was reissued with a new cover image – a child on a swing – aimed at a summer reading market.

Add-ons

Extra value can be created with add-ons such as a CD-ROM or minidisc included in the book, or internet links in the text. It would now be unusual to publish a major textbook without an associated website offering extra resources. Videos, tests, quizzes, and games may be available for educational texts, with lesson plans for the teachers. For academic textbooks, lecturers may be provided with a full course of lecture slides and, for major texts, a full range of resources including student assessment. Ebooks can contain extra features such as videos and animations.

Price

Marketing will be involved in setting the prices for new books. Factors affecting the book's possible published price include its perceived value to end-users; their ability to pay low or high prices (for example high-earning professionals); and the price of competitors' books, especially if the book can be compared against similar books in shops, rather than stand alone by advertised mail order. Sometimes a book has a uniqueness that can let it command a premium price. Other factors include whether the book will be bought primarily by end-users or by libraries or businesses; and whether there are established price ceilings in the market which, if breached, could reduce sales (for example to an impulse buyer, gift buyer, student or school).

The raising of the published price would usually lead to a fall in demand, whereas lowering the price would usually (but not always) lead to a rise in the quantity sold. Products which are thought to be *price inelastic* – changing the price has only a limited effect on the level of demand – tend to be highly specialist and professional titles. The book may convey need-to-know information – such as how to use a software package – for which a business professional is happy to pay a higher price. Consumer books, especially paperbacks, which may be bought on impulse, and many textbooks tend to be *price elastic* – changing the price has a greater effect on the level of demand. Price elasticities vary according to the type of book. It can be difficult, for example, for an editor to persuade an academic or professional book author that lowering the price will not open the gates to a flood of eager readers.

A cost-based approach to pricing is now less common – this involves a standard mark-up from the unit cost of the book. Instead publishers will price to the market with a keen eye on the relevant competition. For trade fiction, pricing to market will override considerations such as the book's length. There are common price points in the market for given categories of books, such as general hardbacks, trade and mass-market paperbacks. This is also true for academic textbooks: for example, the price points for humanities and social sciences paperback texts are lower than those for management and STM titles. Periodically brave publishers break the prevailing price points, by lifting the price or lowering it to undercut competitors.

Trade publishers may have to price with a view to the discounts offered by retailers to consumers. Christmas bestsellers will have their recommended price set in the full knowledge that retailers will reduce the price considerably. A book priced by the publisher at £25 may be sold at up to half price by retailers if a price war develops in the market.

The level of discounts given by publishers to booksellers is a marketing cost to the publisher. It determines the amount of money the publisher actually receives from sales made by the retailer. The trade publishers, which are highly dependent on retail exposure, give booksellers the highest discounts. Most sales in a bookshop are made within the first 20 to 30 feet of the entrance, and this is the prime location where offers to consumers are displayed, such as '3 for 2'. Retailers ask publishers for especially high discounts to participate in their promotions, and for additional sums to secure window displays and prominence in catalogues.

Electronic products can be difficult to price when there are no set price points in the market. Publishers may resort to cost-based approaches in order to recoup their investment, or keep prices low initially in order to encourage early orders. The prices of ebooks may match those of printed books or be lower, say two-thirds or a half. Books are free from VAT, but it is payable on electronic products such as ebooks, CD-ROMs, DVDs and online content.

Place

A full view of a book's distribution and the different channels through which books are sold is provided in later chapters. From the point of view of the marketer, they need to understand fully the markets into which books are sold, both the needs of consumers and the different sales channels. The growth of sales through supermarkets and the internet, for example, are key trends affecting the marketing of books. Marketing managers need to assess the likely audience for a book and work out, with the sales department, how it can be made available through the relevant channels, as well as promoted to the relevant decision-makers and consumers.

Promotion

The aim of promotion is to make the media, the book trade, and consumers conscious of the company and the products it offers; and to stimulate demand.

The work may be divided by task. In some publishers, especially consumer, specialists deal solely with public relations, or with the development of promotional and point-of-sale (POS) material for retailers, or with catalogues, or with space or outdoor advertising or copywriting; or with emarketing. In some academic and professional publishers, the work may be divided between textbooks, mail-order sales or journals promotion. Publishers of all kinds also hire advertising agencies (especially for major projects or authors), freelance publicists, direct mail and website specialists. While in-house designers and production staff are sometimes used, marketing staff make extensive use of desk-top publishing (DTP) and may commission freelance designers and buy print themselves because these suppliers are not those producing the books. Some major publishers have adopted content management systems to facilitate catalogue and website production.

The promotional material produced and the interest generated help the sales staff to sell to the book trade, or to schools or colleges, and the rights staff to their customers. Details of the promotional spend and activities will help with subscription levels. Home and overseas customers use the promotional material as a reference source for ordering.

Emarketing

The development of emarketing has revolutionized promotion and the whole marketing function. At the start of the century many publishers' websites were in early stages of development and were beginning to perform a range of functions. For example, those that delivered content online were present in the advanced professional and journal publishers (charged-for content), or on sites linked with textbooks (free or password-protected). Some of these publishers established associated networking and updating services for professional groups, ranging from school teachers to high-level research communities.

For most book publishers, however, their sites at the outset performed the direct marketing function of providing information on their titles, in effect they were an extension of their print-based catalogues, increasingly with an online facility for ordering printed books and as a prelude to ordering ebooks. Some publishers in the consumer field embellish their web pages, for example with author interviews and interactive material, such as activities or games linked to particular books or children's characters. In 2007 Macmillan Children's Books launched a service offering wallpaper and ringtones, available to download from their author sites. Publishers of consumer books written by brand-name authors face the challenge that their imprint name is a sub-brand to that of their authors in the public's mind. In order to co-ordinate the promotion, such publishers may offer to host their authors' websites. In academic publishing, email marketing to lecturers, with RSS (really simple syndication) feeds, has grown significantly.

The presence of Amazon and Google in the marketplace offers both opportunities and threats to publishers. Academic publishers have welcomed the opportunity to display their books through Google Book Search, since they believe their titles have exposure they would not otherwise receive. Readers can view sample pages and then click through to buy the book. Amazon has such a service with Search Inside, and some major publishers have started similar schemes. Other publishers are less sure of the benefits of having their books digitized by such major players as Google and Amazon. Nigel Newton, Chief Executive of Bloomsbury, warned of the napsterization of publishing:

> It's terribly short sighted to see this as a marketing opportunity. It may lead to a sales increase in the short term, but in 20 years' time it may result in no sales. We don't know, once they have this material, what they will do with it.
> (*The Bookseller*, 21 April 2005)

Internet marketing does have huge potential for the niche publishers both large and small. Specialist and academic titles are unlikely to be widely stocked in bookshops. The publishers can establish specialist interest, internet communities around their publications to whom they can directly sell their titles. For some of the well-known academic and specialist publishers, direct sales of their books from their websites grew quickly, along with sales via internet booksellers. The internet means they can keep in touch with their market, and mail to a highly relevant audience in a cost-effective way.

Word of mouth

Publishers have long recognized that an important influence on sales is the elusive word of mouth (WOM). Sales are generated by personal recommendations from friends, family or booksellers. Sometimes bestsellers can appear from nowhere, such as *Captain Corelli's Mandolin* (1994) by Louis de Bernières and *Eats, Shoots and Leaves* by Lynne Truss (2003). Publishers cannot guarantee a buzz around a book, but they are constantly trying to encourage it through obtaining coverage in the media or making sure the book is stocked prominently in bookshops. Today the internet provides opportunities for viral marketing, spreading an idea, a joke, or information around a social network. Text messaging provides another route. Publishers are experimenting with placing content and information on blogs and social networking sites in order to generate attention for titles. Dorling Kindersley created an interactive 'widget' for *Complete Reflexology for Life* (2007) by Kevin Kunz – this showed how areas of the hand connect up to parts of the body. The widget could be emailed to friends or added to the user's page in Facebook.

In 2007 Richard Dawkins appeared in a video on *Second Life* to mark the launch of the paperback of *The God Delusion*

When *The Observer* newspaper compiled a list of the most powerful players in publishing in 2006, the person who came top was Amanda Ross. She

> runs Cactus TV with her husband, Simon Ross (brother of Jonathan), and together they produce Richard & Judy, the daytime chat show which, through its insanely popular Book Club, more or less dictates what is in the bestseller lists. The Book Club was Ross's idea – inspired by the Oprah Winfrey show – and she is the one who selects the titles featured on it . . . Since it started in 2004, in fact, the Book Club has been responsible for the sale of more than 10 m books and has generated more than £60 m for publishers. What this means in practice is that the sales of one in four books sold in this country are now based on Amanda Ross's recommendations. It also means that, almost single-handedly, she has turned at least 10 authors into millionaires. (telegraph.co.uk, accessed 1 June 2007)

The success of reading groups represents an opportunity to influence book sales. (Reading groups are also called clubs, and this can lead to confusion with the direct sales organizations long known as book clubs.) Publishers produce information packs and web resources around leading authors to encourage reading groups to adopt their titles. Other influences on book sales can include winning a major literary prize such as the Booker (Table 10.3) or when a novel, for example, is adapted for television or film. Classic as well as contemporary authors receive a boost in their sales when the latest adaptation makes it on to the screen.

The Booker Prize for Fiction was first awarded in 1969, and Man Group became the sponsor of the prize in 2002

The author plays a prominent part in promoting their books, from appearances at book signings or literary festivals to sending out flyers with their Christmas cards and adding a link to the relevant Amazon page to their email signature. Amongst the largest literary festivals are the ones held at Edinburgh, Hay-on-Wye and Cheltenham.

Table 10.3 Man Booker Prize for fiction winners 1998 to 2007

Year	Author	Title	Publisher
1998	Ian McEwan	*Amsterdam*	Jonathan Cape
1999	J. M. Coetzee	*Disgrace*	Secker & Warburg
2000	Margaret Atwood	*The Blind Assassin*	Bloomsbury
2001	Peter Carey	*True History of the Kelly Gang*	Faber & Faber
2002	Yann Martel	*The Life of Pi*	Canongate
2003	DBC Pierre	*Vernon God Little*	Faber & Faber
2004	Alan Hollinghurst	*The Line of Beauty*	Picador
2005	John Banville	*The Sea*	Picador
2006	Kiran Desai	*The Inheritance of Loss*	Penguin
2007	Anne Enright	*The Gathering*	Jonathan Cape

The book club at Newtown, Newbury, reading *I'm Not Scared* by Niccolò Ammaniti. It is estimated that there are 50,000 people in reading groups in the UK

Deckchairs for the Hay Festival, Hay-on-Wye, Wales. Held annually, the festival attracts both writers and celebrities, from Ian Rankin and Wole Soyinka to Bill Clinton and Ken Dodd. The town has over 30 bookshops selling new, old and out-of-print books

As the novelist Jane Rogers writes:

> Books are promoted to us endlessly, through adverts, reviews, adaptations,
> through glossy attention-grabbing covers in bookshops, and wild claims
> on jacket sleeves. They are set texts for exams; they are hyped by prizes and
> awards; or they are written by celebrities. But in the end, every reader knows,
> probably the most compelling reason for picking up a book which is new to
> you, is when a friend tells you, 'Read this, it's really good.' (page vii)

Promotion and publicity techniques

Before running through the promotion and publicity techniques that are
applicable to many books, we will take a quick look at the way the marketing
department of a consumer book publisher would set about promoting a major
lead title. Most of the promotion budget and staff time goes on titles envisaged as
bestsellers.

The first priority of the marketing department – many months in advance
of publication – is to plan and undertake trade-focused promotion. The aim is to
persuade the book trade that the book will deliver a flood of customers to their
stores during the set publication slot; that they will need to display it prominently
and order large quantities. The central buyers of the retailers are courted. They
might be invited to meet the famous author or visit the exotic location of the book.
They are sent early reading copies and other devices to captivate their attention,
from free gifts to DVDs with author interviews.

Much of the marketing budget that is directed at the book trade is spent on
the main retailers to ensure they place the book in the prime spots in their stores
and take it as part of their promotions (for example 3 for 2; monthly, summer and
Christmas selections). Other techniques designed to increase their order quantities
are developed, such as bespoke competitions for each retail chain and point of
sale material to maximize the book's presence in their stores. The marketing
department then follows through with their consumer-focused promotion – the
big bang advertising campaign to potential readers occurring closer to the book's
publication. The publisher's consumer marketing spend, which is known to
the book trade in advance of their ordering, demonstrates that the publisher is
backing the title to the hilt and reinforces the book trade's confidence to order
large quantities. Meanwhile, the publisher's publicist has been imaginatively
engineering media interest in the book and author, which manifests itself around
publication. It is then hoped that word-of-mouth recommendations ripple through
the population.

Children's books

Children's books, reaching a general retail market, libraries and schools, combine
the techniques of general and educational publishing. The marketer creates
and mails the catalogue, generates free publicity, organizes exhibitions, attends
conferences and liaises with schools and libraries; and, occasionally, may dress up
as a large, ungainly character for a delighted audience.

We now turn to the variety of techniques used more generally.

Author questionnaire

Around the time of the delivery of the manuscript, the author completes a questionnaire, which is returned via the editor. The author supplies personal information, a biography, a blurb, a short synopsis, and the book's main selling-points and intended readership or applicability to courses. In addition they may supply lists of their affiliations to membership organizations and online forums; and lists of print and broadcast media (and individuals) that might review or publicize the book. Well-connected authors may need to be contacted in person to gain information on media and other contacts. Other information could include relevant festivals, conferences and exhibitions.

Advance information sheet

The marketing department will prepare the book's advance information (AI) sheet, and its electronic equivalent (as a PDF), which contains bibliographic information (title, author, format, extent, illustrative content, hardback/paperback, ISBN, planned price and publication date); a synopsis, the cover blurb, and a contents list; and a biography of the author. The above are the book's features, and it is important that the AI also sets out the book's benefits – i.e. what it will do for the purchaser or reader. A dictionary will help someone with their studies or to work more effectively in business. A travel guide will enable someone to make the best of their weekend away, giving them the key information and guidance they need. Is there a key benefit – the book's unique selling proposition (USP)? For example, for a non-fiction title, is it written by the leading expert in the field; for an educational title, does it match the latest curriculum requirements? The key benefits can be difficult to identify when a book is coming into a crowded market, but the exercise is even more crucial.

The AI is sent well ahead of publication (preferably around nine months before) to all the people who help sell the book: the publisher's sales force and overseas agents, booksellers, wholesalers, and library suppliers. Wholesalers and library suppliers need the information to enter the title in their catalogues and online databases to secure advance orders. Having the book listed on Amazon and in the relevant bibliographic databases is a vital step in making sure the book can be readily identified and purchased.

Cover

The cover is another promotional item used by the publisher's home and export sales departments, wholesalers, library suppliers, internet booksellers and overseas agents. Produced well ahead of publication – preferably six to 12 months – it will be used to secure advance orders from bookshops. Publishers find that books sell better on Amazon if they appear with a cover, and dummy front covers may be used when the book is first listed, ahead of the completion of the final version. The cover blurb is written by the editor, marketing department, or an in-house or freelance copywriter.

Catalogue

Catalogue preparation is a major task: it involves gathering book information from all round the firm, updating it, collecting illustrations, copywriting, briefing a

Marketing fiction

Claire Squires, author of *Marketing Literature: The Making of Contemporary Writing in Britain* and Senior Lecturer in Publishing, Oxford International Centre for Publishing Studies

E★PERT

Publishers have always made efforts to promote, distribute and sell fiction, but the late twentieth and early twenty-first centuries have been a period of marketing intensification. Campaigns for potential bestsellers combine a range of generic marketing materials (catalogues, point-of-sale, bound proofs) and targeted marketing strategies to support the journey of novels from the author to the eventual reader.

The traditional marketing method for fiction – literary journalism and press coverage – still has its place, but doubts about the impact of reviews on book sales, and the diminution of review space in most national newspapers have prompted publishers to attract customers in other ways. In 1969, the Booker Prize was established by The Publishers Association, and since this date, literary prizes have had a crucial impact on book sales. Alongside the rise of literary prizes, there has been a growing meet-the-author culture, through events in bookshops, libraries, and literary festivals. The expansion of reading groups has also presented publishers with opportunities: publishers mail advance copies to registered groups, and create online reading guides. Equally, novels have microsites, and many authors have their own websites. Print, broadcast and new media-based reading groups have pushed book sales, with the Richard and Judy Book Club achieving unprecedented media exposure and sales for a range of fiction and non-fiction titles.

The post-NBA retail environment has led to heavy discounting practices. Fiction features prominently in price promotions such as 3-for-2s, and the welcoming atmosphere of the superstores encourages browsing, frequently with cappuccino in hand. Branding, however, is difficult in fiction – titles by market-leading authors may sell immediately, with the help of the brand identity of cover design – but for most novels publishers have to work hard to differentiate their products in a very crowded marketplace. Cover design has been an important selling tool particularly since the paperback revolution in the 1930s: the browser in the bookshop judges new books by their covers, and backlist titles are revivified through rejacketing. Multimedia synergies also push fiction sales, with film and TV tie-in editions produced with cover stills.

In the early twenty-first century, there is a vibrant reading culture in Britain, owing in no small way to the marketing activities surrounding books. Despite the Long Tail potential offered by online retailers, recent marketing has meant a concentration on a small number of highly successful titles, forcing midlist authors to the margins. In this period, the marketing Holy Grail has been word of mouth, with many fiction titles benefiting from chains of recommendation fostered by social networks. A novel such as Louis de Bernières's *Captain Corelli's Mandolin*, however, while a quintessential word-of-mouth bestseller, also had a substantial marketing campaign behind it, an iconic cover design, and an author fully engaged in promotion.

designer, sometimes print buying, and carrying through all the production stages, as well as database management.

The maintenance of the publisher's in-house database covers each title's current status (future or actual publication dates, whether it is reprinting or out of print), current prices, its coding by product category or subject, and additional information on each title built up over time (such as long and short promotional and contents copy, and reviews received). More extensive data will cover contractual matters, such as the rights held and the rights available for sale or licensed to others. The advantage of such a database is that it is a central repository of definitive information about the publisher's titles. It allows the publisher to retrieve and manipulate information in forms most suited to the intermediaries and end-users, in print and online (especially for the web catalogue).

The twin aims of a catalogue are to present the firm and its products attractively to buyers – the book trade and consumers; and to act as an informative, readily understandable and accurate reference so that products can be ordered easily through the supply chain at home and abroad.

Consumer book publishers normally produce imprint catalogues announcing their forthcoming books geared to their six-monthly selling cycles. The autumn/winter catalogue appears in time for the preceding mid-summer sales conference; the spring/summer catalogue appears for the preceding Christmas sales conference. Consumer publishers may issue monthly catalogues or stocklists. Catalogues are distributed to all members of the supply chain and to main libraries, to the public (via booksellers to account customers), and to review editors and the media. The stocklists covering new and backlist books and their prices which accompany catalogues are used by the publisher's sales representatives (reps) and the book trade for ordering.

Educational, academic, STM and professional publishers usually arrange their new book catalogues (and selected backlist) by subject or subject groupings. Different subject catalogues may be produced for different levels of the education system, and books within a textbook catalogue (which includes selected backlist) may be arranged or classified by the age group, or examination or academic level served. Catalogues are produced annually to cover the following year's publications, or six-monthly or more frequently. Although the catalogues are mailed to selected booksellers, wholesalers, library suppliers and exporters, they are aimed primarily at teachers, academics, and professionals – those who decide to purchase or adopt the books. They are distributed to schools, academic libraries, institutions, departments; and, where appropriate, to targeted subject specialists or professionals, and to industry.

Publishers have experimented with the abolition of printed catalogues and stocklists, on the basis that the information can be accessed online. This has met with mixed success and most publishers have retained print versions in some form. Publishers sometimes produce complete printed catalogues containing summary information on all new and backlist titles. As the main reference source of the publisher's output, it is used by the book trade, libraries and others at home and overseas.

Bibliographic information: 'invisible marketing'

Supplying the main bibliographers with accurate information in the standard format (BIC BASIC new title record) on each new title is essential. This can be done by sending the AI or using an agreed electronic format such as ONIX (Online Information Exchange).

> ONIX is both a data dictionary of the elements which go to make up a product record and a standard means by which product data can be transmitted electronically by publishers to data aggregators, wholesalers, booksellers and anyone else involved in the sale of their publications. (editeur.org, accessed 22 August 2007)

This is a low-cost means of promoting the book worldwide, and facilitates its ordering through the supply chain. Information given to the bibliographers – the main ones are Nielsen BookData (UK) and Bowker (USA) – nine to six months ahead of publication lists the new title on their electronic databases. There are differing levels of service from a free listing of basic bibliographic information through to a fuller description with author biographies and covers.

Bibliographic Data Services is the leading supplier of bibliographic information to libraries and suppliers. It specializes in the promotion of new title information in MARC (Machine Readable Catalogue Format), a data standard used by libraries to store and exchange information. It also supplies the Cataloguing in Publication (CIP) data to the British Library's weekly addition to the definitive British National Bibliography (BNB) and other products, accessed worldwide. You can see the CIP data for a book on its title-verso page.

Legal deposit is the act of depositing published material in designated libraries. Publishers in the United Kingdom and Ireland have an obligation to deposit published material in the six legal deposit libraries, which collectively maintain the national published archive of the British Isles. The six libraries are:

- British Library,
- Bodleian Library, Oxford University,
- Cambridge University Library,
- National Library of Scotland in Edinburgh,
- National Library of Wales in Aberystwyth, and
- Library of Trinity College, Dublin.

Reviews

A review list is prepared, tailor-made for the title, taking account of the author's ideas and contacts. Review copies may be bound, uncorrected proofs or printed books. They are sent out with a review slip, press release or letter which gives the details of the title and requests a review. Any review clippings received are circulated in-house and to the author. Reviews have declined in importance in their influence on book sales, and greater attention has been directed to the PR for a title. John Sutherland writes:

Old hands will hark back nostalgically to the days when Arnold Bennett could clear a whole edition with an enthusiastic epithet in the London *Evening Standard*. Now the literary editor, David Sexton, could disembowel himself, Mishima-style, on the roof of his building and it would not generate a ripple of interest among book buyers. (*Financial Times*, 9 October 2004)

Reviews can still be crucial for biographies or academic works, for example, where potential readers may want to gauge the quality of the work ahead of their purchase. Reviews on Amazon may be written by enthusiastic readers or friends of the author.

Public relations

Public relations (PR) include generating free publicity and furthering a company's brand image with authors and the media. By comparison to the big budgets elsewhere in the marketing department, publicists operate with little expenditure. Engineering free publicity in the print and broadcast media is vital in consumer book publishing, and spreads word-of-mouth knowledge about the book. For titles which do not receive marketing expenditure, PR can propel sales, and smaller publishers will use it to compete effectively with the major players. On some major titles prior to contract, the publisher's innovatory publicity ideas (and promotional spend) may persuade the author to write for their particular company, rather than for competitors. Publicists can develop strong bonds with authors, and become close friends.

The publicist, also called the press and PR officer, is in constant contact with press and magazine editors, journalists, radio and television producers. With so many books and authors competing for media space, a book or author has to be carefully positioned in the marketplace.

At the manuscript stage, the publicist targets the market, and formulates a publicity plan to commence six months before publication. A key part of the task is to meet with the author and discuss their book, interests and promotional ideas. The publicist identifies the appropriate media that would be interested in the book, and helps them come to a decision to cover the title by suggesting suitable angles.

New authors may be positioned in terms of established writers – the 'new Catherine Cookson', for example

The stimulated coverage should occur around publication. Coverage is gained from features, author promotions which authors may be contractually obliged to fulfil – tours, literary festivals, signing sessions, radio and television appearances, accompanied by the publicist – press releases, and launch parties. Around the time of publication, authors will appear in newspapers and magazines outlining their typical day or answering questionnaires about their likes and dislikes. New authors may need coaching in media awareness and interview techniques. Authors themselves may come up with innovative ways to promote books. In 2006 Margaret Atwood launched the LongPen, a device which enables books to be signed by the author even on another continent, over the internet (longpen.com).

Signing sessions, competitions for booksellers, and joint promotions with booksellers, especially the main chains, are arranged in close conjunction with the sales department. Sales staff are warned about any impending coverage so that they can inform the booksellers who are thus more likely to stock the book which in turn sells more copies. Major TV or film tie-in titles receive cross-media promotion involving the link-up between the publisher and the media company for mutual benefit. Film and TV adaptations work wonders for the sales of classic authors as well, increasing their sales by three or four times.

Other PR involves informing the trade press (*The Bookseller* and *Publishing News*) about the company and forthcoming titles, distributing bound proofs to influential people, entering titles for literary prizes, helping to plan and attend exhibitions (including the publisher's own sales conferences), maintaining contact with The Publishers Association, Booktrust and the British Council (all of which promote books) and sometimes answering queries from the public, teachers, librarians and booksellers.

News stories can be a good way of getting books on to the front page, or into the radio or television. For the new edition of a major dictionary, for example, stories will be given to the press about the latest words to enter the language:

> Once, you might have been stuck for the word to describe an unsightly tummy bulge protruding over low-rise jeans. But 'muffin top' is one of hundreds of new words and phrases, along with 'wag', 'size zero' and 'hoodie', that have entered the language and are listed in the *Collins English Dictionary*'s 9th edition, published today. (*The Guardian*, 4 June 2007)

Serial rights

In consumer book publishing, publicity staff instead of the rights department may sell serial rights to their contacts in the press and magazines. Extracts or serials should appear around book publication and produce income and publicity. See also Chapter 12, 'Rights sales'.

Paid-for promotion

Point-of-sale material

Eye-catching material – posters, display kits, copy holders, presenters, brochures, badges etc. – is designed to focus booksellers' and readers' attention on major books, series or brand imprints; to make shops more enticing; and to capture display space both at home and abroad. Produced mainly for consumer books (but sometimes for major reference books and textbooks), most is declined or thrown away by booksellers. Nevertheless, it shows the publisher's commitment to the book and assists advance selling to the book trade and customers abroad. Sometimes a publisher may provide major retailers with spinners or special shelving for a series, but books are usually displayed on tables or standard shelving in the larger shops.

Media advertising

For most books, the high cost of advertising in the press, magazines, or on television or radio, or by poster would not be recouped by the sales generated. It has to be used very selectively, and short-lived, large-scale consumer advertising is restricted to major consumer books. The large publishers spend most of their budget on press and outdoor advertising, especially adverts on the London Underground and buses. Although its effectiveness is intangible, it encourages the book trade to buy and display the book and pleases authors and agents. Consumer

Outdoor advertising for books includes ads on London buses

Marketing

An interest in the firm's books and the ability to identify the editorial reasoning and sales potential are necessary. Creativity is needed in originating ideas for promoting a wide range of titles, as well as an understanding of the relationships between costs and expected sales in maximizing the profit potential of each title, within budget. Marketing is a strategic activity, and knowledge is required of competitive behaviour and the market environment. Qualifications can be obtained through the Chartered Institute of Marketing (CIM).

Good personal relations inside the company (particularly with editors) and outside the company are vital, as are administrative and planning skills.

The development of promotional material engages copywriting (which can be learnt by literate people who appreciate the different styles demanded for different lists and books), editorial, production and DTP skills. In direct mail promotion or selling, the marketer acts like a detective – working out where the people are and how to reach them. PR work involves living on one's wits, exchanging favours with the media, establishing a rapport and trust with all kinds of media and authors, knowing when to hype and when to hold back, being able to talk oneself in and out of situations fast, having supreme self-confidence and a high tolerance of rude people and working anti-social hours.

book publishers also advertise to the book trade in *The Bookseller* or *Publishing News* – advertisements usually appear two to four months ahead of publication so that the sales force has time to follow up. The non-consumer book publishers advertise selectively in specialist magazines, and journals (especially their own) – ostensibly to sell books, but also to please authors and attract new ones.

The main tasks involved in advertising are conceiving selling ideas from editorial concepts, relating advertising to the other promotions, copywriting and working with the designer or agency, negotiating the best rates and positions, and maintaining tight budgetary control.

Direct marketing

In order to write effective copy, a useful acronym to remember is AIDA: attention, interest, desire, action

The preparation and mailing of brochures or leaflets direct to targeted specialist audiences forms a large part of the work of promotion staff in educational, academic, STM and professional book and journal publishers. The relevant audience could be teachers in schools, university lecturers and librarians, or business and legal professionals. Together with mailed subject catalogues (and to some extent reviews) it is the main promotional means by which these groups can learn about new and related backlist titles (monographs are normally promoted only once). Together with the editor, the promotion controller works out the scope of the market, the best approach, what kind of mailing piece is appropriate including email, the time it should be distributed (usually around publication) and to whom, i.e. which mailing list to use, within the allocated budget.

The controller writes the copy, often designs it, and carries through the production stages. Depending on the export arrangements, material may be mailed direct to libraries, teachers, academics and booksellers in selected countries. Other promotional material includes flyers or showcards which authors can distribute or display at conferences, exhibitions or other events.

Textbook promotion

Teachers and academics are unlikely to prescribe a book for student use unless they have examined a copy first. Titles that are expected to be ordered in bulk for schools or placed on a reading list of books which students should buy (excluding monographs and professional reference titles) are marked in catalogues and leaflets which contain inspection copy order forms. Inspection copies can also be ordered or downloaded from the publisher's website. The teacher, having placed the order, is asked to supply comments on the suitability of the book. If the book is adopted for student purchase, the lecturer is asked whether it is the core text or to be used alongside other titles, or merely recommended, and fill in the number of students on the course and the name of the supplier. If adopted, the recipient keeps the book for free; if not, they pay for it or return it – although policies differ according to the publisher. Some publishers will send unsolicited free desk copies of textbooks to influential teachers. The feedback and response rates are used for market research. In academic publishing the information is passed to the sales staff, who contact lecturers directly and alert the campus booksellers through which the books are purchased and the library, which may order copies. Textbook publishers of all levels build databases of adoptions (institution, course, student numbers) for subsequent follow-up and targeting. In school textbook publishing the UK schools ordering class sets directly are recorded.

Lecturers' reading lists, which may be available on the internet, are the key determinant in a student's choice of books. According to a research study for The Publishers Association in 2005, 83 per cent of students who received a strong textbook recommendation from their lecturer purchased a book, compared to 30 per cent of those who received a weak recommendation (openbooksopenminds. co.uk, accessed 12 June 2007). The research showed a low propensity to buy books which are not recommended – 74 per cent said they had not bought any other new books.

Direct sales

Most books are sold via booksellers (including Amazon) to end-users. Some booksellers, especially the specialist, sell by mail order and may produce catalogues. The book clubs (general interest and specialist), direct selling companies and internet booksellers are the main mail-order channels. But some publishers sell a proportion, or indeed a major proportion, of their products directly to end-users.

In the consumer market, *Reader's Digest* is best known for its large-scale direct marketing campaigns. College textbook publishers, in response to declining campus sales and the growth of internet purchasing, are encouraging direct purchase by offering incentives to students. The publishers of high-priced reference or online works sell directly to defined professional markets (for example legal, accountancy, finance and business), though some of their products, such as books, pass through booksellers and library suppliers. The academic and STM publishers likewise actively solicit direct orders – or through intermediaries – of high-level books from academics, scientists and professionals. Publisher displays at conferences can also be an effective method of reaching these markets.

Journal publishers promote their journals directly to researchers and librarians primarily to secure institutional subscriptions from libraries. The bundling of electronic journals now leads librarians to choose packages that offer the best value. However, journal publishers also offer subscriptions at much lower rates for personal use, which are supplied directly. Their aim is to convert personal subscriptions into full-priced institutional subscriptions. The schools market is ideal for the direct marketing of books and new media, since schools may buy multiple copies with repeat purchases direct from the publisher. Discounts are given by quantity rather than to any intermediary.

Consumer publishers rarely solicit direct orders because most are unable to identify readers and addresses, and many of their books are priced for the retail outlets, too low for their distribution systems to supply one paperback book cost effectively by mail order.

The direct marketing vehicle may be a space advertisement, an insert in a magazine or book, a mailed item (a catalogue or leaflet and personalized letter) or an email. Whatever the means, the promotion controller encourages direct purchase (sometimes by special offers) and includes a response facility which eases ordering and payment (by freepost, telephone, or email, and using a credit card) or which facilitates, for example, a journal subscription via the library. By assessing the response rates, direct marketing allows the statistical testing of the effectiveness of different offers and creative approaches (such as the design of the envelope, letter and leaflet), their timing and frequency, and of the vehicle.

The mailing list is of prime importance. It should be accurate, up to date, and appropriate for the product. List brokers may be used, lists are rented or acquired free, and are tested initially. Lists may be gathered from firms which specialize in constructing lists in educational, academic and professional areas, from associations, journal subscribers, and conference delegates, and from authors. In time the best lists are the publisher's own, built from successive sales and recorded and coded into the publisher's own database or customer relationship management (CRM) system. Sometimes they are rented from, or to, other publishers. The most likely customers are targeted regularly with the most appropriate titles, and varying amounts are spent to acquire and keep different levels of customer.

Postal mailings can still be done very cheaply and, for example, some publishers use mail houses in India. While email provides a highly cost-effective method of mailing, companies must ensure that its use stays within the law. The advice from the Information Commissioner's Office is that:

> You must not contact individuals without their prior consent unless you have obtained their details in the course of a sale or negotiations of a sale, you only contact them about your own similar products or services and you give them the opportunity to opt out of receiving further marketing messages each time. (ico.gov.uk, accessed 4 June 2007)

Direct marketing sells books quickly (most feedback is usually in weeks, not many months) and a response rate of 1 or 2 per cent would be thought a success, though

Best practice is to ask individuals to opt in to receiving marketing messages rather than opt out

rates of up to 5, 10 or 15 per cent plus are possible. If poorly executed, much money can be lost even though the books are sold at full price or at modest discount.

Telemarketing, by a publisher's own staff or by a retained agency, is sometimes used to follow up a mailshot, for example, to reach teachers and professionals at their place of work. It may be used to follow up renewals of journals and online reference subscriptions. However, it plays a relatively minor part in the marketing mix.

Now read this

Alison Baverstock, *How to Market Books*, 4th edition, Kogan Page, 2008.
Philip Kotler, Veronica Wong, John Saunders and Gary Armstrong, *Principles of Marketing*, European Edition, Prentice Hall, 2004.

Sources

Eileen Armstrong, *Boys into Books*, School Library Association, 2007.
BML (Book Marketing Limited), *Expanding the Market*, February 2005.
Jenny Hartley, *The Reading Groups Book*, revised edition, Oxford University Press, 2002.
LISU, *Annual Library Statistics*, Loughborough.
Mintel, *Books*, 2005.
Mintel, *Books, Music and Video Retailing*, 2007.
Angus Phillips, 'How Books Are Positioned in the Market', in Nicole Matthews and Nickianne Moody (editors), *Judging a Book by Its Cover: Fans, publishers, designers, and the marketing of fiction*, Ashgate, 2007.
Angus Phillips, 'Jane Austen Gets a Makeover', *Logos*, 18:2, 2007.
Al Ries and Jack Trout, *Positioning: The battle for your mind*, McGraw-Hill, 2001.
Jane Rogers (editor), *Good Fiction Guide*, Oxford University Press, 2001.
Claire Squires, *Marketing Literature: The making of contemporary writing in Britain*, Palgrave Macmillan, 2007.
John Sutherland, 'Brave New World', *Financial Times*, 9 October 2004.

Web resources

www.literacytrust.org The National Literacy Trust is a charity dedicated to 'building a literate nation'.
www.themanbookerprize.com Man Booker Prize for Fiction.
www.noonebelongssheremorethanyou.com Website for author Miranda July, which makes clever use of the top of her refrigerator.
www.openbooksopenminds.co.uk Research into the textbook market commissioned by The Publishers Association.
www.publisherspublicitycircle.co.uk Publishers Publicity Circle – holds monthly meetings for publicists from publishers and freelance PR agencies.

CHAPTER 11

Sales and distribution

While it is the job of marketing to understand the needs of the market and promote books to the relevant audiences, it is the sales staff who stimulate demand through the various retail channels. They realize income by sustained face-to-face selling to key intermediaries. With the decline in independent bookselling, the dominance of the chains and their shift to central buying, and the rise of supermarket and internet sales, the focus of sales staff has altered in recent years. Publishers have redesigned job roles to create key account managers, who deal with the chains and other key customers, and there is less emphasis on visiting individual bookshops. Publishers have reduced the number of their field sales representatives, and redefined their roles to focus on marketing and customer relations.

In the area of distribution, the larger publishers run their own operations. Small- and medium-sized enterprises (SMEs) do their own distribution or use third parties – larger publishers or independent distributors.

SALES

Rights sales
are covered
separately in
Chapter 12

Publishers typically derive most of their sales revenue from a small number of customers, and small revenue from a great number. This so-called Pareto effect suggests that 20 per cent of customers might account for 80 per cent of total sales. In consumer book publishing, the bookselling chains have tended to dominate, followed by wholesalers and library suppliers. But a big order from a supermarket can put a book amongst the bestsellers, and the importance of the chains has been challenged by the supermarkets and internet booksellers.

The internet also provides a route to sell the 'Long Tail' – the books that are not regularly stocked in bookshops (see Chapter 13). Customers searching online for a relevant title can come across slow-selling backlist titles as well as the current bestsellers. Certainly publishers have to ensure that their books are listed with sufficient information online, and they are using services such as Google Print and Amazon's Search Inside as ways of attracting purchasers.

Since independent booksellers rely on the trade wholesalers with their own sales forces, many have lost face-to-face contact with publishers. However, they

Using Google to sell more books

Pete Shemilt, Sales and Marketing Director (EMEA), Academic
and Professional Books, Cambridge University Press

EXPERT ★

The book publishing industry has a love–hate relationship with Google. In fact
it has also been a litigious affair, with the Association of American Publishers
(AAP) famously filing a law suit against the media giant in October 2005 claiming
infringement of copyright by the Print Library Project: Google's plan to digitize
books held by some of the world's major academic libraries.

But despite this, publishers of all sizes remain keen to work with Google
and the reason, of course, is search. Google's dominance in this market is
compelling, and optimizing search results on key words and phrases associated
with books, authors and content is a core component in any marketing strategy
– driving Internet users extremely cost effectively to the point of purchase. In
addition, Google AdWords offers a paid search option.

Google Book Search (books.google.com) takes this revolution in marketing
efficiency a significant step further. The Partner Programme allows the full text
of books to be searched at no cost to the publisher (except the cost of delivering
the book for scanning by Google). Publisher copyright is respected as there
are constraints that limit the extent of a book that can be read online for free
by a consumer. For publishers this is also a modest potential revenue stream
as a share of income is received on advertising displayed against their content.
Future models may include selling or renting access to the content to provide an
additional revenue stream for publishers and Google.

Google Book Search is particularly powerful for books outside the bestseller
lists: the 'Long Tail' of a publisher's portfolio. Academic and professional
publishers like Cambridge University Press derive much of their revenue from
many thousands of different books targeted at very specific niche markets. What
Google Book Search enables is discovery of this content and also reassurance
that it is relevant: the publishing equivalent of being able to walk around a
car, look under the bonnet and kick the tyres before making the decision to
purchase.

For niche books, visibility is key and Book Search also provides a compelling
call to action in the form of a click through to the publisher website or to a choice
of online retailers. Backlist books which would otherwise be difficult to find
have certainly benefited tremendously. Cambridge University Press studied the
difference in sales between 2003 and 2006 for books that were published before
the year 2000. They discovered that in the United States, books in the Google
Book Search programme had a sales rate 20 percentage points higher than those
not included. Cambridge enjoys over a million book visits per month on titles in
Google Book Search.

So whether you believe that Google is true to its motto 'don't be evil' or are
suspicious of their ultimate motives, the impact on potential sales is impossible
to ignore. As Google's own publicity states: 'you would sell a lot more books if a
lot more people knew about them'.

may deal with selected publishers from which they receive higher discounts than from wholesalers.

With the UK market relatively mature, publishers look to overseas markets to boost sales of English editions. Sales staff will make visits to key markets and use local distributors and agents as the route to market. If the market is sufficiently strong, the company may set up its own office in the country. Publishers may also have joint ventures – companies set up in partnership with domestic publishers – or copublication deals – where they co-operate with domestic companies on particular projects – in export markets.

Sales forecasting and inventory control

Sales forecasting and translating it into the actual number to print of a book, especially one of expected high sales volume, is part of the risk decision for the publisher. The view of the sales department is critical. Printing too many copies at the outset would lead to large stock write-offs if the book does not sell; printing too few and being unable to fulfil demand quickly enough on reprint would lead to lost sales and antagonize the book trade and readers. For consumer book publishers, the all-important Christmas market of short intensity is the most difficult to predict, with surprise and often quirky bestsellers popping up each year.

In theory, the sales department of a consumer book publisher should receive the orders from the book trade three months ahead of publication – in practice, orders often arrive after the publisher has set the print run quantity. Therefore the publisher has to forecast. The management of the sales department has conventionally based their forecasts on judgement and experience, historic data of the firm's similar books, and the conversations they have held with the book trade's senior buyers. More recently they have the aid of forecasting software, either the publisher's own or supplied by specialist firms.

Tom Holman writes:

> Plenty of printing decisions are still based on what publishers hope they will sell rather than cold calculation – but the availability of high quality data and market intelligence means predicting demand has become a much more exact science. The improvements are due in large part to the rise of Nielsen BookScan, which has given publishers far more accurate records of how many copies of their books are selling, as well as where and when. Basing future sales on past performance isn't always reliable, but publishers credit BookScan with transforming forecasting. Combined with the publisher's own sales data, it has reduced the likelihood of rash overprints, improved the timeliness of reprints and cut back on returns. (*The Bookseller*, 9 February 2007)

The international college textbook publishers, academic and STM publishers face the challenge of managing stock levels in their warehouses throughout the world and the shipping of stock between them. For example, the UK sales office in the early new year would have forecast the adoption demand of a college textbook in the UK and northern Europe to be purchased by students in the autumn and would have the stock (printed in China during the summer) to meet that demand.

But in September, at the critical UK buying period, another publishing centre overseas receives an unexpected and large direct order from an institution, likely to be repeated annually thereafter, which they cannot fulfil. The stock earmarked for UK and Europe is immediately shipped out of the UK to the overseas centre, dangerously lowering the UK stock levels. But they may have other warehouses elsewhere with small quantities of available stock from which they can replenish the UK.

Roles in the sales department

The sales director, usually supported by a UK sales manager and often by a European sales manager, plans and organizes the sales effort, and negotiates terms of trade with the main customers. The sales management comments on editors' new book proposals – forecasting sales and advising on pricing – and is involved with reprinting and repricing decisions, and with the disposal of overstocks by remaindering or pulping.

In-house sales staff, sometimes called key account managers, propose the purchase of titles three to six months ahead of publication to the buyers of key accounts, and discuss the plans for promotions to be run by the publisher or retailer. These could be based around 3-for-2 or half-price offers, summer reading or back to school campaigns. Although some chains delegate purchasing decisions to branch buyers, who are called on by publishers' sales representatives (reps), most buy centrally and relate order quantities to the sizes and character of their branches – the process of scaling out orders. *Scale-outs* apply to new books and promotions. In some chains, the local managers still have the ability to increase orders. Supermarkets are serviced exclusively by wholesale merchandisers or buy centrally from publishers.

Another sales role is the special sales manager, who will sell to non-book wholesalers, major non-book retailers, direct selling companies such as the Book People, newspapers and magazines (for example cover mounts), and sometimes to remainder or promotion book imprints. They may also sell to book clubs. In academic, STM and professional publishing, special sales encompass direct supply deals made with institutions and businesses, such as bulk sales of textbooks to universities. Special editions may be printed for companies to give away to staff or their customers. Furthermore, some reference and directory publishers sell advertising space in their books and on their websites to supplement copy sales income.

In medium to large publishers the UK sales manager (supported by in-house staff) runs the sales force. Small publishers may not be able to afford the high cost of employing their own reps. Lists may be sold by freelance reps, who are paid a commission of 10 to 12 per cent on net receipts from sales, or by marketing and sales firms, or by the sales force attached to their distributor, or by a larger publisher. But preferably a publisher employs its own full-time reps. Each rep covers a discrete area (a territory), is supplied with a car, a laptop, and receives expenses and a salary. Some publishers, more often the consumer firms, pay bonuses for exceeding sales targets. The reps, who usually live in their territories, meet together with the in-house staff only at the sales conferences (two to four times per year), where they learn about the new books, promotional plans and

Chains with strong central buying do not allow visits by reps to individual stores

EXPERT

How to manage winning a major literary prize

Richard Knight, Operations Director, Nielsen BookScan

What can we learn from looking at the sales of the Man Booker and Costa (formerly Whitbread) prize winners? Analysis of the Nielsen BookScan retail sales data reveals some interesting lessons for a publisher whose author wins a major literary prize.

Firstly, because of the timing of the award, winning the Man Booker means that whatever the sales in the winning week you will get an almost identical sales peak 10 weeks later at Christmas (see graph below). The first two weeks of sales after the win will gross 12 to 15 times the sales of the pre-win seven-week average but then the sales decay quickly.

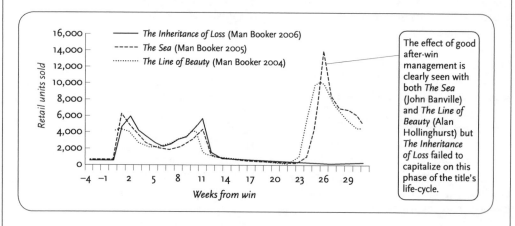

The Inheritance of Loss (Man Booker 2006)
The Sea (Man Booker 2005)
The Line of Beauty (Man Booker 2004)

The effect of good after-win management is clearly seen with both *The Sea* (John Banville) and *The Line of Beauty* (Alan Hollinghurst) but *The Inheritance of Loss* failed to capitalize on this phase of the title's life-cycle.

This rule of thumb applies to both Man Booker and Costa (Whitbread) award winners where a title is not already popular. However, the Costa awards tend to favour more popular titles that have already caught the public eye. Where the average 7-week figure for pre-win sales is high, around 2,000 units per week or more, the sales effect of winning is much reduced with typical uplifts of around two or three for the winning weeks.

Looking at the last three winners of both awards, the sales shape and volume vary little between the successful titles over the winning period. What does affect the sales volume of the winners is what happens *after* the win. Those titles where paperback editions are already in existence when the win is achieved, or where they are rushed out shortly after, can soar to massive heights following the initial surge in sales.

If the peak rise in sales when the win is announced is the measure of the importance of a prize winner – although of course it is prestige that matters more to most authors and publishers – then most winners will be disappointed. Typically between 1,000 and 6,000 copies will be sold. However, it is the publicity surrounding the prize that makes the difference. Should an author have any choice about the prize for which they are entered, they should go for the one with the biggest publicity budget not the biggest prize money!

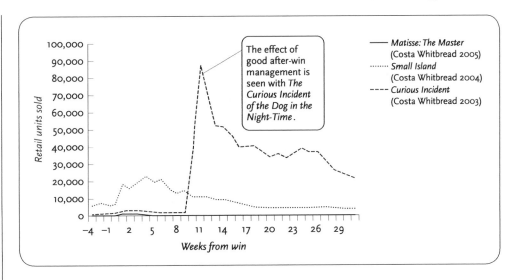

Publicity sells books and the combination of good publicity plus good after-win publishing to get additional copies and formats released quickly to the market can bring about meteoric rises in sales that dwarf the actual win uplift. *Small Island* by Andrea Levy sold 424,000 copies and *The Curious Incident of the Dog in the Night-Time* by Mark Haddon 1.4 m copies in the 52 weeks following their Whitbread prize wins because of good after-win management. By comparison *The Inheritance of Loss* by Kiran Desai sold 117,000 copies in the 48 weeks following its Booker win in 2006, and *Matisse: The Master* by Hilary Spurling sold only 12,000 units in the 52 weeks following its 2005 Whitbread win. Both titles failed to capitalize on the after-win market.

Certainly winning a prize does not guarantee to turn a slow-selling book into a fast-selling one and it is not the role of the judges to select on bestseller potential. The 15 times uplift from a win is similar for all titles and a book that would not be expected to sell in large numbers – such as *Matisse: The Master* – will have a much smaller total uplift than a very popular title like *Small Island*. Finally, another outcome of a prize win is the effect on the author's backlist – even titles six to eight years old can start selling again.

priorities. The reps are sent all the promotional material (advance information sheets, jackets and covers), publicity and marketing details, and feedback orders and reports on their activities, and on the response of customers.

Terms of sale

Publishers sell books to customers on the following terms. The definitions are open to variation, but the important distinction is between firm orders and sale or return. The risk for publishers is lower with firm orders, while the risk for booksellers is lowered if there is the guarantee that they can return unsold stock. If a book is returned to the publisher, the bookseller usually pays for the return delivery, unless otherwise agreed.

Firm orders

On firm orders the bookseller agrees to accept the books, to pay for them (preferably on one month's credit, unless otherwise agreed) and not to return them for credit without prior permission from the publisher. The bookseller takes the risk that the books may not sell and that the publisher may sometimes refuse returns. Powerful booksellers will request a higher discount on firm sales and are likely to be more cautious on the quantity ordered.

Sale or return

Consignment sales are one form of sale or return (SOR). Publishers prefer consignment sales to the simplest form of sale or return. With books sold on consignment – sometimes called *see-safe* orders – the bookseller can within a specified period return books (provided that they are in saleable condition) for credit, or in exchange for other books. The bookseller's account is charged at the time of supply, and payment is due at the expiry of the credit period. Under an alternative arrangement, the bookseller within a specified period can return books and no charge will be raised. Payment is not usually due until the end of the specified period, or when the books are sold. Amazon runs a scheme called Advantage, which can be used by small publishers or authors who self-publish. Publishers give the retailer 55 per cent discount, and Amazon keeps in stock quantities as low as two copies. At the end of each month, Amazon pays the publisher for sales in the previous month.

Sometimes an individual large order for a new book placed by a branch book buyer or an independent bookseller may be firm in part, the remainder bought on consignment. The terms of trade between publishers and their customers – discounts, credit periods and levels of returns – are in a state of flux. As the large retailers have gained in strength, the consumer publishers essentially trade with them on a sale or return basis on longer credit terms (typically 60 days). Small independents may get 30 days credit. Discounts are discussed in more detail in Chapter 13.

Selling in

It is important to realize that good sales staff do not merely walk into the head offices of the chains or into individual shops with a bag of new titles to sell, authorize the return of unsold books and leave. In a rapidly changing world, affecting publishing and retailing, and of changing consumer preferences, the retailers must concentrate their time and effort on marketing and selling the right titles to their customers. The role of the rep or key account manager extends to representing the constituent parts of the publisher – the sales and marketing departments, and the editorial thinking behind projects – to the retailers, and helping them market and sell them to their customers effectively.

Key account managers will discuss forthcoming titles with the major booksellers, looking to push those books most suitable for each chain. Sometimes a book is seen as, for example, a Waterstone's title, one that could do especially well in their shops. Promotional plans will be discussed, both those planned by the publishers and suitable promotions being run by the bookseller. Promise of a

Sales

S K I L L S

Common features of all good sales staff are their energy, self-motivation and discipline which gets them out of bed very early, and makes them work long hours and withstand the physical rigours of driving and carrying heavy bags. They should have clean driving licences and be happy to drive many miles. Being alone, field reps need to be well organized to keep up with the emails and manage their own time.

A good field rep knows the books and the customers' businesses and their customer profiles, interests and systems. If allowed, they call repeatedly and regularly with good warning, appear on time, introduce the books well, succinctly and enthusiastically, gain the buyer's confidence and trust, get the order and are welcomed back. Although reps are given priorities, their skill is to determine which books are best for their area and each outlet, and what size of orders is suitable. They gain the confidence and respect of buyers by recommending books that prove themselves.

On meeting buyers of differing levels of seniority, sales staff need to be alert and make a good first impression. Listening and watching they adjust their selling style and procedure to a buyer's character and mood. They need to be flexible, pitching their style within a range from soft to hard sell, and sense when – and when not – to talk. They are part amateur psychologist, part actor. Strong negotiation skills are required, and they should present their firms honestly, be diplomatic and have authority. When a buyer asks for special terms, or some other favour, a sales manager must be able to make decisions which are best for the company but at the same time attractive for the customer. Their marketing and customer service skills give the publisher a competitive edge.

Educational and college reps must have a lively interest in education and the ability to get on well with the kind of people in those professions and understand their attitudes, mindsets and the conflicting pressures they work under. Overt hard selling is inappropriate. Rather a rep needs to be able to talk about the problems faced by teachers, the kinds of materials used, and the ways a teacher likes to use them, and then has to be able to suggest and promote a suitable book or service. Increasingly they need skills in demonstrating online and other services, and in the higher education sector they need to understand the purchasing systems of the institutions.

decent marketing spend can be required to get a title taken seriously by the major chains. While a retailer may bear the cost of a promotion themselves (in 2007 WHSmith self-financed a 3-for-2 offer on all books in store), more often extra discount is required from the publisher to secure a place for a book in a promotion, and payment may be required from the publisher to secure a prime position in a chain's Christmas campaign.

A consumer publisher's senior in-house staff see the main book buyers twice a year around nine months ahead of the main seasons – in February/March for September to January titles, in August/September for the February to August titles. They prioritize the lead titles which are part of major promotions, discuss other new books and important backlist. Monthly presentations to the key accounts follow, around five months ahead of publication.

What has changed the practice of selling in is the widespread use of sales data. Booksellers can check on an author's track record, and will not be impressed by wild claims by the publisher. When they are unsure about a new title, they will want to check the author's previous sales to firm up their opinion. As Kate Kellaway writes,

> In the past, publishers could fudge sales figures. Now, thanks to the Nielsen BookScan, there is nowhere to hide. It is possible to look up sales data on any novelist faster than you can say Zadie Smith. And if a book flops commercially, or, to use publishing parlance, 'doesn't work', a postmortem can be briskly conducted. Equally, if it does 'break out' (desperado publishing slang for success), the scale of its popularity can be precisely assessed. (*The Guardian*, 25 March 2007)

Those field reps who visit individual accounts will keep a file on customers, listing their interests and opening hours. By appointment, they visit mainly booksellers – the branches of the chains and significant independents – any wholesalers or library suppliers within their areas, and other outlets which justify the high cost of calling. The reps prepare their own folders with clear plastic sleeves containing neatly placed covers, and other information to show buyers. The folder contains the covers of forthcoming books over, for instance, the following two, three or more months, and the lead titles are usually at the front. They use the folder as a visual aid to sell books on subscription (in advance), and the catalogue for covering the backlist. They rarely carry finished copies, apart from exceptions such as children's illustrated books.

Publishers provide their reps with laptops, which allow them to provide current information on stock availability, order status, and sales history, and to send information, such as orders and reports, back to their publishers in the evening.

Advance orders are called subscriptions

A rep's aim is to obtain advance orders (or *subscriptions*) on forthcoming books usually three months ahead of publication from all the main bookshops, in time to inform the print run decision. As most independents place orders electronically, and not through the reps, the reps want the orders to be sent to their publishers, not via higher discount wholesalers. During a call they will cover the new books to be published in a certain period and take up the new books from that point in a subsequent visit. However, smaller and infrequently visited bookshops may be sold new books post-publication.

The meeting with the bookshop buyer takes place in an office, the stock room or on the shop floor. The first few minutes are spent discussing trade gossip and the shop. Reps provide the main contact between booksellers and publishers, and should be able to supply the most recent information on all the firm's titles and to determine what information would be useful, and what marketing and promotions the bookseller could use.

The rep usually leads off with a major, strongly promoted title. The prime aim is to put the buyer in a positive buying frame of mind. Two to three minutes are spent in presenting a lead title. Showing the cover, the rep talks about the book and author, covering such aspects as its contents, what part of the market it is aimed at, why it is good, and sometimes the competition, previous books by the author, and the promotion. Although more time is devoted to the main titles, the rep generally has under a minute per title, just one or two sentences, to sell it. One approach is to have a key positioning line, which helps place the book in the mind of the buyer. The 'new Harry Potter' is overused, but similar lines can be created. If the book is of local interest or is going to receive other publicity, this is mentioned. Mention of participation in the Richard and Judy book club, for example, will guarantee a good subscription. Reps keep records of orders, so that they can remind buyers of orders placed on authors' previous books.

Training is usually required to sell well, both in negotiation and interpersonal skills. To avoid diluting the buyer's interest the rep, aware of his or her buying pattern and customers, concentrates on those titles likely to sell in that particular shop – retailers' customer profiles differ greatly. There is a common understanding between an experienced rep and a good buyer with regard to the titles and order quantities that can be sold in that particular shop. Weak buyers need help. A good buyer is often aware of the books before the rep calls and can estimate within a few seconds the number of sales. But a buyer may want a larger quantity than the rep had in mind or conversely may place an order which the rep feels is too low. Knowing that the book is selling well elsewhere or sensing that the buyer does not appreciate some aspect, the rep mentions that and suggests a higher quantity. If the rep is trusted, the buyer may increase the order. Part of the persuasion may involve the rep in allowing greater freedom on returns within the firm's overall policy. But selling too many copies which are merely returned erodes the bookseller's and publisher's margins.

While there are bookshops which expect reps to do their stock checking and re-ordering for them, booksellers' electronic stock control systems should in theory override their intervention. In practice reps may tactfully remind buyers of new and backlist titles missing from the shelves, reshelve misplaced titles or mention a title that is gaining media attention. When visiting the branch of a chain, the rep will check that the store is complying with the display and positioning of key titles as agreed with head office.

Backed up by attractive POS material, the rep tries to persuade the bookseller to mount special window or instore displays offering incentive terms if necessary. They will receive a weekly email from head office with news of media coverage which is relevant to titles on the list. The bookseller may ask the rep to arrange an author signing session in the shop. Reps also feed back promotion needs requested by customers or promotion ideas used by other publishers which could be emulated; and occasionally reps make editorial suggestions. They may also chase debts.

Academic sales

Academic sales forces are smaller than those of consumer book publishers. Reps visit a limited range of bookshops, such as campus stores, which stock their titles, and may call on specialist mail-order booksellers and library suppliers which supply books to home and export markets.

Additionally they may visit campuses in order to identify courses and the lecturers who make the decisions to recommend textbooks. While to a limited extent they encourage academics to order personally, or through their library, monographs and reference books (and sometimes journals and online services), their main thrust is to secure textbook adoptions. Using the promotional material and occasionally bound copies, they present the most relevant texts to individual lecturers who, if interested, are followed up by email and are sent inspection or gratis copies. They may also demonstrate any supporting electronic resources, arrange for password access for the lecturer, and promote any customization possible of the company's titles. The major publishers employ specialists to conduct technical demonstrations. The rep also undertakes market research, such as looking at reading lists to check new and old adoptions or recommendations and discussing with lecturers trends in subjects generally and particularly in relation to the firm's and competitors' titles. Sometimes they pick up new ideas and potential authors, to be developed by editors.

There is a great disparity amongst publishers regarding the proportion of the reps' time spent visiting booksellers and campuses. Many firms rely on direct mail promotion and reps devote most time to booksellers, whereas the reps of the larger textbook publishers may emphasize college calling. Owing to the difficulty of combining bookseller and college calling cycles, they may separate the activity. The busiest time of college-related shops (which derive 70 per cent of sales from five months of the year) is from the start of the academic year through to Christmas, followed by a secondary peak in the New Year to serve semester course starts. Thus the rep's key period, from mid-summer onwards, is the run-up to September. Although good booksellers forge links with lecturers and solicit reading lists around May, reps alert buyers to adoptions from information gathered from campus visits and from inspection copy reply cards and inform librarians. There are online reading list services such as the one run by Blackwell (readinglists. co.uk).

Reluctant buyers are eventually triggered into building up their stock by the students. Only a small number of booksellers stock monographs and high-priced reference books; such books are supplied by bookshops in response to orders. However academic reps also sell titles more dependent on retail exposure – these may be used by students as background reading or for reference. One example is OUP's series of Very Short Introductions. A crucial aim is to get bookshops to stock and display the books – otherwise sales are lost. Booksellers are encouraged to distribute promotional material and to mount special displays at back-to-college time. Another activity is setting up and attending exhibitions at academic conferences. Large firms employ full-time staff solely for UK and European conferences. Against the background of the decline in campus bookstores and the reluctance of booksellers to hold stock of academic titles, conference exhibitions provide an opportunity for academics to see the publishers' main titles.

Sales in schools publishing

School textbook publishers and some children's book publishers employ a core of full-time educational reps supplemented with term-time reps – often parents or ex-teachers. The large publishers have separate sales forces covering primary and secondary schools, and possibly the further education sector. Additionally, they may appoint specialist advisers (ex-teachers) in the major subject areas. They provide product training for reps, give talks to teachers and promote to local advisers. A rep of a large company may cover just two counties while one in a small company may have to cover a whole region.

During term time reps usually visit two to three secondary schools per day or up to five primary schools. Large primary schools warrant coverage similar to a secondary school. The number of schools visited per day is related to their proximity.

Educational publishers usually hold two or three sales conferences a year, before the opening of terms, at which the commissioning editors present the new books and digital resources. The marketing/sales manager directs the priorities. The reps relate what they are told at the centre to their particular areas and schools. Conferences enable the reps to report on sales, and on the response from their schools.

The key period and busiest time for reps is the spring term when teachers select what they will use for the next school year – their financial year usually begins on 1 April. The summer term is quieter; the winter term becomes progressively more important towards the end. Educational reps carry heavy cases of books (sometimes several hundred titles), and the promotional material, including advance information on forthcoming titles. In small primary schools, headteachers usually choose the materials to be used; in secondary schools and large primary schools departmental heads have the most influence. Thus a rep will try and see them, sometimes by appointment to talk about forthcoming titles, but mainly to show them finished copies. Teachers are asked what they are using and whether they are satisfied. If it is a competitor's book and there is a sign of hesitation, this provides an opening for a rep to discuss the merits of his or her books.

Experienced reps know the content not only of their own books but also of their competitors too, and recount the experience of teachers in other schools. If a teacher shows sufficient interest a rep will ask for an inspection copy to be sent. Occasionally copies of key books are left behind. Although priority is given to new books, especially those introducing a comprehensive course of study for National Curriculum core subjects, the promotion of the backlist is vital. In those schools which manage their own budgets, reps encourage direct orders to the publisher, offering incentive discounts on sizeable quantities if necessary.

Market research includes the regular feedback of information such as teachers' suggestions, the response of teachers to their own and competitors' books, information on competitors, buying policies, local authority guidelines affecting purchases, and gaps in the market. Sometimes reps suggest ideas for books to the commissioning editors, give advice to teachers who are considering authorship and discover new authors. The market for digital content has been stimulated by the government's provision of eLearning credits over a five-year period up until 2008; in response publishers have developed a range of CD-ROM and online products, including those for interactive whiteboards.

Apart from visiting schools, reps ensure that their books are included in the school library, maintain contact with inspectors and local authority advisers, and sometimes conduct seminars. They are also involved in setting up and staffing local exhibitions, and the major exhibitions linked to national subject conferences held in vacations. Generally speaking, reps who work long hours during term time benefit from the school holidays.

INTERNATIONAL SALES SKILLS

There are various ways of organizing export sales staff within a publishing house. In small firms the sales director may be responsible for home sales and for export arrangements, spending perhaps one or two months abroad annually. In larger firms there are separate export departments headed by an export sales manager, who reports to the sales director. An export manager may be supported by office staff. In still larger firms, there may be an international sales director in charge of staff such as regional sales executives or area export managers who look after all the group's lists in specific areas of the world, such as mainland Europe, or are possibly concerned with particular lists of the group. They are usually responsible for all export sales within their designated areas and for the arrangements made with various kinds of overseas agents. Their direct selling may also extend to major importers and bookshops.

A characteristic of staff in international sales is that they are usually expected to spend anything from three to six months abroad. Medium and large publishers may employ British sales representatives who cover parts or the whole of Europe or other areas of the world. Broadly, the larger the company, the smaller the geographical area covered by each representative; but compared to the home market their territories are vast and their calls to importing book trade customers far less frequent. They are either home-based, travelling regularly, or resident overseas. Some of the major publishing groups station UK nationals in small offices in countries outside the fields of operation of their overseas firms. They are

SKILLS

International sales

The ability to speak preferably two or more languages is invariably needed, but is not a top priority: most customers can speak English to some extent. But linguistic ability enables you to understand and relate that much better to the market and customers. Fluency in one or more of the European languages such as French, German, Spanish and Italian, and semi-fluency in some is ideal. Standard Arabic and Chinese are sometimes particularly desirable for certain firms.

Export sales staff have a commitment to publishing and exporting, and have to enjoy working with books. First and foremost sales people, they have a burning desire to ring up the till, to increase profitable turnover. Most of the personal skills required for selling to the home market are paralleled in export selling; but exporters face the complexities of understanding many different and diverse markets and need an appreciation of the political, social, economic and cultural factors pertaining to each country, as well as a sensitivity to and enthusiasm for the market. Good exporters are able to sell and adapt to different environments and situations fast.

Sales staff must like travel, have the self-motivation to work far away from headquarters, take high-level decisions on behalf of their firms, and cope with loneliness. Exporting calls for tough survivors. Some of the overseas postings made by non-general firms are in less-developed countries with arduous climates.

mainly concerned with promoting the firm's books, liaising with and supervising arrangements made with local distributors, opening up the market and, when appropriate, employing local representatives. The export-orientated ELT divisions of major publishers typically have their own export sections deploying all of the above methods. Publishers may also employ full-time local nationals in some areas to represent their interests.

Distribution arrangements

The staff numbers of UK export departments are paradoxically far smaller than the home sales side because much of the work of promoting and selling books is carried out abroad. The main export arrangements are as follows.

Sister companies and branches

In countries where there are firms connected through ownership with the UK publisher, such sister firms usually have the exclusive right to publish the UK firm's output. For example, Oxford University Press has a number of branches around the world. Nevertheless, certain UK titles may be licensed to, or distributed by, other firms. Branches or sister companies may develop publishing operations aimed at their own domestic market and for export throughout the group.

Closed market

Within a territory (a country or region), a stockholding agent usually has the exclusive distribution rights for part of, or the whole of, the publisher's output – the market is closed. The agent services the orders originating from customers within the territory and collects the money. Normally the agent carries out the promotion and sales representation as well. Such agents may be wholesalers, booksellers, importers or branches of other UK publishers. Sometimes, exclusivity is restricted to part of the publisher's output or important named customers within the territory deal directly with the publisher – the market is semi-closed.

Open market

In the open market – countries outside the closed markets of the exclusive stockholding agents (and of the publisher's overseas firms) – the publisher deals directly with the local book trade. However, non-exclusive distribution arrangements may be made with certain local 'preferential' stockists (such as wholesalers) which receive more favourable terms from the publisher. The local booksellers can order either directly from the publisher or from the stockist. Some stockists also promote and sales-represent the publisher's books.

Sales on commission

Independent reps or firms ('bag-carrying agents') are appointed to promote and represent the books in specified countries – usually but not always in open markets. Carrying many publishers' lists, they are based in the UK or abroad. They receive a commission of from 10 to 15 per cent on net sales revenue from the territory. In mainland Europe, especially, such reps face a loss of commission on orders sent to UK wholesalers instead of via the rep or direct to their publisher, and also on internet sales.

Penguin India, started in 1987, publishes a range of fiction and non-fiction books, predominantly by Indian authors. It also publishes in local languages

Terms of trade

The agents, wholesalers and booksellers trading in the books receive discounts, usually off the UK published price, and sometimes higher than home discounts, from the publisher. They then add their costs and profit which can result in book prices being higher than those in the UK. Compared to the UK, customers' credit periods are longer (90 days from date of invoice) but can extend to six months or more from slow-paying parts of the world. Wherever possible 'firm sales' are made, though some unsold books are returned (especially general paperbacks).

There are different terms that apply to the shipping of books:

- *ex-warehouse* – the customer bears the cost from the publisher's (or printer's) door. This is a common basis for trading.
- *free on board (FOB)* – the publisher delivers the books free to the buyer's appointed UK shipping agent. Buyers within a country may co-ordinate and nominate a UK export company that will consolidate orders.
- *cost, insurance and freight (CIF)* – the publisher bears all the costs up to their arrival in a port or town. In return for saving the customer cost and (if the goods are sent air freight) time, the discount and credit period may be cut back.
- *on consignment* – the customer pays only on sales made and has the right to return unsold stock. This may be used for substantial orders.

Other export sales not under the control of the publisher are made by the UK and US export wholesalers, booksellers, and library suppliers. The largest are internationally based and promote, sell and distribute books worldwide – such firms are major 'home' customers of academic and STM publishers. Some end-users seeking the cheapest source of supply (especially libraries) 'buy round' the publishers' arrangements by ordering books from library suppliers or US exporters which ignore exclusive territorial markets. Furthermore, internet bookselling is breaking down national frontiers for the trading of different kinds of books in different languages.

International sales staff who are selling into open markets, for example Europe, will be keen to publish UK trade editions ahead of the equivalent US editions. Some consumer publishers believe that translation deals encourage the sales of English language editions.

Promotion and personal selling

Communication with the international network is vital. People abroad must be persuaded to concentrate on promoting and selling the firm's titles rather than those of others. Constant contact takes the form of the supply of information through mailings, email, telephone calls and overseas visits.

The advance information sheets, catalogues, leaflets, covers, and point-of-sale material cascade on to the agents and representatives who use that material to publicize the publisher's titles within their markets. Some agents prepare their own catalogues from information supplied, while others send out UK originated material. Agents may generate free media publicity, secure reviews, mail catalogues, sometimes place advertisements, attend exhibitions and operate a textbook inspection copy service.

The UK publisher too may mail promotional material direct to wholesalers, booksellers, libraries, British Council offices, academics and professionals, send books for review to learned journals, send complimentary copies of textbooks to influential people and operate an inspection copy service from the UK. The promotion efforts of publisher and agent may overlap. Of equal importance is the quality and regularity of the response from agents and representatives. They provide feedback on their activities and on market conditions, and specific feedback on individual titles, such as requests for more material.

Overwhelmingly, however, export sales are generated by personal selling. The senior sales staff give presentations to agents and main customers on their visits to the UK, at book fairs, and in their own countries. Their trips may last two, three or more weeks, and encompass half a dozen countries, 30 to 40 customers or just one. They primarily sell to agents' sales managers or directors concerned with imports and may brief the agent's reps at a conference. They discuss all aspects of their trading relationship and assess agents' effectiveness.

More junior sales staff, the reps, usually sell to the book trade in open markets. They try to get subscriptions for new books, do not overlook the backlist, respond to complaints and collect debts. When appropriate they supply promotion copy for inclusion in the catalogues of wholesalers or retailers, check orders in order to avoid expensive distribution mistakes, and sometimes co-ordinate booksellers' ordering. Academic reps may call on lecturers and librarians in order to secure textbook adoptions, facilitate inspection copy orders, and encourage booksellers to carry out joint promotions and exhibitions. ELT reps promote and sell courses directly to private language schools, state schools and to government agencies.

While the *Harry Potter* series sells well across international markets, other titles may have variable patterns of sale. What goes well in one country may not work in another market. Book formats and covers may have to be varied to take account of international differences in taste. International sales staff view titles with their markets in mind, and may join both editorial and covers meetings.

The top 10 countries for exports of books from the UK are shown in Table 11.1.

Table 11.1 Top destinations for UK book exports 2006 (*source*: The Publishers Association, *UK Book Industry in Statistics*, 2006)

Country	Value of sales (£m)
USA	215.6
Irish Republic	133.3
Germany	92.2
Australia	80.0
The Netherlands	79.5
France	58.8
Spain	48.2
Japan	47.3
South Africa	46.2
Italy	42.3

Diane Setterfield's gothic novel, *The Thirteenth Tale* (2006), had modest initial sales in the UK despite reaching the top of *The New York Times* bestseller list

DISTRIBUTION

The distribution of books, journals and new media products is critical to the publisher's role of getting its product into the customers' hands at the right time and in the right quantities. The key aspects of distribution (sometimes called logistics) are:

- customer care,
- accuracy in order fulfilment,
- speed and reliability in dispatch,
- physical protection of the product, and
- economies in dispatch.

Failings in these areas lead to lost sales, diminished retail display, increased cost to the publisher and loss of confidence by bookseller and reader; improvements give the publisher a competitive marketing edge.

Book distribution is an enormous challenge and exhibits unusual characteristics. Many other kinds of goods produced by manufacturers (often on continuous production lines) are supplied directly to wholesalers and then on to the retailers. But publishers hire printers to manufacture the books which are delivered to the publisher or its distributor; and for their size carry an enormous range of new and backlist products stored for a long time. In the main, publishers supply retailers – individual shops or their centralized warehouses – directly. Despite the growth of the wholesalers, book wholesaling in the UK is concentrated on consumer books. The customers for books extend beyond the retail trade – to schools and to individuals needing single copies (for review, inspection, mail-order sales). Publishers receive massive numbers of small orders, the profits from which may not cover the distribution and credit cost. Yet book retailers demand faster and more reliable distribution in order to compete against other kinds of products. UK publishers export vigorously and distribute to most countries from the UK via a myriad of arrangements and carriers. In material handling terms, book distribution presents extremes, ranging from one or more titles of varying size or other media products up to a container load.

Publishers face the return of unsold books from the book trade (typically in the range of 10 to 20 per cent of sales), which are credited accordingly; and if the books are damaged or of low value they destroy them. KPMG in 1998 estimated that the average cost of publishers' distribution was amongst the highest in industry and represented 13 per cent of sales, while that of a consumer goods manufacturer was 6 per cent.

ISBN and EDI

The foundation stone on which all book trade electronic transactions and information systems are based was the introduction in 1967 of the standard book number (SBN). By 1970 it had become internationally accepted. The ISBN incorporates the language of origin, the publisher, and the unique identifier of each book or edition. The last digit is a check to ensure the preceding digits are correct. ISBNs are also used by publishers to identify other kinds of products such as audiobooks, CDs and ebooks. The digital identifier for journals is the international standard serial number (ISSN).

In 1979, TeleOrdering was launched by Whitaker. This enabled booksellers to transmit orders electronically overnight into publishers' computers. TeleOrdering was the book trade's first proprietary electronic trading system deploying an early form of electronic data interchange (EDI). EDI facilitates the exchange of data between computer systems, saving trading partners' time, errors and cost by avoiding the use and handling of paper and making it unnecessary to rekey information.

By the mid-1980s standards were developed to convert the ISBN into the European article numbering (EAN) bar code. This appears on the back cover of books. By the early 1990s most main UK bookshops had installed electronic point of sale (EPOS) systems which read the bar codes. The collection of EPOS data from the UK general retail market by Nielsen from the late 1990s aided the management of stock during the rise and fall of a title's sales.

The allocation of ISBNs in the UK is made by the UK International Standard Book Numbering (ISBN) Agency. On 1 January 2007, the ISBN changed from 10 to 13 digits, and all existing ISBNs were prefixed by 978. The resulting 13-digit number is identical with the EAN-13 number that is currently encoded in the bar code. The 979 prefix will be introduced when the current stock of numbers is exhausted.

A bookseller in Holland, BGN, has introduced radio frequency identification (RFID) into its stores. Called a smart bar code, a RFID tag can be inserted into a book, enabling fast scanning of the books within a store. This raises the possibility of smart shelving, which recognizes what stock is sitting there, and for customers to go through self-service tills. For the moment the system is being used to speed up the shelving of books when they arrive into the shop, and to put back stock that has wandered to other parts of the shop.

Industry standards

In the drive towards electronic ordering, invoicing, information gathering and transmission, Book Industry Communication (BIC) was founded in 1991 by The Publishers Association, The Booksellers Association, The Library Association (now Chartered Institute of Library and Information Professionals – CILIP) and the British Library. BIC aims to develop and to promote standards for ecommunication and ecommerce, and to aid supply chain efficiency, in the UK and internationally. Its membership embraces publishers, distributors, retailers, wholesalers, library suppliers, bibliographic providers, system suppliers and shipping organizations. The adoption of 'standards' is critically important to the trading of physical and digital products, and there are many agencies in the UK, Europe and in America working on standards for the description and trading of different categories of products. However, for the publishing industry and the intermediaries, BIC focuses on three main areas.

Product information

Firstly, the development of standardized product information – a classification system whereby publishers describe the bibliographical details of their products consistently – and the technical and procedural standards whereby they electronically communicate that information and its updating to others, such as to the bibliographic providers, wholesalers and retailers (see Chapter 10).

Supply chain

The second area relates to the supply chain and covers bar codes; B2B ecommerce transacted through EDI (orders, acknowledgements, delivery notes, invoices, credit notes, and price and product availability); and the standardization of returns authorization procedures in order to reduce costs. The industry returns initiative (IRI) has led to returns requests being sent by booksellers electronically, with credits taking place automatically when stock is returned. There is no precise data, but the IRI is believed to have made reductions in the cost of returns, compared to the situation at the time of a KPMG study in 1999. Under the IRI, no returns will be authorized until three months after publication or once 15 months have elapsed since the title was last supplied to the shop.

Digital publishing

As publishers license and sell their products online either via intermediaries or directly to end-users from their digital warehouses, there is a need for common standards to facilitate electronic copyright management in order to trigger payment systems. For instance, an intermediary may want to print on-demand a publisher's title or to customize a product including chapters from a range of book sources, or a researcher may want to follow-up an electronic journal reference in an article from another publisher's journal server.

The classic digital identifiers – the ISBN and ISSN – are the basis for electronic rights management systems at the macro level. The Association of American Publishers sponsored the concept of a micro-level identifier – the digital object identifier (DOI) which is now promoted by the DOI Foundation. The ideas behind the DOI are that it is a simple or dumb number which can be attached by the publisher to an object, such as a journal abstract, author's name and address, or book chapter, or piece of text or an illustration – whatever the publisher considers could be reusable or tradable. The publisher maintains a continually updated directory, which acts as a routing system where the dumb number is associated with the publisher's internet address. The publisher's database stores the most accurate information about the DOIs such as the copyright ownership, terms and conditions of sale and prices. The journal publishers were amongst the first publishers to deploy DOIs, though the take-up in other areas has been slow.

Warehousing and distribution

The major publishing groups run their own distribution and generally place the facility in the country away from the headquarters, while the very small publishers do it from home. Small and medium publishers either distribute themselves or use independent distributors (such as Central Books or Turnaround); they also may use the larger publishers (or wholesalers) – all of which are eager to increase their turnover. Some may use a mixture, supplying direct sales themselves but using third parties for trade and export sales. Third-party distributors offer to publishers the complete service of bulk storage, invoicing, customer service and cash collection, and delivery for which they charge around 12 per cent of sales: less for larger publishers and more for smaller publishers.

> In logistical terms, the difference between a wholesaler and distributor is that a distributor will provide additional services, while a wholesaler will traditionally give 'sale without transformation' (although wholesalers have been seeking to add to their offer in recent times). (*The Bookseller*, 30 March 2007)

The supply chain for books

Books can be supplied directly from the publisher or through a distributor or wholesaler (see the figure below). Smaller bookshops source the majority of their stock from the wholesalers.

The independent third-party distributors occasionally go bust, which can be a disaster for the publisher if unable to retrieve its cash and books from the receiver. The trend is towards fewer and larger distributors. Size gives to the distributor the turnover to invest in expensive electronic book handling and warehouse systems, the ability to bulk up order values, greater leverage in debt collection, and the securing of lower rates with carriers. The distributor TBS (The Book Service Ltd), owned by Random House, handles orders for publishers such as Faber & Faber and Quercus. Bookpoint and Littlehampton Book Services are owned by Hachette. With the development of faster and more reliable transportation systems, including air freight, there is a movement away from overseas stockholding agents to direct supply from the UK, giving a greater opportunity to price books more competitively in many markets.

The 'trade side' of distribution is concerned with processing received orders, raising invoices and documentation. Not all publishers can accept teleorders, and many orders are received in writing or by fax, telephone, or email. Once orders are received, the invoice is raised, and the documentation, labelling and physical distribution begin. There are many standardized codes which tell a customer a book is unavailable for various reasons. UK booksellers are identified by the

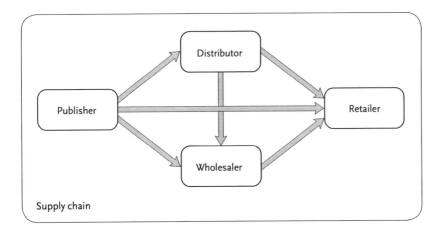

Supply chain

standard address number (SAN) which is a unique identifier of the delivery address. New books or reprints not yet in stock are recorded on a 'dues listing' and dispatched when available unless otherwise instructed. Export orders need additional documentation to coply with the receiving country's import regulations and taxes, such as VAT. On orders to mainland Europe some publishers invoice in Euros or local currencies and offer banking arrangements. Mistakes in export orders incur severe penalties. Pro-forma invoices may be sent to unsafe customers before the books are dispatched. Most publishers supply books to UK booksellers carriage free, whereas mainland European publishers charge carriage to their booksellers.

The customer services department resolves queries from sometimes irate booksellers regarding problems of distribution and of accounts. The textbook inspection copy service and mail-order or subscription sales are usually handled by separate departments.

The warehouse includes the bulk store of books and journals (and of any raw paper reserves), into which deliveries are made, and a 'picking' area where titles and back-up stock are positioned for easy location (new books and fast-selling titles in prime sites). The invoices may include the location of titles in the order in which they are 'picked'. The collated orders move to the packaging and dispatch area. Dispatch involves knowing the most economic, speedy and reliable method (road carrier, shipping, air freight, post) and negotiating bulk deals with carriers. If the publisher bears the cost, the incentive is to lower costs to increase profitability; when the customer pays (for example on FOB export orders) the incentive is to assist them to save money, a marketing service. In order to treat mainland Europe as an extension of the home market and to compete against US publishers, some UK publishers are using pan-European delivery networks operated by the same carriers as used in the UK. In so doing, the publisher controls the level of service door-to-door, avoids dealing with dozens of carriers and attains economies.

While the computer monitors stock levels, there are staff who physically check the stock and check the returns (the bar codes can aid the task), liaising with the sales office where appropriate. The application of computers to order-processing, distribution and dispatch provides key information for management, such as reports on dues, sales by title, by area, by representative (and comparative monthly reports), type of customer, discount structure, return levels, stock and re-order levels, method of dispatch, carriage charge analysis, and debtors.

Print on demand

The advent of print on demand (POD) reduces the need for a publisher to store stock of very slow moving backlist titles. Indeed for highly specialist titles or customized books, it removes the need to hold any stock. A book is produced in response to an order and the publisher's POD supplier dispatches it direct. Third-party distributors serving publishers risk being cut out and some are installing their own POD facilities.

Print on demand: a perfect storm?

David Taylor, Managing Director, Lightning Source UK and Senior
Vice President Global Sales

Genuine print on demand (POD) is the ability to print and distribute a single
copy of a book from a file that is held digitally. Sell book, print book has started to
replace print book – then try to sell it.

The traditional publishing model is characterized by the offset printing
of inventory at levels based on best guess sales estimates and its storage in
distribution centres. The sales effort is geared to the stimulation of orders. A key
aim for the publisher's production function is achieving the lowest unit cost for
the number of copies that the publisher wants to hold in stock.

Printing too many copies runs the risk of writing off stock; printing too few,
the risk of losing sales. The acronyms RPUC (reprint under consideration), RP
(reprinting) or TOS (temporarily out of stock) all add up to one thing: a missed
sale and an unhappy customer. The print-on-demand model means that a book
is always available.

There is little doubt that POD is becoming an increasingly important part
of inventory and supply chain management for traditional publishers and their
distributors. Market trends and advances in digital print capabilities are set to
accelerate the take-up over time. Traditional publishers use print on demand in a
number of different ways, and here are just a few:

- keeping titles in print and capturing sales that otherwise would have been lost,
- bringing titles back into print from OP (out of print) status,
- issuing titles in paperback for the first time,
- reducing inventory levels and the cash tied up in the business,
- reducing warehousing needs,
- import and export via printing in the sales market, and
- development of new products and revenue streams (for example, large print
  editions).

However, print on demand is having another major impact in the global book
trade and one that is fuelling a rapid rise in the number of titles that are in print.
Genuine print on demand allows a publisher to operate a virtual stock policy with
titles being printed only when there is an order. This model removes the need to
tie up capital in speculative inventory, and the need for real estate warehousing
and distribution facilities.

Lightning Source, for example, offers fulfilment systems that allow not
only publisher/distributor direct ordering but also a buy/sell relationship with
wholesalers and internet retailers. In this scenario, a publisher need not carry
any inventory or indeed physically handle the book to fulfil an order. Inventory
is printed from a digital file only when an order is received. The only entry cost
for the publisher is the setting up and management of the digital file and its
associated metadata.

The effect of this model is to reduce dramatically the barriers to entry in
terms of capital for a start-up publisher; this in turn has stimulated an explosion

in new publishers entering the market for whom print on demand is core to their whole business model. This new type of publisher is fundamentally a selling/marketing model with a very different looking balance sheet to the traditional publisher and its requirement to hold and finance speculative inventory.

In addition, print on demand has allowed completely new publishing models to emerge. In the US in particular, there has been an explosion in the field of self-publishing in the last five years, underpinned by both the print-on-demand model and the ability to support and market these titles via the internet bookselling model.

The other major new model to emerge on the back of print on demand is the content aggregator. Such an organization brings books back from the out-of-print graveyard. An out-of-copyright title can be scanned and reissued as a facsimile of the original, even dropped into a generic cover, and made available in the market via the provision of metadata about the title to the book trade.

Print on demand allows publishers to meet single copy demand for their content in a phenomenon that has come to be known as the 'Long Tail'. The internet bookselling model allows the consumer to find obscure titles not usually stocked in bookshops. The coming together of POD, the Long Tail and the internet bookselling model is starting to look like a perfect storm.

Ebooks

Christoph Chesher, Group Sales Director of Taylor & Francis Group and Honorary Professor of Publishing Studies, University of Stirling

New technology has brought threats to traditional business models, but for those prepared to accept the challenge it also provides the prospect of exciting new developments. There are a myriad of opportunities – both to disseminate content to a wider audience and to create new and incremental income streams.

The new technology associated with ebooks has enabled publishers to develop new business models: from offering content on a chapter-by-chapter basis to allowing users to compile their own ebooks or rent titles for a specific period (a week, month . . .). For publishers, there remains the question whether these new business models provide useful incremental income or simply cannibalize existing full price sales. All the indicators suggest that they provide income that would otherwise not be realized. Take, for example, Taylor & Francis's ebook rental scheme. Feedback from users suggests a typical profile of students searching for material for their projects, often at short notice and often at night. Whilst they are unlikely to contemplate purchasing two or three monographs at $100/£50 each, they seem perfectly relaxed about a paperback price point (sub £10/$20), no matter that they only receive access for a week or so and will never own the title.

A successful area for the sale of ebooks to individuals is to professionals, particularly those in medicine, law, computing or engineering, where the

E★PERT

portability of key handbooks on handheld PDAs is of key advantage to them whilst they are on the move.

Ebooks are an important source of income to Taylor & Francis, but their sale to individuals represents a relatively small percentage of overall online income compared to sales through the academic library channel. Although libraries still purchase the majority of their book titles as print (the general consensus in the industry being that ebooks account for between 6 and 8 per cent of sales to libraries in 2006/7), the market is definitely in transition with many publishers quoting growth rates of 40 to 60 per cent per annum. Significant growth in the market share taken by ebooks seems likely. Taylor & Francis ebooks are also available through a number of intermediaries such as Amazon, eBooks.com and Sony Connect and through ebook aggregators such as ebrary, eBL, MyiLibrary and Dawsonera, all of which supply the academic library market.

Publishers have had to grapple with building their own online platforms, and for many the decision to invest significant sums is far from clear cut at a time when ebooks occupy a small share of the overall books market. However, those that have taken the plunge are finding that the technology can help to make a significant contribution in other areas originally unforeseen. The cost of distributing print books as inspection copies to lecturers is a substantial but necessary cost and the ability to provide inspection copies electronically offers potential savings. Many publishers (including Taylor & Francis) now offer the option of an eInspection Copy.

Ebook files are increasingly being used in advertising as well. Publishers supply many bookseller websites with cover images and sample pages in order to help stimulate demand. More recently Amazon's SITB ('search inside the book') programme has taken this to a new level, to the benefit of both customer and publisher. The customer can find the book that best fits their need, whilst the scheme increases the overall propensity of the consumer to purchase. Google Book Search and Microsoft Live also provide publishers with the opportunity of extra exposure for their books within the framework of the main search engines. Both companies assert that trials indicate that the greater percentage access that a publisher allows to its books, the higher the usage and click through to bookshops (see the box, 'Using Google to sell more books'). For the publisher, however, there is the dilemma of assessing at what level free access provides a taster and at what level it effectively provides users with a free library service. In the same way that in the early twentieth century recording companies at first felt threatened by the advent of commercial radio and then grew to love the exposure it provided, publishers are likely to grow more relaxed about legitimate online preview schemes. Indeed publishers are experimenting with innovative preview schemes themselves. The ebook widget allows a publisher to benefit from viral marketing in ways never previously envisaged. The ebook widget can be emailed to anyone and can also be lifted and embedded on to any site or blog. It consists of the book cover which, when clicked upon, reveals, through a pop up, several pages (as many as the publisher wishes) and a 'buy the book' button which will take the user to the publisher's ecommerce site. What is certain is that publishers will constantly need to consider new and non-traditional ways of both generating income and delivering their material.

Online content and ebooks

Some publishers have built their own platforms for the delivery of online content; others use third parties. High levels of investment are required to develop online services. The majority of sales are to institutions. For ebooks, publishers may distribute through a third party, referred to as a digital asset distributor (DAD), or opt for direct supply. Content is sold as entire books or by the chapter. Libraries prefer ebooks on a common platform and there are companies such as ebrary that will supply content from a variety of publishers.

Ebooks will have to grow from a very small base – estimated at less than 1 per cent of the US market for books in 2005 – yet some publishers are definitely expanding this market. Trade publishers such as Macmillan and Random House produce new titles in ebook formats. In the area of academic publishing, Taylor & Francis generate 5 per cent of their book sales from ebooks (DOC, 2006). Launched in the US in 2007, CourseSmart is a joint venture between six publishers, including Pearson and Wiley, to provide ebooks of higher education textbooks. Students can purchase ebooks for a set period, with prices below those of the printed texts. This may encourage students away from purchasing second-hand editions. Other products have been developed for students, such as memory sticks which hold key textbooks as well as free memory.

Now read this

Chapter 13, The sales channels for books in the UK.
Barney Allan, *Guide to Export for UK Book Publishers*, The Publishers
    Association/UK Trade & Investment, 2004.

Sources

DOC (Digitisation of Content Group), *Brave New World*, November 2006.
Supply Chain and Your Business, Supplement to *The Bookseller*, 9 February 2007.
Simon Linacre, 'Wholesale Changes', *The Bookseller*, 30 March 2007.

Web resources

www.bic.org.uk BIC (Book Industry Communication) – develops and promotes
    standards for electronic commerce and communication in the book and
    serials industry.
www.booksellers.org.uk The Booksellers Association.
www.publishers.org.uk The Publishers Association.

CHAPTER 12

Rights sales

The author–publisher contract sets out the scope of the publisher to license various kinds of rights to other firms: the licensing business model. These rights allow other companies to exploit the book in different ways – media, territories and languages. Rights sales can be important to a publisher since the income attracts little in the way of direct costs and is often simply extra profit. In consumer book publishing the contract is frequently drawn up by the author's agent and sets out the rights available to the publisher.

The large publishers maintain separate contracts departments which put into the contractual detail the outcome of the agreements reached with authors, agented authors and with publishers from whom they have bought, and with licensors to whom they have sold rights. There are also contract specialists who offer their services to publishers and agents.

The selling of rights may be done by editors and sales staff. However, medium to large publishers employ specialists to sell rights actively. A small department consists of a rights manager and assistant; larger ones have staff who specialize in particular rights or regions of the world. A publisher may use rights selling agents abroad (for example in mainland Europe, the USA and Japan) who receive a commission of, say, 10 per cent on sales made.

A report published by The Publishers Association in 2006 put a value on the rights sales for the larger publishers in the UK. The total income in 2004 was £128.5 m, with 56 per cent from co-editions and 44 per cent from the sale of other rights. Foreign language co-editions accounted for 64 per cent of co-edition sales; the remainder are English language co-editions. For foreign language co-editions, 52 per cent of sales were in western Europe, 13 per cent were in Nordic countries, 12 per cent in central and eastern Europe, and 9 per cent in Asia. For English language co-editions, 56 per cent of sales were to USA and Canada, and 44 per cent in the UK, including book clubs. Under the sale of other rights, the embryonic area of electronic rights totalled £4.2 m, mainly in the sectors of academic and reference publishing (publishers.org.uk).

Rights staff may also check and monitor the contracts made between the publisher and authors, and offer their expertise on copyright and media law. Separate permissions staff may carry out necessary reactive work, which involves responding to requests for copyright permission to reproduce material (such as extracts of text, tables, technical illustrations) from the firm's books. They are usually granted a *non-exclusive licence* to reproduce the material for a particular use, with due acknowledgement, for a specified edition, quantity and in a specified language throughout the world, though the territories may be limited. The applicant is charged a fee, usually equally shared by the originating publisher and author. The Copyright Licensing Agency (CLA) facilitates the collection of fees from educational and other organizations wishing to copy extracts for class sets and other uses. Such 'collective' – or 'secondary' – licensing schemes are used by publishers when it is not possible or practical for them to license users directly.

> A non-exclusive licence allows a publisher to enter into agreements with other third parties

The majority of books have no significant rights sales income, but some (such as in consumer publishing, especially in adult and children's highly illustrated colour books) earn much or depend on rights deals for viability. Where agents are involved, many rights may be reserved and not available to the publisher, limiting what then can be sold. For example, a publisher buying volume (essentially print) rights for a specified territory will not be able to sell translation rights. By contrast, the non-consumer publishers acquire all rights from their non-agented authors. As the major publishers consolidate their position worldwide, they gain the capability of publishing books themselves in foreign languages rather than licensing translation rights to others. The major STM publishers, in particular, are increasing their ability to sell their products digitally and directly to end-users without the use of intermediaries.

Rights work involves close contact with the editorial, production, promotion and sales departments, and accounts. Selling to customers, who are mainly editors or directors of other firms, has to be carried out in a regular and personal way, and good negotiation skills are required to negotiate deals and contracts. Foreign travel includes at the very least attending the major book fairs in Frankfurt and – for children's books – Bologna. Staff who sell many books of international appeal, such as highly illustrated colour non-fiction, travel widely and frequently, making

The Frankfurt Book Fair is held in October of each year

Copyright Licensing Agency

Kevin Fitzgerald, Chief Executive of the Copyright Licensing Agency

The Copyright Licensing Agency Ltd (CLA) was set up by UK authors and publishers to perform collective licensing on their behalf for the copying of extracts from publications.

CLA was established in 1982 by the Authors Licensing and Collecting Society (ALCS) and the Publishers Licensing Society (PLS) to license the limited photocopying and scanning of books, journals and magazines. Visual creators are also represented through an agency agreement with the Design and Artist Copyright Society (DACS).

CLA licenses organizations from the business, education and government sectors and permits limited copying under blanket licences, in most cases in return for one single annual fee.

Through reciprocal agreements with sister organizations in other countries, our licences also include rights to copy from titles published in all major overseas territories. CLA is always looking to expand its licensed repertoire and in 2006 new agreements were reached to add territories such as Argentina, Belgium and Mexico.

In the financial year 2006/7 over £49 m was collected in licence fees and record distributions of that revenue were made to copyright owners within the same year with authors and publishers benefiting to the tune of £47 m. This money is allocated to individual copyright owners on the basis of the titles copied in the relevant period.

This core licensing activity connects creativity with industry by ensuring that copyright owners receive a fair reward when their works are copied as well as providing easy, legal access to a wide range of publications – such as trade and consumer magazines, journals, books, law reports and press cuttings – for businesses, schools, colleges, government and public bodies.

Recently, in collaboration with copyright owners, CLA has faced the new challenge of licensing the re-use of born-digital publications. There is demand from our licensees in many sectors – especially Higher Education and the pharmaceutical industry – for a 'comprehensive digital licence' (CDL) that will allow print-to-print, print-to-digital (scanning), digital-to-digital and digital-to-print re-use of extracts from publications. In order to engage authors, visual creators and publishers with the issues surrounding the collective licensing of digital originals, CLA hosts a number of sector-specific information days and consultation events as well as pursuing dialogue with individual publishers. As ever, the objective is to provide collective solutions that complement the primary business of copyright owners.

To be eligible to benefit from CLA's licensing activity, authors and artists must be members of ALCS and DACS respectively and publishers should have given their mandate to PLS. By supporting copyright owners in this way, CLA plays a part in maintaining the value of their work, thereby sustaining creativity and the creative industries in the UK which provide over 8 per cent of the UK GDP and generate millions of jobs.

E★PERT

Book fairs

Lynette Owen, Copyright Director, Pearson Education Ltd

E ★ PERT

Book fairs are key events in the publishing world calendar, providing a meeting place for publishers, agents, distributors and retailers to pursue their business on a face-to-face basis; authors may also attend for book launches and cultural events. Some book fairs admit the public, who can attend literary events and in some cases purchase books at a discount.

Rights trading is a major feature of many book fairs. Although this business is conducted year-round by letter, telephone and email, book fairs provide a focus for new titles on offer. The key fairs for rights business are: Frankfurt, held in October and covering all types of publication and featuring exhibitors from all over the world; Bologna, from 2008 held in late March and covering children's books and some educational publications; and London, now held in mid-April.

BookExpo America, held in early June and alternating between New York and other US cities, is primarily an event for US publishers to showcase their new publications to the US book trade, but it provides an opportunity for British and other publishers to meet US publishers on home territory.

Other fairs in western Europe have varying roles: Salon du Livre (in Paris in March) and Göteborg (late September) are largely cultural events, whilst Liber (held immediately before Frankfurt and alternating between Madrid and Barcelona) is primarily a forum for Latin American publishers to meet Spanish publishers.

In central and eastern Europe there are now many fairs, although most are 'selling fairs' for local publishers to sell books to the visiting public. The Warsaw fair, held every year in May, provides a rights forum, whilst the Moscow International Book fair (early September) provides an opportunity to meet many Russian publishers who do not always attend western book fairs. Fairs have also been established in Prague, Budapest and the Baltic states, where the book fair rotates between Estonia, Latvia and Lithuania. In the Balkans there are fairs in Belgrade, Bucharest and most recently in Thessaloniki.

Further afield there are book fairs in Calcutta and Delhi (sales rather than rights events), Seoul, Tokyo and Beijing. Beijing is a major rights fair and Tokyo is seeking to build up this aspect of its business. In Latin America, Guadalajara is being promoted as a rights event. The Cape Town book fair, first held in 2006, is hoping to establish itself as a pan-African rights forum.

Literary agents and publishing rights staff start work on book fairs early and appointments are planned and confirmed many weeks before the event itself. Random callers may be accommodated, but prebooked appointments are now the order of the day.

Rights sellers attend book fairs armed with information and material on existing and forthcoming projects and work under considerable pressure; usually no more than half an hour is available for each appointment. Traditionally, sellers remain based on their own stand or in an agents' centre, whilst buyers move around the fair from meeting to meeting. The physical conditions at some fairs leave much to be desired! A rights appointment will usually start with a discussion of any outstanding business, followed by a presentation of new projects; the rights seller will aim to select titles appropriate to the customer and may be switching languages from appointment to appointment. Projects may be offered on the basis of an exclusive option (more common for academic and professional titles, where the potential buyer will need time to obtain specialist reviews), multiple submission to more than one potential buyer, or a full-scale auction where would-be buyers will have to compete with each other on the basis of terms set by the seller.

Although rights trading is conducted all year round and has been much facilitated by email, book fairs remain extremely important as much rights business depends on personal relationships, knowledge of the taste of the potential buyer (particularly important in trade publishing) and face-to-face discussions. Business is often extended beyond a full working day at the fair with breakfast meetings, receptions and dinner after the fair; publishers are social animals and many a deal has come about as a result of a chance encounter in less formal circumstances than a fair appointment. Much business, particularly for trade titles, may be conducted before and after the fair itself in hotels and offices.

The period after a book fair is usually extremely busy, and traditionally the onus is on the rights seller to follow up with each customer promptly after the fair, confirming what has been agreed, drawing up contracts for any deals finalized at the fair and providing any information or sample material promised to the potential buyer. For educational, academic and professional titles, decisions tend to be taken some weeks or months after the fair itself – for trade titles, decisions may be made more quickly.

In the age of the internet, conference calls and videoconferencing, the future value of book fairs has sometimes been questioned, but most publishers would agree that they remain hugely important events and that 'virtual' events would not be an adequate substitute for regular personal contact and the buzz of a well-run book fair.

sales trips to countries in addition to their attendance at relevant fairs. There is a great deal of paperwork – correspondence, maintaining customer mailing lists, and record keeping after fairs and sales visits. Rights managers have to keep track of trends around which countries are likely to be fruitful sources of business – for example, China has assumed much greater importance in recent years as the economy and the publishing sector there have experienced fast growth. In Europe, there are variations between countries in terms of the number of books bought per head of population. Those countries with a tradition of cheap paperback publishing are likely to have higher sales per capita.

As in other areas, rights selling is aided by technology. For example, there are specialist rights sales software programs, such as Bradbury Phillips, and the international book fairs are creating their virtual equivalents for the trade of rights. Selling may be done by telephone or email, using a variety of print materials, such as advance information sheets, sample pages and the catalogue, or using a laptop. Many customers still want to see physical material, including manuscripts, proofs or printed copies.

The rights department may get involved with a title before the author has signed the contract. An editor may ask the rights manager to assess the title's

rights sales potential particularly if that affects the author's advance, or the viability of the book depends on rights sales. Sample covers and page spreads may be shown at the Frankfurt Book Fair to gauge the likely interest in a proposal. Around the delivery of the manuscript, the titles are assessed and a strategy is drawn up regarding the choice of possible customers, and how and when they will be approached. There are many kinds of rights and the deals struck are both intricate and varied. The main rights are described in the following pages. Sometimes, the author's approval is needed before deals are concluded, and it is any case a courtesy to keep them informed.

Reprint paperback rights

With the emergence of consumer book publishers that publish both hardbacks and paperbacks, the selling of reprint paperback rights by originating hardback publishers to separate paperback publishers is now rare. But a small or medium size publisher while capable of selling a trade paperback itself, may not be able to sell a mass-market paperback edition demanding different distribution channels. Thus it could access that market by licensing that edition to a larger publisher. *The No. 1 Ladies' Detective Agency* by Alexander McCall Smith was first published in 1988 by Polygon, a small Scottish publisher, before appearing as an Abacus paperback in 2003.

The key features of such deals are as follows. The seller defines the rights granted, i.e. the exclusive right to publish a particular kind of edition in specified territories is stated and the duration of the licence is delimited (for example eight years). The buyer reprints its own edition and pays royalties on copies sold to the originating publisher. These royalties are shared between the author and the publisher, for example, 60/40 or 70/30 respectively. A rising royalty scale – where the royalty rate increases when sales reach a certain figure – and the size of the advance (representing a proportion of future royalties) are negotiated. The advance payable is usually split, payable on signature of the contract and on publication. The buyer will pay the originating publisher an *offset fee*, not shared with the author, for the right to reproduce the text prior to printing, and sometimes a fee for use of the digital file of the illustrations. The timing of reprint paperback publication is set so as not to undermine the originator's other sales.

North American rights

Authors' agents, on behalf of authors, and book packagers may retain US rights or North American rights (the USA plus Canada). But if held by the publisher and the book is not to be sold via the publisher's North American firm or through a distribution arrangement, the rights may be licensed. The USA is by far the largest and richest English language market. According to Lynette Owen, 'The American market is undoubtedly the single most significant overseas English-language market for British publishers for both trade and academic titles' (Owen, page 103). Sometimes US publishers request Spanish language rights.

Selling to US editors is carried out at a distance or personally when they visit the UK en route to the Frankfurt or Bologna Book Fairs, or at such fairs. The London Book Fair has grown in importance. Sometimes, the rights manager attends the annual US book fair, BookExpo, or visits New York to see a number of publishers. UK-based scouts of US publishers may be used; and UK editors are also in contact with US publishers. The submission method may be simultaneous – the chosen editors receive the material together – or occasionally auctions are held. Editors may be given the proposal, manuscript, or proofs. Depending on the stage reached, the rights manager uses the author's previous sales figures, the jacket and blurb, pre-publication quotes, the UK subscription order, reviews and details of other rights sales to stimulate interest.

There are essentially two types of deal. In the first, the US publisher manufactures its own edition, pays royalties and an advance which are shared by the UK publisher and author – usually the larger part goes to the author, for example 75 to 80 per cent. In effect the UK publisher acts as the author's agent. Additionally the US publisher may pay for the use of a digital file of the illustrations, or an offset fee if it does not edit or Americanize the book. This type of *royalty exclusive* deal tends to be used on most fiction and on some illustrated books of considerable US interest.

In the second, the UK publisher co-prints the UK edition with the US publisher's edition. This is an English language co-edition. The bound copies are sold at a small marked-up price; and the author's royalty of say 10 per cent of the UK publisher's net receipts is included in the price paid. This type of deal can apply to any illustrated consumer book, and to academic books published by UK firms without a strong US presence. The $–£ exchange rate can affect the viability of co-edition sales to the US market.

Whichever applies, the US publisher is granted an *exclusive licence*, sometimes for the full term of copyright. The US publication date is stated, the UK publisher is obliged to supply the material by a set date, and the US publisher, too, to publish by a certain date. Attempts are made to forestall premature release of an

An offset fee is payable in order to reproduce the original setting of a book

The *Literary Market Place* is a useful guide to US publishers and book clubs, and the *International Literary Market Place* lists foreign language publishers; as do fair catalogues

ensuing US paperback or remainder, which could jeopardize export sales of a UK paperback. The price paid or the royalty rates, and advance, are negotiated as well as the territories. The US publisher is granted exclusively the USA (with Canada open to negotiation), is excluded from the UK publisher's territories (e.g. the Commonwealth and mainland Europe), and has the non-exclusive right to publish in other countries. The US publisher may be granted other rights, such as book club or serial, and pays a proportionate sum from such sales to the UK publisher. This is then shared with the author like the royalties. With some co-edition deals the US publisher may be territorially limited to North America, and the subsidiary rights granted may be fewer.

Rights

SKILLS

Rights staff preferably know French or German, and if concerned with co-editions especially, Italian and Spanish as well. But negotiations are mostly in English. However senior, the work can involve much administration.

The essential prerequisite of selling is knowing the books and the customers. Editorial insight of the firm's new titles and lateral thinking aids the assessment of rights prospects and their worth, the drawing out of salient points and the realization of sales revenue. With highly saleable titles, skilled judgement is needed on the kind of approach and its timing to selected customers.

The perception of customers' needs entails an understanding of the way they run different kinds of businesses – for example their product range, markets, business models, and financial structure – in different cultural, political and economic contexts. It is also important to recognize personal interests and tastes – especially in fiction and children's publishing – and national reading trends.

Dealing with relatively small numbers of senior people regularly and personally demands the development of good and close relations. Sales skills encompass the enthusiastic promotion of titles in writing, on the telephone and in person, even when there is scant information available on a new title. Where customers are in competition or when time is short in co-printing, they have to be pressured and manoeuvred to clinch deals quickly.

Negotiation skills allied to experience, numeracy and fast thinking help a rights person to tell if a customer is offering too low an advance or too little in a co-printing deal. The full implications and catches in customer contracts must be spotted and adverse clauses removed or modified.

Where physical or digital elements are supplied, a knowledge of production processes and of terminology is required. As so much of the job involves remembering and recording which books are on offer and who is looking at what, a meticulous, methodical mind which registers fine detail is essential – the consequences of selling the same book twice in the same territory are horrendous.

Long working days precede and follow the major fairs, such as Frankfurt, at which customers are seen on half-hourly appointments during the day, and informally into the nights, over a week. The job calls for immense stamina and a strong voice box.

Translation rights

With the continued globalization of publishing, sales of translation rights are expected to grow. Acquiring translation rights gives the purchaser the right to publish a work in a particular language. In the case of adult consumer books, translation rights (for some or all foreign languages) are often retained by agents. But if they are held by the publisher, the titles are promoted abroad by email and telephone, and personally at major book fairs or through sales visits. Publishers within a language market area are selected and sent material simultaneously. Academic titles take some time to be reviewed. Foreign language editions may increase export sales of the English language edition owing to the book's increased exposure, but there is also the argument that the translation rights should be withheld, for example in Europe, to encourage the sales of the English language edition. Continental European publishers will want to race their translations of consumer titles through to capitalize on the original publication and to avoid loss of sales from purchasers of the English edition.

The foreign publisher translates and produces the book, and pays royalties and an advance. There may also be a charge for the digital files of the illustrations. The advance is usually lower than for English rights, and some publishers work on an advance equivalent to half of the royalty earned on the first print run. Occasionally

Agatha Christie's books have been translated into over 40 languages and have sold over 2 billion copies worldwide

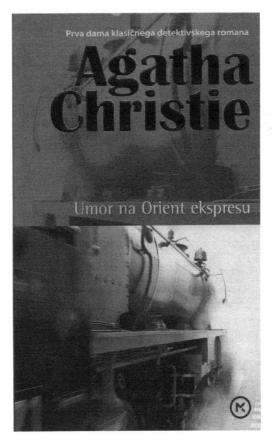

The Slovenian edition of Agatha Christie's *Murder on the Orient Express* (Mladinska Knjiga)

a lump sum is requested to reproduce a set quantity. This can be a good arrangement for those territories where the customer may not provide accurate or regular data on the number of copies sold. The purchasing publisher may be granted an exclusive language licence for a particular edition, and other rights, for a set period throughout the world. Sometimes, on a consumer book, a Spanish or French publisher is excluded from Latin America or Quebec, respectively, and rights can be sold separately in different territories for the same language. The author receives say 50 per cent of the royalties if academic, or up to 80 or 90 per cent if popular trade. There are some novelists whose sales in translation greatly exceed their English language sales – for example the US novelist Jonathan Carroll. The rewards to academic authors from translation are usually in terms of prestige and the dissemination of their work, rather than financial.

UNESCO has a historical database of translations which can be consulted

Table 12.1 Top 10 translated languages (*source*: http://databases.unesco.org/xtrans/xtra-form.shtml, accessed 17 May 2007)

Original language	Number of translations
English	920,595
French	172,104
German	156,536
Russian	91,382
Italian	51,327
Spanish	39,618
Swedish	28,494
Latin	15,477
Dutch	14,721
Danish	14,438

Table 12.2 Top 10 target languages (*source*: http://databases.unesco.org/xtrans/xtra-form.shtml, accessed 21 May 2007)

Target language	Number of translations
German	249,411
Spanish	192,833
French	184,106
English	107,379
Japanese	104,371
Dutch	99,129
Portuguese	69,806
Russian	61,431
Polish	59,725
Danish	50,383

online (see Tables 12.1 and 12.2). A search on the Index Translationum reveals the most popular original languages, with English heading the table. This clearly gives UK publishers an advantage when it comes to selling translation rights. What is often commented on is the small number, by comparison, of translations into English. Translation sales lead the way into emerging markets such as Eastern Europe, the Baltic countries and Asia.

Co-editions

The alternative to a translation deal, which is used for many highly illustrated colour books and children's picture books, is for the foreign language publishers to supply the digital files of their translations to fit around the four-colour illustrations. This is a foreign language co-edition. Several language editions are printed together by the publisher or packager in order to gain economies of scale. The printing press usually has five cylinders carrying the printing plates. Four cylinders carry the plates which print the four-colour illustrations (made up of yellow, magenta, cyan and black), and the fifth cylinder carries the plate of the text printed in black outside the areas of the illustrations. The press operator changes the fifth plate for each language edition printing. The ordered quantities, carrying each publisher's imprint, are usually supplied royalty inclusive.

English and foreign co-edition deals are central to the work of rights staff of highly illustrated adult and children's publishers and packagers. They usually initiate deals well in advance of publication with English language publishers and book clubs, using the future book's contents, and mock-ups of the jacket and blads of selected double-page spreads. The co-printing of foreign language editions follows because these publishers translate from the final English proof or the bound copy. The English and foreign language co-printing of children's books of few words can coincide. Negotiations with customers on the price paid per copy for the books, the timing of the deals and their combined printing are critical. Co-editions may be combined with TV tie-ins, own-brand titles and sponsorship deals. The complexity of these deals, involving close contact with the production department, makes it very difficult for authors' agents to enter this form of rights selling. Peter Usborne, founder of the children's publisher Usborne, comments about co-editions:

> You have to invest in each of the books you produce – you have to create something that is more expensive than your partner can afford to create so that they will buy it from you rather than making it themselves. (*The Bookseller*, 19 October 2007)

A blad is a sample printed section

Book club rights

In the UK, Book Club Associates (owned by Bertelsmann) is the major operator. The book club sector has declined severely in the face of competition from discounting by retailers, both terrestrial and online. Book club rights are normally granted to the publisher by the author. A book club editor selects the books for a club's programme. They are sent sample material, often manuscripts, sometimes proofs. The publisher's aim is to secure a firm bulk order from the club early enough, so that the club's edition can be co-printed with that of its own – an English co-edition – thereby lowering the per copy cost of production to the benefit of the margin on the trade edition, especially on illustrated colour books. A major club will sell the book to its members at a significant discount off the publisher's catalogue price. It therefore seeks a high discount off the publisher's catalogue price of 75 to 80 per cent. The author's royalty is included in the price paid by the club, and is usually either 10 per cent of the publisher's net receipts or 50 per cent of the manufacturing profits. Some book clubs, however, offer royalty-exclusive deals where the publisher receives a royalty of 5 to 7.5 per cent based on the club price and on copies sold.

A book club may itself reprint the book under its imprint with the publisher's permission, in which case it also pays a royalty on the club price. The royalty paid to the publisher is likewise shared with the author. In such royalty-exclusive deals the rights manager negotiates the advance payable and charges the club an offset fee (not shared with the author) for the right to reproduce the publisher's typography. There is a trend for clubs to print their own editions.

The quality paperback clubs take run-on paperback copies of the publisher's hardback edition printing and typically price their same size paperback edition for club members at 50 per cent off the publisher's hardback catalogue price. The publisher makes minor changes to the cover of the book club's edition, such as deleting its own imprint, bar code and price.

Other permutations include a club purchasing a small quantity of a book from a publisher's existing stock, and the licensing by a publisher to a club of a hardback edition of a title which the publisher could sell itself only in paperback.

A book club is usually granted the right to sell its English language edition in the UK, and sometimes other overseas territories in which it operates, but is excluded from North America.

Electronic rights

The licensing of electronic rights has become important for publishers in some areas, such as reference and academic publishing. If the companies do not have the resources and skills to publish digital versions of their products, they will look to sell to third parties. Even for bigger players, the sale of electronic rights may provide useful external income. Customers could be new media companies rather than other publishers, and the possibilities of the internet and mobile technology are still being explored. In China and Japan, for example, hand-held dedicated readers are produced for reference works such as dictionaries. The ebook is gaining in popularity, although sales remain low. There is growing interest in travel content and language phrasebooks being available on mobile phones. Journal and reference articles and whole books may be licensed to *aggregators*, such as EBSCO and ProQuest, which offer content from a variety of publishers to academic or public libraries and other institutions.

Academic publishers may offer site licences for their electronic services to institutions such as universities – the licences outline the conditions under which the service is to be used. In the USA, libraries have formed consortia to negotiate the terms for access to online databases. In the UK the Joint Information Systems Committee (JISC) arranges licences for databases and ebooks on behalf of UK

Licensing electronic rights – a starter for 10

David Attwooll, Director of Attwooll Associates Ltd, a publishing consultancy and licensing agency specializing in electronic media

E★PERT

Finding the right customers in the area of electronic rights usually requires active hunting, and there are technical issues around delivering content. Electronic rights deals can be very time-consuming and, as with all rights, can be done in-house or outsourced to a specialist agency. Here are some pointers:

1. Electronic markets are more various than book markets, and can be segmented in similar ways. But they can also sorted by ebusiness type, including:

- library 'aggregators' of data,
- ebook companies,
- internet service providers (ISPs) and portals,
- hardware manufacturers,
- elearning vendors,
- company websites, and
- mobile phone companies.

2. Understanding your ecustomer's business model facilitates successful licensing deals – for example, do they charge subscriptions, sell individual ebooks, or rely on advertising revenue?

3. What do you actually own? What rights do you have to sell or license? Conducting an audit of your intellectual property assets (including image rights) is a critical first step.

4. Information-based content works well on screen and in searchable databases, especially non-fiction and learning materials not organized in continuous prose. Any metadata enabling users to find immediately what is relevant to them is extremely valuable: the structure and formal tagging of content (including images) are key elements.

5. Electronic file formats are becoming more generic. Using a flexible data structure such as XML facilitates many deals. Many e-customers (especially ebook companies) will also take adapted PDFs.

6. There are some industry norms for electronic licensing deals. Firstly, licensing deals are non-exclusive. The definitions of e-rights granted will not usually be territorial or by retail sales channel (as for print rights), but by specific product, platform and market. Definitions should prevent data being reused in other products (possibly in small chunks) by the same e-companies. Regarding payment terms, for licences to aggregators of larger data products, advances or minimum annual guarantees and a royalty based on usage are often achievable. By contrast, ebook agreements are distribution deals, so revenues are retrospective, and should be seen as net of an agreed discount (rather than a royalty).

7. Online users expect up-to-date content, and publishers may be required to provide updates. This is both an organizational problem and a commercial opportunity to add greater value.

8. Licence periods should be short and some control over the start date should be specified (since launches are often delayed).

9. Security of data is essential and should be covered in the contract. Similarly, it does not make sense to license unabridged, valuable data to a paying customer who is then giving it away free on the web. Smaller subsets are usually sufficient here.

10. Acknowledgements and feedback: in addition to full publisher and copyright credits it is often possible to negotiate links to the publisher's website. Analysis of actual usage can be specified in the agreement and is extremely useful in improving editorial content.

higher and further education (jisc-collections.ac.uk). Access will be passworded and there may be limits on the number of concurrent users. Increasingly universities have negotiated off campus access, using the Athens authentication system (athens.ac.uk).

Publishers selling electronic rights will protect themselves by granting short-term, non-exclusive or narrow exclusive licences, in particular languages, limited to specific formats or platforms, with performance guarantees and advances. Licensing on a non-exclusive basis means that new companies and new technologies can be tried out. Strict controls on the use of the publisher's brand may be written into the contract to minimize any damage to its reputation. In the days of the dotcom boom, sizeable money could be on offer for the right content but those sums are now harder to negotiate. The publisher may prefer fixed annual fees to royalty deals based on untested business models. Alternatively they may enter into joint ventures in which costs and income are shared in agreed proportions. Advances are unlikely on ebook deals.

Extra value will come from higher levels of structure and metadata in the content for sale. Publishers seeking to sell electronic rights need to ensure that they hold their content in a suitable form such as XML. Such files can be returned from the typesetter or planned from the outset. PDF files may be sufficient for ebooks.

Serial and extract rights

First serial rights are more valuable since the extracts appear before the book's publication

Selling serial rights is granting the right to a newspaper or magazine to publish extracts from a book. Serial rights can be sold for a large sum of money in the case of celebrity or political memoirs. First serial rights are the most valuable because they appear before the book's publication, and can offer a national newspaper or magazine a scoop of some kind. These rights are often but not always retained by authors' agents. Sometimes first serial rights can be sold to two different publications; for example David Blunkett's memoirs, *The Blunkett Tapes* (2006), were serialized in both *The Guardian* and *Daily Mail*. The second and subsequent serial rights appear after the book's publication and may be sold to a succession of regional or evening newspapers, or magazines, at rates equal to or above that paid for original articles of comparable length, or for zero on the basis that the coverage will stimulate sales of the books. Ideas for extracts, which may come from the editor, are marked on the manuscript or proof and sent to chosen feature editors of newspapers and magazines some months ahead of the book's publication. The author's share of first serial rights (often as much as 90 per cent) may be offset against the advance, so as well as providing valuable publicity for the book the sale of such serial rights is particularly valuable financially. In some consumer book publishers, the marketing department sells serial rights instead of the rights department.

Film, TV and audio rights

Publishers are often unfamiliar with selling rights to film and TV production companies, whereas the larger agenting firms have developed an expertise in this area. Usually production companies will acquire an option in a novel, which gives them the right to come back within a fixed period and purchase the full rights to take a film into production. Lynette Owen comments on the chances of a work making it on to the screen:

> The proportion of films based on literary works should be seen in the context that between 5 per cent and 10 per cent of options are exercised and of those perhaps one in ten finally proceeds to production; television options have a higher success rate than film options. Since options should be paid for rather than granted free of charge, the income is nevertheless welcome. (Owen, page 252)

Film rights to *The Horse Whisperer* (1995) were sold for $3 m before the author Nicholas Evans had even finished the novel

On the
insistence of
J. K. Rowling,
the audiobooks
of Harry
Potter, read
by Stephen
Fry, are wholly
unabridged

Preferred partner arrangements with production companies enable publishers to sublicense film and TV rights and in turn acquire the rights to publish books of upcoming programmes and films.

Audiobook rights can be licensed exclusively in two forms: abridged and unabridged. Some of the main trade publishers operate their audio divisions which often abridge their own books, or license titles from agents or other trade publishers which do not have their own audiobook lists. There are also independent and specialist audiobook publishers. Unabridged audiobooks tend to be produced by specialist publishers supplying public libraries, which may also publish large print books – another right available for licensing. There is growing interest in making audio titles available for digital download on to devices such as iPods and mobile phones. Books can also be licensed for reading or dramatization on radio.

EXPERT

Audiobooks

Nicholas Jones, founder and director of Strathmore Publishing Ltd

In 1935, the Royal National Institute of Blind People recorded (on 16 rpm shellac discs) a reading of Agatha Christie's *The Murder of Roger Ackroyd*. This was the first 'talking book'.

Audiobooks (a term not finally accepted universally until this century) continued to be seen as 'books for the blind' well into the 1990s. In the US, Caedmon released recordings for a general market as early as 1954, particularly of poets reading their own work. In the UK, EMI and Argo experimented with spoken-word recordings in the 1970s. In the late 1980s, the BBC launched its Radio Collection – selections from its archives on cassette tape. Thus began a public awareness of 'radio on demand', but it was not until the 1990s that mainstream publishers launched audio lists – Penguin, Hodder, HarperCollins, Random House and Orion. Once audio was in bookshops rather than record shops, it began to be appreciated by the general public as a valid medium in its own right rather than as second-best or a substitute for those unable to read printed books. There was clearly a demand: sales grew at about 20 per cent per year from 1995 to 2001, although they have now levelled off.

Technological developments helped. The Sony Walkman players, first cassette and then CD, encouraged multi-tasking and listening whilst travelling. By 2005 cassettes were almost totally superseded by CDs, and audiobooks are now online at sites such as audible.co.uk – downloads are perhaps 10 per cent of the market in 2007, a share growing fast. In 2008, Amazon acquired Audible to enhance its capability to sell content in all formats: print, ebook and audiobook. Although this will increase awareness of audiobooks, audio publishers in both the UK and US are concerned about the further concentration of the download market; rivals like audioVille and Spoken Network have very small shares of the market, and the Amazon/Audible merger makes it even more of a David–Goliath struggle.

Most high street sales are of abridged titles, skilfully cut back to between three and eight hours (30,000 to 70,000 words); unabridged titles often run to 20, and there is a version of *War and Peace* that is over 60 hours long. Library sales are usually unabridged. Downloading has removed the physical constraints which made unabridged difficult to market, and compared with sales on CD, a far higher proportion of online sales to the consumer market are unabridged.

Audio is a small proportion of the UK consumer book industry: hard sales figures are difficult to obtain, but according to 2006 industry association surveys, the UK market is about £70 m – 2.8 per cent of the approximately £2,500 m UK consumer book market. However, even this modest share is at odds with the mere £21 m that shows up in the Nielsen figures; the balance is presumably made up by library and mail-order sales of unabridged books.

Audio is proportionately better established in the US, with $870 m retail sales – say £435 m at current exchange rates; the US population is 300 m, the UK, 60 m. The US consumer market is about $12,200 m; audio is therefore about 7 per cent. According to a 2007 survey by the Audiobook Publishing Association, only 8 per cent of the adult population of the UK have listened to an audiobook in the past year; the US equivalent figure is 25 per cent.

Job opportunities in audio lie in deciding what to publish and acquiring rights, with perhaps some involvement in the casting of readers; all production is outsourced to a small number of established producers and studios who specialize in the field.

Other rights

Examples of other rights include condensation (a right sold mainly to Reader's Digest), promotional reprint rights (low-cost editions for a mass market), large print, Braille (generally granted for free), and English language paperback licensing rights to export territories. Material may also be licensed for use in coursepacks or customized textbooks for college courses.

Now read this

Lynette Owen, *Selling Rights*, 5th edition, Routledge, 2006.

Sources

Literary Market Place, Bowker Annual guide to the US publishing business.
International Literary Market Place, Bowker 'For book publishing contacts on a global scale'.
Lynette Owen (editor), *Clark's Publishing Agreements: A book of precedents*, 7th edition, Tottel Publishing, 2007.

Web resources

www.theapa.net Audiobook Publishing Association.
www.audiopub.org US Audio Publishers Association.
www.cla.co.uk Copyright Licensing Agency.

CHAPTER 13

The sales channels for books in the UK

Publishers can operate through a variety of sales channels, and the choice of channel will depend on the sector in which they operate. The sales success of consumer books, for example, depends on retail exposure. As we saw in Chapter 10, an important purchase prompt is being visible in the shops. The booksellers are the consumer publishers' most important customers and the sales channel at which they direct most of their marketing and sales effort. But publishers also have to pay attention to the growth in sales from the supermarkets and through the internet. Table 13.1 shows the market share *by value* of different retail outlets in the UK – volume figures (units sold) show higher shares for the supermarkets and online. Over time the trend has been for the share of supermarkets and the internet to grow, and for independent bookshops, bargain bookshops and book clubs to suffer a decline (Table 13.2).

Philip Kogan, Chairman of the independent publisher Kogan Page, writes about the need for a publisher to have a full understanding of the relevant sales channels:

> Today the smell of a title in the publisher's nostrils is not enough. One has to know and be sure of the channels of sale before committing to publication.

Table 13.1 The market share in the UK book trade (2005) based on value of sales (*source*: Competition Commission, 2006)

Retail outlet	Percentage share
Waterstone's	24
Other bookshops including Borders and Blackwell's	15
Other stores including WHSmith	19
Supermarkets	8
Internet	8
Book clubs and other distance sellers	15
Other outlets including bargain bookshops	10
Total	100

Table 13.2 Change in sales from 2001 to 2005 (*source*: www.booksellers.org, accessed 25 October 2007)

Outlet	Percentage change
Chain bookshops	+18
Bargain bookshops	−14
Independent bookshops	−16
Supermarkets	+90
Other retail	−12
Direct mail	−25
Internet	+183

Except for the occasional wild success, which can come from a small or large company, the conventional book trade is a hard sell nowadays . . . We look at all possible sources of revenue in internet selling and online publishing, in the new audio forms of publishing and the rest. While wishing to work with our first love, the bookshops, we also know that to survive we have to engage in sponsored publishing and sell ad space in books and online. (Kogan, 2007)

The UK book trade has seen a great many changes over the last 25 years. These include the collapse of the Net Book Agreement in 1995 (the official end came in 1997), which led to price discounting, and the development of large chains on the high street. Smaller shops have closed and medium-sized businesses have been swallowed up by their larger rivals – for example, Borders bought Books Etc in 1997; Waterstone's acquired Ottakar's in 2006. The late twentieth century saw the arrival of the superstore concept from the USA – large, welcoming shops with a wide range of stock (typically 50,000 to 80,000 titles) and coffee shops. The first Borders superstore opened in Oxford Street in 1998; and Waterstone's in Piccadilly in 1999.

Both Borders and Waterstone's would be sitting pretty in the retail market were it not for the growth in sales through the internet and supermarkets. In 2007 came the news that Borders had sold their UK operation to Luke Johnson (the Chairman of Channel 4) and his private equity firm, and Waterstone's announced plans to close some of its bookshops.

The supermarkets have become so significant to consumer publishers that in 2007 HarperCollins launched a new mass market list called Avon, aimed at time-pressed women. Called 'channel publishing', the list was to take 'a supermarket-style approach, identifying the three most popular genres for [the] audience: chick lit, romance, and crime/thrillers' (*The Guardian*, 31 March 2007). Supermarkets can call the shots, as they do in other product areas, demanding large discounts as well as payments to remain preferred suppliers. Publishers have to respond not only by changing what they publish but also by forming larger groups, which can offer a constant supply of likely bestsellers.

The independent bookshops have had a torrid time faced with price discounting not only in the high street chains but also online and by the supermarkets. A

E★PERT

Independent bookselling in the twenty-first century

Patrick Neale, co-owner of Jaffé & Neale bookshop and café, Chipping Norton, Oxfordshire

Why would anybody buy books in an independent bookshop these days? They are notoriously the most expensive, often smell of boiled cabbage and are run by ex-teachers who took early retirement with no knowledge of retail fundamentals. Is this really the case or is there a fantastic opportunity for independent booksellers opening up right now?

The channels from which customers can buy books are many compared to 20 years ago. This is obviously a great benefit to customers. They can pick up bestsellers at the supermarket, train station, petrol station, or airport – or have them delivered to their door having purchased online.

Previously one would have visited WHSmith or one of the old-established independent retailers and put up with whatever service was thrown at you. Then came the new high street players, Waterstone's, Borders and Ottakar's (now part of Waterstone's), making bookselling exciting and vibrant. The Net Book Agreement collapsed and Amazon and the supermarkets waded in, making the book market even more dynamic. Most customers have welcomed these developments.

This is the environment in which independent booksellers have to operate and it is no surprise that 50 are going out of business every year. Competition is strong and so there is no point trying to face these big businesses head on. Butchers and greengrocers have already witnessed the 'heartless' way customers have chased bargains and convenience and neglected their traditional shopping locations. Rather it is wiser to play to your strengths and recognize where the large chains and online retailers cannot compete.

One could feel very pessimistic and fear the death of independent bookselling. The questions asked in the House of Commons about the price of the Harry Potter books and the shouts of 'it's not fair' may raise the spirits of some. But customers are always right and they will not take kindly to any return to price fixing.

So how do independents respond to this tough environment? The exciting news is that sales in the independent sector have actually increased. So it is not all gloom.

Independent booksellers have realized that customers want personal service. They want recommendations from people they know and trust, not from a chain that demands a payment to display books at the front of the store. Independent booksellers put books at the front of their shop because they have read them and can advise buying them with their integrity intact. The independent bookseller can create an environment where customers feel welcome and known. They can get to know each customer's preferences and recommend exactly to the tastes of those individuals. This 'boutique' style of retailing is not the cheapest but can give the customer the feeling of individuality in an often soulless high street. Book clubs and author events are increasingly becoming the domain of the independent as they are seen as unprofitable to the big chains. On this note authors are keen to champion independent bookshops as they may well have supported them before the author was famous.

Independent bookshops can tailor their shop to the exact requirements of the community making it the meeting place. Our bookshop acts as a head office for the 'Keep the Local Lido Open' campaign and is a drop-off point for a group of people to collect their organic eggs. There seems to be shift from, and a suspicion of, the big players in the retail sector. In the same way that people are going to butchers who can tell them exactly where their meat comes from, they want to get their books from people who know the pedigree of the books they are selling.

There is definitely a future for cleverly located and well-run independent bookshops. They must be run by book lovers who understand their market and want to give customers an experience they will remember and pay a little more for. Independent booksellers can lead the vanguard in bringing the soul back to Britain's high streets.

Jaffé & Neale
bookshop and café

bookseller may find it cheaper to buy a book from Tesco than directly from the publisher. By April 2007, there were 1,424 independent bookshop members of The Booksellers Association, compared to 1,839 in April 1997. There is some evidence that independents have now stabilized their position. The ones that survive have sought to make a niche for themselves by offering excellent service, prompt ordering, and stressing their place in the community. Just as consumers are being encouraged to buy from local suppliers in other product areas, the independents are emphasizing their value in an increasingly homogenized high street.

Other book outlets of significance to particular kinds of publishers include airport terminal shops, especially at Heathrow and Gatwick, which sell enormous quantities of paperback fiction, travel and business books (flight delays are a boon for book sales).

Research suggests, unsurprisingly, that 97 per cent of heavy book buyers are comfortable going into bookshops; there is a lower figure of 78 per cent amongst light book buyers (BML, 2005). Table 13.3 shows that bookshops remain the most popular retail outlet for books, but also the importance of other channels.

Table 13.3 Retail outlets for book purchases – percentage of consumers who had bought from each type of outlet (*source*: Mintel, *Books, Music and Video Retailing*, 2005)

Source of purchase	*Bookshop*	*Supermarket*	*Book club/direct sales*	*Internet*
Percentage	44	32	11	22

THE CHAINS

There is no doubt that bookselling has become much more professional in the last 30 years. There are shops on many high streets which offer a good range of stock amongst pleasant surroundings. Yet as Robert McCrum writes:

> Since the abolition of the Net Book Agreement in 1997 the transformation of the bookshops has been bought at a cost: a highly visible minority of books sell very well indeed, and probably better than ever, while the majority struggle to perform. The profits from fewer and fewer mega-selling titles are required, more than ever before, to carry the losses sustained by the rest of the list. (*The Observer*, 1 July 2007)

The chain booksellers differ in their character, and have aimed to develop distinctive brands. For example, WHSmith has the aim to be Britain's most popular bookseller, stationer and newsagent. It has shops on virtually all the main high streets in the UK, and sells 40 m books a year. A valuation of its airport and railway shops in 2007 came up with a figure of £500 m, although sales through these outlets have a lower proportion of books (20 per cent) than the high street shops (estimated at between 25 to 30 per cent) (*The Bookseller*, 25 May 2007). WHSmith is popular with two age groups in particular, from 15 to 19 and from 45 to 54.

Waterstone's, part of the HMV Group, has more than 300 shops. An average-sized Waterstone's store has a range of around 30,000 to 40,000 individual books, with 150,000 titles in the largest store. During the 1980s Waterstone's and Dillons competed fiercely with each other, opening well-designed branded stores, typically carrying a much larger range of stock than traditional bookshops. They tended to be called 'up-market' booksellers, exemplified by their wide range of hardback and trade paperback titles and the depth of backlist titles stocked. However the size of these stores became dwarfed in the late 1990s by the opening by Waterstone's and Borders of flagship superstores carrying upwards of 150,000 titles. Waterstone's has a large audience amongst ABC1s, readers of broadsheet newspapers, and users of the internet. In 2007, announcing plans to close some stores, the Managing Director of Waterstone's, Gerry Johnson, said there would be 'more emphasis on novels, cookery and children's books and less on "academic and humanities" areas, which he said could still be bought online' (*The Guardian*, 14 March 2007). Previously Waterstone's had given up on its own independent online operation, and worked with Amazon, but in 2006 it started its own website again.

The original Dillons shop was founded in 1936 by Una Dillon (1903–93). The chain was sold to HMV in 1998 and put under the Waterstone's brand in 1999

In the UK Borders has around 70 stores; it has an urban bias, with a strong customer base amongst the 35–44 age bracket and the AB socio-demographic

The interior of Waterstone's in Piccadilly, London. Europe's largest bookshop. It has over eight miles of shelving and 150,000 titles in stock

group. In the USA, Borders has nearly 500 superstores, while its main rival, the world's largest bookseller Barnes & Noble, has over 700. During the 1990s these chains were credited with transforming US bookselling.

The medium-sized chains usually operate smaller stores and tend to be weighted to fast-moving frontlist titles, concentrating on the top-selling 5,000 titles. However, amongst them are the academic-orientated stores of Blackwell, which together with Waterstone's, dominates the ownership of campus-related bookstores. For publishers of high-level academic and professional titles, Blackwell is a major customer owing to its UK retail and library supply businesses, as well as its leading position in exporting specialist titles. Blackwell has over 60 outlets in the UK. One issue for academic shops is how to attract footfall outside the two peak sales periods of the autumn and the new year. Some campus shops now stock stationery, music, and gift items. Neil Broomfield, Sales and Marketing Director for Higher Education at John Wiley, said: 'Given that campus stores will find it challenging to compete with online stores for price and range, they need to focus on their key assets – proximity to the student body, outstanding product knowledge and excellent service' (*The Bookseller*, 18 August 2006). Ottakar's, which concentrated on opening shops in smaller county towns, was sold to Waterstone's in 2006.

How the chains operate

A major chain such as Waterstone's operates centralized buying, that is book buyers at head office select titles presented to them by the publishers' sales or key account managers. This usually prevents the publishers' sales representatives from selling titles directly into their branches. In some cases, chains mix centralized buying with some discretion for the branches to purchase stock locally. The ways in which the chains manage their purchasing decisions are in a state of flux. In 2008 Waterstone's planned to open a new centralized distribution centre, which would supply all the stores across the company. This opened the question of firm sale on stock from publishers, since unsold stock could be transferred to other branches rather than returned to the publisher.

WHSmith is its own wholesaler – it operates centralized buying from publishers and its own warehouse at Swindon, which receives stock from the publishers and then distributes the books to its branches.

The major bookselling chains have central marketing departments which organize, often in collaboration with publishers' sales and marketing staff, consumer advertising, instore promotion, and author signings in the branches. In 2007, for example, Borders launched a scheme aimed at readers in book groups, who were able to buy selected titles at discount. Extra material about the titles is supplied on the company's website.

SUPERMARKETS AND THE INTERNET

Supermarkets and other non-book retailers

Other kinds of big retail chains, such as the supermarkets, buy centrally and receive their stock either directly from publishers or via wholesalers. The supermarkets often offer massive discounts on bestsellers, usually up to 50 per cent of the recommended price. In 2007 *Harry Potter and the Deathly Hallows* was sold by Asda at £5.00 compared to the recommended retail price of £17.99. Although the supermarkets' share of the overall book market is still limited, their share of sales can reach 50 per cent for top bestsellers, which explains why they can

Supermarkets and books

Joel Rickett, Deputy Editor of *The Bookseller* and author of a weekly column in *The Guardian* about books and publishing

Since Tesco and Sainsbury's first started selling books in the early 1990s, various myths have been spun about supermarkets and books. The first myth is that these giant retailers use books as a 'loss leader' – discounting below cost price to lure customers who will then pick up (more profitable) groceries. A few blockbuster books are sometimes used in this way, but the supermarkets actually make a profit on 99 per cent of the books they sell – even on those £3.50 paperbacks and yes, even on Harry Potter.

The second misconception is that supermarkets only stock a handful of bestsellers. That may have been true a decade ago, but now any large Asda, Tesco or Sainsbury's has a surprisingly deep and varied book range (Tesco's biggest stores have up to 5,000 different paperbacks). No less an authority than James Daunt, founder of the upscale London bookshops Daunts, once remarked to me that he personally would be happy to read nothing but books from the shelves of his local Tesco for the rest of his life.

This brings me to the third myth, namely that supermarkets are only interested in commercial fiction by brand name authors, trashy celebrity autobiographies or 'misery memoirs'. They certainly do a roaring trade in these areas, but they also shift big numbers of literary classics, cookery, history, biography, children's picture books and even cult fiction. Tesco sold more copies of Ali Smith's experimental novel *The Accidental* than Waterstone's; in 2007 it promoted the Man Booker Prize shortlist.

Finally, people suggest that the supermarkets reach an entirely new demographic who never usually buy books. The fact that they are hoovering up market share across most genres suggests that many avid readers also pick up books while on their weekly shop. The edited range in supermarkets helps these people choose quickly – and the influence of media book clubs (particularly Channel 4's Richard & Judy show) supplants the role of informed booksellers.

Many independent bookshop owners complain bitterly about the industry terms' structures that have enabled supermarkets to gain such ground. Publishers can certainly be accused of naivety in the early days, giving away margin too easily; now they are faced with demands for payments of up to £3 m to become 'preferred suppliers'. Yet it is hard to argue with such scale – Tesco turns over the annual sales of the entire UK book trade every 20 days.

We ain't seen nothing yet. Supermarkets have a 12 per cent share of total UK book sales by volume (BML/TNS 2006), but only a small proportion of their shoppers ever pick up books. The main players Tesco and Asda have plans to expand their ranges; others with bookish ambitions include Sainsbury's, Woolworths, Morrisons, Wilkinsons and Costco. For them all, books generate customer goodwill, add quality by association, and sell at a high price per item. In the most optimistic assessment, this shift could empower publishers, spread the reading habit, and perhaps even help the finest local bookshops to flourish in opposition, as have delicatessens and farmers' markets.

E★PERT

ask for discounts as high as 65 per cent. One in five of Tesco's customers bought a book there in 2005, and the range stocked by the supermarkets has grown to include biography and other non-fiction. In 2006 Tesco stocked books in over 650 of its stores, with up to 5,000 titles available in its larger shops. Merchandisers, for example Entertainment UK (owned by Woolworths) and Handleman UK, stock the shelves in supermarkets and monitor stock levels.

Books are available in many other kinds of retail outlets, which the publishers reach through wholesalers. For example, the merchandising wholesalers serve newsagents, convenience general stores, ferry port outlets, and motorway service stations. They will check and replenish stock of mass-market paperbacks, and remove slow-selling titles for destruction. There are wholesalers dedicated to supplying garden, DIY and leisure centres, and specialist shops such as computer stores and toy shops.

Online bookselling

In the UK online bookselling still means Amazon. In 2007, over 80 per cent of visits to book websites were made to amazon.co.uk or amazon.com (*The Bookseller*, 4 May 2007). With an international brand, heavy discounting on a large range of titles, 24/7 access, features such as giftwrapping and recommendations based on your purchase history, the internet bookseller has built up a powerful presence in the UK market. The range of titles dwarfs the selection that can be found in any terrestrial bookshop, opening up a window for smaller publishers, which may be struggling to get their titles into the chains, and for backlist titles.

The concept of the 'Long Tail' was coined by Chris Anderson in relation to books and music. Usually books that are not selling in sufficient numbers are returned to the publisher. Yet the internet provides a means of marketing and selling these titles. If we add up this Long Tail of slow-selling books, Anderson suggested that it could add up to a greater source of revenue than the bestsellers prominent in bookshops. This idea strikes a chord with publishers, which have seen internet bookselling open up a new channel for backlist books which had disappeared from terrestrial retail display. The book return rates are much lower, and the internet provides a good route for the fulfilment of low-value single book orders.

The original model was for Amazon to source books from the wholesalers, avoiding the need for a large investment in warehousing. By 2008 the company ran four of its own distribution centres – two in Scotland, one each in England and Wales – enabling it to provide fast supply of bestselling lines. Other internet retailers, such as Tesco.com, use the wholesalers.

For some the internet will never match the experience of browsing in their local or high street bookshop, but especially for those without ready access to a bookshop, the internet provides a convenient and cost-effective method of obtaining books. A 2007 study looked at attitudes to buying online, and found that the profile of the online consumer had changed from being a young and wealthy male to one that is 'far more reflective of the general shopping population: more of them are women, older and from lower socio-demographic groups' (PricewaterhouseCoopers, page 1). Looking at different product types, the research found that books were the second most popular item for online purchase. Amongst online shoppers, 71 per cent buy books at the moment, and 88 per cent were likely to buy online in the future. Factors influencing the decision to buy online included price, convenience, ease of search, and 24-hour access.

Although Amazon dominates internet bookselling, there is increasing competition from Play.com, Waterstone's, Tesco, and smaller operators including independents with their own websites (sometimes provided by the wholesalers). Based in Gloucester, the Book Depository aims to service the Long Tail. Rather than hold stock, it meets customer orders from the optimal source – publisher, wholesaler or distributor. Innovations around a hybrid model of 'clicks and bricks' have also been developed by some chains – there may be a facility to reserve books online and pick them up from a store. Publishers are showing renewed interest in selling direct to consumers – for example in 2007 Random House launched a site offering discounted and signed copies.

Bargain bookshops

Of declining importance are the bargain bookshops, which occupy high street positions, sometimes on short leases granted by stressed landlords. Joel Rickett writes:

> Ten years ago you'd see so-called bargain outlets on the high street, festooned with permanent 'closing down' signs. They offered a garish mix of remainder stock and specially produced titles – hobby books, cookbooks, maps, children's books – for a few pounds each. Publishers saw them as convenient dumping grounds for overambitious print runs. But with books now being sold for a few quid everywhere from eBay to Tesco to Waterstone's, the bargain shops have struggled. (*The Guardian*, 17 February 2007)

Publishers have a long history of ridding themselves, albeit quietly, of their mistakes in printing too many copies. When a title's sales are insufficient to cover the cost of storage, it may be pulped or remaindered. Some publishers never remainder in the home market, or at all. A publisher having sold a book to a book club is restrained from remaindering. Remainders commonly stem from speculative or poor publishing decisions on new books, or from the one reprint too many of good books. While a title may no longer sell in hardback or paperback at full price, it may sell well when released at a bargain price. The publisher needs to convert its dead stock into cash.

A publisher's sales manager sells the titles either directly to bargain chains or to a remainder dealer usually at a price well below the cost of manufacture. The booksellers, who cannot return such books, sell them to the public at a heavily discounted price. Dealers also export remainders. A publisher may remainder only part of the stock (partial remaindering); if the publisher has a one-year stock plan and holds two years' stock, the balance is off-loaded to free warehouse space. A dealer may purchase from a publisher's warehouse, or distributor, pallets of mixed titles which have been returned from bookshops.

The promotional book publishers provide the bargain chains with a ready supply of newly created low-priced books. Such publishers and the remainder dealers are well represented at the London and Frankfurt Book Fairs, and have their own London fairs, organized by Ciana, in January and September. A bargain chain may also sell new titles at deep discounts alongside remaindered titles, and may sell other goods such as stationery and artist's materials.

WHOLESALERS AND INTERMEDIARIES

Trade wholesalers

Many of the independent bookshops stock from 12,000 to 20,000 titles. Most purchase their stock from the two largest trade wholesalers, which offer next-day delivery. Gardners, based in Eastbourne, stocks over 700,000 titles from more than 4,000 publishers. Bertram Books, based near Norwich, has over 500,000 titles from around 4,000 publishers. It was purchased in 2007 by Woolworths, which had previously bought the wholesaler THE in 2006. Around 30 per cent of the wholesalers' sales comes from independent bookshops. Wholesalers can also act as distributors for small publishers, and they have installed POD facilities as another service to publishers.

From the late 1980s, the trade wholesalers revolutionized the speed and efficiency of book distribution through their supply to the independent bookshops, which were faced with a myriad of publishers' invoicing systems, and publishers' warehouses which could be slow and inefficient. The wholesalers' growth was grounded in their focus on customer service to booksellers. They offered the convenience of dealing with just a few invoicing systems, rather than those of dozens of publishers; of online bibliographic information systems (including marketing and purchasing advice); of online ordering; and of consolidated orders with fast and reliable delivery. The wholesalers became the booksellers' stockroom. If the trade wholesalers had restricted their ambitions to the independent booksellers they too would have faced eventual decline. But they extended their reach into serving some of the retail chains and supermarkets, entered the school library supply market (long restricted to specialist suppliers) and began to export. At the end of the 1990s, they received a fillip from the emerging internet booksellers, such as Amazon UK, which initially drew their stock from the wholesalers. Bertram Books supplies waterstones.com.

In 2006 around 20 per cent of books sold by retailers in the UK were sourced through a trade wholesaler. By 2007 consolidation meant that the two major wholesalers, Bertrams and Gardners, had over 80 per cent of this market (OFT).

Book market information

The retail outlets summarized above account for most of the UK retail sales of books. The publishers sell their new titles directly to the retailers (or via wholesalers). But the data of actual sales made by the retailers to their customers is of critical importance to the retailers, wholesalers and publishers. The installation by retailers of electronic point of sale (EPOS) systems, reading the bar codes on covers when sales are made, enables the retailers to monitor the rate of sale of titles and to control their inventory (by reordering the titles which sell or by returning unsold titles to the publisher). The effect of EPOS installations was that booksellers placed smaller orders more frequently (provided that a title was stocked in the first place) and expected faster deliveries.

Nielsen BookScan collects the sales data by title from almost all of the different kinds of book retailers from across the country and from internet booksellers, and produces various bestseller charts which are published in *The Bookseller* weekly. Data is also sold to interested parties. Thus, for example, publishers can not only monitor the sales performance of their own titles – their rise and fall – but also that of competitors. Publishers armed with that information are in a far better position to respond to the needs for quick reprints or not. However, the data cannot help publishers' sometime over-optimism or misjudgement of printing too many copies of a new title at the outset, or that of booksellers' stocking too many copies in the knowledge that they can return unsold stock.

Returns

The return of unsold books to publishers from retailers and wholesalers is an expensive and wasteful characteristic of the book business, which was estimated by KPMG in 1998 to cost the industry £100 m. Current estimates are that 15 per cent of books (by sales value) are returned to the publisher, and book wastage is still approaching 20 per cent of production. This is raising increasing concern about the connected ecological issues. Is it right to have such a culture of wasteful distribution within the book industry? Mark Williams, Managing Director of the distributor TBS, commented: 'Green issues are going to be a major driver in the future, and we want to reduce the expense of moving product around. People talk about air miles or food miles – we have book miles' (*The Bookseller*, 17 August 2007). In 2007 Hachette announced that it would move to firm sale on its backlist for environmental reasons.

Library suppliers

The public, academic and corporate libraries are supplied by booksellers and library suppliers. The UK public library market has been difficult and long gone are the days when library sales supported hardback runs of new titles. There has been a continued consolidation amongst the main library suppliers. Following the collapse of the Net Book Agreement, the public libraries sought higher discounts – above 30 per cent – through collective regional purchasing consortia, while still demanding a large amount of bibliographic selection support and book processing from the suppliers such as Askews, Holt Jackson and Peters (which specializes in children's books). The entry of the trade wholesaler Bertrams into the public library market, through the purchase of Cypher, caused consternation amongst the library suppliers and publishers, who have conventionally segmented this channel through different discounts and terms. In 2007 Gardners purchased Askews, and in 2008 Holt Jackson, in a further consolidation of the wholesaler and library supply market.

Blackwell, Dawson and Coutts (owned by the giant US wholesaler Ingram) serve academic markets. The library suppliers export, especially academic and STM titles, sometimes under tendered contracts, to national and regional government libraries, and university and corporate research libraries.

E★PERT

Public libraries

J. Eric Davies, Consulting Senior Research Fellow, Department of Information Science, Loughborough University

Public libraries represent a significant component of the information chain which connects authors and readers. The United Kingdom is served by over 4,500 service points, including mobile libraries and more than 60 per cent of the population is recorded as holding library membership. They are managed by local government authorities and are funded from local taxes. In the 2005–6 financial year, overall spending by the 149 public library authorities reached £1.1 bn. Public library services are generally free at point of use and provide the community with access to a range of information products and supporting services including lending, reference and enquiry services as well as reading development and lifelong learning initiatives. Through specialized services, they cater for a range of people within the community including children and visually impaired people.

The public library collection will typically be wide ranging in terms of subject coverage, publication dates, and format. In 2005–6 the total book stock in UK public libraries amounted to 104,863,207 books, representing 1.75 books per head of population. Increasingly, electronic information is being exploited in public libraries and the *People's Network* – a national initiative which connects public libraries to the internet – has been a significant success. Around 40,000 networked PC terminals are available in libraries for public use – in the majority of cases, free of charge.

Public libraries account for a considerable volume of sales of books and other published media. Public library spending on information materials amounted to some £134 m in 2005–6 with almost £80 m being spent on books. Over 12 m books were added in 2005–6. The budget for library materials represents around 12 per cent of total public library spending and this proportion has been declining. In 1999–2000 it was almost 14 per cent, and in 1995–6 it was over 17 per cent.

Book issues, the staple of public libraries, totalled over 323 m in 2005–6, but the number has also been declining. Book issues were over 514 m in 1995–6, and 430 m in 1999–2000. Some of this trend is attributed to library users turning to audiovisual materials and electronic sources of information. Visits to libraries, on the other hand, have shown a recent upward trend, reaching almost 340 m in 2004–5.

The legal basis for the library service is the Public Libraries and Museums Act 1964 which confers a duty on library authorities to provide a 'comprehensive and efficient library service'. Central government oversight of the service is in the hands of the Secretary of State for Culture, Media and Sport, who is empowered under the Act to superintend the delivery of library services and to promote the improvement of public libraries. Since 2001 a suite of service standards has been introduced by government to monitor performance. The lead strategic government agency for libraries is the Museums, Libraries and Archives Council (MLA) launched in 2000. Through its *Framework for the Future* programme it promotes the development of libraries for the future. A key component of this programme is the *Better Stock, Better Libraries* initiative which has its foundations in a commissioned study of acquisitions practices undertaken by PricewaterhouseCoopers for the MLA. The initiative is aimed at reducing substantially the cost of buying books and other stock through collective purchasing, closer working with book suppliers and streamlining acquisitions processes. Pilot projects are under way.

Increasingly the emphasis is on libraries demonstrating value for money through a high level of performance and on achieving visible social, cultural and economic impact in the community.

Discounts

Publishers sell their books to retailers and intermediaries at different discounts off their recommended retail prices. They aim to keep their discounts secret and by law must not collude with rival companies. The main factors affecting discount levels are:

- the type of book – hardback or paperback, trade or non-trade,
- the role and value the intermediary plays in the supply chain,
- the balance of power between the buyer and seller,
- historical precedent, and
- the size of order on a particular book or group of books.

For some publishers, the best discount is zero. The intermediaries are cut out of the supply chain entirely or are dealt with on low, or 'short', discounts. For example, the learned journal publishers may grant a discount to the subscription agents of 0 to 5 per cent. The highly specialist publishers producing very high-priced information products sold directly to professional markets may grant a discount of 10 to 20 per cent on an order received from a bookseller. The school textbook publishers may grant a discount of 17 to 20 per cent to a school supplier such as a bookseller, specialist school contractor or local authority purchasing organization. In such examples, the publishers generate the demand themselves, and can supply end-users directly – the intermediaries provide a convenience service to the end-users. If schools are supplied direct, a discount of 10 per cent may be offered as an incentive, based on the size of the order or as part of a special offer (for example, if orders are received by a certain date).

The college textbook publishers offer discounts to booksellers in the range 30 to 40 per cent. The publishers argue that they have achieved the adoptions through their own promotion. The terrestrial booksellers argue that they are physically stocking the titles for student purchase and displaying other titles that they might buy. Textbook discounts have risen to some extent from the pressure exerted by the chains, especially Waterstone's. However, the retailers' leverage on the textbook publishers for increased discounts is far less than on the consumer publishers. The major publishers are resistant and are building their direct supply capabilities.

In consumer books, the discounts are more varied and are the highest in the world. Anthony Cheetham, Chairman of Quercus, writes:

The chains have gone about as far as they can in squeezing better terms from suppliers. Average discounts are around 60 per cent. Unsold stock can be returned for credit. Any significant commitment of shelf space is billed to the publisher as an additional cost. (*The Bookseller*, 15 June 2007)

A small publisher might give a discount of 40 per cent to Waterstone's and 55 per cent to a wholesaler, but the question then arises as to how widely their titles will be stocked. To get shelf space a larger publisher will offer deeper discounts and will pay for its titles to be prominently displayed. These charges can amount to many thousands of pounds, and can be asked for by other retailers such as the supermarkets. In 2007 a leading chain was asking £45,000 for a book to appear at Christmas in window and front-of-store displays, and in their national advertising campaign. The terrestrial retailers argue that their expensive display space generates the sales for the publishers; smaller publishers become frustrated by their inability to access the system.

OTHER SALES CHANNELS

Direct sales

A proportion of children's publishers' sales and a very high proportion of educational publishers' sales do not pass through retailers. Furthermore, some publishers, especially those issuing specialist academic and professional titles, sell them directly to end-users by conventional means or through the internet, and there are other sales channels available, such as those used by the highly illustrated and promotional book publishers.

Book clubs

Sales to book clubs are handled by publishers under rights deals. Book clubs have conventionally occupied a major segment of mail-order sales to consumers. Founded in 1966, Book Club Associates (BCA) is the UK's largest book club operation with a variety of clubs including World Books, History Guild and Books for Children. The club is owned by Bertelsmann. Another club is the Folio Society, founded in 1947, which specializes in handsome illustrated hardbacks in a range of bindings.

BCA has found it difficult to retain members in the face of the retail competition offering deep discounts. For example, Amazon emails information about new or discounted titles to customers with the relevant profile. The fundamental strategy of a club is to focus the members' attention on a selected and small number of recommended titles which are deeply discounted, and clubs are migrating to the net too with more people joining by the internet or ordering online. Publishers supply the clubs with non-returnable bulk quantities of the books at very high discounts, perhaps 75 per cent, or the clubs reprint their own copies, paying a royalty to the publisher.

Direct selling companies

Some companies sell books (and other products) directly to customers in their workplaces or homes. They employ hundreds of 'agents' who receive a percentage on sales, and who allow customers time to examine the books before they purchase. The companies order very large quantities of selected titles from publishers on a non-return basis, and sell them at say a 70 per cent discount off the publisher's price, usually six months after publication. The pre-eminent company is the Book People. Through the internet or the telephone, or through its distributor network in 30,000 workplaces, customers buy at deep discounts off the recommended price.

Children's books

Children's books sell well when displayed face out alongside other kinds of products, whether in the multi-product WHSmith chain, or amongst groceries or toys, where parents are likely to have their children in tow. They are available in supermarkets, toyshops, and internet retailers. Like the educational textbook publishers, children's publishers also supply their books directly to schools when their books are used to support the National Curriculum.

The school is an important outlet for children's books, providing a setting where children's books leap through the adult sales barrier and important word-of-mouth recommendations amongst children themselves take place. School book fairs have grown enormously and involve the supplier providing the school with upwards of 200 titles displayed face out. The school benefits from a sales commission or free books. Scholastic is the largest seller of children's books through schools.

Used books

Worthy of note in any discussion of the sales channels for books is the burgeoning second-hand or used book market. In 2006 22 per cent of adults bought books from a charity shop or other second-hand outlet (Mintel, 2007). Oxfam has 100 specialist bookshops, alongside its sale of books in its other retail outlets. The internet has revolutionized the search and sale of second-hand books: Amazon sells second-hand copies through its Marketplace scheme; and AbeBooks lists over 100 m new, used, rare, and out-of-print books from more than 13,500 booksellers. As John Sutherland comments,

> Most purchased books (look at your shelves) are read once, if that. Particularly with classics, canny readers are buying used copies off the web. In the course of time, the web may well function like a 19th-century circulating library, giving books multiple leases of life. (Sutherland, 2004)

Publishers are concerned about the impact of second-hand sales on the sales of new books, and authors of course receive no royalties on sales past the initial purchase. Textbook publishers have to issue new editions on a regular basis to counteract the attractions for students of buying second hand. There is also concern about the sale of used books described as being like new. These could be unwanted review copies or returns that have found their way into the second hand market. There are other channels for used books, including initiatives such as BookCrossing, which encourages readers to leave books in a public place to be picked up by others. Started in 2001 BookCrossing asks readers to tag a book before releasing it 'into the wild', enabling the book's progress to be tracked (bookcrossing.com).

Online content

In sectors such as professional and journals publishing, the model for publishing has shifted from the delivery of books and printed journals to the supply of content online. Educational publishers produce CD-ROM, website add-ons, and online subscription services for schools. Many publishers will sell through third parties and use rights sales to take advantage of online markets, but some have committed themselves to a digital future by building the necessary platforms to sell directly to their markets. Companies such as ProQuest CSA and EBSCO offer sales channels for publishers, providing ejournals, ebooks and databases to libraries, companies and other institutions.

Trade publishers have been less interested in supplying content online, but renewed interest in ebooks and the arrival of a fresh generation of readers have stimulated publishers to make available ebook editions. Ebooks can be bought directly from publishers or from a variety of other websites. Publishers are pricing up individual chapters as well as the complete books. Amazon, Google, Microsoft and other big technology companies may become significant retailers of ebook content worldwide.

Audiobooks

Digital downloads of audiobooks are also attracting interest, with titles available from a variety of websites including iTunes, Audible (Amazon) and Silksoundbooks. Some technical book publishers are also selling digital voice audio.

Sources

Anderson, Chris, 'The Long Tail', *Wired*, 12.10, October 2004.

BML (Book Marketing Limited), *Expanding the Book Market*, February 2005.

Competition Commission, *Report into Proposed Acquisition of Ottakar's plc by HMV Group plc*, 12 May 2006.

Tom Holman, 'The Returns Journey', *The Bookseller*, 17 August 2007.

Ben Hoyle and Sarah Clarke, 'The Hidden Price of a Christmas Bestseller', *The Times*, 18 June 2007.

Philip Kogan, 'Independent in a Sea of Conglomerates', *Logos*, 18:2, 2007.

Robert McCrum, 'Fear the Revolution', *The Observer*, 1 July 2007.

Laura Miller, *Reluctant Capitalists: Bookselling and the culture of consumption*, University of Chicago Press, 2006.

Mintel, *Books, Music and Video Retailing*, 2005.

Mintel, *Book Retailing*, 2007.

OFT (Office of Fair Trading), *Report into Completed Acquisition by Woolworths Group plc of Bertram Group plc*, 16 April 2007.

PricewaterhouseCoopers, *The Internet: This time it's for real*, June 2007.

Caroline Sanderson, 'Several Careful Owners', *The Bookseller*, 8 June 2007.

John Sutherland, 'Brave New World', *Financial Times*, 9 October 2004.

David Teather, 'Challenge Amazon', *The Bookseller*, 4 May 2007.

Web resources

www.booksellers.org.uk The Booksellers Association represents over 4,000 retail outlets.

www.booktokens.co.uk Book tokens were first introduced into the UK in 1932; their story is told here.

http://blogs.guardian.co.uk/books/ *The Guardian* blog about books and the book trade.

www.readitswapit.co.uk Readers swap books online.

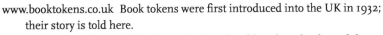

CHAPTER 14

Getting into publishing

Publishing is a popular career choice and there is strong competition to enter the industry. Although many junior jobs that are advertised state that previous publishing experience is necessary, entry to publishing is paradoxically mainly at the bottom. You should therefore snatch any kind of work in any area of publishing, whatever the size of firm. Publishers usually recruit only to fill vacancies which, at the entry level, often occur at no more than a month's notice. Working on a short-term contract, or covering for a permanent employee's maternity leave, can be a good opportunity. Once in, you will be learning, gaining personal impressions of various jobs by talking to people, and, what is more, be in a position to hear about future jobs. From that bridgehead, it is usually easier to obtain a second job than the first, by moving sideways or upwards within or outside the firm.

Do not fear that your first job will necessarily determine your subsequent career. It is best to complete at least a year in the first job, but two to three job changes in the first five years are not uncommon. At the outset, it is preferable to think firstly of the kinds of books you would be interested in publishing and hence the type of publishing company (sometimes it can be problematic to move across publishing sectors); and secondly of the kind of work for which you feel you might have a particular aptitude.

To increase your chances, the ability to drive can be useful and computer literacy is necessary for all jobs. Office and IT skills, and experience of administrative work are desirable. The ability to use publishing software such as Adobe InDesign can be a great advantage, as are proofreading skills. If you are a bookseller and want to move into publishing, two to three years of bookselling is ample. For any newcomer to the industry, work experience at a publisher will help your CV stand out, and a temporary job with a publisher during the summer may lead to the elusive first full-time appointment.

FIRST STEPS

Market research

You must carry out research on publishing in general and on your target publishers in particular, and especially you should research the books these firms publish.

Read the trade press – *The Bookseller* and *Publishing News*; read book reviews; and visit libraries and bookshops to look at publishers' books and to seek advice from librarians and booksellers. For specialist areas visit the appropriate library or bookshop. When visiting bookshops, during their quiet periods try to talk to the manager who deals directly with central office or publishers' reps. When you have narrowed down the field or have secured an interview, you must read the publisher's catalogue and visit their website before any further approach is made.

> The London Book Fair held in April provides a great opportunity to view the output of publishers

Networking

Contacts in publishing can provide insight into particular firms, offering you advice, spreading knowledge of your abilities, and alerting you to impending vacancies. Sometimes these contacts are influential enough to secure you a preliminary discussion or interview, though rarely a job itself. Therefore, first tap your family and personal connections; if you draw a blank there, take the initiative. You can network by joining the Society of Young Publishers (SYP), London and Oxford. It holds monthly meetings, at which senior publishers speak, and publishes the journal, *InPrint*. Membership is not restricted to people employed in publishing. Women in Publishing (WiP) holds regular meetings and training sessions in London and Oxford. Membership is open to women of any age in publishing. You may be able to attend meetings of the Independent Publishers Guild (IPG) in London and around the country (mainly small publishers), or go to events of organizations such as the Oxford Publishing Society (OPuS) or the Publishers Publicity Circle (PPC).

QUALIFICATIONS

Most entry into publishing requires an undergraduate degree, and common subjects are English, History and Modern Languages. People with degrees in science, mathematics and other specialities, such as law or medicine, are at a premium for publishers in those areas. A teaching background or experience in English language teaching is particularly useful for educational and ELT publishing, and African studies or experience of working for Voluntary Service Overseas for international educational publishers. Some legal background is useful for rights and contracts positions. Language degrees are desirable for rights and export sales departments of all kinds of publishers. The level of degree is less important. Those with doctorates seeking their first junior job may face the difficulty that they are that much older than competing younger applicants.

Some of the major publishers offer graduate recruitment schemes. For example, under the long-running Macmillan scheme, five or six graduates are selected each year and are given an accelerated, diverse and international experience to shape them for management positions.

Pre-entry qualification

Traditionally the only departments in which formal vocationally orientated qualifications are highly desirable are graphic design and production. More recently some publishers like to see a qualification from the Chartered Institute of

Marketing (CIM) for marketing posts. The pre-entry publishing courses used to concentrate on copy-editing and production skills, but now they cover the business and marketing aspects of publishing. At undergraduate level, students can choose to study publishing along with other disciplines. There has been a large increase in the range of courses available at undergraduate and graduate levels, with student places around several hundred per year. Their links with publishers, various work experience schemes for students, and the rise of their former students into management positions have undermined the traditionalist view that pre-entry vocational training is a waste of time.

Attaining a BA or MA in Publishing does not guarantee a job in publishing but it substantially increases the chances – the established courses score impressive success rates. Some publishers, recognizing the quality of graduates from the main programmes, advertise job openings directly on their websites.

Work experience

There are some websites that advertise work experience, and some of the larger publishers have established mechanisms for recruiting students keen to gain, mostly unpaid, placements. You can write to the HR departments or if you have any contacts inside a publisher, use them to find out who it would be best to contact. Work experience is an excellent preparation for a career in publishing. By working in different departments you can gain first-hand experience of the different functions, find out about your aptitudes, and build a network of contacts.

Other experience which increases a job applicant's attractiveness includes editing your school or college magazine, website work and short-term work in a bookshop.

FINDING VACANCIES

Recruitment agencies

There are a variety of agencies that recruit for publishers. Examples are Judy Fisher, JFL Search & Selection, and Inspired Selection. Some, such as Meridian Search and Selection, specialize in more senior positions and will help headhunt staff from rival companies. The agencies regularly advertise junior positions on their own and other websites. Some of the agencies encourage job hunters to register with them, offer free advice, and they will forward the details of likely candidates when a vacancy occurs.

Publishers also use agencies to recruit for temporary positions. There is always a demand from publishers for temporary staff to fill jobs vacated by people on holiday or ill. In London this is a good way of getting the feel of different publishers and can lead to a permanent job.

Advertisements

Advertisements for publishing jobs appear in the trade press (*The Bookseller* and *Publishing News*) and the national press (mainly *The Guardian* on Mondays and

Saturdays). Publishers outside London may advertise locally. The very high cost of press advertising has prompted some publishers to advertise jobs on free websites, such as those of the IPG, SYP, and the Oxford International Centre for Publishing Studies. Some employers have also created vacancy areas on their own websites. Many jobs, especially in trade publishing, are not advertised at all. Publishers prefer to use word-of-mouth recommendations.

YOUR APPLICATION

Preparing your CV and covering letter

To secure an interview you must attract the publisher's attention by submitting a compelling and immaculately tailored CV and covering letter, without spelling mistakes, inconsistent punctuation or ungrammatical sentences. Many new entrants applying for their first publishing jobs, as well as those applying for subsequent jobs, fail on these points at this initial hurdle.

A typical CV (or résumé) will have the following headings:

- personal details,
- personal statement – a short description of your attributes and personal qualities,
- education,

- relevant previous employment and work experience, paid and unpaid – other employment can be moved later on in the CV,
- skills and qualifications,
- personal interests, and
- references.

The CV is an organized summary of the key facts (not opinions) about yourself. Bullet points may be a useful way of emphasizing essential points about a job or your degree. While emphasizing your assets, the CV must be truthful. Each element should prove to the publisher that you have the qualities and skills for the job: omit those that do not. It should not be longer than two A4 pages. For those with little work experience, the chronological CV laid out in a form style is usually the best approach. The information is listed in chronological order under headings.

Under personal details give your full name, contact address with home and mobile telephone numbers, email, date of birth, and nationality. The education section lists college and school details, with dates, courses taken, grades achieved, special projects, scholarships, prizes. Spotlight any occupational training courses which show relevant skills.

If you have relevant employment and work experience, you will want to put this near to the top of the CV, usually in reverse chronological order – the most recent first. Provide employers' names, your job titles with duties and responsibilities, promotions, special awards, and accomplishments (for example ideas that reduced costs, increased profitability, streamlined administration) – a few key points for each job. Relevant work outside publishing should be emphasized, for example office, library or bookshop work, preparing a firm's literature or magazine, compiling mailing lists, public and customer relations, teaching, and work overseas.

Whatever the CV format, the skills emphasized may be those pertaining particularly to specific jobs, for example design or proofreading, and those which are more generic, such as computer literacy, website development, driving, languages, numeracy, administration, communication (for example, presentations, telesales). At management levels, applicants often start their CVs with a personal statement highlighting their achievements, skill and experience. This is followed by sections on their career history and key skills.

Activities and interests may be incorporated under the above headings or listed separately. If you are about to leave full-time education, your skills and keen interests (for example, photography, sport) assume great importance because with little work experience they mark you out. You should list your leadership or administrative positions, and achievements.

The CV usually ends with the names and telephone numbers of your two or three referees who can convey your character, stability and competence to perform the job. Brief them beforehand. One should act as a character reference. You can state, if necessary, that they should not be contacted without prior consultation. It is increasingly common is to say that references are available on request.

Use factual, concise simple language – without abbreviations or jargon – and active verbs. Have someone who is literate or familiar with recruitment to check and edit your CV. It is vital to avoid basic spelling and grammatical errors: for example, check your use of apostrophes and avoid mixing up their and there. Use good quality white paper (avoid colour printing and coloured paper). Set good margins with adequate spaces top and bottom. Leave one line space between sections. Try not to break a section at the bottom of the first page (a heading should be followed by at least two lines of text, or carried over). Number the two sheets. Insert your name at the top of page two.

COVERING LETTER

The covering letter accompanies the CV. Its purpose is to show the publisher the benefits of employing you, to whet the publisher's appetite to learn more about you – to read your CV and to call you to interview. The letter should be no longer than one page of A4, say three to five short paragraphs, printed on white A4 paper (the same as the CV). If you are applying for your first job in publishing you will not have space, nor would it be desirable, to expound at length on your love of books and reading.

The letter should be headed with your name and contact details and addressed to the head of the department to which you are applying, to the HR department, or, if replying to an advertisement, to the person stated. It is vital to spell correctly the names of the manager and publisher.

Start with a brief and simple statement of your reasons for writing – for example that you are applying for position X, advertised in journal Y, on Z date, or are seeking work, or mention a mutual contact referral – and that you enclose your CV.

Orientate the letter to the job, firm, your suitability and enthusiasm:

- State briefly your current position, for example about to leave college with expected qualifications.
- Show your research of the publisher by referring to recent or future books or promotions.
- Stress your motives and suitability: your relevant experience, skills and enthusiasm. Link your attributes to those specified in the advertisement, and you may want to use similar phrasing. Convey your enthusiasm by anchoring it to some credential, or a relevant fact.
- Give positive reasons for making the career step and for your keen interest in the job.
- Sign off using 'Yours sincerely' and sign your name above your printed name.

Use relatively short paragraphs rather than a few long ones; use plain English, concise and precise language, and the active voice. Avoid clichés and unappealing abruptness. To judge tone, try reading the letter aloud the next day, or ask someone else, such as a tutor or senior colleague, to read and proofread it. Ask them what overall impression you have conveyed in the letter – employers welcome the right level of enthusiasm. Remember you are trying to persuade a stranger to interview you.

APPLICATION FORM

Some publishers supply application forms. Make copies of the form if not supplied electronically. Follow the instructions and read it right through twice before starting. Take particular care with your full answers to the major open-ended questions or 'other information'. Use the photocopies for drafting and layout. If necessary, attach an extra sheet. You may be allowed to attach your CV and a covering letter.

What to do now

If you have been shortlisted, the publisher will contact you to arrange the interview. You may receive a rejection – like the majority – or worse, hear nothing. Difficult as it is, do not let depression and frustration colour future applications. No application is wasted: elements can be reused and modified. Some publishers hold strong but rejected applicants on file.

Direct approach to publishers

Since many publishing jobs are not advertised, writing speculatively to publishers can work; but be prepared to write a large number of applications. Many publishers have high staff turnover at junior levels or need to cover maternity leave and these continually create new opportunities.

Because so many humanities graduates apply to the London consumer book publishers and their editorial departments, you increase your chances if you apply to other sectors and departments. There are many opportunities in sales, marketing and production, as well as in the out-of-London educational, academic, and journal publishers.

Some publishers do not reply to speculative approaches, others hold impressive candidates on file, to be approached later if a job arises. Some will call you for a preliminary discussion which may lead to an interview, or are prepared to offer advice, possibly recommending you for interview in another house. If you hear nothing or receive a letter of rejection, yet are still very keen on that publisher, telephone the manager and persuade him or her to give you a short chat. People whose commitment to publishing is so strong and who persist usually get in.

INTERVIEW

Before the interview

If you are called to interview, acknowledge quickly. If you decide not to go, say so, and give others the opportunity. Publishers often shortlist between six and a dozen, with possibly a few marginal reserves. Prepare thoroughly beforehand. First, research the publisher, its books or promotions. 'Why do you find them interesting?' This greatly improves your chances. Second, think of answers to probable questions. As a publisher, what would you be looking for? What are your particular strengths? From your research, you should be able to deal with questions that relate to your interest in the job and test your knowledge of the publisher. Also you should be prepared to discuss what you think are the most important skills needed. You may be asked what you feel would be the most mundane or frustrating parts of the job and how you would cope with them.

The thinking you put into your CV and letter is apposite to questions such as:

- Why do you want to go into publishing? (Don't just say 'I love reading and books'.)
- How is your previous experience applicable?
- Why do you think you are suitable?
- What are your major strengths?
- What makes you think you will be good at this job?
- What are your interests or hobbies?
- What books do you read? – asked especially by consumer book publishers. Cite books which correspond to their interests and be prepared to analyse briefly why you think they work.

Be prepared for questions which probe facts, explore your feelings, judgement and motivation. You may well be asked to explain why you left a job. Do not blame the previous employer or specific individuals. Acceptable reasons include: 'I left for a better opportunity' or 'for more challenging work', or 'to broaden my experience'. Redundancy, even if no fault of your own and a common affliction of many in publishing, can be related to the circumstances of the particular firm. Beware of quoting shortcomings that may be applicable to the new job.

You will need to show that you have thought of medium-term career goals, while stressing your preparedness to commit yourself to the job for an effective time-span. Many new entrants apply, for example, to the marketing and sales departments, with the ambition of becoming editors. You may confess that legitimate target to a manager of another department but you must show strong commitment to the job applied for, otherwise you will be rejected.

Book publishing is an ideas business from start to finish. 'What ideas do you have?' may be asked of any applicant in any department. Do not sit dumbfounded. There may be no 'correct' answer – the question is more of a test of initiative and of common sense.

Come up with your own questions to ask the interviewer. The best ones relate to clarifying features of the job and showing your knowledge of and keen interest in the publisher. Questions relating to the job include its main aspects, what factors promoted its creation, limits of authority, responsibility and independence, whom you would be working with most closely, terms and conditions, and future prospects. Those relating to the publisher (such as on new developments) could arise from your research. However, you should ask only a few questions – you are the one being interviewed. You could ask questions to which in part you can guess the answer and which will elicit a positive response. Be careful not to ask questions that are out of your depth, or cheeky, or ask the publisher to give you unreasonable special treatment.

You may want to take samples of printed material on which you have worked – for example a college magazine, book, or promotional material. By recounting quickly the brief, the decisions and initiatives taken, the problems overcome, the people involved, you can reveal your analytical, decision-making and organizational abilities, your ideas and effectiveness in dealing with people and your success.

Interview

Before the interview, you will need to judge your standard of dress. The style and atmosphere of publishers can differ markedly, and some departments, such as accounts, may be more formal than others. On the whole it is best to appear businesslike and well dressed and groomed.

You must not be late so allow plenty of time, and make sure you know the exact location of the interview. Some publishers are difficult to find. If you are unavoidably delayed, telephone and apologize. On arrival announce yourself to the receptionist and if time allows examine the publisher's material in the showroom.

While some interviewers will greet you at the door, your first test may be to enter the room confidently (an important skill for most jobs). You should greet the interviewer and shake their hand positively. First impressions count, so don't forget to smile, and make sure you come across as confident and relaxed. Throughout the interview try to mention those assets which reveal your suitability and enthusiasm, anchor your skills in hard evidence, and ground accomplishments by giving examples. Reveal your research of the publisher, but do not over-praise or lecture.

Maintain eye contact with the interviewer and listen to the questions. Do not mumble yes/no answers. Answer questions fully, but judge the length and depth of your reply by watching the interviewer's verbal and non-verbal cues, and interest level. Be prepared for the interviewer's follow-up questions. When stating views make sure your reasoning is sensible and fairly firm, not vague, arrogant or inflexible.

The danger of talking too much, apart from boring the interviewer, is to go beyond the question and introduce irrelevant facts or opinions, either of which inadvertently reveal weaknesses. Indeed an interviewer may keep quiet and let you hang yourself. Interviewers tend to form negative impressions more readily, and on less information, than they form favourable impressions; their judgements are apt to be coloured by one or two striking attributes of candidates; and they tend to reject on negatives rather than select on positives.

A quality that most interviewers want to see, which can illuminate all others, is enthusiasm. It means having a positive outlook that shines through whatever subject is being discussed. Do not give the impression that you are not really interested in the job. The more nervous you become, the faster you may talk. Strive for measured animation. Undue modesty will conceal you, while boasting is damaging. If you have been dishonest in your CV or overstated the case you will be unable to substantiate your claims.

Depending on the job, you may want to take along a portfolio of your design work or journalism. You will need to judge in the interview how much importance to give the portfolio, depending on the level of interest shown by the interviewer.

Finally, the most intangible and important part of the whole exercise is whether the interviewer likes you and thinks you will fit in because most publishers are relatively small businesses (or profit centres within a large

> First impressions count at interview, including your appearance, body language and tone of voice

corporation) and publishing is a personal business. Some managers set great store on their quality of life expressed by the work they do and the people they have around them.

Having asked your own questions, by the end of the interview you should have a clear idea of what the job entails, what will happen next, who will make the next move, and the timescale. Publishers typically use either one or two interview stages. If called to a second interview, be armed with ideas that might help the publisher – but do think them through.

YOU'RE IN!

When the publisher is pretty sure it wants you, your references may be checked – but not always. If you are the chosen candidate reply quickly if you decide either to decline or accept the offer. There is usually little or no room for negotiation on salary in junior jobs. A question you may be asked at interview or subsequently is 'What salary are you expecting?' It is preferable to pass the responsibility back to the publisher to make the first offer by asking, for instance 'What are you planning on paying the best candidate?' Publishers rarely state salaries in advertisements and there is great variation in salary ranges between different publishers.

Publishers differ markedly in style of management and atmosphere. The first months at work are a crucial period for quickly assimilating the politics of the organization and learning how to work within it, how to get things done, how to win and retain the regard of new colleagues. Tactics such as throwing your heart into the new job and being seen to arrive early and leave late will establish an enduring reputation.

Career paths

It was mentioned earlier that the first jobs within the first few years may not necessarily determine a career path. Many new entrants have little idea of the work of the departments they join and may find they develop a forte and liking for the work. It is possible to move across to other departments and areas of publishing, but over time it becomes progressively more difficult: there are usually candidates who have acquired specialist knowledge of that particular area of publishing.

In small firms with few staff and less departmentalism it may be easier to move around the firm and learn different jobs, sometimes simultaneously. But such knowledge may not be considered by a larger firm to be specialist enough. In contrast, junior staff in large firms while often finding it more difficult to cross the more pronounced departmental boundaries, may gain in-depth expertise afforded by the greater resources of the publisher. People move from small to large firms, which usually pay much higher salaries at the top, and vice-versa: for example, middle-ranking staff of large firms may attain more senior jobs in smaller firms. The promotion of staff with little management experience to departmental management positions is common.

Unlike huge industrial concerns and the civil service, not even the largest publisher has a big enough staff pyramid to be able to fill staff vacancies from within at the time they occur. Publishers are not rash enough to advertise career pathways which cannot be fulfilled but in some large firms there are visible grade progressions within departments.

Although some staff progress upwards in publishers, a few rapidly, it has become rare to spend a whole lifetime with one firm. Rather most people move from one publisher to another, sideways or hopefully in an upward direction. The possibility of getting stuck in any job at any level is ever present.

In moving around companies, most people tend to stay with the type of work in which they have acquired expertise. If moving between functions is far from easy, moving across the major types of publishing is even more difficult. Generally speaking people stay within consumer, educational or academic publishing (unless, that is, they have more transportable administrative and ICT experience). Many have expertise that is applied to the publishing of books and associated products for certain markets and their contacts inside and outside publishing are orientated accordingly.

Some people in their early 30s with much experience want to change direction, for instance, to move from academic to consumer book publishing, or vice-versa. But they are up against people already in that area so their chances of getting a job at the same level of seniority and salary are much more remote. As you increase your expertise of an area, the more valuable that expertise becomes and the more difficult it is to throw it aside and turn to something else. There are always exceptions. People do move between departments and types of publishing at all stages of their careers up to and including managing directors but they are in a minority.

Corporate reorganizations and takeovers inevitably affect careers. Employees unfortunately cannot choose their new owners. After a takeover, staff from the acquiring company may enhance their position in the larger organization, whereas the former management of the bought company is realigned. The managers may stay, leave or be downgraded. The more junior staff may leave as the new owners rationalize the departments, for example, by cutting out competing editorial units, merging production and design and rights departments, amalgamating the sales forces, centralizing HR, accounting and distribution services, and relocating offices (even across the Atlantic). Many staff who leave with their redundancy payments reappear in other publishers, start their own businesses in specialist services or consultancy, or go freelance.

Freelance work, for example in editorial, design or web design, offers the freedom of working at home without the rigours and costs of commuting to work. Outside the general hubbub of a publishing house, and with fewer interruptions, freelancers may be able to work faster and plan their day to their own rhythm. But forced to maintain a flow of work and pressured to meet deadlines, the freelancer's day often extends far into the night, to weekends and public holidays. The best ways of obtaining work are through personal recommendation, professional contacts, or by personal approach. Industry bodies such as the SfEP (Society for Editors and Proofreaders) and the Society of Indexers maintain registers of freelancers. The National Union of Journalists recommends hourly rates for editorial work such as proofreading.

Many people in their 30s reach a plateau below management level and fear that their rapidly approaching fortieth birthday is their last chance to make a change. With increasing age the possibilities of movement diminish. However, many senior jobs are filled by people roughly between the ages of 37 to 45. After that, unless an individual is particularly well known or brilliant or specialized, changing companies becomes progressively more difficult. By the age of 50, with the same provisos, it becomes very difficult indeed – there may be no alternative but to stay put until retirement.

Another factor that may constrain intercompany movement is the housing market and your accessibility to a range of firms. House prices in the south-east region are higher and increase at a proportionately faster rate than in the rest of the country; they rise particularly steeply towards the centre of London. A company away from the centre may offer to pay relocation expenses, but you should consider the possible career step after that. If you move home too far out, you may be taking a one-way rather than a return ticket.

Staff of commercial publishers are very attractive to the many public, private and voluntary sector organizations operating their own publishing. Moreover, the contacts made and skills learnt in publishing can be applied to other commercial enterprises, not necessarily concerned with publishing.

In commercial and not-for-profit publishing, staff have been traditionally recruited from within the industry; and publishing staff tend to be retained unless they leave voluntarily or are forced out. It has been a relatively closed world. However, with the growth of digital publishing and the highly commercial outlook of most publishers, the industry now also looks outside for fresh talent. Managers may come from other industries, as well as staff with IT and logistics backgrounds. Publishing businesses have changed dramatically over the last decades and will continue to do so at accelerating speed.

Post-entry training

Most people in publishing learn on the job by observing the successes and mistakes made by themselves, colleagues, and other publishers, and applying that experience to each new project: knowledge is passed on or reinvented.

Few publishers give sufficient emphasis to training of their junior staff in their early 20s, or for that matter of senior staff who, while having specialist knowledge of their field, may often lack a broad overview of the business and general management knowledge; let alone an MBA. Publishers may then complain that they face shortages of talent when recruiting for senior posts. If you are fortunate enough to work in a firm that trains, take all the opportunities offered. But if not, the initiative is yours to seek out relevant meetings such as those of the SYP and WiP, and to make the time to attend courses. There are numerous courses offered part-time by the main teaching institutions and by professional organizations such as ALPSP (Association of Learned and Professional Society Publishers) and the SfEP. The Publishing Training Centre in London offers the greatest range of short vocational courses for the industry, and sets the national occupational standards.

Salaries

Within book publishing there is a great variation in salaries and no trade-wide statistics are available. Estimates of the typical starting salary in publishing in 2007 were around £18,000. Traditionally, the many junior jobs in publishing, particularly in editorial, have low starting salaries, in part a consequence of large numbers chasing few jobs. Some people argue that the incidence of low pay and the high proportion of female employment at junior levels are not unconnected.

Those who move jobs on a regular basis may find they have increased their salaries above the levels of those who are content to stay for a long time in the same company. The law of supply and demand affects salaries across different types of publishing. For example, publishers wanting staff with a humanities background have a large choice and tend to pay lower salaries than legal and medical publishers, which may find it difficult to recruit staff with the relevant academic qualifications or experience. Moreover, some people like to work in areas which they see as having intrinsic interest and accept lower salaries than if they worked in other fields of publishing. This has applied particularly to those in the literary and prestigious end of publishing.

On the marketing and sales side, salaries have been approaching those of general commerce; but at the top end, the salaries of most directors of publishing companies do not equate with those earned by the heads of large fast-moving consumer goods industries. At the very top, chief executives earn salaries many times those of the lowest paid staff, in some cases more than 15 times.

Diversity in publishing

There is a high proportion of women in pre-entry courses and in publishing, particularly London consumer book publishing, to the extent that publishers are wondering how to attract more men into the profession. About 70 per cent of the workforce is female. In senior management there is a higher proportion of men than in the publishing workforce as a whole, but the position of women has improved at board level. There are a number of women in senior positions across the industry.

The study *In Full Colour* (2004) found that only 8 per cent of the publishing profession believed the industry to be culturally diverse – 47 per cent said it is not. A later study (*Ethnic Diversity in Publishing*, 2006) found that 92.3 per cent of employees within the publishing industry are from a white background, while 7.7 per cent are from a black and minority ethnic (BME) background. Although this matches the proportions within the UK as a whole, it did not reflect the ethnic make-up of London (71.2 per cent white/28.8 per cent BME), where most of the respondents were based. There is a clearly an opportunity for publishers looking to broaden the readership for their books. Helen Fraser, Managing Director of Penguin, said: 'A workforce that mirrors the population, especially urban populations where the majority of books are sold, will be able to tap into the whole market' (Kean, page 11).

Now read this

Alison Baverstock, Susannah Bowen and Steve Carey, *How to Get a Job in Publishing*, A & C Black, 2008.

Sources

BML (Book Marketing Limited), *Ethnic Diversity in Publishing*, September 2006.
Danuta Kean (editor), *In Full Colour*, Supplement to *The Bookseller*, 12 March 2004.

Web resources

www.alpsp.org Association of Learned and Professional Society Publishers.
www.ipg.uk.com Independent Publishers Guild.
http://www.macmillan.com/grad.asp Macmillan Graduate Recruitment Scheme.
www.opusnet.co.uk OPuS (Oxford Publishing Society).
www.prospects.ac.uk Official graduate careers website.
www.brookes.ac.uk/publishing Oxford International Centre for Publishing Studies.
www.publishers.org.uk The Publishers Association.
www.publisherspublicitycircle.co.uk Publishers Publicity Circle.
www.train4publishing.co.uk/careers Publishing Training Centre's pages on careers.
www.careersatrandom.co.uk Random House Group's careers website.
www.sfep.org.uk Society for Editors and Proofreaders.
www.indexers.org.uk The Society of Indexers.
http://www.thesyp.org.uk/ Society of Young Publishers.
http://www.wipub.org.uk/ Women in Publishing.

Glossary

This glossary is a simple look-up guide to key UK publishing terms, abbreviations and acronyms. The list is not exhaustive and no attempt has been made to provide lengthy definitions.

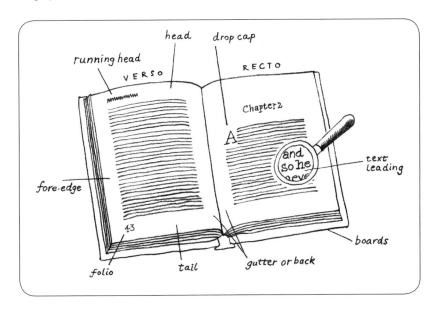

add-on extra value added into a product, for example a CD-ROM in the back of a book

advance a sum paid in advance to the author in anticipation of the author earning royalties from sales of their work. Advances can be paid on signature of contract, delivery of the typescript, and on publication

advance copy the printed copy available once the book is printed and ahead of publication. Advance copies will be sent to the author and used in marketing

Aga saga a novel set amongst the Aga-owning English middle class

agent a literary agent may act on behalf of an author and negotiate the contract for a book with the publisher. An agent can also be a third party acting for a publisher in an export market

aggregator   an aggregator will license the rights to distribute content online from a variety of publishers

AI   the advance information sheet which contains essential bibliographic and marketing information

AIDA   (in marketing) attention, interest, desire, action

airport edition   the export paperback edition of a book sold airside at airport shops ahead of the main paperback edition

ALPSP   Association of Learned and Professional Society Publishers

APA   Audiobook Publishing Association

BA   The Booksellers Association

backlist   a publisher's established titles; compare *frontlist*

BAPLA   British Association of Picture Libraries and Agencies

BCA   Book Club Associates

BIC   Book Industry Communication

big deal   a bundle of journals sold by a publisher as one package

blad   a sample printed section

blog   an online journal

blurb   the selling copy that appears on the back cover or front jacket flap of the book

book club   traditionally a mail order bookseller; now also a reading group

breadcrumbs   the links on a web page that enable the user to retrace their route back through the site

bulk   a paper's thickness

burst binding   see *slotted binding*

chick lit   a genre of fiction principally aimed at single women in their 20s or early 30s

CIF   cost, insurance and freight

CIP   cataloguing in publication [data]

CLA   Copyright Licensing Agency

CMS   content management system

co-edition   an additional part of the print run sold to a third party. There are both English and foreign language co-editions

commissioning   creating a new project and signing up an author; or acquiring the rights to publish a work from the author, their agent or another publisher

contract   the legal agreement between the author and publisher, outlining the rights acquired by the publisher and the responsibilities of both author and publisher

copublication   publication by arrangement between two companies. This could mean the use of both imprints and dividing the profits on the title. It could also extend to sharing development work and using joint branding, for example with a coursebook published in an overseas market

copy-editing   editing the author's manuscript with regard to style and consistency to eliminate errors and improve the text for the reader

copyright   the protection which gives authors and other creative artists legal ownership of their work – it establishes their work as their personal, exclusive property. © is the copyright symbol

coursepack   a collection of materials, usually photocopied, for use in the classroom

cover   a paperback is bound with a cover. The design may be adapted from the hardback jacket or be completely new

cover mount   a book or other product packaged with a newspaper or magazine

CRM   customer relationship management

crossover title   a children's book with an adult market

CSR   corporate social responsibility

CTP   computer to plate

CUP   Cambridge University Press

depreciation   reducing the value of stock in the company's accounts

Digital Rights Management (DRM)   the technical means by which publishers control access to digital content

discount   publishers give retailers a discount off the recommended price to encourage them to stock their titles. In consumer publishing discounts can reach high levels

DK   Dorling Kindersley

DNB   *Dictionary of National Biography*

DOI   digital object identifier

DTD   document type definition

DTP   desktop publishing

dues   the orders collected by the publisher before publication

dummy   a mock-up of the final printed book, mainly used for selling illustrated books to retailers or overseas customers

ebook   an electronic book

EDI   electronic data interchange

EFL   English as a foreign language

ELT   English language teaching

emarketing   use of the internet for marketing. Activities include search engine optimization, email marketing and website promotion

EMEA (sometimes EMA)   Europe, the Middle East and Africa

end-matter   the pages at the end of a book with, for example, the appendices and index

EPC   Educational Publishers Council

EPOS   electronic point of sale

EPS   encapsulated PostScript

extent   the length of a book, expressed in number of words or printed pages

firm sale   books sold on the basis of firm sale are paid for and cannot be returned by the purchaser, for example a retailer

FOB   free on board

folio   a page number

frontlist   a publisher's new titles; compare *backlist*

goodwill   assets that contribute to a publisher's competitive advantage, including its brand and employees

house style   the set style imposed during the editing of a text – elements include spelling, grammar, capitalization and hyphenation

HTML   HyperText Markup Language

imprint   a list of books within a publisher's overall publishing programme. Each imprint will have its own flavour and direction. The imprint may be represented visually with a logo on the spine and title page of each book

institutional repository   a digital collection of research papers by members of an institution such as a university

intellectual property (IP)   a publisher's IP includes its copyrights and licences

IPG   Independent Publishers Guild

IPR   intellectual property rights

IRI   industry returns initiative

ISBN   international standard book number

ISP   internet service provider

ISSN   international standard serial number

jacket   the dust jacket wrapped around a hardback book

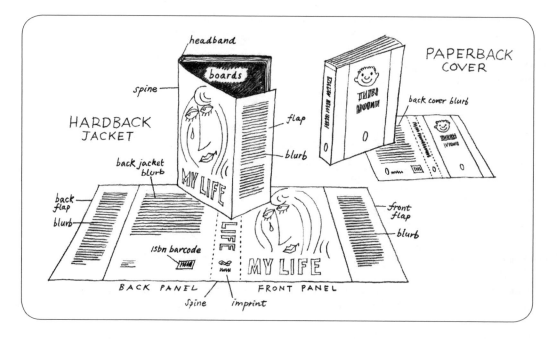

JISC   Joint Information Systems Committee

JPEG   joint photographic experts group

leading   the spacing between lines of text

licence   a licence gives a publisher the sole, exclusive right to publish an author's work and sell it as widely as possible. The publisher also licenses a book to other publishers, for example for translation. A *non-exclusive* licence enables the publisher to sell content – for example for digital use – to a number of companies

list-building   taking a strategic view of commissioning in order to create a new publishing list or expand the present publishing programme

literal   error introduced in keyboarding a text; also called a **typo**

litho   offset lithography. This form of printing is still common for many books

LMS   learning management system

Long Tail   first proposed by Chris Anderson in 2004 in *Wired* magazine, the idea that there is greater total value in the Long Tail of less popular products (available over the internet) than in the more widely available hits

manuscript (ms) the author's version of the work. Now often referred to as the *typescript*, it was originally handwritten

marketing mix product, price, place and promotion

mass-market paperback A format paperback – 178 × 110 mm; compare *trade paperback*

metadata data about data. This enables content to be categorized and found more easily in online searches

monograph scholarly work based on the author's primary research

moral rights additional to copyright, these statutory rights granted to the author are the right to paternity, the right of integrity, the right to prevent false attribution and the right to privacy

NBA Net Book Agreement

net receipts the revenue received by the publisher after a discount has been given to a wholesaler or retailer. Also called net sales revenue (NSR)

notch binding see *slotted binding*

NSR net sales revenue

OA open access

OCR optical character recognition

OEBF open ebook format

OED *Oxford English Dictionary*

offset fee a fee payable to reproduce the original setting of a book

on-screen editing copy-editing on screen rather than on a paper print-out

OP out of print

OPuS Oxford Publishing Society

OUP Oxford University Press

outdoor advertising advertising on billboards, buses and trains

overheads the ongoing costs of running a business, for example office costs and salaries

PA The Publishers Association

packager separate from a publisher, a packager supplies an edited and designed book for the publisher to market and sell

pay per view users of an online service pay for access to individual articles, chapters, pages

PDA personal digital assistant

PDF portable document format

Perfect binding the binding method used for cheap paperbacks. The spine folds of the sections are cut off and the spine edge of the now individual leaves roughened. Glue is applied to hold the leaves together and to stick on the cover

PLS private language schools

POD print on demand. Digital printing enables the economic printing of short runs. True print on demand is the ability to print single copies to order

podcast a series of digital or audio files available for syndication or download

POS point of sale

positioning placing the product in the mind of the consumer

postprint a journal article after peer review. This is the version that is typeset and published

PPC Publishers Publicity Circle

PR   public relations

prelim pages   the first few pages of a book, usually paginated with roman numbers

preprint   a journal paper before peer review

print run   the number of copies printed of a book

production values   the quality of the paper, design, printing, binding and cover of a book

proofreading   reading proofs of a book in order to spot mistakes missed at the copy-editing stage as well as any errors introduced in the design and production stages. Proofs can be read against the original copy or 'read blind' (with no reference to the original version)

proposal   a document outlining the content and market potential of a proposed title. Elements include the book's coverage, target audience, level of readership, any competing titles and an author biography

PS   PostScript

puff   the endorsement used on the book's cover, ahead of the book being reviewed

RAE   research assessment exercise

recto   a right-hand page

returns   unsold books sent back to the publisher by the retailer

RFID   radio frequency identification

RP   reprinting

RSS   really simple syndication. Content distributed to users by regular feeds

running head   the heading at the top of each page – for example, the chapter or book title

see safe   books sold on a see-safe basis, for example to a retailer, are paid for under credit terms. If they are unsold, their return may be authorized by the publisher and credited against future orders

SEO   search engine optimization

serial rights   the right to sell selections from a work to a newspaper or magazine. *First* serial rights cover extracts before the book's publication; *second* serial rights are for extracts published on or after publication

SfEP   Society for Editors and Proofreaders

site licence   granted to an institution, for example a university, it permits usage of software or an online service on a number of computers

slotted binding   a method of binding in which the spine folds of the sections are perforated during sheet folding. The binding machine injects the adhesive to hold together the folded sections, applies the cover and trims the book. Also known as *notch* or *burst binding*

SOR   sale or return

spine   the backbone of a book. Most books are displayed spine out

STM   scientific, technical and medical

subscription   the sales on subscription are made in advance of the book's publication. These are then recorded in the publisher's ordering system as dues

subsidiary rights   the rights a publisher can acquire in addition to the basic publishing rights – examples are translation and serial rights

SYP   Society of Young Publishers

TIFF   tagged image file format

trade paperback   B format paperback – 198 × 129 mm; compare *mass-market paperback*

trade publishing   the publishing of books that are sold through the book trade; also known as consumer publishing

typo   error introduced in keyboarding a text

Unicode   an encoding system which gives a unique identity to each character, 'no matter what the platform, no matter what the program, no matter what the language' (unicode.com, accessed 1 October 2007)

USP   unique sales proposition – what makes a book stand out from the competition

VAT   value added tax

verso   a left-hand page

viral marketing   spreading a marketing message using social networks

visual   mock-up of cover or jacket design

VLE   virtual learning environment

wasting   disposing of unsold stock

Web 2.0   the new generation of the web in which users upload as well as download

web press   press that prints on to a reel of paper

widget   a mini web plug-in with sample content that can be emailed or copied on to the user's social networking pages. This is an example of viral marketing

wiki   a collaborative website. The name derives from the Hawaiian word *wikiwiki* – quick

WiP   Women in Publishing

WIPO   World Intellectual Property Organization

WOM   word of mouth

XML   Extensible Markup Language

Bibliography

The relevant sources and suggestions for further reading are given at the end of each chapter. This list pulls together key texts and resources.

Journals and periodicals
The Author
The Bookseller
Learned Publishing
Logos
Publishing News
Publishing Research Quarterly

Industry databases and internet resources relevant to publishing
Amazon
Book Facts Online
booktrade.info (book2book)
Google Book Search
GPI Country Reports
Mintel
Nielsen BookData
Nielsen BookScan

Industry data is also available from the websites of the industry associations:
www.booksellers.org.uk   The Booksellers Association
www.publishers.org.uk   The Publishers Association

Books
Barney Allan, *Guide to Export for UK Book Publishers*, The Publishers Association/ UK Trade & Investment, 2004.
Chris Anderson, *The Long Tail: How endless choice is creating unlimited demand*, Random House, 2006.
Diana Athill, *Stet*, Granta, 2000.
Tricia Austin and Richard Doust, *New Media Design*, Laurence King, 2007.
Phil Baines, *Penguin by Design: A cover story 1935–2005*, Allen Lane, 2005.

Phil Baines and Andrew Haslam, *Type and Typography*, Laurence King, 2005.

David Bann, *The All New Print Production Handbook*, RotoVision, 2006.

Alan Bartram, *Making Books: Design in British publishing since 1945*, British Library, 1999.

Alison Baverstock, *How to Market Books: The essential guide to maximizing profit and exploiting all channels to market*, 4th edition, Kogan Page, 2008.

Alison Baverstock, Susannah Bowen and Steve Carey, *How to Get a Job in Publishing*, A & C Black, 2008.

Eric de Bellaigue, *British Book Publishing as a Business*, British Library Publishing, 2004.

Carole Blake, *From Pitch to Publication*, Pan, 1999.

Clive Bloom, *Bestsellers: Popular fiction since 1900*, Palgrave Macmillan, 2002.

Robert Bringhurst, *The Elements of Typographic Style*, version 3.1, Hartley & Marks, 2005.

Judith Butcher, Caroline Drake and Maureen Leach, *Copy-Editing: The Cambridge handbook for editors, copy-editors and proofreaders*, 4th edition, 2006.

Bill Cope and Angus Phillips (editors), *The Future of the Book in the Digital Age*, Chandos, 2006.

Gill Davies, *Book Commissioning and Acquisition*, 2nd edition, Routledge, 2004.

Dictionary of Printing and Publishing, 3rd edition, A & C Black, 2006.

Simon Eliot and Jonathan Rose, *A Companion to the History of the Book*, Blackwell, 2007.

Jason Epstein, *Book Business: Publishing past, present, and future*, Norton, 2002.

John Feather, *A History of British Publishing*, 2nd edition, Routledge, 2005.

David Finkelstein and Alastair McCleery, *The Book History Reader*, 2nd edition, 2006.

Jenny Hartley, *The Reading Groups Book*, revised edition, Oxford University Press, 2002.

Barbara Horn, *Editorial Project Management*, Horn Editorial Books, 2006.

Barbara Horn, *Copy-editing*, Horn Editorial Books and Publishing Training Centre, 2008.

Ros Jay, *The White Ladder Diaries*, White Ladder Press, 2004.

Hugh Jones and Christopher Benson, *Publishing Law*, 3rd edition, Routledge, 2006.

Andrew Keen, *The Cult of the Amateur*, Nicholas Brealey, 2007.

William Kasdorf (editor), *The Columbia Guide to Digital Publishing*, Columbia University Press, 2003.

Marshall Lee, *Bookmaking: Editing, design, production*, 3rd edition, Norton, 2004.

Lawrence Lessig, *Free Culture*, Penguin, 2004.

Jeremy Lewis, *Penguin Special: The life and times of Allen Lane*, Viking, 2005.

Ruari McLean, *The Thames and Hudson Manual of Typography*, Thames and Hudson, 1980.

Keith Martin, *Creative Suite 3 Integration*, Focal Press, 2007.

Tom Maschler, *Publisher*, Picador, 2005.

Nicole Matthews and Nickianne Moody (editors), *Judging a Book by Its Cover: Fans, publishers, designers, and the marketing of fiction*, Ashgate, 2007.

Laura Miller, *Reluctant Capitalists: Bookselling and the culture of consumption*, University of Chicago Press, 2006.

Michael Mitchell and Susan Wightman, *Book Typography: A designer's manual*, Libanus Press, 2005.

Ian Norrie, *Mumby's Publishing and Bookselling in the Twentieth Century*, 6th edition, Bell & Hyman, 1982.

Lynette Owen (editor), *Clark's Publishing Agreements: A book of precedents*, 7th edition, Tottel Publishing, 2007.

Lynette Owen, *Selling Rights*, 5th edition, Routledge, 2006.

Alan Powers, *Front Cover: Great book jackets and cover design*, Mitchell Beazley, 2001.

Paul Richardson, *Publishing Market Profile: The United Kingdom*, The Publishers Association, 2007.

Paul Richardson and Graham Taylor, *A Guide to the Publishing Industry*, The Publishers Association, 2008.

R. M. Ritter, *New Hart's Rules: The handbook of style for writers and editors*, Oxford University Press, 2005.

R. M. Ritter, *The Oxford Style Manual*, 2003.

R. M. Ritter, Angus Stevenson and Lesley Brown, *New Oxford Dictionary for Writers and Editors*, 2005.

Lucienne Roberts and Julia Thrift, *The Designer and the Grid*, RotoVision, 2002.

André Schiffrin, *The Business of Books: How international conglomerates took over publishing and changed the way we read*, Verso Books, 2001.

Claire Squires, *Marketing Literature: The making of contemporary writing in Britain*, Palgrave Macmillan, 2007.

Rachael Stock, *The Insider's Guide to Getting Your Book Published*, White Ladder Press, 2005.

John B. Thompson, *Books in the Digital Age*, Polity Press, 2005.

Thomas Woll, *Publishing for Profit*, 3rd edition, Chicago Review Press, 2006.

World Intellectual Property Organization, *Managing Intellectual Property in the Book Publishing Industry*, WIPO, 2008.

Gabriel Zaid, *So Many Books: Reading and publishing in an age of abundance*, Sort of Books, 2004.

Directory of publishing organizations

Association of Learned and Professional Society Publishers (ALPSP)
Blenheim House, 120 Church Street, Brighton BN1 1AU
www.alpsp.org.uk

Arts Council England
14 Great Peter Street, London SW1P 3NQ
Tel: 0845 300 6200
www.artscouncil.org.uk

Audiobook Publishing Association
email: info@theapa.net
www.theapa.net

Book Aid International
39–41 Coldharbour Lane, Camberwell, London SE5 9NR
Tel: 020 7733 3577
www.bookaid.org

The Booksellers Association
Minster House, 272 Vauxhall Bridge Road, London SW1V 1BA
Tel: 020 7802 0802
www.booksellers.org.uk

Booktrust
Book House, 45 East Hill, London SW18 2QZ
Tel: 020 8516 2977
www.booktrust.org.uk

CILIP (Chartered Institute of Library and Information Professionals)
7 Ridgmount Street, London WC1E 7AE
Tel: 020 7255 0500
www.cilip.org.uk

Copyright Licensing Agency
Saffron House, 6–10 Kirby Street, London ECIN 8TS
Tel: 020 7400 3100
www.cla.co.uk

English PEN
6–8 Amwell Street, London ECIR IUQ
Tel: 020 7713 0023
www.englishpen.org

Independent Publishers Guild (IPG)
PO Box 93, Royston SG8 5GH
Tel: 01763 247014
www.ipg.uk.com

National Literacy Trust
68 South Lambeth Road, London SW8 IRL
Tel: 020 7587 1842
www.literacytrust.org.uk

The Poetry Society
22 Betterton Street
London WC2H 9BX
Tel: 020 7420 9880
www.poetrysociety.org.uk

The Publishers Association
29b Montague Street, London WCIB 5BW
Tel: 020 7691 9191
www.publishers.org.uk

Publishing Scotland
137 Dundee Street, Edinburgh EHII IBG
Tel: 0131 228 6866
www.publishingscotland.org

Reading Agency
PO Box 96, St Albans ALI 3WP
Tel: 020 7278 8922
www.readingagency.org.uk

The Society of Authors
84 Drayton Gardens, London SWIO 9SB
Tel: 020 7373 6642
www.societyofauthors.org

Society of Indexers
Woodbourn Business Centre, 10 Jessell Street, Sheffield s9 3HY
Tel: 0114 244 9561
www.indexers.org.uk

Society for the History of Authorship, Reading & Publishing
email: members@sharpweb.org
www.sharpweb.org

UK Serials Group
PO Box 5594, Newbury RG20 OYD
Tel: 01635 254292
www.uksg.org

Welsh Book Council
Castell Brychan, Aberystwyth, Ceredigion SY23 2JB
Tel: 01970 624151
www.cllc.org.uk

Networking opportunities

Independent Publishers Guild (IPG)
PO Box 93, Royston SG8 5GH
Tel: 01763 247014
www.ipg.uk.com

OPuS (Oxford Publishing Society)
email: secretary@opusnet.co.uk
www.opusnet.co.uk

Publishers Publicity Circle (PPC)
65 Airedale Avenue, London W4 2NN
Tel: 020 8994 1881.
email: ppc-@lineone.net

Society for Editors and Proofreaders (SfEP)
Riverbank House, 1 Putney Bridge Approach, Fulham, London SW6 3JD
Tel: 020 7736 3278
www.sfep.org.uk

Society of Young Publishers (SYP)
Society of Young Publishers, c/o *The Bookseller*, Endeavour House,
189 Shaftesbury Avenue, London WC2H 8TJ
www.thesyp.org.uk
Oxford branch: www.thesyp.org.uk/oxford

Women in Publishing (WiP)
Membership c/o Susan Gunasekera, No. 4 Harston, Burritt Road, Kingston,
Surrey KT1 3HT
email: membership@wipub.org.uk
www.wipub.org.uk

Training organizations

Association of Learned and Professional Society Publishers (ALPSP)
Blenheim House, 120 Church Street, Brighton BN1 1AU
www.alpsp.org.uk

Chapterhouse
16 Magdalen Road, Exeter EX2 4SY
Tel: 01392 499488
www.chapterhousepublishing.co.uk

London School of Publishing
David Game House, 69 Notting Hill Gate, London W11 3JS
Tel: 020 7221 3399
www.publishing-school.co.uk

Marketability
12 Sandy Lane, Teddington, Middlesex TW11 0DR
Tel: 020 8977 2741
www.marketability.info

Oxford International Centre for Publishing Studies
Buckley Building, Gipsy Lane Campus, Oxford Brookes University, Oxford OX3 0BP
Tel: 01865 484957
www.brookes.ac.uk/publishing

Pira International
Pira House, Cleeve Road, Leatherhead, Surrey KT22 7RU
Tel: 01372 802000
www.piranet.com

Publishing Scotland
137 Dundee Street, Edinburgh EH11 1BG
Tel: 0131 228 6866
www.publishingscotland.org

Publishing Training Centre
Book House, 45 East Hill, London sw18 2qz
Tel: 020 8874 2718
www.train4publishing.co.uk

Society for Editors and Proofreaders (SfEP)
Riverbank House, 1 Putney Bridge Approach, Fulham, London sw6 3jd
Tel: 020 7736 3278
www.sfep.org.uk

Society of Indexers
Woodbourn Business Centre, 10 Jessell Street, Sheffield s9 3hy
Tel: 0114 244 9561
www.indexers.org.uk

Scholarships and grants

Book Trade Benevolent Society (BTBS) – the book trade charity
The Foyle Centre, The Retreat, Kings Langley, Herts WD4 8LT
Tel: 01923 263128
www.booktradecharity.demon.co.uk

Tony Godwin Memorial Trust
c/o 38 Lyttelton Court, Lyttelton Road, London N2 OEB
www.tgmt.org.uk

Worshipful Company of Stationers and Newspaper Makers
Secretary, Mr J. P. Thornton FCA, The Old Dairy, Adstocksfields, Adstock,
Buckingham, MK18 2JE
email: jpt@jptco.co.uk
www.stationers.org

Recruitment agencies and careers advisers

Astron Limited
1 Berkeley Street, London W1J 8DJ
Tel: 020 7016 8812
email: reception@goastron.com

Bookcareers.com
Career development and coaching
PO Box 1441, Ilford, Essex IG4 5GH
www.bookcareers.com

Inspired Selection
2nd Floor, Hedges House, 153–5 Regent Street, London W1B 4JE
Tel: 020 7440 1500
First Floor Offices, Golden Cross Court, 4 Cornmarket Street, Oxford OX1 3EX
Tel: 01865 260270
www.inspiredselection.co.uk

Intelligent Resources Ltd
No. 1 White's Row, Spitalfields, London, E1 7LF
Tel 020 7375 0085
www.intelligentresources.com

JFL Search & Selection
27 Beak Street, London W1F 9RU
Tel: 020 7009 3500
www.jflrecruit.com

Judy Fisher Associates
7 Swallow Street, London W1B 4DE
Tel: 020 7437 2277
www.judyfisher.co.uk

8 Haymarket, London, SW1Y 4RF

ing.com

...dian Search and Selection
2 Southwick Mews, Paddington, London W2 1JG
Tel: 020 7402 6633
www.meridian-recruit.com

Sue Hill Recruitment
Borough House, 80 Borough Hill High Street
London SE1 1LL
Tel: 020 7378 7068
www.suehill.com

University publishing courses

Undergraduate publishing courses

Bangor University
www.bangor.ac.uk
BA English with Publishing

Coventry University
www.coventry.ac.uk
BA Graphic Design and Illustration

University College Falmouth
www.falmouth.ac.uk
BA Graphic Design

University of Gloucestershire
www.glos.ac.uk
BA Publishing; BA English and Publishing; BA Film and Publishing;
BA Marketing Management and Branding and Publishing – other combinations
available

University of Huddersfield
www.hud.ac.uk
BA Educational and Children's Publishing

Loughborough University
www.lboro.ac.uk
BA Publishing with English

Middlesex University
www.mdx.ac.uk
BA Publishing and Media

Napier University, Edinburgh
www.napier.ac.uk
BA Publishing Media; BA English and Publishing

North East Wales Institute of Higher Education
www.newi.ac.uk
BA Design: Illustration for Children's Publishing

Norwich School of Art and Design
www.nsad.ac.uk
BA Graphic Design

Oxford Brookes University
www.brookes.ac.uk/publishing
BA Publishing Media; BA English and Publishing Media; BA Marketing and
Publishing Media; BA Film and Publishing Media – other combinations available

University of Reading
www.rdg.ac.uk
BA Design for Graphic Communication; BA Typography and English;
BA Typography and History; BA Typography and History of Art and Architecture

Swansea Institute of Higher Education
www.sihe.ac.uk
BA Graphic Design

University of Wolverhampton
www.wlv.ac.uk
BA Graphic Communication

Graduate publishing courses

City University
www.city.ac.uk/journalism
MA/Diploma Publishing Studies; MA Electronic Publishing

Kingston University
www.kingston.ac.uk
MA/Diploma Publishing; MA Publishing and the Creative Economy;
MA Creative Writing and Publishing

London College of Communication
www.lcc.arts.ac.uk
MA/Diploma Publishing

Napier University, Edinburgh
www.napier.ac.uk
MSc/Diploma Publishing

Oxford Brookes University
www.brookes.ac.uk/publishing
MA/Diploma Publishing; MA/Diploma Digital Publishing; MA/Diploma
International Publishing; MA/Diploma Publishing and Language; European
Master in Publishing

University of Plymouth
www.mapublishing.co.uk
MA/Diploma Publishing

University of Reading
www.rdg.ac.uk
MA Theory and History of Typography & Graphic Communication

Robert Gordon University, Aberdeen
www.rgu.ac.uk
MSc/Diploma Publishing

University of Stirling
www.pubstd.stir.ac.uk
MLitt Publishing; MSc International Publishing Management

University College London
www.publishing.ucl.ac.uk
MA/Diploma Publishing

Index